Disrupt or Be Disrupted

Disrupt or Be Disrupted

A blueprint for change in management education

GRADUATE MANAGEMENT
ADMISSION COUNCIL

A Wiley Brand

Jacket design by Adrian Morgan
Cover art by Shutterstock (RF)

Published by Jossey-Bass
A Wiley Brand
One Montgomery Street, Suite 1200, San Francisco, CA 94104-4594—www.josseybass.com

Jossey-Bass books and products are available through most bookstores. To contact Jossey-Bass directly call our Customer Care Department within the U.S. at 800-956-7739, outside the U.S. at 317-572-3986, or fax 317-572-4002.

Wiley publishes in a variety of print and electronic formats and by print-on-demand. Some material included with standard print versions of this book may not be included in e-books or in print-on-demand. If this book refers to media such as a CD or DVD that is not included in the version you purchased, you may download this material at http://booksupport.wiley.com. For more information about Wiley products, visit www.wiley.com.

Library of Congress Cataloging-in-Publication Data
Disrupt or be disrupted : a blueprint for change in management education / Graduate Management Admission Council. – First edition.
     pages cm
  Includes bibliographical references and index.
  ISBN 978-1-118-60239-3 (hardback); 978-1-118-65354-8 (ebk.); 978-1-118-65363-0 (ebk.)
  1. Management–Study and teaching.   2. Business education.   I. Graduate Management Admission Council.
  HD30.4.D576 2013
  650.071–dc23

                                    2013018277

Printed in the United States of America
FIRST EDITION
HB Printing   10 9 8 7 6 5 4 3 2 1

CONTENTS

FOREWORD

The MBA program, the flagship of business schools, was the greatest educational innovation of the twentieth century. I base this claim on at least three characteristics of the program: the case method, the transformational experience, and internationalization. Although business schools did not pioneer the case method—law schools did so—they made the case method discussion into a dynamic experience that brought a slice of real life into the classroom. In addition, the MBA was not just an educational experience but a transformational one. Both in the classroom and through the increasingly important extracurricular activities, students found their capabilities stretched not just technically but in terms of personal development. Graduates of good business schools found themselves transformed as people. More recently, the rapid internationalization of the student population of many full-time MBA programs, combined with the emphasis on group work, has given students a far more multicultural experience than those provided by other educational programs.

In the twenty-first century, the MBA and business schools face many challenges, most of which are ably addressed in this book. In this foreword I focus on the challenges that concern me the most. I do so based on my experience as regular or visiting faculty, and dean or associate dean, at top business schools on three continents.

The central ongoing challenge for a business school is that it is both a business and a school, a much stronger challenge than faced by other academic fields. Business schools have two audiences: academics and business practitioners. Furthermore, because academics are outside of business organizations, we cannot directly participate in or easily observe what is happening inside them. In contrast, just comparing ourselves to other professional subjects, a medical academic does research on the same human bodies on which doctors practice, a legal academic uses the same legal materials as does a practicing lawyer, and an engineering academic researches the same bridge structure as may be built by a practicing engineer.

This dual audience of business schools requires dual roles, which in turn may create a misalignment of the interests of the school and of individual faculty members. A school prospers by satisfying both its business and its academic audiences—and financially by attending to the business audience. In contrast, a faculty member can do very well focusing on just the academic audience. This split from practice is getting worse as more and more new faculty members start off in nonbusiness disciplines such as economics and psychology. Being embedded in universities drives this phenomenon. Interestingly, in Europe, where many schools have started outside of universities, most of the highest-ranked schools are stand-alone or have very loose links with a parent university (eight of the top ten in the *Financial Times* ranking of 2012).

This duality lies at the heart of the challenge to the sustainability of the business model of business schools, as discussed in a number of chapters in this book. The drive for research that seldom feeds directly into teaching means that less than half, in some schools much less, of faculty time is relevant to teaching. This effect holds up a high-cost umbrella for potential disruptors. Duke Corporate Education was the pioneer in leveraging teaching stars developed by the investments of other business schools. Certainly, in nondegree programs, we can expect to see more such disruption, and soon in degree programs also.

The duality also makes the role of the dean of a business school increasingly difficult. More than in other fields, the dean of a business school is trying to run a business. Typically, the dean's role is to close the gap between faculty interest in academic research and the need to deploy faculty for practitioner engagement. Schools often seek to appoint former practitioners as their deans, with risky results. Recently, three of the top European business schools had to replace their new nonacademic deans within two years of their appointments.

The final issue I raise is the 900-pound gorilla in the room: rankings. The first widely followed ranking, that by *Bloomberg Businessweek*, quickly generated changed behavior by business schools. But because that ranking used only three measures, there was a limited amount that schools could address. The advent of multiple-item ratings, especially those of the *Financial Times*, has given much more scope for redesign of programs that can improve a school's ranking. I know, because as the academic dean for the MBA program at London Business School, I redesigned the program in a way that helped lead the MBA to the number one ranking in the world for three years in a row. Rankings create a virtuous cycle of increased applications, more revenues, better teaching and research, back again to better rankings. But chasing rankings can be a Faustian bargain.

This book does a great job of tackling the many different issues facing graduate business schools today. The authors represent a wide range of schools and perspectives. It is essential reading for all those involved in the leadership of business schools, not just faculty but also those executives who sit on advisory boards and governing bodies. I recommend that deans give copies of this book to all their board members.

George S. Yip
May 2013

George S. Yip is a professor at China Europe International Business School and a visiting professor at Imperial College Business School. He is former dean of Rotterdam School of Management, Erasmus University, and former associate dean at London Business School.

Disrupt or Be Disrupted

INTRODUCTION

The Change Imperative

Brooks C. Holtom
Georgetown University

Lyman W. Porter
University of California, Irvine

Since the late 1980s, dramatic advances have led to completely new ways of interacting, sharing, learning, and doing business. In today's world, relentless change is the norm as organizations strive to stay in front of new competitors, economic fluctuations, globalization, and technological developments. Because graduate business schools face these same pressures, it is no longer enough to maintain the status quo, or even to make incremental improvements. In the face of such demands, the role of business school deans has become broader and more strategic. Responding to today's challenges while balancing relevance, value, and reputation requires unprecedented strategic thinking, creativity, stakeholder engagement, and interpersonal effectiveness.

To help both business schools and their deans to thrive, this book takes an evidence-based approach to navigating changing times and to creating platforms that leverage schools' unique comparative advantages in ways that are tailored to today's business realities.

1

Throughout this volume, we discuss the challenges schools currently face (some of which are touched upon later in this chapter) and identify strategic insights and recommendations the authors offer to position graduate business schools for the future. Each chapter analyzes specific challenges and opportunities that business schools will confront as they continue to cope with the massive changes in the external environment. The forces for these changes can, and most likely will, have a significant impact on graduate management education in the years ahead.

Graduate Management Education's Major Challenges: An Overview

Financial Pressures

Concerns about the cost of management education are escalating. The problems manifest themselves in a number of ways. American universities have raised their tuition five times as fast as inflation since the mid-1980s (*Economist*, July 9, 2011). In 2012, student loan debt in the United States exceeded credit card debt, and, for the first time, student loan debt delinquency rates exceed those for credit card debt (Mitchell, 2012). Cost concerns are not exclusive to the United States. Since 2010, students have organized protests in response to government proposals to increase fees and tuition in Canada, Chile, Germany, and the United Kingdom.

On the other side of the financial equation for business schools is a precipitous decline in government funding—a trend that is not expected to reverse (Korn, 2011). Between 2008 and 2012, total state funding for higher education in the United States dropped by 15 percent, adjusted for inflation, as states struggled with budget deficits. In some hard-hit states, cuts have surpassed 25 percent (Nicas & McWhirter, 2012). These well-publicized cuts are an acceleration of a long-term decline in government support, which has fallen from 40 to 50 percent of a typical state school's operating budget in the 1980s to about 10 percent in recent times. Given public resistance to raising tuition, politicians in Canada, Chile, Germany, and the United Kingdom have also sought to balance budgets by cutting spending.

For schools of all kinds, endowment income is not always a reliable source of needed financial relief. As Figure I.1 shows, among U.S. schools in the *Financial Times*'s Top 100 institutions worldwide, endowments at public institutions average 40 percent of those at private institutions (Palin, 2012).

Thus, economic downturns affect these institutions differently. Market crises hurt well-endowed schools when endowment earnings are severely curtailed; however, this is generally a short-term effect. In contrast, schools with small endowments are generally forced to depend heavily on the aforementioned uncertain state funding. To balance the books, "schools are leaving faculty positions unfilled and eliminating programs that are not delivering a positive return" (Palin, 2012).

This is not surprising. When it is not possible to continue to raise tuition faster than inflation, government support remains steady or declines, and endowments cannot keep up, business schools must carefully consider where to invest scarce resources. First-rate scholars, for example, are an increasingly expensive component of budgets. So, should these scholars migrate to the few schools that can afford them? Should students access the insights of these scholars via Massive Open Online Courses, or MOOCs? Should some schools declare themselves to be primarily teaching or research institutions and not pretend to be both?

Responses to these challenges will most likely be many and outwardly focused (for example, expansion of specialty master's programs, development of additional custom executive education, global partnerships) and inwardly focused (for example, redesigning the curriculum). These efforts have only increased and diversified the competitive landscape, which we discuss next.

Figure I.1 Endowments, Budgets, and Tuition Fees at Leading U.S. Business Schools 2008–2012

Fees and Funding

How leading private and public US business schools have fared during the economic downturn

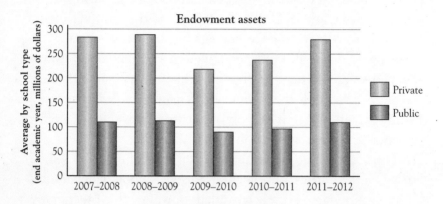

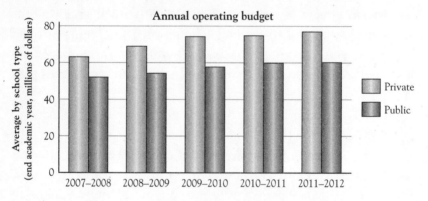

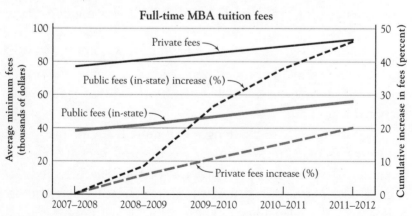

Source: Palin, 2012.

Shifts in Student Origin and Age

There are numerous signs of just how much the market for graduate management education has changed around the world. One clear indicator concerns geographic trends. For example, the early part of the twenty-first century has seen increased demand for the GMAT® exams in Asia. In 2012, 30 percent of exams were taken by Asians, an increase of 59 percent since 2004. (See Figure I.2.) However, fewer candidates are applying to U.S.

Figure I.2 GMAT® Score Reports in Asia 2008–2012, by Program Type

GMAT® Trends Tracker 2012: Testing Data

Asia (Citizenship Group)

Asian citizens took a total of 110,737 GMAT exams during Testing Year (TY) 2012. This level represents an increase of 39,588 exams or 56 percent from the 71,149 taken in TY2008.

During TY2012:
• Women: **50%**
• Younger than 25: **58%**

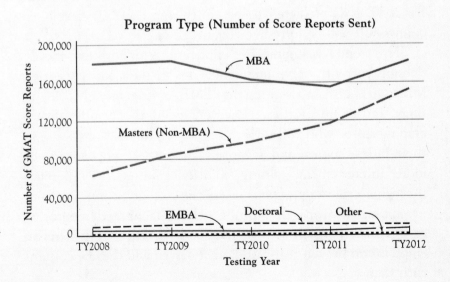

Source: GMAC, 2012b.

schools (down 6 percent from 2004 to 2012; Schlegelmilch & Thomas, 2011). The decline is due in part to heavy investment in business education in Asia and Western Europe. For example, according to Association to Advance Collegiate Schools of Business (AACSB) estimates, there are 1,500 business schools in India (*Economist*, October 15, 2011). Furthermore, a number of Western schools, including INSEAD and MIT, are opening campuses in Asia. Although these trends will play out over many years, mid-level U.S. schools are already feeling the effects, with enrollment down by more than 20 percent since the turn of the century (*Economist*, October 15, 2011).

Another indicator of change concerns the age of students considering graduate management education. As Figure I.3 shows, from 2008 to 2012, the greatest growth in GMAT test takers was in the younger-than-twenty-five-year-old age group, who in 2012 represented 47 percent of all test takers.

However, there was also a significant uptick in test takers who were more than forty years old (GMAC, 2012b). The aging of the population is another fundamental demographic change that will shape educational markets in the coming decades. In 2005, the average age of the world population was twenty-eight. By 2050, it is predicted to be thirty-eight, and in developed countries it will be forty-five (Bach, 2012).

This trend has a number of implications for business schools. Schools currently serve undergraduates in their early twenties, MBAs in their late twenties, and EMBAs (executive MBAs) in their thirties and forties. However, given the coming demographic shifts, who will serve the growing number of people in their fifties, sixties, and seventies? Will these populations be more interested in gaining additional knowledge (perhaps through certificate programs or custom executive education) or in sharing it (through business school–facilitated mentoring or socially responsible start-up incubators)? Will they demand an emphasis on proven real-world practices, or will they be content with theory?

Figure I.3 GMAT® Exams Taken Globally 2008–2012, by Age

GMAT® Trends Tracker 2012: Testing Data

Worldwide (Citizenship Group)

Global citizens took a total of 286,529 GMAT exams during Testing Year (TY) 2012. This level represents an increase of 39,572 exams or 16 percent from the 246,957 taken in TY2008.

During TY2012:
- Women: **43%**
- Younger than 25: **47%**

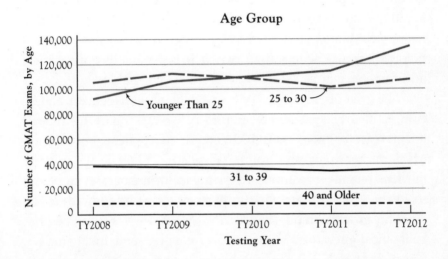

Source: GMAC, 2012b.

Changes in Program Numbers and Types

Shifting student markets are giving rise to a host of new competitors. As of 2011, AACSB estimated that there were 13,725 business schools (includes undergraduate schools) worldwide. The largest numbers were found in India (2,000), the United States (1,624), China (1,082), and Mexico (1,000). Of the 1,270 AACSB member schools, 57 percent were public (722), and 43 percent were private (541). Of the 649 AACSB-accredited schools of business, 488 were found in the United States, and

161 were outside the United States. This number grew 105 percent from 1984 to 2011. In regions outside the United States, which are dominated by other accrediting agencies such as EQUIS, AMBA, and ACBSP, growth was even more pronounced over this period (Datar & others, 2010).

The market for the full-time MBA, the historical driver of graduate management education, shows signs of decline. A shift has occurred from full-time programs to part-time programs and continues unabated, in part due to escalating tuition costs. The majority of part-time students continue to work and thereby avoid the steep opportunity costs associated with the full-time degree. Similarly, students have been turning to one-year programs that are cheaper than two-year programs in both tuition and forgone salaries (*Economist*, October 15, 2011).

The area of greatest growth in graduate management education is, clearly, specialized master's programs. Figure I.4 reveals an increase of more than 100 percent in applications to non–MBA master's programs from 2008 to 2012. Overall, the number of MBA test takers went down during that time period, and more so in the United States than other markets (GMAC, 2012b).

The growth trend toward non–MBA master's degrees has been most pronounced in Asia, as can be seen in Figure I.5. Given that in 2012 the number of Asian test takers approximated the number in the United States—and that growth in test takers in Asia was 56 percent from 2008 to 2012, compared to a decline of 7 percent in the United States—these are trends that cannot be ignored (GMAC, 2012b).

In terms of programs, the master's program that grew fastest from 2008 to 2012 was finance, as can be seen in Table I.1.

Another sign of change appears in the market for executive education. It has grown tremendously since the start of the twenty-first century and, consequently, has become increasingly important to many schools' bottom lines. Revenues at representative top-tier schools have increased impressively since the turn of the century. At Harvard, for example, total executive educa-

Figure I.4 GMAT® Score Reports Globally 2008–2012, by Program Type

GMAT® Trends Tracker 2012: Testing Data

Worldwide (Citizenship Group)

Global citizens took a total of 286,529 GMAT exams during Testing Year (TY) 2012. This level represents an increase of 39,572 exams or 16 percent from the 246,957 taken in TY2008.

During TY2012:
- Women: **43%**
- Younger than 25: **47%**

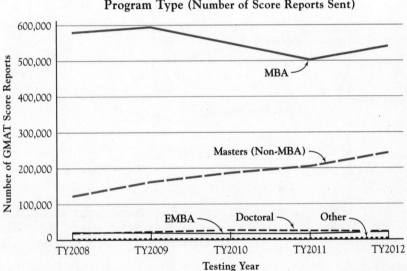

Program Type (Number of Score Reports Sent)

Source: GMAC, 2012b.

tion revenues were US$71 million in 2001 and US$113 million in 2010 (Harvard Business School Annual Report 2001, 2010). During that time period at Duke Corporate Education (CE)— ranked first in the world by the *Financial Times*—revenues grew more than 200 percent, from US$12 million in fiscal year (FY) 2001 to US$38 million in FY 2010. Custom programs have grown most quickly on a percentage basis and, as of 2012,

Figure I.5 GMAT® Score Reports in Asia 2008–2012, by Program Type

GMAT® Trends Tracker 2012: Testing Data

Asia (Citizenship Group)

Asian citizens took a total of 110,737 GMAT exams during Testing Year (TY) 2012. This level represents an increase of 39,588 exams or 56 percent from the 71,149 taken in TY2008.

During TY2012:
* Women: **50%**
* Younger than 25: **58%**

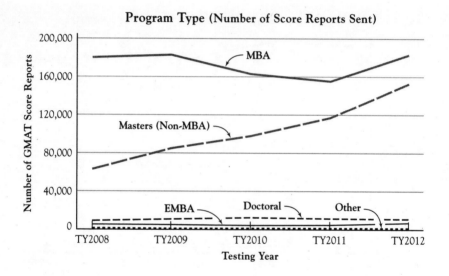

Source: GMAC, 2012b.

accounted for a majority of revenues at some institutions. For example, at IMD, 45 percent of total revenue was derived from programs created and delivered exclusively to individual clients (Tanikawa, 2012).

Not surprisingly, executive education, one of the most lucrative lines of business for management schools, is facing increased competition from a variety of providers. For example, graduate schools in fields such as international relations, public affairs,

Table I.1 Change in GMAT® Score Reports 2008–2012, by Program Type

Program	Change in Number of GMAT Scores Sent	Percentage Change
EMBA	−200	−1%
MBA, full-time, fewer than 2 years	775	3%
MBA, full-time, 2 years or more	−21,257	−6%
MBA, part-time, evenings and weekends	−33,622	−27%
MBA, distance or online	2,256	22%
MA/MS/MSc in accounting, accountancy, or taxation	28,053	68%
MA/MS/MSc in business or management	4,166	83%
MA/MS/MSc in finance	25,615	164%

Source: GMAC, 2012a.

law, and journalism are developing executive education courses, particularly in niche areas that are not covered by traditional business schools. Stand-alone leadership development centers, such as the Center for Creative Leadership, have also increased markedly in numbers and revenues since the 1990s.

Moreover, new institutions such as Hult International Business School have quickly gained traction, in part because their one-year format is both relatively unique in the U.S. market and enables students to recoup their investment more quickly than other programs do. Hult has been ranked number one in postgraduation salary increase and number one in return on investment by *The Economist* (*Economist,* October 15, 2011). But the ascent in the rankings (number 21 in the United States and number 31 worldwide, according to *The Economist*) is also attributable in part to the nimbleness afforded a school that is not tied to a larger university bureaucracy.

As another example, the South African Council for Higher Education plans to create a two-tier MBA with different levels of academic rigor. This will put the country at odds with the rest of the world, according to one knowledgeable observer (Bisoux, 2011). Further blurring the boundaries is the wide-scale proliferation of certificate programs. But in less-developed markets, in particular, will people distinguish between a diploma and alternatives such as certificates? For example, in India will Stanford's name mean more to applicants and employers than the difference between a certificate and a degree? We may soon find out. Stanford Ignite, a part-time certificate program for entrepreneurs, based in Bangalore, launches in July 2013.

Technological Opportunities—and Threats

Further complications are growing out of the effects of technology on collaboration, teaching, and learning. For example, traditional competitors are now teaming up in a university consortium to offer small online courses. Duke, the University of North Carolina at Chapel Hill, and Northwestern are among the universities that will join together in fall 2013 to offer about thirty online courses. The courses are available both to their own students and to others who must apply, be accepted, and pay more than US$4,000 a course. This will further allow students to get access to the best courses or faculty talent regardless of location. Put differently, the rich will likely get richer, and the poor will likely get poorer.

Another innovative use of technology is Massive Open Online Courses, called the "single biggest change in education since the printing press" (Chubb & Moe, 2012). The courses are offered for free by leading institutions (such as Harvard, MIT, and Stanford) and have enjoyed overwhelming enrollment success. For example, a course at Stanford enrolled more than 150,000 students worldwide in fall 2011. MOOCs obviously offer great opportunities to students and have the potential to transform graduate management education.

However, such developments are not without their critics. For example, detractors are quick to point out that both attrition and costs are steep. How schools can sustain this model is unclear, given the costs to develop and deliver the content. In the Stanford case, only 7,000 people passed the course, and it brought in no revenue. Even so, that number is still larger than the population of Stanford undergraduates, and learning on a large scale clearly occurred. Furthermore, many traditional business school subjects, such as statistics and accounting, may be very well suited to long-distance learning. If accreditation standards can be developed and tests can be administered by a related or independent organization, then students may be able to demonstrate competencies without ever having to earn a traditional diploma. Could these new formats provide a viable substitute for an MBA degree someday?

Cornell University took a two-step approach toward this outcome with a MOOC it started offering in early 2013 through eCornell. The class, called "Marketing the Hospitality Brand Through New Media: Social, Mobile, and Search," is available for free and takes roughly a month to complete. After finishing, participants may enroll in the second part of the class for $1,200, which results in a certificate in hospitality marketing and new media strategies for revenue growth (Hassan, 2013).

The University of Wisconsin goes yet another step further by offering a bachelor's degree to students who take online competency tests based on what they know. Students do not have to attend classes on campus or even take an online course. The degree is based on knowledge, not credits—the traditional currency of universities (C. Porter, 2013).

Clearly, these and other technological developments will have profound effects on the role of faculty and the need for full-time faculty and brick-and-mortar facilities. Just as L. W. Porter and McKibbin (1988) could not have predicted the emergence of the Internet or what its impact could be, today's business school leaders cannot assume that MOOCs are the only technology threat on the horizon. We simply do not know what is next. However, we can be certain that technology will continue to evolve in ways that let people to share information more effectively than before. We can also be sure that there will be dramatic gains—such as when the poor get access to previously unavailable world-class instruction—and significant challenges— such as figuring out how to protect intellectual property and maintain incentives to create it. Business school leaders must confront the possibilities as they emerge and examine how technological advancements fit holistically within their schools' missions, portfolios, and plans.

The Ongoing Importance of Relevance, Value, and Reputation

Although the market will determine the fate of many of the varied experiments of today and tomorrow, one thing is almost guaranteed: New competitors and products starkly demonstrate that standing still is unlikely to be a sustainable strategy. Schools must proactively demonstrate relevance, value, and reputation, which means rethinking how they conduct research, select and train faculty, design curriculum, engage students, and measure quality.

There is no shortage of societal challenges that business schools could help to analyze and address. Affordable health care, nominal and relative national debt levels, and innovations in products and services are just a few areas that would benefit from the skilled application of best practices and principles by management school graduates. Yet, many critics argue, current MBA models are losing their relevance. In addition, scandals such as Enron have undermined faith in the finance profession, and the 2008 global economic crisis occurred while major financial institutions such as Lehman Brothers were led by MBAs. As David Garvin has said, "A decade ago, the MBA was the 'golden ticket' to the job of your choice, but the future of business schools is not as rosy as it used to be" (Bisoux, 2011, p. 24).

Some contend that public funding is supporting research that could be better accomplished within think tanks or similar entities. A renowned business school scholar maintains that "employees of purely discovery-focused corporate R&D groups and government research institutes are inherently more cost effective than university scholars, who must split their time between research and instruction and whose explorations are not market driven" (Christensen & Eyring, 2011, p. 350).

To a troubling degree, some business school activities still seem relatively impervious to change. Among the most important of these are the way doctoral education is carried out and the continuing intensive emphasis on specific functional areas such as accounting, finance, and marketing—emphasis that at times hinders attempts to achieve more integrated approaches to solving business problems. This functional area emphasis is evident in the way teaching and research are organized in both the broader academy and individual schools. Despite substantial overlap in the way the knowledge is applied in the real world, management and operations are taught in separate departments, and the latest research about accounting and finance are presented in separate academic conferences. Curriculum committees design "integrative" courses, but on the shifting sands of what constitute the core, or essential, concepts that underpin management education. The lack of agreement on a clear paradigm of management education undoubtedly contributes to the difficulty of making the case that business education leads to superior management or organizational performance (Mintzberg, 2004).

What Follows in This Book

In sum, formidable challenges face the leaders of graduate management education. Following the Ford Foundation and Carnegie Corporation reports from 1959 and the AACSB Porter and McKibbin report of 1988, this book marks another quarter-century step in the development of the field. Because constraints and challenges are often key drivers of innovation, we are hopeful about the future. The strategic investment of considerable thought and effort will differentiate the winners from the losers. The chapters that follow are designed to inform that thinking.

As a starting point, in Chapter One Dierdorff, Nayden, Jain, and Jain pose a question that anyone involved in providing graduate management education needs to be able to answer: *Why does this type of education matter?* Can we demonstrate that it provides measurable value-added? If so, how do we know? Another way to put the topic of the chapter in perspective is to ask: Will graduate management education remain relevant for the remainder of the twenty-first century? The authors examine this question from the perspective of individuals who will be students in the future, organizations that will hire graduates of business programs, and, especially, society at large. In the latter part of the chapter, the authors put forth ideas for changes that will be necessary to increase the effectiveness and relevance of graduate management education in the years ahead.

Chapter Two delves into a basic issue that schools of all sizes and types face: *how to position the school for the future.* Hay provides a strategic examination of a set of positioning questions (such as, whom does the school serve?) that each school must answer for itself, given its own unique environment and circumstances. The questions are important, and, if faced directly and openly, the answers should reveal whether a school has a foundation of clarity and conviction about its current positioning and what changes it might want to make in the future. The chapter, in effect, provides any school with an early basis for a revealing look in the mirror.

In Chapter Three, Kang and Stark look at specific examples of different business schools' financial models. They do so by drawing on interview data from deans at a wide range of schools. Their focus is on such critical input variables as funding sources, the importance and role of research, and the development of reputation and how that opens doors to key resources. The chapter concludes with a discussion of *how a school might be able to change its financial model* if it wants to do so and what the advantages might or might not be.

Spender and Khurana in Chapter Four focus intensively on four exemplar management schools—at Harvard, Chicago, Carnegie Mellon, and Yale—and *how each has placed its own intellectual signature on doctoral education for future faculty members who go on to careers at major universities around the United States and overseas.* The chapter's central proposition is that "a school's doctoral program is a litmus test of the research ability and productivity of its disciplinary and intellectual signature." The authors visit the long-standing rigor-relevance issue and strongly encourage broader use of different research methodologies and a wider approach to selecting research topics in doctoral studies.

Curriculum is the subject of Chapter Five, by Rynes and Bartunek. The fundamental question examined here: *Is the typical curriculum of today's MBA programs meeting the needs of organizations and society as we move further into the twenty-first century—and, if not, what needs to be changed?* The authors cite research indicating that two areas of the curriculum especially need increased attention: the leadership and management of human capital, and decision making and problem solving. In addition, the areas of ethics and corporate social responsibility appear to merit more examination. However, as the chapter makes clear, no matter how desirable these curricular changes might be, there are formidable obstacles to implementing them that schools must appreciate and consciously overcome.

In Chapter Six, Brown, Arbaugh, Hrivnak, and Kenworthy examine the challenges involved in *increasing the quality of teaching and delivery of course content* in order to facilitate and enhance student learning. Among the important issues they cover are ways to maximize the potential of various delivery approaches, such as online instruction and experiential learning exercises. The role of schools in staffing, training, motivating, and rewarding instructors is emphasized, as is the necessity to give concerted—but often overlooked—attention to course design.

The recipients of graduate management education—the students—are the central focus of Chapter Seven by Feldman. In particular, the analysis highlights the factors that affect how engaged students become in their classroom education, in their extracurricular activities, and in their own posteducation professional development. The chapter takes a decidedly student-as-agent perspective. It emphasizes *the choices management schools face regarding how much and what kinds of engagement they want to encourage* and how their approaches to student selection can affect the amounts and types of engagement. As the author stresses, more engagement is not necessarily better engagement.

Finally, how should the quality of graduate management education be measured? Chapter Eight by Rubin and Morgeson describes a comprehensive approach to measuring that quality. More specifically, the authors propose *a well-developed and workable alternative to the much-criticized rankings of business schools by various media outlets.* That alternative approach, labeled the "Quality Content Model," is based on a meticulous examination of the multidimensional nature of graduate management education and hence on the different criteria that contribute to its overall quality. Within the new approach, subject matter experts determine the relative importance of each of the different criteria. Then ratings, not rankings, can be made of a specific school on each criterion. As the authors conclude, "The time has clearly come for the academic community to move beyond mere criticism of media rankings as indicators of [graduate management education's] program quality." In this chapter, the authors have indeed outlined a specific way forward that *does* move beyond those criticisms. This is a matter for both individual schools and the field in general to address when contemplating the path to a successful future.

Since the 1960s, business schools and graduate management education have made some impressive advances overall and have introduced more constructive changes than many would have predicted (L. W. Porter, 1997). Despite these accomplishments, critics abound, and many of them have had considerable influence over the ongoing dialogue about how to improve and, indeed, reinvent graduate business education. (See, for example, Mintzberg, 2004; Khurana, 2007; and Datar, Garvin, & Cullen, 2010.) In various respects, these critics see business education heading in the wrong direction and still in need of a major overhaul. Their calls do not go unheeded, but collectively they do not necessarily coalesce around a unified new direction for business schools. The need to make fundamental changes in graduate management education is the central theme in these critiques. How to get from here to the future is the overriding issue, one that is addressed throughout this book.

References

AACSB. Business School Data Trends and 2012 List of Accredited Schools, 2012. http://www.aacsb.edu

Bach, D. "We Need to Rethink . . . Everything." *BizEd*, September/October 2012, pp. 18–24.

Bisoux, T. "Re-Envisioning the MBA." *BizEd*, September/October 2011, pp. 22–30.

Christensen, C., & Eyring, H. *The Innovative University.* San Francisco, Calif.: Jossey Bass, 2011.

Chubb, J., & Moe, T. "Higher Education's Online Revolution." *Wall Street Journal*, May 30, 2012. http://online.wsj.com/article/SB1000142405 2702304019404577416631206583286.html

Datar, S., Garvin, D., & Cullen, P. *Rethinking the MBA: Business Education at a Crossroads.* Boston, Mass.: Harvard Business Press, 2010.

Economist. "How to Make College Cheaper." Business. July 9, 2011. http://www.economist.com/node/18926009

Economist. "Trouble in the Middle: Is Time Running Out for Business Schools That Aren't Quite Elite?" Briefing. October 15, 2011. http://www.economist.com/node/21532269

GMAC. GMAT *test-taking data (unpublished), 2008–2012.* Reston, Va.: Graduate Management Admission Council, 2012a.

GMAC. GMAT *Trends Tracker 2012.* Reston, Va.: Graduate Management Admission Council http://www.gmac.com/market-intelligence-and -research/research-library/gmat-test-taker-data/gmat-trends -tracker-2012.aspx, 2012b.

Harvard Business School Annual Report 2001. http://www.hbs.edu/annualreport/2001/pdf/HBS-Annual-2001.pdf

Harvard Business School Annual Report 2010. http://www.hbs.edu/annualreport/2010/pdf/HBS-Annual-2010.pdf

Hassan, C. "Cornell University MOOC Helps Students Earn Professional Certificate." U.S. News University Connection. January 9, 2013. http://www.usnewsuniversitydirectory.com/articles/cornell-university-mooc-helps-students-earn-profes_12866.aspx

Khurana, R. *From Higher Aims to Hired Hands: The Social Transformation of American Business Schools and the Unfulfilled Promise of Management as a Profession.* Princeton N.J.: Princeton University Press, 2007.

Korn, M. "The State of a State School." *Wall Street Journal*, October 6, 2011, B6. http://online.wsj.com/article/SB2000142405311190490090457655440048694 4150.html

Mintzberg, H. *Managers Not MBAs: A Hard Look at the Soft Practice of Managing and Management Development.* San Francisco, Calif.: Berrett-Koehler, 2004.

Mitchell, J. "Federal Student Lending Swells." *Wall Street Journal*, November 28, 2012, A1. http://online.wsj.com/article/SB1000142412788732446930457814509 2893766844.html

Nicas, J. & McWhirter, C. "Universities Feel the Heat Amid Cuts." *Wall Street Journal*, June 14, 2012. http://online.wsj.com/article/SB1000142405270230373420457746647085037 0002.html

Palin, A. "Business Schools See Their Funding Begin to Run Dry." *Financial Times*, December 10, 2012. http://www.ft.com/intl/cms/s/2/e6363828-3df7-11e2-91cb-00144feabdc0.html#axzz2EfVpj0M4

Porter, C. "College Degree, No Class Time Required." *Wall Street Journal*, January 25, 2013, A3. http://online.wsj.com/article/SB1000142412788732330110457825599237922 8564.html

Porter, L. W. "A Decade of Change in the Business School: From Complacency to Tomorrow." *Selections*, 1997, 13(2), 1–8.

Porter, L. W., & McKibbin, L. E. *Management Education and Development.* New York: McGraw-Hill, 1988.

Porter, M. "What Is Strategy?" *Harvard Business Review*, November 1, 1996. http://hbr.org/product/what-is-strategy/an/96608-PDF-ENG

Schlegelmilch, B., & Thomas, H. "The MBA in 2020: Will There Still Be One?" *Journal of Management Development*, 2011, 30(5), 474–482.

Tanikawa, M. "Designing Business Education for a Custom Fit." *New York Times*, May 17, 2012. http://www.nytimes.com/2012/05/18/world/asia/designing-business-education-for-a-custom-fit.html

1

ENSURING AND ENHANCING FUTURE VALUE

Erich C. Dierdorff
DePaul University

Denis J. Nayden
Oak Hill Capital Management

Dipak C. Jain
INSEAD

Subhash C. Jain
University of Connecticut

Key Topics Covered in This Chapter

- Value of graduate management education for individuals, organizations, and society
- Challenges and pressure facing future success
- Imperatives for future relevance, effectiveness, and value

Consider for the moment that there is not a single occupation in the vast world of work for which the MBA is a mandatory entry requirement. Yet, even the most casual observer of business schools would note the substantial growth in graduate management education's popularity since its inception more than a century ago. This juxtaposition suggests that although graduate management degrees may not be strict occupational prerequisites, they are indeed perceived as worthwhile investments.

But what exactly *is* the value of graduate management education? As it turns out, the answer may not be entirely self-evident and is most certainly taken for granted by various business school stakeholders. In fact, uncovering a cohesive narrative that articulates the value of graduate management education is quite difficult. This does not mean that significant scholarship does not exist. However, this body of work is not rooted in a particular academic domain and is challenging to comprehensively grasp and clearly explicate. With this in mind, our primary aim is to convey the central case for why graduate management education matters. Building this case is not only crucial for a deeper understanding of the current state of graduate management education but also for addressing the myriad challenges that lie ahead if it is to continue to be a valuable mechanism for professional education.

We also believe the time is ripe to remind ourselves that graduate management education has broad implications for individuals, organizations, and society. We say "remind ourselves" because the value provided by graduate management education is not often extolled in either the popular press or scholarly literature. Consider, for example, that the past two decades of scholarship regarding graduate management education have been absolutely replete with criticism. These frequently scathing critiques have ranged from the philosophical (for example, Ghoshal, 2005) to the functional (for example, Mintzberg, 2004). Even a blithe perusal of this literature is likely to cause one to ask, Does graduate management education do anything well? We believe the answer is resoundingly affirmative. Further, we maintain that too often, the critiques of the past decades have failed to generate ways to enhance graduate management education. In other words, we contend that it is critical to simultaneously recognize that what we do has value, but that it also needs meaningful improvement. Only a balanced perspective can bring a reinvigoration in the way graduate management education is delivered in contemporary business schools.

To fulfill our primary aim, this chapter seeks to accomplish three general goals:

1. To build a case for the value of graduate management education at the individual, organizational, and broader societal levels

2. To outline several pressures that are likely to amplify the need for innovation in the way we currently conceptualize and approach graduate management education

3. To describe a key set of imperatives for business school policy-makers and faculty to address in order to sustain and enhance the value of graduate management education.

Ultimately, we hope not only to establish the clear value proposition of graduate management education but also to compel business schools to recognize that the time is now to reexamine the fundamental tenets on which graduate management education is built.

But before we begin, let us briefly acknowledge a few premises from which our ensuing discussions flow. First, we assert that the raison d'être of graduate management education involves (a) inculcating individual competence in managing various organizational resources (financial, technological, and human capital) and (b) fostering a particular set of values that shape the way individuals view and interpret the world of work. This initial assertion naturally leads to another premise, which is that graduate management education has its most direct impact on individuals. This means that its influence on organizations and ultimately society occurs through a compilation process in which individual competence and values exert bottom-up effects. Simply put, graduate management education starts with people. Finally, although we recognize that graduate management education encompasses a variety of programs (for example, master of science, executive, and joint degrees), we concentrate much of our discussion on MBA programs. This acknowledges both the predominance of the MBA degree in graduate management education and the fact that the vast majority of previous scholarship has exclusively focused on the MBA.

The Impact of Graduate Management Education

Why would someone pursue graduate management education? Why would organizations seek to hire those with graduate management degrees? What are the implications of graduate management education for society at large? Such questions are fundamental to the ultimate purposes of today's schools of business. Still further, questions about the value proposition of graduate management education undergird many of the recent criticisms of business schools and, at the same time, overlay the very reasons that renovations of our current practices are critical. In the sections following, we discuss the various ways graduate management education shapes individuals, organizations, and society.

Individual Value

Here, the question of value centers on the potential individual-level benefits that coincide with graduate-level training in business schools. Considering the substantial investments of time, money, and effort that graduate-level business training requires, one would hope there would be evidence to support a viable value proposition. Indeed, there are ample reasons to suggest the value of graduate management education for individuals.

At a general level, graduate management education holds perceived value for individuals across a number of business school stakeholders. For example, prospective students frequently indicate that graduate management education will bring them increased job opportunities, salary potential, and business-related knowledge and skills (Graduate Management Admission Council [GMAC], 2012a). Such positive perceptions hold after graduation, when the vast majority of MBA alumni indicate that, knowing what they know now, they would pursue the degree again (GMAC, 2013). Among the key benefits these alumni frequently cite are opportunities to develop management knowledge and technical skills, network and form relationships of long-term value, and expand their career options (Bruce, 2010). In addition, potential employers consistently recognize the value of graduate management education when they recruit graduates, acknowledging that it instills competencies needed for successful job performance (GMAC, 2010).

In addition to perceptions of value, there is evidence that graduate management education has significant competency and career consequences for individuals. For example, graduate management education is capable of increasing cognitive and interpersonal competencies related to managerial effectiveness (Boyatzis, Stubbs, & Taylor, 2002; Hoover, Giambatista, Sorenson, & Bommer, 2010). MBA programs typically require coursework that, at a minimum, touches the key competencies required for managerial performance, including managing human capital, strategy and innovation, decision-making processes, administrative activities, external constituents and context, and logistics and technology (Rubin & Dierdorff, 2009). MBA programs generally include instruction on additional key areas of business management, such as integrative or systems thinking (Atwater, Kannan, & Stephens, 2008). The personal competence that is gained from graduate management education benefits individual careers in both the long and short term (Zhao, Truell, Alexander, & Hill, 2006). For instance, longitudinal studies show that individuals who complete the MBA report greater early career success than similarly qualified individuals without the degree (Inderrieden, Holtom, & Bies, 2006). Finally, building social capital and increasing networking opportunities are frequently listed as advantages of pursuing graduate management education (Vaara & Fay, 2011).

Graduate management education also provides significant economic consequences for individuals. For example, those who complete their MBAs stand to earn as much as 81 percent more after graduation than before they entered the MBA program, and employers report a five-year stable salary premium of US $40,000 for an MBA graduate over someone with a bachelor's degree (GMAC, 2012b). Such findings are consistent with other research showing that MBA salaries and rates of return are substantial (Connolly, 2003). As a result, some have concluded that the "MBA yields an excellent return on investment for nearly everyone, regardless of the type of program, the race of the student, or even the ranking of the school" (Holtom & Inderrieden, 2007, p. 36).

This discussion strongly suggests that graduate management education holds both perceived and actual consequences for individuals. This is not to say that current models of graduate management education are without need of improvement, a point to which we return later in the chapter. However, graduate management education does appear to be a fruitful, systematic training ground for managerial competence that brings with it numerous personal benefits coinciding with its completion.

Organizational Value

Given the consequences of graduate management education for individuals, the question becomes whether or not organizations benefit as well. There are several reasons to believe they do. For example, graduate management education offers cross-functional exposure that is difficult to either imitate or systematically implement in other organization-specific training settings. In addition, graduate management education serves as a filter of sorts; organizations can reasonably assume that individuals who apply and eventually matriculate from business schools possess demonstrated ability and motivation that underlies effective job performance. Finally, the intent of graduate management education is to train individuals in evidence-based, state-of-the-art management practices that help solve complex organizational problems. By continuing to hire MBAs, organizations give the impression that they perceive such value in graduate management education. As an example, a 2012 survey of 1,096 employers found that nearly four in five companies planned to hire at least one MBA candidate (GMAC, 2012b).

Beyond simple market demand, there are other reasons to believe such training adds value to organizations. For instance, at their essence, MBA programs are formalized management development programs, and research has consistently demonstrated the effectiveness of formal programs in promoting managerial competence (see Burke & Day, 1986; Collins & Holton, 2004). Of particular value to organizations is the fact that managerial competence has been linked to a variety of outcomes. These outcomes include reductions in large employee-related costs such as turnover (Griffith, Hom, & Gaertner, 2000) and counterproductive behaviors (Greenberg, 1990); increases in employee and team performance (Judge & Piccolo, 2004; Stajkovic & Luthans, 2003) and organizational citizenship (Podsakoff, MacKenzie, Paine, & Bachrach, 2000); and improved overall commitment and satisfaction (Podsakoff, Bommer, Podsakoff, & MacKenzie, 2006). Still other research suggests that when it comes to outcomes such as revenue and environmental sustainability, companies led by executives with graduate management education often outperform companies with executives who do not (Jiang & Murphy, 2007; Slater & Dixon-Fowler, 2010).

Another way in which graduate management education benefits organizations is through management practices that are first taught to students and then transferred to the students' eventual employers. Not only do many of these strategies defy the "commonsense" approaches routinely found in contemporary organizations (Pfeffer & Sutton, 2006), but evidence also indicates that effective management practices are quite rare in industry (Bloom, Sudun, & Van Reenen, 2012). For example, the evidence is rather clear that downsizing seldom, if ever, makes a firm more competitive (see Cascio, 2005; Datta, Guthrie, Basuil, & Pandey, 2010), yet the practice is commonplace in today's organizations. Other specific management practices, such as internal promotion or succession planning, have been convincingly linked to better organizational performance on a variety of financial, customer, and productivity measures (see Combs, Liu, Hall, & Ketchen, 2006; Huselid, 1995). Large-scale research spanning multiple countries indicates that well-run companies engage in management practices that ensure rigorous monitoring, set challenging targets, and use contingent rewards (Bloom & others, 2012). The impact of graduate management education on organizations comes, then, from teaching these types of evidenced-based practices. In fact, graduate management education seems highly beneficial in this regard when one considers that MBA coursework regularly covers (a) statistical and data analysis tools, important for monitoring performance; (b) the connections between operational and financial concepts (for example, output and gross margin), critical for setting interdependent performance goals; and (c) merit-based incentives (for example, raises, bonuses, and promotions), helpful in promoting employee motivation and commitment (Homkes, 2011).

Societal Value

Up to this point, we have discussed the various forms in which graduate management education contributes value to individuals and organizations, contributions that are usually in more direct or explicit ways. Yet, graduate management education also holds potential value for the society in which both individuals and organizations operate. At a general level, a substantial body of literature has shown that higher levels of education in a given society are associated with numerous economic and social benefits. For example, education has been linked to broader economic growth in societies (Temple, 2001) as well as social consequences such as better health, less crime, more community and civic participation, and social cohesion (Baum & Ma, 2007; McMahon, 2001; Wolfe & Haveman, 2001). These benefits have also been attributed to higher or tertiary education (Gemmel, 1996).

In specific respect to graduate management education, it is important to remember that a central tenet underlying the formation of university-based business schools was the notion of producing professionals with expertise to develop better functioning businesses aligned with the "broader interests of society" (Khurana, 2007). The primary rationale here is that, to be prosperous, societies require well-functioning organizations. These linkages between organizations and society, organizational effectiveness and societal prosperity, are wholly consistent with the focus and promise of graduate management education—a promise that entails training individuals to effectively manage organizations of any kind. Although this latter fact is often overlooked, it is important to recognize that the competencies taught in graduate management education generalize beyond the typical "business" organization (that is, for-profit entities). Indeed, one would struggle to identify *any* organization—large or small, profit or nonprofit, public or private—that does not require effective management of people, money, and technology to both thrive and survive.

Certainly there is room for debate about how well graduate management education has promoted an alignment between societal and organizational interests (a point we return to later). Yet it is undeniable that the majority of advocates of this alignment reside in institutions of graduate management education. Consider the early influential work of Freeman (1984) on stakeholder theory, in which he explicitly argued the case for business impact on entities beyond stockholders alone. The same scholarly attention can be seen in more recent work on "shared value" creation, most notably outlined by Porter and Kramer (2006; 2011), where value is defined as the intersection between economic benefits and meeting societal needs and challenges. Still others have argued for rebuilding organizations with a greater sense of community (for example, Mintzberg, 2009). The growth of research and educational programs around social entrepreneurship, sustainability, and ethics in business schools further indicates the continuing relevance of graduate management education to society (Audebrand, 2010; Bruce & Edgington, 2003; Stead & Stead, 2010). When we consider all these contributions collectively, we seriously wonder, Where else would individuals be exposed, concertedly and systematically, to the notion that organizations and society are inextricably interdependent if not in programs of graduate management education?

Waning, Sustaining, or Gaining Value in the Future?

Despite escalating criticism of graduate management education, the case for its value to individuals, organizations, and ultimately society is compelling. Few educational endeavors have enjoyed such an impressive record of growth over the past several decades. For example, since the advent of graduate management education, the number of graduates in the United States grew at an average annual rate of 12 percent; by 1981, the output of graduates was greater than that of law and medical schools combined (Rosett, 2008). Current estimates by the Association to Advance Collegiate Schools of Business (AACSB) show that approximately 13,670 institutions, of which AACSB accredits 633 schools across 41 different countries, offer MBA degrees globally (Trouble in the Middle, 2011). Although growth has somewhat stabilized in the United States, outside the United States interest in graduate management education continues to grow, with an 8.8 percent increase in the number of non–U.S. citizens taking the GMAT exam between 2006 and 2011 (GMAC, 2011).

Yet there are reasons to believe that graduate management education faces new pressures and challenges that are unprecedented in its century-long history. As outlined by Holtom and Porter in this volume, these include pressures from new technology (for example, massive open online courses, or MOOCs), changing applicant demographics, and financial constraints. Moreover, the shifting global economic landscape offers both challenges and opportunities for graduate management education. Consider, for instance, that nearly 4 billion consumers live at what is considered the "bottom of the economic pyramid" (BOP) and earn less than $3,000 a year in local purchasing power. Yet their aggregate purchasing power is substantial, providing enormous opportunities for companies who can deliver products that this $5 trillion BOP market demands at prices they can afford (Jain, 2011). Furthermore, organizations must serve these emerging constituents in an environment of limited natural resources, which will force more efficient and responsible use of resources. According to McKinsey Global Institute, by 2030, resource productivity opportunities worldwide will total $2.9 trillion. These opportunities will include reducing food waste, deploying efficient irrigation systems, and improving the energy efficiency of buildings (Dobbs, Oppenheim, & Thompson, 2012). Needless to say, such complex tasks will require competent managers with a range of critical capacities to lead organizations in addressing these complexities. Graduate management education can and should be largely responsible for helping future leaders develop these capacities.

In addition to recognizing these external pressures, we have reason to suspect that the traditional approach to graduate management education is insufficient to address the growing complexity of the world of work. As business school insiders have exhaustively detailed over the past two decades, there are numerous areas in which graduate management education falls short of meeting its promises of value contribution. For example, some contend that graduate management education is too detached from workplace issues and emphasizes theory to the detriment of applied knowledge (for example, Ghoshal, 2005). Others argue that current models increasingly encourage students to generate hasty solutions to complicated problems (for example, Mintzberg, 2004). Still others assert that the current approach requires significant retooling to enhance a global mind-set, deepen cross-cultural understanding, and promote social concerns such as global poverty and income inequality and ethical awareness (for example, Datar, Garvin, & Cullen, 2010). Taken as a whole, these assessments call into question both the philosophy and methods underpinning current models of graduate management education and raise concerns that graduates are increasingly incapable of managing complex, multicultural organizations in ways that meet stakeholders' expectations (Khurana, 2007).

Stakeholders beyond business school insiders appear concerned about the current approach to graduate management education. In the United States, public perceptions of businesses and those who run them have consistently fallen over several decades—perceptions exacerbated by numerous headline-making corporate scandals, such as Enron, Worldcom, Hewlett-Packard, Lehman Brothers, and so on. For example, the 2009 Edelman Trust Barometer found that 84 percent of Americans held businesses responsible for the global financial crisis (Edelman, 2009). Other stakeholders, such as employers, also indicate they want more from graduate management education, including graduates with greater competence in areas such as strategic thinking, interpersonal skills, and leadership (GMAC, 2004). As part of writing this chapter, one of the authors interviewed nine senior human resource executives from large multinationals that hire MBAs and eleven corporate recruiters from different-sized companies. Among the challenges they identified for graduate management education included providing:

- A more values-driven education that emphasizes doing the right thing for the long term, operating with a high level of integrity and trust, investing in people, and helping communities to be as successful as the companies themselves
- A "borderless orientation" that stresses collaboration and knowledge sharing, both internally (across functions or units) and externally (across geographies)
- Networking skills that promote collaboration as well as personal and career development

- Enhanced creativity and innovation that emphasize experimentation, calculated risks, and integrating consumers and producers into the value chain

What this discussion of external pressures and internal critiques exemplifies is that graduate management education must undergo a serious renovation, not only to *ensure* its current value but also to *enhance* its future value in the world's economies. The ultimate outcome, however, will rest upon how we conceptualize and deliver graduate management education. Many of the chapters in this volume focus on specific ways to renovate current models and practices, such as curriculum content and delivery, student engagement, faculty development, and quality enhancement. With this mind, we turn our attention toward four key imperatives that underlie the recommendations presented in later chapters. These fundamental imperatives lie at the core of how we conceptualize graduate management education rather than processes of implementation or delivery per se. Yet they raise questions that we must address a priori because they guide how we both generate and select subsequent actions to improve graduate management education. Of course, these imperatives are by no means an exhaustive list; rather, they are some of the big issues we feel are most immediately salient.

Imperative 1: Increasing the Effectiveness of Graduate Management Education

One point the previous decade of critiques has made is that we can do better. Although graduate management education has demonstrable benefits for individuals, organizations, and society, there is still a substantial need to increase its efficacy as an effective training ground for managerial competence. A dual focus on enhancing learning and promoting the transfer of this learning into practice is essential.

Several scholars have noted that a key means to enhance learning within graduate management education, including MBA programs, is to bolster instructional relevance (Bennis & O'Toole, 2005; Pfeffer & Fong, 2002). For example, Rynes and Bartunek (this volume) outline several specific challenges that beset graduate management education, including the need to substantially infuse more ethics and leadership into the curriculum. The evidence clearly shows that, even though they provide training that spans the full scope of required managerial competencies, the majority of MBA programs underemphasize competency instruction on the very skills practicing managers deem most essential (see Rubin & Dierdorff, 2009). Moreover, multiple business school stakeholders—including faculty, administrators, alumni, and recruiters—recognize both the importance of these competencies and the fact that they are currently underemphasized. This has led Rubin and Dierdorff (2011) to conclude:

> MBA programs have adopted a form of pluralistic ignorance in which stakeholders seem to privately agree what competencies ought to be emphasized, but fail to manage such agreement in practice, inevitably maintaining the curricular misalignment that remains so persistent. (p. 154)

In addition to the opportunities to enhance the scope and relevance of curricula there is significant room for improving the manner with which we deliver graduate management education. Among the pressing needs here are to reduce reliance on a single dominant instructional method (such as lecture or case study) within a given institution and to better integrate technology to boost learning itself rather than merely reduce costs. Brown and his colleagues (this volume) describe in detail several curriculum delivery needs and recommend specific practices to increase the effectiveness of particular instructional techniques and learning technologies.

The ultimate goal of any educational program—especially applied programs such as those in graduate management education—is to ensure that learning takes place and then is effectively transferred to other contexts. Meeting this goal involves promoting the transfer of knowledge and skills that students learn in graduate management education to the managerial roles where they eventually work. Pfeffer and Sutton (2000) referred to such transfer as bridging the "knowing-doing gap," which is fundamental to the success (or failure) of graduate management education. At least part of the challenge of bridging this transfer gap can be addressed by aligning curricula to managerial realities and using more hands-on instructional techniques such as behavioral modeling. However, in all likelihood we also need to rethink the type of knowledge graduate management education seeks to inculcate. Along these lines, improving the transfer of graduate management education requires moving beyond building conceptual and procedural knowledge (*know about* and *know how*, respectively) to building a deeper capacity for *applied management knowledge*. Baldwin and his colleagues (2011) described applied management knowledge as

> beyond knowing how to effectively execute management actions to also include determination of when and under what circumstances it would be appropriate to take such actions. . . . Put another way, [applied management knowledge] determines how well managers identify and execute proper courses of actions in contextual situations, without directions or response cues, amidst the noise and competing demands that typically characterize authentic management roles. (p. 585)

These authors go on to describe specific ways to increase applied management knowledge in business schools—ways that include focusing on fundamentals, introducing counterintuitive pedagogy, encouraging perspective taking, and increasing knowledge accessibility.

Graduate management education has undeniable effects on individual learning, but as the discussion indicates, our current approaches leave abundant room for improvement. In addition to meeting the needs addressed in later chapters, enhancing effectiveness in the future will entail increasing the alignment of curricula to managerial realities, augmenting and revising current instructional techniques, and refocusing attention on forms of learning that can better boost the transfer of graduate management education to practice. Even .further impetus for improvement comes from evidence showing the paucity of effective management practices in all types of organizations as well as the disconnect between evidence-based recommendations and actual practice (for example, Bloom & others, 2012; Rousseau & McCarthy, 2007; Rynes, Brown, & Colbert, 2002; Rynes, Giluk, & Brown, 2007).

Imperative 2: Defining and Differentiating Within Graduate Management Education

Historically, the purpose of graduate management education was to train a professional class of individuals who were technically skilled in quantitative methods and functional areas. Two prestigious studies sponsored by the Ford Foundation (Gordon & Howell, 1959) and the Carnegie Corporation (Pierson, 1959) laid the groundwork for what became the traditional two-year MBA program. For more than four decades, the major thrust of MBA programs has been to inculcate knowledge of general administration, including accounting, economics, finance, operations, statistics, and principles of general management. As Khurana (2007) notes, the basic intention of graduate management education has been to

> give students a wide-ranging exposure to many forms of knowledge and discourage a narrowing of focus—the notion being that as graduates moved higher in their organizations and into posi-

tions of greater responsibility, they would require familiarity with a broad array of corporate functions and find themselves managing people from a variety of corporate functions. (p. 295)

This prevailing focus on *breadth* over *depth* reinforces contemporary notions of the MBA graduate as a *general manager*. The intended outcome is essentially a transportable degree that applies across industries, organizations, and occupations. To date, the logic of such an approach has been reinforced by placement data that show MBA graduates employed in a variety of managerial roles across industries. For example, in a survey of 2,060 alumni, only 28 percent reported that they did not fulfill a "manager or supervisor" role in their current organization (GMAC, 2004). Moreover, employers report that of the graduates they hire, 87 percent will be placed into "mid-level" or "senior-level" positions (GMAC, 2012a).

Over the past three decades, however, several important changes in the business education environment have led to a reconsideration of the general management approach. The trend toward viewing knowledge as a commodity has pressured many business schools to placate hiring organizations by producing students who, rather than being broadly knowledgeable, are well versed in narrow tools and techniques (see Trank & Rynes, 2003). Moreover, amid growing criticism, the capacity of the standard two-year MBA to be sufficiently responsive to the worlds of industry and commerce that graduates enter has been questioned (see Podolny, 2009). Finally, the flattening of the growth trend in overall MBA enrollment (GMAC, 2013) has further heightened attention in business schools to growth opportunities in other degree program offerings, which hold the potential to offset this slowing demand for MBA education.

One reaction to these pressures appears to be an increase in specialization within graduate management education. The result of specialization has been twofold: (a) rapid growth of myriad educational vehicles designed to deliver joint degrees and narrow terminal master's degree programs and (b) increased learner choice in the courses that constitute the MBA (for example, fewer "lockstep" curriculum programs). For example, a large-scale study of 576 universities providing graduate management education found that 66 percent offered at least one MS degree, and 34 percent offered at least one joint degree such as an MBA/ JD (Dierdorff & Rubin, 2009). MBA programs also now routinely reduce required core coursework to allow students to focus on highly specific content areas frequently referred to as *concentrations, areas of focus, specializations, career tracks*, and so forth. More than half of the schools examined by Dierdorff and Rubin (2009) offered at least one MBA concentration, with an average of more than seven concentrations across the 576 sample schools.

The increase in degree program variety and MBA specialization are not necessarily problematic per se—both promise a closer alignment of graduate training with future occupational demands. The concern instead lies with the rapid proliferation of such changes without apparent thought as to what they actually mean to various business school stakeholders. It is critical to recognize that conferred degrees are not meaningless; they carry significant weight in the eyes of employers and society at large. To say that an individual received an MBA or an MS degree implies that he or she acquired a certain knowledge and skill base. Graduate degrees also communicate specific meaning to stakeholders and establish a certain value for one form of education over another. Thus, it is imperative for business schools to ensure that their various program offerings are indeed aligned with the needs of individuals, organizations, and society rather than merely leveraged as additional sources of revenue.

To do so, business schools must realize that offering multiple degrees will certainly involve trade-offs that are both strategic and operational in nature. It is true that specialized training can be a better match for specific occupational requirements. However, differentiation also requires a given institution to allocate resources across a variety of programs, and, to be most effective in an instructional sense, such allocations cannot simply mean repackaging existing coursework into bundles that the institution can fit equally well into either the more general MBA or more specialized MS degrees.

Program differentiation also requires that business schools actively manage external perceptions and understanding of different degree programs. Although more research is sorely needed, there is some evidence that as curricula have grown more varied the result has been increased confusion in the marketplace among recruiters (GMAC, 2008). For some narrow specialized master's degrees, potential marketplace confusion may be much less likely to exist. This certainly would seem to be the case for degrees that are closely linked to particular occupations, such as MS degrees in finance, accounting, or human resources. These types of MS degrees also correspond with well-established professional certifications (for example, CFA, CPA, SPHR). However, an unambiguous understanding of other widely offered MS degrees (for example, MS in management) does not seem as likely to exist. Moreover, MS degrees in newer specialty areas, such as entrepreneurship or sustainability management, would seem even less likely to be clearly understood by external stakeholders.

With increases in program variety, it should come at no surprise that external stakeholders (and business school faculty for that matter) might not be able to clearly define and differentiate a school's various offerings. The increased popularity of MS degrees and the shift away from a conventional MBA toward a reduced core with increased concentrations leads to a host of fundamental questions that must be addressed. What is the *real* difference between an MS degree and an MBA with an equivalent concentration, such as an MS in finance versus an MBA with a finance concentration, or an MS in entrepreneurship versus an MBA with an entrepreneurship concentration? If both the MBA and the MS in management are meant to provide general management training, precisely how and why do they differ? To what extent are MS degree students exposed to general business acumen outside their specialties? How much, if any, cross-functional training coincides with various MS degrees? How comparable is an MBA degree from one institution to another given the pronounced increase in course customization?

It is crucial for institutions to clearly articulate what their degrees mean in real curricular or programmatic terms. This need is made even more urgent by recent evidence of the increased hiring of individuals with more specialized graduate management training (GMAC, 2013). At first blush, addressing questions such as those described might seem to be a purely "academic exercise." After all, both potential students and employers do not seem to be complaining. Yet, it is essential to realize that applicant and employment demand do not speak to issues of educational quality or the long-term consequences of ambiguity in graduate management program offerings. To use a business education analogy, would we ever teach our students that the most effective companies are those that only focus on demand without a concern for product or service quality, customer understanding, and the unique value added by different company products or services?

Overall, we believe the most effective way forward for graduate management education involves a deeper understanding of the variety of degree programs that are offered. A focus on defining and differentiated the unique purposes, structures, and values of a school's various offerings is vital. For the MBA degree, this involves an emphasis on a cross-functional breadth of education, whereas the emphasis is on a technical depth of education for MS degrees. Clearly, the demand for management generalists still exists. Even in rapidly expanding high-technology sectors like biotechnology or renewable energy, managerial roles continue to emerge (Dierdorff & others, 2011).

Just as critical to addressing this imperative is understanding the types of individuals that could be best suited for different educational programs. For instance, some contend that the MBA be reserved for individuals with high levels of work experience, perhaps those already with managerial experience (for example,

Mintzberg, 2004). High levels of work experience are also relevant to program success in other business school offerings, such as executive MBA or executive education programs (Garvin, 2007). For specialized MS degrees, such extensive work experience may or may not be as salient. This collectively suggests that one way to differentiate various program offerings is to tailor them toward particular student profiles with regard to work experience, career maturity, and desired occupational outcomes. Indeed, some of this segmentation already seems to be naturally occurring in the applicant marketplace, where data show that compared to applicants to MBA programs, nearly double the number of applicants to MS programs are under twenty-four years of age and tend to be seeking to establish their careers rather than switching careers (GMAC, 2012c). Thus, the MBA might be better positioned as a "higher-level" degree for either those with considerable managerial experience or perhaps those with ample work experience and possessing other graduate-level degrees (for example, MS in engineering fields). MS degrees would be better positioned for individuals more recently finishing undergraduate studies or those seeking to enter very specific occupational roles such as tax accounting, financial analysis, and so forth.

Imperative 3: Recognizing and Expanding Our Espoused Values

As we noted at the beginning of this chapter, part of the purpose of graduate management education is to foster a particular set of values that shape the manner with which individuals view and interpret the world of work. Some might argue that graduate management education does not (and cannot) teach a set of core values and to do so would assume the existence of a universal set of values. However, it is undeniable that we already promote a particularistic set of values in graduate management education, regardless of country and institution, and these values are quintessentially economic and financial in nature (Augier & March,

2011; Ghoshal, 2005; Khurana, 2007). Moreover, the problems associated with these dominant values and the theories on which they are based have been well documented, including both a lack of supporting evidence for theoretical conjectures and several unintended consequences such as increased self-interest, greed, and free-riding (Ferraro, Pfeffer, & Sutton, 2005; Ghoshal & Moran, 1996; Pfeffer, 2005; Pfeffer & Sutton, 2006; Podolny, 2009; Rocha & Ghoshal, 2006; Wang, Malhotra, & Murnighan, 2011). Giacalone (2004) called attention to the imperative of addressing the values we espouse when he remarked:

> What ideals should our students aspire to achieve? Aspiring doctors and psychologists are socialized to strive for newer and better techniques to improve our physical and mental health. Aspiring engineers strive for better techniques and newer approaches to improve society. They are socialized into professional lives that will leave behind something worthy of their time on the planet. Their professional goals are not solely financial, but transcendent, and help them aim for something more than a financial bottom line. (p. 416)

Ultimately, the question is this: What types of values *should* be emphasized in graduate management education? At the very least, business schools must first recognize that they do indeed impart a certain view of the world, one that holds unintended, and often negative, consequences. Then business schools must inculcate the fact that there are multiple value propositions of equal importance to organizations and societies, and that these necessarily extend beyond mere economic or financial success. As Wang and colleagues (2011) succinctly observed, we must ensure that students know when they "only focus on financial analyses and the line items on balance sheets, their decisions may ignore other social consequences" (p. 657).

Graduate management education can accomplish much of this work by taking seriously the inclusion of courses that teach these fundamental principles (see Rynes and Bartunek, this volume, for curriculum recommendations). Yet, additional space in the curriculum will work only if everyone responsible for graduate management education, not just the faculty who teach specific courses, emphasizes and espouses organizational obligations and societal connectedness. This may not be as difficult as some believe. For example, one hallmark of graduate management education is teaching individuals how to manage organizational capital that is inherently multidimensional (financial, technological, human) and interdependent in nature (Atwater & others, 2008). Numerous concepts and models incorporate these types of multifaceted views of organizational performance, such as shared value creation, the balanced scorecard, sustainable enterprises, and the triple bottom line. In this sense, it seems quite feasible to expand the set of values that graduate management education promotes to include a broader arena of impact.

What if graduate management education maintains the status quo? We believe there are serious ramifications if we fail to collectively act. For instance, if graduate management education continues to be associated with the general public's distrust of business (or, worse yet, seen as the cause of "bad business," as some have suggested), then the perceived value of such training will almost certainly diminish. Podolny (2009) portended this potential consequence and concluded, "Business schools can regain society's trust by emphasizing values as much as they do analytics and by encouraging students to adopt a holistic approach to business problems" (p. 63). In addition, the expansion of emerging markets in underdeveloped economies will undoubtedly lead to times when either meeting or failing to meet societal and business needs will be clearer to stakeholders (especially when the markets are in developing nations most in need of well-functioning organizations). Finally, there is evidence that graduate management education is not yet contributing as much as it could to the functioning of noncorporate organizations. Recent surveys indicate that fewer than 10 percent of MBA alumni work in governmental or nonprofit organizations (GMAC, 2012d). Although some of this underrepresentation could be dismissed as a lack of MBA hiring, an alternative reason could be the lack of value institutions of graduate management education place on service to others and society.

Imperative 4: Fulfilling the Promise of Professionalism

We intentionally call this final imperative *fulfilling the promise* because, despite the fact that professionalism is in the DNA of graduate management education, it is far from achieving professional status. This unfulfilled promise has not only set adrift the focus of contemporary graduate management education, but it has also impeded the renovation needed to guarantee its ongoing value for individuals, organizations, and society. In his meticulous articulation of the historical development of American business schools, Khurana (2007) observed the centrality of professionalism in the underlying purpose of graduate management education:

> University business schools were originally created to be "professional schools" not in the loose sense in which we now use the term to refer to graduate schools in any area outside the arts and sciences, but in another, more complex sense reflecting a very specific, historically grounded understanding of what constitutes a "profession." This notion comprised, among other things, a social compact between occupations deemed "professions" and society at large. Business schools were thus intended not just to prepare students for careers in management but also to serve as the major vehicles of an effort to transform management from incipient occupation in search of legitimacy to a bona fide profession. (p. 7)

This quote makes it clear that the imperative of professionalism cuts across the previous three imperatives we set forth for graduate management education. In fact, the astute reader probably noticed the use of the term *professional* in each of the preceding sections. This is because the concept of professionalism carries specific meaning that can shape the way in which graduate management education is designed, implemented, and evaluated as well as the types of values, standards, and practices it instills. The imperative of professionalism is arguably most relevant when considering the predominate degree in graduate management education, the MBA. While other more specific degree programs in business schools have made strides toward professionalism through means such as certification (for example, CFA for financial analysts, CPA for accountants), such professionalizing has eluded the MBA.

Of course, the notion of management as a profession is not without detractors. Some argue that management simply cannot be a profession nor can business schools be professional schools (for example, Barker, 2010). However, the empirical evidence rather convincingly points to the contrary. For example, one defining characteristic of all professions is a common body of knowledge requisite for occupational performance. Five decades of focused research have repeatedly shown a striking consensus about what managers do and what makes them successful, and such competencies remain consistent regardless of occupation or industry (see Dierdorff, Rubin, & Morgeson, 2009). MBA education also draws upon multiple academic disciplines, such as mathematics, economics, psychology, philosophy, and sociology. This is a characteristic shared by other established professions such as medicine, which relies on fields like biology, chemistry, and psychology (Bennis & O'Toole, 2005). Here, too, there is consensus regarding the foundational subjects to be instructed, which is clearly reflected in the required coursework by literally hundreds of business schools (Rubin & Dierdorff, 2009). What MBA program does not insist on courses in accounting, finance, marketing, and management? The problem with failing to recognize consensus in both competencies and curricula is that it opens up MBA education to virtually any combination of courses business schools see as adding value, regardless of whether the content is relevant to the profession of management (O'Toole, 2009).

Fulfilling the promise of professionalism also means focusing on commonly held ideals that typically espouse a social compact, where values such as service to others or to society are empha-sized (Khurana & Nohria, 2008; Trank & Rynes, 2003). As we outlined in the preceding section, business schools have a sub-stantial need to recognize that particular values are already being promoted in MBA education, and these values are rather limited in scope and quite disconnected from business schools' historical emphasis on serving both organizational and societal needs. Thus, the benefit of treating management as a profession is that it forces us to identify and address the values we espouse; to take a concerted look at the types of ideals we deem important enough to instill. Like other professional schools, which influence the conduct of people in related occupations by inculcating particu-lar values (for example, impartial counsel, doing no harm, or serving the greater good), business schools must similarly infuse ideals, beginning with the notion of shared value through effec-tive management for individuals, organizations, and society (Podolny, 2009).

The first step toward fulfilling the promise of professionalism is to agree on a common set of principles, content domains, and experiences that will exist within any graduate management education program. In other words, we must articulate a common set of competencies toward which our programs will direct spe-cific coursework and learner experiences. This is especially the case for the MBA. As we discussed, there is already substantial consensus around what is required to perform managerial roles as well as the domains currently covered by business schools. Such existing conditions strongly suggest that it is indeed pos-sible to agree on what our students must learn, and to claim otherwise rings rather hollow.

It is also important to point out that establishing a core curriculum does not in any way impede creativity in the way a particular institution delivers learning or even in the types of mission-driven activities that supersede such a common core (for example, electives, co-curricular activities, internships, and so on). Certainly, there is variability in the ways medical or law schools deliver courses in gross anatomy or constitutional law; yet, can anyone seriously imagine producing an MD or JD who has not mastered such subject matter?

Indeed there are multiple ways to move toward professionalism in management, such as through existing accrediting bodies or by establishing new associations for certification purposes. Underlying any of these efforts is the necessary recognition that claiming professionalism in management *does not* mean that one must possess the MBA to be a successful manager, but rather that the MBA confers a particular level of expertise concomitant with particular foundational training. In this regard, the arguments often put forth against establishing post–MBA professional certification, such as the inability of certifications to guarantee managerial success, lack a convincing rationale. Certifications are simply validations of the requisite knowledge and skill that subsume managerial roles, not predictors of job performance. Who would argue that possessing a CPA or a professional engineer (PE) certification guarantees high performance as an accountant or engineer? Regardless of the specific actions taken toward professionalism in management, it is certain that without collective action it is very likely that the legitimacy of graduate management education will continue to be questioned, and ultimately its value will diminish.

A Unique Opportunity for Action

In this chapter we sought to articulate the case for why and how graduate management education is valuable to the individuals who choose to pursue it, the organizations that eventually select its graduates, and the societies within which both reside. We believe building such value propositions are necessary for several reasons, not the least of which is to remind ourselves of the substantial and meaningful influence graduate management education can and does have on multiple stakeholders. Moreover, the past few decades have seen a rise in questions about the legitimacy of graduate management education in terms of its effectiveness, the purposes of its existence, as well as the constituents it serves and fails to serve.

Toward this end, we extended our explication to a discussion of the types of pressures that currently face graduate management education. Pressures such as those we discussed, as well as those described throughout this book, represent forces that will either facilitate or inhibit the future value of graduate management education. To be sure, the nature of this impact is in our collective control. We believe to adequately meet these challenges business schools must strive to realize the promise of professionalism, whereby the education we provide fulfills the dual functions of instilling managerial competence and supporting social responsibility. The times in which we live present a unique chance to reconceptualize the purposes and desired consequences of graduate management education. This opportunity not only carries the promise of improving graduate management education through innovation and renovation of current models and practices, but also the looming threat of diminished relevance if we fail to collectively act in this regard. Put bluntly, the time is now to create a new future rather than critique the past if the value of graduate management education is to flourish into the next hundred years.

Summing Up

- Evidence clearly demonstrates that graduate management education is valuable to individuals. Positive outcomes include business acumen, managerial competence,

economic benefits (salary), and other career-related
consequences.

- For organizations, graduate management education holds
value by promoting managerial effectiveness that is
associated multiple organizational outcomes (for example
less turnover, increased performance, and so forth) as well
as inculcating effective management practices that are all
too rare in industry at large.

- Societies require well-functioning organizations to be
prosperous. The linkage between organizations and society,
organizational effectiveness and societal prosperity, are
wholly consistent with the focus and promise of graduate
management education, which is to train individuals to
effectively manage organizations of any kind.

- Graduate management education today faces
unprecedented pressures and challenges. Pressures from
external forces include challenges of learning technology,
the shifting global landscape, and financial constraints.
Internal pressures require meeting the challenges associated
with heightened criticism about both the legitimacy and
effectiveness of current approaches.

- The effectiveness of graduate management education
necessitates a greater alignment among what is taught and
occupational and organizational reality, augmenting
instructional techniques, and refocusing attention on forms
of learning that promote transfer to practice.

- The variety of program offerings that continue to
proliferate in graduate management education must be
more defined and differentiated. This requires deeper
understanding of the unique purposes, structures, and
occupational relevance of different programs in order to
better serve all business school stakeholders.

- The promise of professionalism in graduate management
education must be fulfilled, which requires taking collective

action and recognizing and expanding our currently espoused values.

References

Atwater, J. B., Kannan, V. R., & Stephens, A. A. "Cultivating Systematic Thinking in the Next Generation of Business Leaders." *Academy of Management Learning & Education*, 2008, 7, 9–25.

Audebrand, L. K. "Sustainability in Strategic Management Education." *Academy of Management Learning & Education*, 2010, 9, 413–428.

Augier, M., & March, J. G. *The Roots, Rituals, and Rhetorics of Change: North American Business Schools After the Second World War.* Stanford, Calif.: Stanford University Press, 2011.

Baldwin, T. T., Pierce, J. R., Joines, R. C., & Farouk, S. "The Elusiveness of Applied Management Knowledge: A Critical Challenge for Management Educators." *Academy of Management Learning & Education*, 2011, 10, 583–605.

Barker, R. "No, Management Is Not a Profession." *Harvard Business Review*, July–August 2010, pp. 52–60.

Baum, S., & Ma, J. (2007). "Education Pays: The Benefits of Higher Education for Individuals and Society." The College Board. collegeboard.com/trends

Bennis, W. G., & O'Toole, J. "How Business Schools Lost Their Way." *Harvard Business Review*, May 2005, 96–104.

Bloom, N., Sudun, R., & Van Reenen, J. "Does Management Really Work?" *Harvard Business Review*, November 2012, pp. 3–7.

Boyatzis, R. E., Stubbs, E. C., & Taylor, S. N. "Learning Cognitive and Emotional Intelligence Competencies Through Graduate Management Education." *Academy of Management Learning & Education*, 2002, 1, 150–162.

Bruce, G. D. "Exploring the Value of MBA Degrees: Experiences in Full-Time, Part-Time, and Executive MBA Programs." *Journal of Education for Business*, 2010, 85, 38–44.

Bruce, G. D., & Edgington, R. "Ethics Education in Business: Effectiveness and Effects." *International Journal of Management and Marketing Research*, 2003, 1, 49–70.

Burke, M. J., & Day, R. R. "A Cumulative Study of the Effectiveness of Managerial Training." *Journal of Applied Psychology*, 1986, 71, 232–245.

Cascio, W. F. "Strategies for Responsible Restructuring." *Academy of Management Executive*, 2005, 19(4), 39–50. Reprinted from 2002, 16(3).

Collins, D. B., & Holton, E. F. "The Effectiveness of Managerial Leadership Development Programs: A Meta-Analysis of Studies from 1982 to 2001." *Human Resource Development Quarterly*, 2004, 15, 217–248.

Connolly, M. "The End of the MBA as We Know It?" *Academy of Management Learning & Education*, 2003, 2, 365–367.

Combs, J. G., Liu, Y., Hall, A. T., & Ketchen, D. J. "How Much Do High Performance Work Practices Matter? A Meta-analysis of Their Effects on Organizational Performance." *Personnel Psychology*, 2006, 59, 501–528.

Datar, S. M., Garvin, D. A. & Cullen, P. G. *Rethinking the MBA: Business Education at a Crossroads*. Boston, Mass.: Harvard Business School Press, 2010.

Datta, D. K., Guthrie, J. P., Basuil, D., & Pandey, A. "Causes and Effects of Employee Downsizing: A Review and Synthesis." *Journal of Management*, 2010, 36, 281–348.

Dierdorff, E.C., Norton, J.J., Gregory, C.M., Rivkin, D. & Lewis, P. "*Greening of the World of Work: Revisiting Occupational Consequences.*" Washington, D.C.: U.S. Department of Labor: Educational and Training Administration, 2011. http://www.onetcenter.org/reports/Green2.html

Dierdorff, E. C., & Rubin, R. S. "The Relevance, Requirements, and Ramifications of Specialized MBA Programs." Project technical report presented to the MERInstitute of the Graduate Management Admission Council, McLean, Va., 2009.

Dierdorff, E. C., Rubin, R. S., & Morgeson, F. P. "The Milieu of Managerial Work: An Integrative Framework Linking Work Context to Role Requirements." *Journal of Applied Psychology*, 2009, 94, 972–988.

Dobbs, R., Oppenheim, J., & Thompson, F. "Mobilizing for a Resource Revolution." *McKinsey Quarterly*, 2012, 1, 28–42.

Edelman. *2009 Edelman Trust Barometer Executive Summary*. http://www.scribd.com/doc/11484809/Edelman-Trust-Barometer-2009-Summary

Ferraro, F., Pfeffer, J., & Sutton, R. I. "Economics Language and Assumptions: How Theories Can Become Self-Fulfilling." *Academy of Management Review*, 2005, 30, 8–24.

Freeman, R. E. *Strategic Management: A Stakeholder Approach*. New York: Cambridge University Press, 1984.

Garvin, D. A. "Teaching Executives and Teaching MBAs: Reflections on the Case Method." *Academy of Management Learning & Education*, 2007, 6, 364–374.

Gemmel, N. "Evaluating the Impacts of Human Capital Stocks and Accumulation on Economic Growth: Some New Evidence." *Oxford Bulletin of Economics and Statistics*, 1996, 58, 9–28.

Ghoshal, S. "Bad Management Theories Are Destroying Good Management Practices." *Academy of Management Learning & Education*, 2005, 4, 76–91.

Ghoshal, S., & Moran, P. "Bad for Practice: A Critique of the Transaction Cost Theory." *Academy of Management Review*, 1996, 21, 13–47.

Giacalone, R. A. "A Transcendent Business Education for the 21st Century." *Academy of Management Learning & Education*, 2004, 3, 415–420.

Gordon, R. A., & Howell, J. E. *Higher Education for Business*. New York: Columbia University Press, 1959.

Graduate Management Admission Council. *Global MBA Survey Overall Report*, 8. McLean, Va.: GMAC, 2002.

Graduate Management Admissions Council. *MBA Alumni Perspectives Survey*. McLean, Va.: GMAC, 2004.

Graduate Management Admission Council. *Corporate Recruiters Survey: Survey Report*. McLean, Va.: GMAC, 2008.

Graduate Management Admission Council. *Corporate Recruiters Survey*. McLean, Va.: GMAC, 2010.

Graduate Management Admission Council. *Profile of GMAT Candidates, 2006–07 to 2010–11*. Reston, Va., 2011.

Graduate Management Admission Council. *2012 mba.com Prospective Students Survey Report*. Reston, Va.: GMAC, 2012a.

Graduate Management Admission Council. *2012 Corporate Recruiters Survey Report*. Reston, Va.: 2012b.

Graduate Management Admission Council. *2012 Application Trends Survey Report*. Reston, Va.: 2012c.

Graduate Management Admission Council. *2012 Alumni Perspectives Survey*. Reston, Va.: 2012d.

Graduate Management Admission Council. *Alumni Perspectives Survey*. Reston, VA: GMAC, 2013.

Greenberg, J. "Employee Theft as a Reaction to Underpayment Inequity: The Hidden Cost of Pay Cuts." *Journal of Applied Psychology*, 1990, 75, 561–568.

Griffith, R. W., Hom, P. W., & Gaertner, S. "A Meta-analysis of Antecedents and Correlates of Employee Turnover: Update, Moderator Tests, and Research Implications for the Next Millennium." *Journal of Management*, 2000, 26, 463–488.

Holtom, B. C., & Inderrieden, E. "Go for the MBA." *BizEd*, January/February 2007, 36–40.

Homkes, R. (2011). "The MBA Advantage." *Bloomberg Businessweek*, July 11, 2011, pp. 45–47.

Hoover, J. D., Giambatista, R.C., Sorenson, R.L., & Bommer, W. H. "Assessing the Effectiveness of Whole Person Learning Pedagogy in Skill Acquisition." *Academy of Management Learning & Education*, 2010, 9, 192–204.

Huselid, M. A. "The Impact of Human Resource Management Practices on Turnover, Productivity, and Corporate Financial Performance." *Academy of Management Journal*, 1995, 38, 635–672.

Inderrieden, E., Holtom, B., & Bies, R. "Do MBA Programs Deliver?" In C. Wankel & R. DeFillippi (eds.), *New Visions of Graduate Management Education* (pp. 1–19). Greenwich, Conn.: Information Age, 2006.

Jain, S. C. "Bottom of the Pyramid Market: Theory and Practice." In S. C. Jain & D. A. Griffith, (eds.), *Handbook of Research in International Marketing* (2nd ed., pp. 376–392). Cheltenham, U.K.: Edward Elgar, 2011.

Jiang, B., & Murphy, P. M. "Do Business School Professors Make Good Executive Managers?" *Academy of Management Perspectives*, 2007, 21, 29–50.

Judge, T. A., & Piccolo, R. F. "Transformational and Transactional Leadership: A Meta-Analytic Test of Their Relative Validity." *Journal of Applied Psychology*, 2004, 89, 755–768.

Khurana, R. *From Higher Aims to Hired Hands: The Social Transformation of American Business Schools and the Unfulfilled Promise of Management as a Profession*. Princeton, N.J.: Princeton University Press, 2007.

Khurana R., & Nohria, N. "Make Management a True Profession." *Harvard Business Review*, October 2008, pp. 70–77.

McMahon, W. W. "The Impact of Human Capital on Non-Market Outcomes and Feedbacks on Economic Development in OECD Countries." In J. F. Helliwell (ed.), *The Contribution of Human and Social Capital to Sustained Economic Growth and Well-Being* (pp. 136–171). International Symposium Report. Human Resources Development Canada and OECD, 2001.

Mintzberg, H. *Managers Not MBAs: A Hard Look at the Soft Practice of Managing and Management Development*. San Francisco, Calif.: Berrett-Koehler, 2004.

Mintzberg, H. "Rebuilding Companies as Communities." *Harvard Business Review*, July–August 2009, pp. 140–143.

O'Toole, J. "The Pluralistic Future of Management Education." In S. J. Armstrong & C. V. Fukami (eds.), *Handbook of Management Learning Education and Development* (pp. 547–558). Thousand Oaks, Calif.: Sage, 2009.

Pfeffer, J. "Why Do Bad Management Theories Persist? A Comment on Ghoshal." *Academy of Management Learning & Education*, 2005, 4, 96–100.

Pfeffer, J. & Fong, C. T. "The End of Business Schools? Less Success Than Meets the Eye." *Academy of Management Learning & Education*, 2002, 10, 78–95.

Pfeffer, J. & Sutton, R. I. *The Knowing-Doing Gap: How Smart Companies Turn Knowledge Into Action*. Boston, Mass.: Harvard Business School Publishing, 2000.

Pfeffer, J. & Sutton, R. I. *Hard Facts, Dangerous Half-Truths, and Total Non-sense: Profiting from Evidence-Based Management*. Boston, Mass.: Harvard Business School Publishing, 2006.

Pierson, F. *The Education of American Businessmen*. New York: McGraw-Hill, 1959.

Podolny, J. M. "The Buck Stops (and Starts) at Business Schools." *Harvard Business Review*, June 2009, pp. 62–67.

Podsakoff, P. M., Bommer, W. H., Podsakoff, N., & MacKenzie, S. B. "Relationships Between Leader Reward and Punishment Behavior and Subordinate Attitudes, Perceptions, and Behaviors: A Meta-Analytic Review of Existing and New Research." *Organizational Behavior and Human Decision Processes*, 2006, 99, 113–142.

Podsakoff, P. M., MacKenzie, S. B., Paine, J. B., & Bachrach, D. G. "Organizational Citizenship Behaviors: A Critical Review of the Theoretical and Empirical Literature and Suggestions for Future Research." *Journal of Management*, 2000, 26, 513–563.

Porter, L. W., & McKibbin, L. E. *Management Education and Development: Drift or Thrust Into the 21st Century*. New York: McGraw-Hill, 1988.

Porter, M. E., & Kramer, M. R. "Strategy and Society: The Link Between Competitive Advantage and Corporate Social Responsibility." *Harvard Business Review*, December 2006, pp. 77–92.

Porter, M. E., & Kramer, M. R. "Creating Shared Value." *Harvard Business Review*, January–February 2011, pp. 63–77.

Rocha, H. O., & Ghoshal, S. 2006. "Beyond Self-Interest Revisited." *Journal of Management Studies*, 43, 585–619.

Rosett, R. N. *Business Education in the United States*. Selected Paper No. 59. Chicago, Ill.: University of Chicago Graduate School of Business, 2008.

Rousseau, D. M., & McCarthy, S "Evidence-Based Management: Educating Managers From an Evidence-Based Perspective." *Academy of Management Learning & Education*, 2007, 6, 94–101.

Rubin, R. S., & Dierdorff, E. C. "How Relevant Is the MBA? Assessing the Alignment of Required MBA Curricula and Required Managerial Competencies." *Academy of Management Learning & Education*, 2009, 8, 208–224.

Rubin, R. S., & Dierdorff, E. C. "On the Road to Abilene: Time to Manage Agreement About MBA Curricular Relevance." *Academy of Management Learning & Education*, 2011, 10, 143–161.

Rynes, S. L., Brown, K. G., & Colbert, A. E. "Seven Common Misconceptions About Human Resource Management: Research Findings Versus Practitioner Beliefs." *Academy of Management Executive*, 2002, 16, 92–103.

Rynes, S. L., Giluk, T. L., & Brown, K. G. "The Very Separate Worlds of Academic and Practitioner Periodicals in Human Resource Management: Implications for Evidence Based Management." *Academy of Management Journal*, 2007, 55, 987–1008.

Slater, D. J., & Dixon-Fowler, H. R. "The Future of the Planet in the Hands of MBAs: An Examination of CEO MBA Education and Corporate Environmental Performance." *Academy of Management Learning & Education*, 2010, 9, 429–441.

Stajkovic, A. D., & Luthans, F. "A Meta-analysis of the Effects of Organizational Behavior Modification on Task Performance." *Academy of Management Journal*, 2003, 40, 1122–1149.

Stead, J. G., & Stead, W. E. "Sustainability Comes to Management Education and Research: A Story of Coevolution." *Academy of Management Learning & Education*, 2010, 9, 488–498.

Temple, J. "Growth Effects of Education and Social Capital in the OECD." In J. F. Helliwell (ed.), *The Contribution of Human and Social Capital to Sustained Economic Growth and Well-Being* (pp. 57–101). International Symposium Report, Human Resources Development Canada and OECD, 2001.

Trank, C. Q., & Rynes, S. L. "Who Moved Our Cheese? Reclaiming Professionalism in Business Education." *Academy of Management Learning & Education*, 2003, 2, 189–206.

"Trouble in the Middle." *Economist*, October 15, 2011, pp. 71–73.

Vaara, E., & Fay, E. "How Can a Bourdieusian Perspective Aid Analysis of MBA Education?" *Academy of Management Learning & Education*, 2011, 10, 27–39.

Wang, L., Malhotra, D., & Murnighan, J. K. "Economics Education and Greed." *Academy of Management Learning & Education*, 2011, 10, 643–660.

Wolfe, B., & Haveman, R. "Accounting for the Social and Non-Market Benefits of Education." In J. F. Helliwell (ed.), *The Contribution of Human and Social Capital to Sustained Economic Growth and Well-Being* (pp. 221–250). International Symposium Report, Human Resources Development Canada and OECD, 2001.

Zhao, J. J., Truell, A. D., Alexander, M. W., & Hill, I. B. "Less Success Than Meets the Eye? The Impact of Master of Business Administration Education on Graduates' Careers." *Journal of Education for Business*, 2006, 81, 261–268.

2

FRAMING AND MAKING STRATEGIC CHOICES

Michael Hay
London Business School

Michael Hay acknowledges the contribution of Tom Ryan to the thinking that underpins this chapter and to the writing of the chapter.

Key Topics Covered in This Chapter

- Forces driving change in management education
- Strategic framework for positioning schools for change
- Dimensions of choices and key parameters for change
- Mapping how schools will achieve their target positioning
- Securing stakeholder engagement for effective adaptation

There is no single way to be a successful business school. Although Harvard continues to succeed as a "classic" school, following it and other traditional business schools is no longer a guarantee of success and may well condemn other schools to failure. Numerous viable business models reflect the pressure to change. Duke Corporate Education (Duke CE) has been very successful in executive education with a business model that broke the mold and forced other schools to change how they compete for company-specific programs. China Europe International Business School (CEIBS) in Shanghai has defied the traditional dominance of management education by established schools in North America and Europe. The challenge for deans and senior leadership teams is to determine which model works best in their own context.

Chapters One and Two of this volume serve as a call to arms by highlighting both the forces that require business schools to adapt and the continued value of management education. This chapter seeks to help leaders responsible for implementing change at an individual school by:

- Providing a framework for clarifying the school's future positioning
- Stressing the importance of mapping how the school will move to its target positioning
- Making recommendations for securing the stakeholder engagement required for effective execution

Schools need to clarify their future positioning by developing aligned, internally consistent answers to the following strategic questions:

- Whom does the school serve?
- What does the school do?
- How does the school deliver programs?
- Where does the school deliver programs?
- Who delivers programs?
- How big is the school?
- How is the school organized and managed?
- How is the school funded?

Four Forces That Make Clear Positioning Vital

As described in Chapter One, many forces are driving change in the world of management education. Four in particular are compelling schools to frame, map, and secure stakeholder support for their positioning.

Force 1: Evolving Needs

The worlds of business and management have changed substantially in the past thirty years. Globalization and technological innovation, along with the restructuring of industries and economies, have unleashed ever-increasing competition and uncertainty. Corporations are held accountable by an expanding array of stakeholders, not just shareholders. The command-and-control model of leadership is being replaced by employee engagement and empowerment, bringing with it an increased emphasis on feelings and behavior. People going into business no longer anticipate having a single career in the same organization over the course of their working lives but rather expect multiple careers in multiple organizations. There is an increasing emphasis on lifetime education; people continually attend educational programs that address the new challenges at each stage of their careers.

To ensure that they remain valid in the current environment, business schools need to challenge the assumptions underlying their current programs and activities. Doing so has significant implications for program content and other design parameters.

Force 2: New International Competition

Governments and business leaders in many emerging markets wish to exploit the perceived value of business schools to their economy and to enjoy the status associated with the presence of a respected business school. In some cases, governments have supported leading international schools in establishing campuses in their countries, such as INSEAD in France; in other cases, governments and private promoters have launched new, independent schools.

CEIBS is the leading China-based international business school. It was established in Shanghai in 1994 by the Chinese government with support from the European Commission. Its mission is to contribute to China's economic development by offering students the latest international management knowledge and practices, coupled with clear China expertise. Government also led the creation of the Moscow School of Management SKOLKOVO, which aspires to develop managers with the leadership skills to succeed in rapidly developing markets, launch new businesses, and lead the development of the Russian economy.

In contrast, in 2002 a group of German companies and associations founded the European School of Management and Technology (ESMT) in Berlin as an international business school with a distinctly European focus on technology and leadership. In addition to providing funding, corporate partners support ESMT by sending their employees to executive education programs, recruiting the school's graduates, providing visiting speakers, and cooperating with student projects. The Indian School of Business (ISB) was launched in 2001 by Indian diaspora with support from the Wharton School, Kellogg School of Management, and London Business School; the school develops young leaders who understand evolving economies and have a global perspective. By 2012, ISB was accepting 767 students to its flagship Post Graduate Programme in Management and delivering a range of open-enrollment executive education programs.

Such changes have numerous ramifications for business schools. The new international schools attract students and executive education participants who might otherwise attend more established schools, particularly in the United States or Europe. At the simplest level, this can reduce demand for programs at established schools. Additionally, it can reduce the diversity of students at these schools and deprive domestic students of valuable international perspectives. Finally, it can lessen existing programs' attractiveness to overseas recruiters, who can more easily and efficiently find suitable hires at schools in their own regions.

Force 3: New Business School Models

Increasing competition among schools and changing user demand have created an impetus for innovation. Business schools have adapted in varying ways, including by changing the nature of their education programs; where they offer them; who delivers them; and how they interact with students, employers, and clients. To facilitate these changes, schools have also adapted how they are organized. Different schools have made different choices about their desired outcomes and how they achieve them. The result is a mix of business models as well as schools that differ significantly in scope.

For example, Duke CE focuses on company-specific executive education; research dominates at the University of Chicago Booth School of Business; London Business School offers a broad range of degree and executive programs; IMD in Switzerland provides a range of executive education but only one degree program. Schools fund themselves in different ways: ESMT is sustained by corporate sponsorship, while Harvard relies primarily on the income its substantial endowment generates. Schools also vary greatly in who delivers their programs: Harvard uses only core faculty; the Indian School of Business relies heavily on visitors from other leading schools; Duke CE uses a pool of adjuncts from other institutions and backgrounds.

In addition, schools respond to globalization in several ways. INSEAD operates from three campuses (France, Singapore, and Abu Dhabi); Kellogg works through partnerships; Spain's IESE offers knowledge transfer to new markets by supporting new schools such as Lagos Business School in Nigeria. Leading schools also vary in the ways they help people to learn. Lectures dominate at Chicago in the same way case studies do at Harvard. The Center for Creative Leadership, while not a business school, competes against them in executive education by using coaching to develop leadership skills. SKOLKOVO Moscow uses projects to achieve the same objective.

The underlying message is this: As some schools adapt to meet the changing needs of specific parts of the market, they make it more difficult for other schools to compete against them in those specific spaces—unless the other schools adapt purposeful strategies of their own.

Force 4: The Arms Race for Talent

Increased competition has created a self-reinforcing cycle. To attract the best faculty, the most successful schools can generate the financial resources they need from student fees and gifts. The best faculty can, in turn, attract the best degree students, who can justify paying higher fees because they are capable of capturing the highest levels of compensation when they graduate. The best faculty can also attract the most senior managers and the most promising "high potentials" to their executive education programs, again allowing their schools to secure higher fees. These higher fees allow the schools to hire more and better faculty.

One of the consequences of this self-reinforcing system is an arms race for the best faculty and the students the schools find most attractive. This can help maintain the status quo and make it hard for other existing schools to improve their quality without a substantial outside injection of funds or innovative approaches. It can also make it difficult for new schools to compete against established schools unless they can deliver a very different value proposition or receive strong financial backing from government or other sponsors.

Framing Choices About Positioning

To aid in dealing with these forces, this chapter seeks to help leaders answer strategic questions about positioning their school on a number of levels. We describe the first level of answers as "elements." For example, degree programs, executive education programs, and research are the potential answers to the strategic question, What does the school do? The elements can be combined in different proportions to determine the character of the school. The next level concerns the parameters decision-makers need to consider for each element, such as the number of years of work experience students should typically have before enrolling in a program. The lowest level—none, three to five years, five to ten years—is described as the "dimension of choice."

Expressed another way, this chapter addresses key elements involved in positioning a business school and provides examples of the parameters that need to be considered and of potential dimensions of choice on each. The elements and examples are intended to be illustrative rather than exhaustive and necessarily include some generalizations.

Whom Does the School Serve?

This is the first question leaders must address to position their school for the future; the answer should underpin every other strategic decision. A school must carefully choose the degree students, executive education participants, employers, and others whom it intends to serve and make sure to address their needs properly. By implication, the leaders must also decide whom the school will *not* serve.

This section focuses on the most direct users of the school. However, a school should not neglect the views of other potential stakeholders, including alumni, faculty, staff, donors, government, and the broader society.

Degree Program Students, Employers, and Recruiters

Degree programs have the potential to serve three groups, or elements, directly: students themselves; employers who fund or support students so they can attend the programs; and recruiters, if students are in full-time programs or are paying for the programs themselves.

More and more business schools are stressing their degree programs' potential impact on the careers and earnings of aspiring managers and business leaders. Increasingly, helping degree program students to find the best jobs is seen as a key role of the schools, especially when the students are not funded by their current employers. That is why schools need to target combinations of students, employers, and recruiters whose interests align and then design programs that meet their needs.

The *degree program students* a school chooses to serve should be relatively consistent on a number of parameters so that schools can pitch their programs to the right level. These parameters include the following:

- Geographic location, with dimensions of choice ranging from local to regional to global. Full-time programs can attract students from anywhere in the world, depending on visa requirements. In contrast, evening programs are most feasible for those living and working locally. Modular and weekend programs have a broader geographic range subject to travel time and cost implications.
- The extent of students' work experience, from none to ten to twenty years of relevant experience.
- Students' academic ability, which ranges from outstanding ability downward.
- Students' career aspirations, from middle management to global leadership; and career interests, from specialization to general management.

- The source of students' funding, which has significant implications for the levels of recruitment and career support services the school will need to provide.

- Students' attractiveness to potential recruiters with whom the school has relationships, which is also a useful parameter when students are not funded by their current employers.

Many *employers* fund selected employees to attend degree programs, or they support the employees in other ways, such as allowing flexibility or time off from work. Because sound relationships with such employers can be a source of students, schools considering which employers to serve should think about parameters that include:

- Geographic location
- The nature of the employer's business, with dimensions of choice based on industry sector
- The employer's approach to talent management, from limited to sophisticated

Recruiters should be considered on a number of parameters similar to those for employers. Schools that want to serve recruiters might find it useful to take into account:

- The career stage at which the recruiters work, from pre-experience through to proven leaders
- The locations for which they recruit, from local to global
- The capabilities and experience the recruiters seek
- The career tracks they offer to business school graduates

Executive Education Program Participants and Employers

Executive education programs need to balance the needs of two elements, or groups: participants and their employers. The relative emphasis will depend on who is paying. Individuals who pay for their own attendance in an open program are more likely to ask, "How will this program help with my career progress?" Company-specific program clients and sponsors of participants in open-enrollment programs increasingly ask, "How will this program help us address the challenges facing our organization?" The most sophisticated are measuring impact and payback from the time and money they invest in programs.

When making decisions based on which *executive education program participants* they wish to attract from those organizations, schools should consider parameters similar to those they apply to degree students:

- Geographic location
- The extent of their work experience
- Their scope of responsibility
- Their academic ability
- Their perceived ability to advance within their employers
- The challenges they face

When deciding which *employers* to target, schools should set parameters similar to those listed for degree program sponsors:

- The employers' geographic location, from local to global
- The nature of their business, with dimensions of choice based on industry sector
- Their approach to talent management, from limited to sophisticated

Government

In many countries, government plays a significant role in funding schools through direct aid, research grants, or scholarships for students. Government may offer indirect support in the form of visas to study and fast-track work permits upon graduation. For example, the government of Singapore established the Finance Scholarship Programme (FSP) to develop the capabilities required to support its positioning as an international financial center.

To the extent that government support is important to a school's success, school leaders must ensure that their programs address the government's needs. Parameters to consider might include:

- The origin of students and participants, ranging from local through regional to international
- Ways in which the school contributes to the country's success, which could include building its capability in strategic industries, improving the competitiveness of domestic firms, and facilitating exports to the home country
- Whether the school's research enhances the global standing of the country or generates insights that improve its international competitiveness

What Does the School Do?

A school can answer this question only after it has decided whom it serves. Business schools primarily do one or more of three things: degree programs, executive education programs, and research.

Degree Programs

Degree programs are designed to develop the business managers, entrepreneurs, leaders, and advisors of the future.

The classic, or traditional, business school degree program is a two-year, full-time MBA for students with several years of appropriate preprogram work experience. The program reflects established choices on the dimensions that apply to key parameters around students, recruiters, and design. The program combines core courses with electives that allow students to tailor it to their individual career aspirations. At Harvard Business School, for example, students are required to successfully complete ten core courses during their first year and ten electives during their second year. For each course, students typically attend classes once or twice per week for the duration of a term (ten weeks) or a semester (fifteen weeks). The average class size varies for several reasons, including learning approach. Harvard uses a section size of about ninety students, but other schools choose to have smaller classes.

Business schools have adapted from this starting point by selecting different dimensions of choice on the following key parameters that address the needs of different potential student audiences:

○ *Program duration* and, by implication, the number of contact hours. The advantage of the two-year approach is that it allows students to complete internships at potential employers, which offers both students and employers a "try before you buy" opportunity. A two-year program also allows students to participate in exchange programs in which they can study overseas for a term. On the downside, it requires students to be out of employment for a substantial time and potentially incur significant debt. Some schools have sought to condense the time commitment. For example, INSEAD in France has long offered a ten-month, full-time MBA that is attractive to students who are not seeking a career change.

○ *Proportion of time* that students are expected to devote to the program. Many schools have introduced part-time and executive MBA (EMBA) programs for people who wish to continue working. Some are delivered during evenings or weekends, which is convenient for those working or living close to the campus but imposes significant travel time and costs on others. This problem has been addressed by the development of modular programs that require attendance in blocks ranging from three days to several weeks. Some of the newer international schools take this approach.

For example, CEIBS offers a two-year modular EMBA in which students meet once a month for four consecutive days, from Thursday morning to Sunday afternoon. ESMT in Berlin offers a twenty-one-month modular EMBA made up of eleven modules alternating three days and ten days each. SKOLKOVO Moscow's modular EMBA can be completed in eight months. It starts with a five-day module and ends with a six-day module, with thirteen modules of four days in between. The modular approach to EMBA programs has allowed broader cooperation between schools so that students can take classes in more than one business and cultural environment (as with the Georgetown-ESADE Global Executive MBA program).

    ○ *Program scope.* Many schools now offer programs that cover only part of the content of a typical MBA program. For example, specialist master in finance programs eliminate aspects that are not immediately relevant to careers in trading or asset management. Other schools offer joint degrees with other institutions. For example, to prepare individuals for complex leadership challenges that balance technical expertise with effective management skills, Harvard Business School has created joint degree programs with Harvard's graduate schools in government, law, medicine, and dentistry.

    ○ *Students' work experience.* The traditional MBA program requires candidates to have several years' experience. Schools such as London, MIT Sloan, and Stanford have long offered degree programs to executives with greater work experience. More recently, schools have started offering master's degrees in management programs to people with little or no business experience.

○ *Program design and pricing.* These two are closely linked. Schools need to decide whether to price programs to be affordable and accessible or to allow them to deliver the highest quality. Schools also must consider whether to use scholarships to support the disadvantaged or to attract the best students.

○ *Market preferences and competition.* A school can position degree programs by selecting different dimensions of choice on key parameters to appeal to different student and employer or recruiter combinations in ways that set the school apart from competitors. For example, Melbourne Business School in Australia (see Figure 2.1) clarified the positioning of its existing academic programs and the launch of new ones by mapping degree programs against two key student parameters: proximity to Melbourne and seniority (personal communication, Melbourne Business School, 2012). The map will be changed by the collaboration between Melbourne Business School and

Figure 2.1 Positioning of Academic Programs at Melbourne Business School

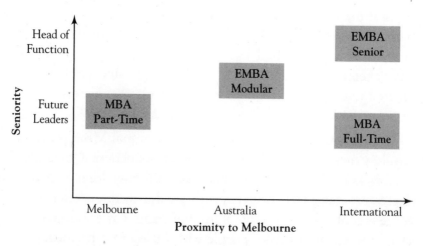

Source: Melbourne Business School: Internal Presentation.

the University of Melbourne's Faculty of Business and Economics that was announced in October 2012.

Executive Education Programs

Executive education is designed for working managers. To make decisions about the design of individual programs and portfolios of programs, schools need to consider a number of parameters:

○ *Program access.* Open enrollment programs, available to the general public, let participants interact with people from different organizations; these programs promote knowledge transfer and new perspectives that supplement the formal content and faculty. In contrast, company-specific programs are restricted to employees of a specific organization. These can be designed to address individual clients' needs, and their closed nature permits discussion of confidential issues.

○ *Program objectives.* Capability programs focus on developing managers by providing insights, transferring skills, and encouraging more effective behavior. Employers are increasingly using capability programs as a key part of their talent management strategy, linking them to specific stages in the development of managers and leaders. In contrast, solutions programs integrate insights and skills into a process that develops a plan to address a current business issue. Open solutions programs are best attended in teams from the same organization; capability programs can be attended by individuals from different organizations.

○ *Program scope.* In capability programs, the dimensions of choice range from functional programs that explore only one topic—such as finance for nonfinancial managers—to general management programs designed to include the key insights, skills, and behaviors required at a given stage of an executive's career. Some schools also offer industry- or sector-specific programs. For company-specific programs, the degree of customization can range from simply renaming existing programs to designing unique solutions that fit a specific corporate agenda.

○ *Participant experience.* Executive education programs are most effective if the participants share comparable experiences and challenges. Schools will need to consider a number of parameters for potential participants. For capability programs, these parameters will typically include the career stage, at which the dimensions might include new managers, those transitioning to general management, and those moving into corporate leadership. The parameters might also include role, level of responsibility, functional experience, and language ability. For solutions programs, the parameters should ensure that participants have a similar level of responsibility and that teams include all relevant functional areas.

Mapping programs against pairs of parameters can identify possible duplications or gaps in a school's portfolio of executive education programs, as I have presented in Figure 2.2 for IMD Switzerland using the information shown on its website in January 2013.

Research

Research focuses on producing generalizable insights. In many schools, faculty are required to publish suitable research in academic journals, such as the *Journal of Finance*, that are read almost exclusively by fellow academics. This is a significant factor in business school rankings. Faculty members' career progress within and outside their current schools often depends heavily on their publication records.

Increasingly, however, questions are arising about the value of academic research and the focus on publishing in academic

Figure 2.2 Positioning of Executive Education Programs, IMD Switzerland

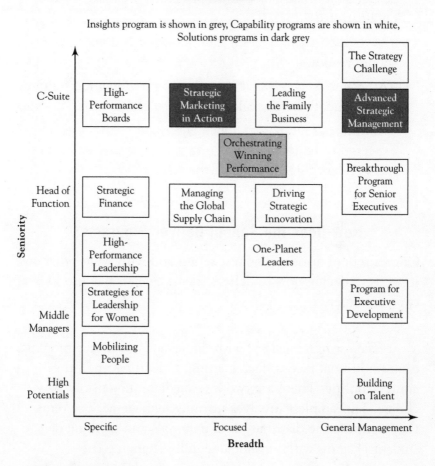

Insights program is shown in grey, Capability programs are shown in white, Solutions programs in dark grey

Source: IMD Switzerland website, 2013.

journals. For this reason, rather than automatically adopting established schools' research policy, leaders need to decide whether they see research as a key element of the school's activities. If they do, then schools should be clear about what choices they are making in positioning research. Schools can make decisions regarding research on a number of parameters:

- *The intended audience:* Where is it to be published: an academic journal, practitioner magazine, or more local publications?
- *The research's aim.* Does it describe what is done or what should be done?
- *The research's scope.* Is it intended to provide understanding of the school's home region or address global issues?
- *The research's future use.* Once published, is the research expected to be incorporated into programs or seen as an independent direct output of the school?

How Does the School Deliver Programs?

Once a school decides whom it serves and with what programs, it needs to decide how to deliver them. Leaders need to look at two parameters:

○ *The use of technology,* with dimensions of choice ranging from traditional face-to-face learning to lectures and other content online. There are two intermediate dimensions of choice. The simplest involves learning management systems that facilitate the distribution of materials and tracking of student progress without fundamentally changing the essentially face-to-face nature of the learning experience. The second is blended learning that combines face-to-face with online learning.

○ *The approach the school uses to help people learn.* There are a number of dimensions of choice schools can use individually or in combination within a program.

The traditional *teaching approach* seeks to transfer knowledge from lecturer to student. At top research-led schools, such as Chicago Booth, this gives students access to rigorous cutting-edge research, frameworks, and techniques. This approach has been applied very successfully to subjects such as finance. However, the teaching approach can leave gaps between knowing and doing. Students may value the insights from faculty research as presented in lectures but find it difficult to incorporate them into their real-life business environments and behavior.

In contrast, the *case study approach* is grounded in the idea of drawing out rigorous thinking from students. Current and future managers are challenged to analyze typical business issues and present compelling solutions based on the information provided. This approach might be described as *accelerating wisdom*. The lecturer's role is to guide the discussion and highlight weaknesses in the thinking and solutions suggested. Harvard is one of this approach's best-known proponents.

One criticism of the case study approach is that it produces people who are convinced they have the right answer even though, in our era of engagement and empowerment, managers also need the interpersonal skills to secure buy-in for decisions and action. Another criticism is that it spoon-feeds students by handing them all the relevant information in a single document— something that rarely happens in the real world.

Project-based learning is a response to this. Students use the concepts and tools they are learning to complete a practical assignment for their employer, a social enterprise, or a corporate client of the school. These projects provide a developmental experience while allowing students to demonstrate their ability to an employer or to make a contribution to an organization that might not otherwise have access to their skill set. Nevertheless, there are a number of challenges in using projects in this way. Many organizations are reluctant to provide confidential information to nonemployees or have it discussed in a classroom. It may also be difficult to reconcile the client's wish for rapid completion with the student's need to fit the project in with other work. In addition, the desire for an academically valid project may conflict with the client's commercial needs.

The teaching approach, case study approach, and project-based learning all regard management as an intellectual exercise. The latest innovation is the *behavioral approach*, which recognizes increased emphasis on feelings and behavior. It relies heavily on self-completed and 360-degree assessment tools as a basis for feedback and coaching, informed by psychology and sociology. Behavioral programs are an increasingly important part of executive education. For example, the Center for Creative Leadership has emerged as a powerful competitor to traditional business schools by focusing on this area. Now a global provider of executive education, it serves more than twenty thousand individuals and two thousand organizations annually.

Where Does the School Deliver Programs?

The answer to this strategic question will grow out of the decisions discussed previously. There are two elements involved: the physical environment and the geographic location.

Physical Environment

Heavily influenced by the type of programs to be delivered and the delivery methods, the physical parameters to consider include:

○ *Types of learning space.* These can be traditional tiered lecture theaters for sixty to 120 students; smaller, flat-floor spaces suitable for more interactive executive education with thirty to forty participants; and breakout rooms designed to accommodate teams of six to eight.

○ *Look and feel of the learning space.* It may range from traditional oak paneling to a contemporary design, such as the state-of-the-art CEIBS Shanghai campus designed by world-renowned architects Pei Cobb Freed and Partners.

○ *Amount of each type of learning space.* Decisions about this are further complicated by the different patterns of demand for lecture space at a business school. Some degree programs have a recurring weekly demand; others require exclusive access to a learning space for blocks of time. When designing the program portfolio, schools need to consider space implications to smooth space demand and avoid excessive peaks and troughs.

In addition to learning and study space, each business school needs to provide appropriate office, catering, exercise, and individual study facilities. School leaders will need to agree on the relevant parameters and dimensions of choice for each.

If executive education and degree programs attract out-of-town participants and students, the school will also need to decide whether to provide residential accommodation on campus or at nearby hotels and what level of facilities are needed, ranging from simple study bedrooms to executive suites.

Leaders need to recognize the uncertainty around the growth of the program portfolio and then design the campus so it can adapt or expand with minimal cost and disruption.

Geographic Location

As a result of globalization, students and corporate clients increasingly expect schools to deliver programs outside their home campus. This creates the need to decide where to deliver programs.

Many business schools use conference or other short-term facilities to offer their degree and executive education programs outside their home campuses without establishing any permanent presence. Harvard has long positioned itself as a global brand with overseas listening posts where faculty can conduct research and develop case studies, but recently it has started offering its executive education programs in China, India, and Europe.

Other schools are more committed to international expansion. Chicago Booth has effectively exported its capability by using home campus faculty to deliver degree and executive programs at facilities it has established overseas. In contrast, INSEAD has expanded from its home campus in France to deliver programs and undertake research with resident faculty on its campuses in Singapore and Abu Dhabi.

Who Delivers Programs?

Decisions about what programs to offer, how to offer them, and where to offer them will drive decisions about the faculty and others who deliver them. A school that provides feedback- and coaching-based leadership programs around the world will require a very different faculty than a school that primarily offers lectures and case studies on its main campus.

Faculty and Associates

A key decision for the leadership team concerns the proportion of programs to be delivered by tenure-track faculty, management practice faculty, lecturers, adjuncts, visitors, and associates. Choices about the degree, executive education, and research outputs will establish the teaching and research load by subject area. Then the number and mix of faculty will be determined by choices around the mix of responsibilities. Some schools aim for faculty who can both teach and conduct research; others are prepared to include people who do one but not the other. Harvard prefers not to use adjuncts or visitors. Duke CE relies almost exclusively on its panel of external lecturers.

Tenure-track faculty are typically career academics who hold PhDs. They will typically receive a base salary in return for an agreed-upon teaching load equivalent to, at leading schools, two to four MBA courses per year. They may receive additional payment for contributions above this level. They may also be allowed to do paid external consulting or to teach at noncompeting schools. They are expected to devote a significant amount of their time to research and to publish in selected journals on a regular basis.

Some schools also have a *management practice* track for people who conduct interesting research that is not suitable for publication in academic journals. Finally, some use *lecturers* who have no research obligations and may be expected to carry a greater teaching load than tenure-track faculty.

Whether tenure-track, management practice track, or lecturers, faculty tend to be based at the school and view this work as their primary activity.

Many schools also use *adjuncts*, who are not career academics per se but may be practitioners. Some schools also use *visitors* to deliver limited but regular teaching with a multiyear commitment to address specific needs. In contrast to faculty, adjuncts and visitors receive fees for teaching on a per course basis and have limited administrative support beyond the immediate needs of the courses they teach.

As business schools seek to increase their academic credibility, they require their core faculty to publish in the leading academic journals, which tend to be specialized and encourage faculty to focus on increasingly narrow topics. This trend is at odds with student and employer demands for greater relevance and applicability of what they learn in business school. The trend has also led to increased use of nonfaculty in program delivery, particularly in executive education. Many schools are hiring people with consulting skills to define, develop, and lead company-specific programs in response to client demand for programs that address the key challenges facing their organizations.

Approaches to Building Faculty at New Schools

To develop their faculty, new schools typically combine three approaches: visiting faculty from other schools, experienced hires, and new PhD graduates.

Many use *visiting faculty from other schools* on a fly-in, fly-out basis. These scholars tend to be attracted by the excitement of the new school and its future. This approach provides flexibility and allows new schools to attract proven faculty with established reputations for the short term. The downside is that visiting faculty may lack familiarity with the local context and are unlikely to conduct locally based research. They can also prove expensive, as the recipient school will need to provide accommodation and pay for travel from their home schools.

New schools also seek to hire *established faculty members* with proven classroom experience and a track record in research. Their reputations can help the school establish its credibility. However, the school may have to provide local accommodations, flights home for faculty and family, and possibly work opportunities for spouses.

Finally, new schools grow their own faculty by hiring *newly minted PhDs* upon graduation or by sponsoring them during their PhD programs. Although this helps to build faculty with interest in and commitment to a school, it can be highly risky. In the short term, such new faculty may lack credibility with students, particularly in executive education programs. In the long term, there is no guarantee that they will become effective teachers or researchers.

At the Indian School of Business, the first programs were delivered by visiting faculty from other schools. Over the past ten years, ISB has built its own core faculty to about thirty, but it still relies heavily on 120 visitors (particularly diaspora) who have long-term relationships with the school. CEIBS has adopted a similar approach, initially relying on visiting faculty before building its own core faculty to sixty-four full-time members while continuing to use visitors with long-term relationships. SKOLKOVO Moscow started with visiting faculty to supplement limited full-time faculty. Today it is growing its own faculty and recruiting through the dean's and faculty's personal contacts. At ESMT in Germany, the initial teaching was done by adjuncts who had delivered custom programs for a predecessor organization. Now ESMT is building a core faculty recruited from leading schools. Some are seasoned; others are fresh from PhD programs.

How Big Is the School?

In addition to defining their school's character by answering the strategic questions discussed, leaders need to decide how big the school should be as measured by the number of faculty or students. For each of these parameters, there may be a critical mass that the school must achieve to be sustainable. Several factors can influence what that critical mass should be and how hard it is to achieve.

For example, if research is seen as a key part of the school's activities, the school needs to attract research-active faculty in the subject areas (such as finance) that it covers. One criterion such faculty often consider when deciding to join a school is whether it employs enough colleagues to stimulate their thinking. In addition, if research output is a significant component of any rankings the school considers important (such as those from *Bloomberg Businessweek* or the *Financial Times*), the school needs enough faculty to publish sufficient research.

Another example relates to the fact that, as noted earlier, degree students expect schools to help them secure suitable career positions. This requires building long-term relationships with selected recruiters, which is easier for a school that offers a larger pool of potential hires. Firms are reluctant to commit to on-campus interviews if they do not see enough potential hires. This creates a need for a critical mass of full-time degree students.

The critical mass in the number of faculty may also establish a minimum requirement for the combined number of degree students and executive education participants a school needs to attract to be sustainable. Faculty costs must be supported by program fees unless the faculty can secure significant research funding.

Despite the obvious appeal of having more faculty supported by more students, it is important to balance quantity with the quality of degree students and executive education participants the school can attract. By relaxing degree program admission criteria to grow intakes, a school may make it harder to place students on graduation. By offering more executive education programs for less experienced managers to support growth, the school may make the audience less interesting to the faculty it needs to attract than more experienced managers with greater responsibilities would be.

Whether school leaders decide they need to grow the school to achieve a sustainable critical mass or shrink it to raise quality, they will also need to decide on the pace at which this can be done. We discuss this topic later in the chapter.

How Is the School Organized and Managed?

Institutional Context

Leaders need to decide on the institutional context in which their school will operate. Should it be part of a larger academic institution such as a university, affiliated with another institution, or independent?

Many business schools, such as Harvard, Chicago, Wharton, and Columbia, were established as part of existing universities. This approach confers immediate academic credibility. In addition, schools founded by or under the care of a leading university often benefit from funding from the central coffers, suitable learning space, faculty from valuable subject areas (such as economics), and management capability. These situations have parallels to the ways incubator centers encourage new entrepreneurial ventures.

Although being part of an established university can provide significant benefits in the early days, certain disadvantages may emerge over time. Business school faculty typically earn substantially more than their colleagues in other subjects. At best, this can be a source of conflict; at worst, it can create a barrier to attracting the best business faculty members if they are required to conform to the university's pay scale. On the positive side, some universities leverage the capabilities of their constituent colleges to offer multidisciplinary programs, as in the case of the joint degrees at Harvard discussed earlier.

Some business schools have responded to the challenge of being part of an established university by becoming quasi-independent. For example, London Business School is a member of the University of London. LBS is accountable to the university for academic standards and relies on it for degree-granting powers, but it is financially and substantially managerially independent.

A third group of business schools has been launched on an independent basis. This typically occurs when the proposed business model is inconsistent with a country's existing academic structures and practices, such as the requirements that have to be satisfied before a degree can be awarded. Examples of independent business schools include INSEAD in France, IMD in Switzerland, CEIBS in China, the Indian School of Business, and ESMT in Germany.

To decide on the best institutional context, a school needs to balance reputational benefits, academic accreditation, and access to shared resources against a possible loss of flexibility for competing in the global business school market.

Academic Partnerships

As discussed earlier, many schools have established partnerships with peer schools. Arrangements such as the one between Georgetown University in Washington, D.C., and ESADE in Spain allow students to study in different cultural and economic environments or to develop complementary skills while supporting improved international research.

In other cases, partnerships allow new schools to benefit from the support of leading international schools. For example, the

Indian School of Business received both know-how and faculty from Wharton, London Business School, and Kellogg—assistance that was likely motivated by a combination of the sense of opportunity in India and the contribution the Indian diaspora had made to those schools. As part of its underlying philosophy, IESE in Spain has supported the development of schools in Africa and South America. These have included the privately funded Lagos Business School in Nigeria, which offers MBA, EMBA (executive MBA), and executive education programs.

Schools need to decide what partnerships, if any, it should establish with other local or international business schools and with other institutions that have additional specializations. In any given partnership, it's important for the school to be clear about what it wants and what it can offer.

The Dean

Because the dean is a key element of every business school, when determining the school's organization and management, leaders must carefully consider both the role the dean plays and his or her background.

Regarding the roles a dean may play, the dimensions of choice include:

- Being the CEO of the school—the one who implements a strategy that puts the school on a sound financial footing while meeting the aspirations of stakeholders
- Serving as an ambassador for the school—by elevating its profile and communicating its vision
- Being the main fund-raiser
- Enhancing the school's intellectual capital base

Note that these roles are not exclusive. But those responsible for appointing the dean must agree on the relative importance of each and how to measure the dean's performance.

Regarding the background of the dean, the dimensions of choice include:

- Academic standing
- Experience as a business leader

Business schools have appointed both academics and non-academics (often ex-consultants) to serve as their deans. Individuals who come from a consulting background, such as Frank Brown at INSEAD and Robin Buchanan at London Business School, offer experience in managing organizations and a commercial focus that an academic may not demonstrate so clearly. However, such individuals may struggle to engage faculty, as often happens when an outsider is recruited into an organization to provide a fresh perspective.

School Management

The answers to the previous questions determine the character, scale, and complexity of a school. Once these decisions are made, each school needs to consider three key parameters related to internal management.

1. *Organizational structure.* With dimensions of choice similar to most businesses, the structure can range from centralized to a series of decentralized profit centers with revenue-generating program activities.

2. *The choice between academics and professional managers in senior management roles.* Academics might be expected to have a better understanding of the "product," but they may also lack experience and expertise in managing people and dealing with clients.

3. *How the school deals with nonfaculty staff.* In the past, business schools may have seen themselves as academic

institutions where nonfaculty were relatively unimportant and easy to replace. The "psychological contract" between schools and their nonfaculty staff reflected this view; staff received lower compensation than they would have in the corporate sector in return for lifetime employment and a relatively easier pace of life. But as the world of management education has evolved, two factors have driven change: Students and corporate clients are expecting an increasingly professional service experience, and, at the same time, schools are seeing the impact of hiring more professional management and staff with meaningful career paths and performance-based pay.

Relationships With Alumni, Recruiters, Clients, and Donors

Business schools are placing more emphasis on professional relationship management with alumni, recruiters, corporate clients, and donors. Increasingly, schools recognize the contributions of these groups by conferring benefits that align with the level of support provided.

The following dimensions of choice regarding benefits to partners are not exclusive.

For *individuals*, benefits can include discounts for graduates on executive education programs, recognition for taking a number of executive education programs, and preferred access to events.

Recruiters may get preferred access to MBA talent. Options include opportunities for profile building through presentations, participation in events, and sponsorship of student events. Recruiters may also get priority access to résumé books, presentation slots, and interviewing schedules.

Partners interested in research may get access to the latest thinking through roundtables, seminars, lectures, research newsletters, and time with faculty.

All *partners* normally get opportunities to network with peers as well as recognition on campus, on the school website, and in printed documents such as the annual report.

Among the types of contributors schools may recognize are donors who give cash or gifts in kind; recruiters or employers who recruit full-time program students; employers that send participants to executive education and EMBA programs; and organizations that allow the school's students to visit them or permit the school's faculty to use them in case studies.

How Is the School Funded?

Profit Orientation

School leaders must decide what level of financial performance they will plan for. Do they want to generate a commercial operating profit, generate a small surplus to reinvest and use as a cushion against tougher times, break even, or run an operating deficit?

In recent years, a number of business schools have been established on a for-profit basis. Examples include the University of Phoenix in the United States and BPP (part of international educational investment company Apollo Global) in the United Kingdom. These schools are run commercially with a view to maximizing shareholder value, which requires generating a surplus in the long run.

These examples, however, are the exception. Most business schools traditionally have been, and continue to be, organized as nonprofits. Many seek to generate a small surplus to provide a cushion against lean times or for future investment, but this can prove difficult because of the demands of various stakeholders, including faculty and students. Newly established schools and those aspiring to increase their quality or scale may need to fund operating deficits so they can recruit additional faculty in anticipation of future demand or invest in marketing to build that demand. Schools may also need to generate funding to invest in new physical facilities.

A related decision concerns the balance among income from degree programs, executive education, research grants, government funding, endowment income, and fund-raising.

Program Economics

The economic profiles of a school's programs are key drivers of overall financial performance and, therefore, the level of funding the school needs to raise from donors or government.

Business schools must decide what level of financial performance they will accept for each of their program activities after deducting only directly identifiable costs (such as advertising for a specific program), after assigning costs clearly linked to a program (such as share of salary for a faculty member who teaches in it), or after allocating all the costs associated with operating the school (such as the dean's salary). The profitability of both degree and open enrollment programs is primarily driven by two factors: class size and program design. Most costs are substantially fixed. As a result, the profitability of degree and open programs is highly sensitive to the number of people in the classroom. This principle does not apply to company-specific programs, which are usually charged on a per-delivery-day basis for the agreed-upon class size. Most costs are, in effect, designed into a program at the start, regardless of the audience.

Before launching new programs, schools need to model the economics and resourcing implications and integrate these into the design process.

Fund-Raising

Although a school can raise funds from a wide range of sources, its leaders must ensure that fund-raising contributes to rather than constrains the school's ability to meet its objectives.

There are a number of parameters to consider in relation to fund-raising:

○ *Whom the school should target:* those who wish to recognize the school's contribution to their own past success, or those who wish to invest in future benefits? The most striking example of the former is 1971 alumnus David Booth, who in 2008 gave $300 million to the renamed University of Chicago Booth School of Business. In contrast, a group of German corporations such as Allianz launched and funded ESMT in 2002 to develop a talent pipeline that would meet local needs.

○ *The size of donations on which the school will focus:* small individual contributions or multimillion-dollar donations? Large donors typically start by making small gifts, so schools often follow a pyramid model in which they pursue a large number of smaller donations but also cultivate individuals with the potential to give much more.

○ *What the donation or resulting investment income can be spent on:* to meet any budget deficit, or for restricted purposes such as scholarships, new facilities, or faculty hires? In the case of endowment funds, it's important to remember that the school can spend only the investment income, not the principal.

○ *How to recognize donors appropriately:* by including them in published lists, naming endowed chairs or buildings for them, or even renaming the school, as with David Booth at Chicago?

How Will the School Move to the Target Positioning?

After answering this question, but before committing to a new position, school leadership teams need to map the strategic journey and ensure that it is feasible.

Many business schools project forward the status quo, sometimes with a little adjustment. However, the best strategies "face the other way." They start with a clear goal and work backward through a logical sequence of steps to reach that goal. This way, the goal and steps are grounded in the reality of the school's market situation, and the resources and elements align.

The strategy's initiatives should be undertaken in phases that move the school from its current position to its target position. It is important to clarify when and how the program and research portfolios will be developed, what the key performance indicators will be, and which people are responsible. The strategy should also identify the key risks to successful implementation and agreed-upon action plans to overcome them.

How Do We Best Make Decisions on Strategic Positioning?

Before addressing strategic positioning questions, school leaders need to improve their chances of successful implementation by deciding what is the best way to make decisions and which stakeholders to involve. The choice of stakeholders depends on the school's perceived purpose and determines the appropriate process for answering the strategic questions.

Conducting Regular Strategic Reviews

It is useful for a school to regularly conduct a thorough review of its strategy and the decisions it has made on the dimensions of choice. In many cases, doing so will confirm that previous choices remain valid and help avoid constant, distracting questions that delay executing the plans. In other cases, a school may recognize a need to readjust some choices in response to changes in the environment.

Engaging the Right Stakeholders

Involving relevant stakeholders is essential because they can make decisions on key parameters and dimensions of choice for each potential element of the school.

Stakeholders to consider include, but are not limited to, faculty, staff, governing board members, students, recruiters, clients, alumni, other donors, government officials, and the wider public.

When deciding which stakeholders to involve at which stage, it is useful to ask three questions:

1. Do they have information that is critical to sound decisions?
2. Is it important to secure their support for the strategy?
3. Do they have a legitimate interest in the decisions being made?

It is also important to manage stakeholders' expectations about what areas they will be involved in and how much they will be involved.

At the end of the process, those responsible for implementation should feel a strong sense of ownership and have a clear sense of priorities. The plan they create should be a living document that the school reviews regularly to assess progress, confirm the validity of earlier choices, and inform the annual budget and target-setting process. The plan should also be realigned when necessary.

Using Charts to Clarify Parameters and Dimensions of Choice

In framing the choices facing a school and increase chances of success, it can be helpful to use strategic maps (such as the one from Melbourne Business School shown in Figure 2.1) and value curves to highlight how the school could position itself on key parameters relative to its rivals.

For example, Figure 2.3 shows how Duke Corporate Education carved out its leading position in company-specific executive education by making different choices on a number of key parameters and turning potential weakness into sources of value for its corporate clients. Duke CE's value proposition is that it

Figure 2.3 Illustrative Competitive Positioning for Company-Specific Executive Education

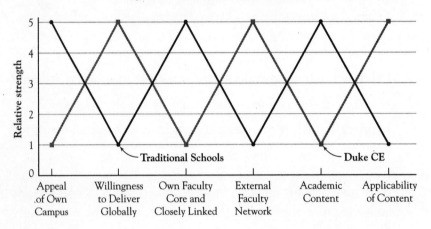

works with clients to create programs that solve challenges and take advantage of opportunities. With its heavy emphasis on relationship management, Duke CE seeks to build deep, long-time relationships with selected clients. It retains a panel of consultants to work with clients to understand their issues and design appropriate programs. Because it has limited faculty of its own, it relies primarily on external faculty and guest speakers to deliver its programs; because it does not have its own campus, it promises to deliver programs anywhere in the world. Traditional schools have struggled to compete against this model, as their faculty often resist using nonfaculty (especially nonacademics) on programs and are often reluctant to travel off campus.

Modeling Financial and Resourcing Implications

Understanding the financial and resourcing implications of different choices helps keep discussions grounded in reality and ensures that choices are valid, consistent, and properly aligned.

Financial and resourcing models that are simple but also robust and flexible can support the strategic planning process by looking farther ahead than normal budgets (perhaps five to seven years ahead) and with less detail (perhaps yearly rather than monthly). Models that use activity-based costing can highlight the elements, parameters, and dimensions of choice a school can change as part of a long-term strategy to deliver the desired outcomes. These models can be simple enough to support exploration of different options in a group discussion. By considering the strategy in aggregate, a school can ensure that it has the resources and capabilities required to execute its plans, that the choices deliver the agreed-upon purpose of the school, and that the financial implications are acceptable.

Such models can be very useful for answering such questions as

- What is the financial impact of changing a program's price?
- What is the impact of increasing or decreasing the number of program participants?
- What is the impact of changing the program structure?
- What is the impact of running an existing program more or less often?

Different Purposes, Different Choices

As we said at the beginning of the chapter, there is no one way to be a successful business school in today's changing environment. Rather, each school needs to develop a strategy and a business model that reflect its own unique situation and aspirations. Some leading schools, supported by their reputations and substantial endowments, will undoubtedly continue to prosper. Other schools that seek to copy the dominant design may be doomed to failure, especially if they attempt to design their strategies to improve their rankings by displacing schools currently ranked above them. In contrast, schools that adopt different purposes and make different choices on key parameters may greatly improve their chances of success.

Imagine, for example, a school that chooses to focus exclusively on entrepreneurial businesses. It might offer a master's in entrepreneurship rather than an MBA. It would target students with a demonstrated appetite for working in smaller businesses rather than investment banks and consulting firms. It would design the curriculum to support the development of a sound business plan and the skills necessary to get things done with limited resources. It would develop relationships with sources of funding for student businesses rather than with potential employers. Much of the coursework would be delivered by practitioners rather than by faculty with a research bias. Its executive education programs would be designed to meet the needs of entrepreneurial and family businesses rather than global corporations.

Such a school might never achieve a high ranking. But it could have a significant impact on economic activity and develop a vibrant school community.

Summing Up

In summary, deans, faculty, and other stakeholders should ask themselves three important questions:

1. Have they developed a clear and viable position for their schools—one that answers key strategic questions regarding whom the school serves, what it does, how and where it delivers programs, who delivers them, how big the school is, and how it is organized and funded?
2. Do they have a clear plan to move the school to the target position?
3. Have they engaged the stakeholders whose support is most necessary for successful execution?

3

MANAGING ASPIRATIONS, RESOURCES, AND COST STRUCTURES

Jikyeong Kang
Manchester Business School

Andrew W. Stark
Manchester Business School

We thank the deans and ex-deans who took part in the interviews, without which whatever insights can be gained from reading our chapter would not be possible. Only one dean declined to be interviewed. All others were generous with their time and gracious in their tolerance of our lines of questioning. Naturally, any misunderstandings of what was said to us are the sole responsibility of the authors, as are the overall conclusions drawn. We did not interview the director/dean of the business school in which we are employed, because we did not want to either run any risk of placing him in a difficult position or jeopardize the independence of our study. The views expressed in the chapter are those of the authors and do not represent those of our employer. We also acknowledge the enormous help provided to us by Joseph Mondello of AACSB International for providing us with much of the data that we have used in the tables and figures included in this chapter.

Key Topics Covered in This Chapter

- Relationships between funding sources and cost structures in differentiating business school models

- Role of research orientation and impact on economics of a business school
- Impact of research orientation on teaching quality and curriculum development
- Strategies used by "young" schools to develop reputation and build brand
- Role of business school autonomy in determining possibilities for change
- Considerations for finding the "right" business school model

Choosing an effective business school business model requires a complex analysis of the interrelationships among existing and potential resources, possible aspirations, and any constraints on a school's freedom to make strategic decisions. Such a close examination is necessary because no one-size-fits-all model works for all business schools in all contexts.

To help with that complex analysis, this chapter points out the main elements of available revenue sources and high-lights the difficulties and costs of attaining certain combinations. As part of this, we explore the potential role of a school's research orientation in determining cost structures and its associated implications for revenue sources.

Our views grow out of an empirical investigation we conducted about business school business models and how they relate to the economics of business schools. We interviewed nineteen deans or ex-deans of business schools around the world. These ranged from schools of long standing to relatively young schools, from schools with little research orientation to ones with high research orientations, from schools with a relatively low focus on graduate business education to those whose main focus is graduate business education. Where relevant, we combine insights from the interviews with statistical data that capture some specific trends affecting business school.

The list of the interviewees and their business schools appears in this chapter's appendix. For a number of reasons, we did not adopt a random sampling strategy. Instead, we used our judgment, and our experience working in and visiting business schools around the world, to come up with the list of included schools. They include nine from the United States, seven from Europe, and three from Asia. In terms of general profile, there are seven public institutions versus twelve private; nine independent versus ten university based. Furthermore, all but one of the business schools have some degree of conventional research activity. This does not imply that all these schools have the same intensity of research activity, however. We regard eight of the schools as being at the stage of actively building up and/ or improving on their research reputations. We conducted semi-structured interviews, mostly face to face but some via videoconference. The individuals we quote on the following pages granted us permission to do so.

The chapter is organized by these topics.

- Possible funding sources available to business schools. We concentrate on support from the state, tuition from degree programs, tuition from nondegree programs, and income from investments and generalized charitable giving. We also discuss issues surrounding access to such revenue streams.
- The important role that research orientation plays in the economics of business schools and the interaction between research orientation and feasible business models.
- Insights into how a number of young schools achieved rapid prominence and related lessons that other business schools can learn.
- Conclusions about the types of business models that are, and can be, adopted by business schools, given the constraints on the freedom to make strategic choices.

Sources of Funding

Business schools can receive funding from a number of places, including:

- The state, whether central or local
- Tuition from degree programs
- Tuition from nondegree programs
- Research grants from state funding agencies and so on, and
- Income from investments and alumni and corporate giving

Our interviews indicated that neither research grants nor research degree programs are seen as significant sources of income. As a consequence, we confine ourselves to discussing the other sources of income.

State Funding

In a 2012 *Wall Street Journal* article, Nicas and McWhirter (2012) state that public research universities in the United States—generally defined as those that compete for research funding and offer advanced degrees—typically depend on federal and state appropriations for more than half of their budgets. Private research universities get about a third of their funding from the government. Unfortunately, some deans either anticipate or have already observed a decline in state funding levels. For example, Dean Judy Olian of UCLA Anderson School of Management expressed the view that state funding of business education has declined in California and will continue to drop. She also suggested that this seems to be a trend in much of the developed world.

According to the same *WSJ* article:

After decades of growth, in the U.S. total state funding for higher education has dropped by 15% since 2008, adjusted for inflation,

to an estimated $72.5 billion this fiscal year, as states have strug-
gled with budget deficits. In states like Arizona, South Carolina,
and New Hampshire, cuts have surpassed 25%. The declines are
even sharper when taking into account increases in enrollment.
Federal funding for university research also has been shrinking,
adjusted for inflation, while such funding in other countries like
China, Japan, and South Korea has grown. Many schools have
responded by jacking up tuition, which is fueling public anger and
inflating student debt levels. Schools are also cutting costs by
increasing class sizes and using more adjunct professors. This
comes after many universities have seen huge growth in their
budgets in recent decades. At the University of Virginia, state
funding has dropped to 5.6% of the total budget this year from
26.2% in 1990. But the university's total budget ballooned during
the same period to $2.58 billion from $678 million. (Nicas &
McWhirter, 2012)

English business schools have long received little or no
funding from the state for postgraduate students of any kind and
now will receive no funding for undergraduate students. As a
consequence, many business schools, although nominally within
the state system, are looking more and more like private business
schools in terms of their funding sources. In contrast, however,
state funding of higher education in Germany and some other
European countries remains fairly stable and is combined with
low levels of tuition.

Tuition From Degree Programs

For the deans who participated in our study, core postgraduate
programs such as the full-time MBA typically provide the schools'
main income. Nonetheless, a few schools see undergraduate education as their main purpose and, consequently, their main
funding source; for these schools, postgraduate education provides additional minor funding.

A number of deans, especially in the United States, commented that tuition in the MBA market has risen sharply over the years, especially at highly ranked schools. This is due in part to continued high demand. For example, between 2004 and 2012, the in-state tuition for a full-time MBA from the Haas School of Business of the University California, Berkeley and the Krannert School of Management of Purdue University grew from $43,024 (Haas School of Business, n.d.) and $25,488 (Steinbock, 2005) to $107,456 (Haas School of Business, n.d.) and $44,632 (Purdue University, n.d.), respectively. Over the period from 2006 to 2012, the tuition at Harvard Business School grew from $79,200 (Levs, 2007) to $126,576 (Harvard Business School, n.d.). Similarly, according to a recent article on the website of the *Economist* (MBA Applications, 2013), MBA tuition at the London Business School has risen from £36,000 in 2000 to £57,000 in 2012. Over the same period of time, tuition at the UCLA Anderson School of Management has risen from $45,000 to $105,000 and at the Hong Kong University of Science and Technology from HK$150,000 to HK$525,000.

Trends in average tuition for full-time MBA programs in different parts of the world are illustrated in Figure 3.1 (Nelson, 2012).

Figure 3.1 suggests that in general, average tuition in the United States is not as high as the examples given previously. This implies that the distribution of tuition is skewed, with highly ranked schools charging substantially more than lower-ranked schools.

Some deans, such as Glenn Hubbard of Columbia Business School, expressed the view that tuition cannot rise any farther, even at the top schools. In the face of still-rising costs, primarily for academic labor (an issue we return to later), there is an implied need to raise money and other resources from elsewhere.

For example, Dean Hubbard said that in the coming years, his job is to raise more money from donors to fill the funding

Figure 3.1 Trends in Full-Time MBA Tuition in Different Regions of the World*

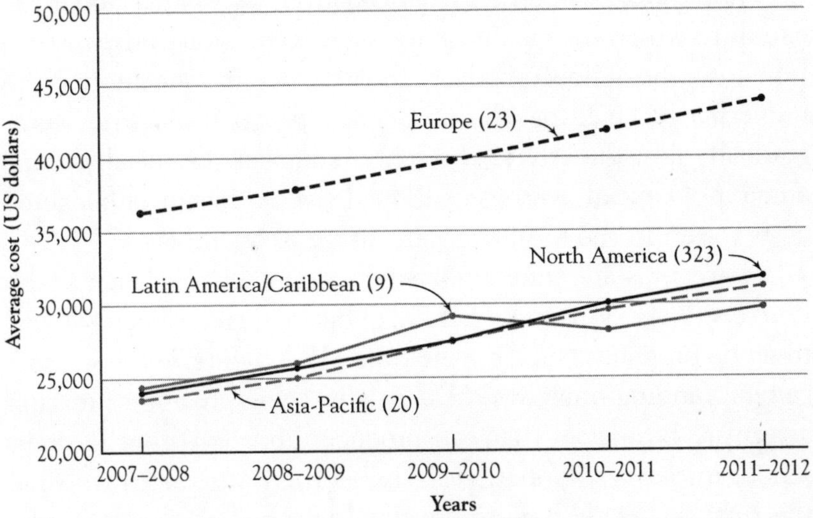

*The numbers in parentheses show the number of schools surveyed for each region.

Source: Reprinted with permission from AACSB International. Nelson, C. (November 28, 2012). Business Schools Cannot Live by Tuition Alone. AACSB International: *Business Education Data and Research Blog.* http://aacsbblogs.typepad .com/dataandresearch/2012/11/business-schools-cannot-live-by-tuition-alone.html

gap. Other schools are moving into specialist, pre-experience, MS programs (such as accounting, finance, and marketing) even though this move is counter to what some scholars have suggested over the years (see Bossard & Dewhurst, 1931; Gordon & Howell, 1959; Porter & McKibbin, 1988; and Khurana, 2007). Such programs are increasingly featured both inside and outside the United States at many business schools, perhaps because they see them as an additional source of funding. However, one dean suggested that such programs represent an opportunity for some of the faculty to get more involved with the business school's teaching activities, with the opportunity to teach more specialist material, often related to and based upon their research interests, than is typically required for undergraduate and MBA programs.

For business schools set in universities, issues arise about the extent to which tuition and state funds feed through the institution into the school's budget. In other words, the money the university receives for offering business programs does not automatically flow directly to the school's budget. Essentially, some amount of central overhead will be deducted as part of budgeted costs (often in the form of a percentage of revenues).

However, some state university business schools (such as the University of Connecticut School of Business) have been allowed to set up programs (such as part-time MBAs) outside the school's general funding framework. Essentially, these programs function as private businesses that can produce funds for other business school initiatives. Nonetheless, issues then arise as to who has the right to decide how to use the additional tuition (the university center or the business school) and how the money can be spent.

We realize from our interviews that revenue-sharing agreements, along with decisions about what a business school can spend money on, rely heavily on context. The arrangements are likely to depend upon negotiations between deans and representatives of the university center, the relative bargaining strengths of the various parties, and, indeed, the strength of the bargainers' personalities. One dean mentioned that a long-time arrangement with one of his "private" programs had been unilaterally renegotiated by a new provost in the name of simplifying and standardizing such agreements institution-wide. Unfortunately, the new sharing agreement has been simplified and standardized to the detriment of his school's budget.

This example demonstrates that, for business schools within universities, budgets may be part of a complex array of implicit and explicit contracts between the school and the university center. Our interviews suggest a diverse range of possible outcomes. Some schools have a high degree of autonomy; as long as they work within the general ethos of the university, the dean has almost total control over the revenues and costs of the school, subject to generating a surplus of a specified size. If such a school can find the money to pursue a new initiative, it is allowed to be entrepreneurial. However, other schools are much more tightly controlled.

The range of budget processes raises a further concern. Do deans of university-based business schools ever wish their schools could be private and independent? The deans we interviewed acknowledged that being part of a wider university had advantages, including enhanced reputation and the reduced cost of shared services, and that any revenue sharing or lack of autonomy was an acceptable price to pay. This should not be taken to imply that all university-based business schools are satisfied with their lots. In an article published in the *Times Higher Education*, Matthews (2012) reported that David Willetts, a U.K. government minister, stated that talks with individual U.K. business school deans suggested that a number of such deans wanted to declare independence from their parent universities as a consequence of the typical "cash cow" status of their schools. The article also suggested that a third of U.K. business schools believed that they were making too much of a contribution to other disciplines.

Conversely, no dean from the independent business schools expressed any great yearning to be part of a university. Perhaps deans self-select into circumstances in which they feel most comfortable.

Tuition From Nondegree Programs

A few deans (for example, CEIBS, Columbia, IESE, IMD, London Business School) identified that tuition from nondegree programs, such as executive education, form a significant proportion of overall revenues. However, schools that are heavily engaged in nondegree programs tend to have one or more of the following:

1. Overall status: when the schools are highly ranked.
2. A clear strategy in which nondegree programs and their needs are given parity with, or indeed primacy over, other activities.
3. Access, early in the life of a business school, to a source of enough nondegree program business to effectively underwrite efforts in this area and allow momentum to build. Such access can grow out of location—especially proximity to a major business center, possibly with limited competition in the market (as with CEIBS in Shanghai)— or a relationship with a major corporation (such as IMD and Nestlé). Once momentum is established, the sources of nondegree program business can expand outward from its original roots.
4. A school governance system that recognizes and rewards selling, managing, and teaching in nondegree programs as well as making conventional contributions to degree program teaching and research.
5. Reliable access to adjunct faculty if regular faculty members are either unavailable or unsuitable.

For those few schools with a high degree of specialization in nondegree programs, recruiting suitable faculty is an issue. Hiring faculty fresh from (the top) business PhD programs, or hiring research-focused faculty from other schools, can create problems. The dean of one school with a heavy focus on executive education said that basing a recruitment strategy in traditional sources is inconsistent with executive education because the school must concentrate on client needs. Fresh PhDs in particular, and research-focused faculty in general, typically have other priorities, such as publishing in highly ranked academic journals. This dean argued that a research focus can conflict with a client focus, especially when the school finds itself competing for clients not only with other business schools but also with consulting companies. As a consequence, the school tends to hire experienced, talented academics for whom academic research is not the be-all-and-end-all. The same dean also emphasized that the reward system for both academics and support staff must be based exclusively on activities that support success in executive education. By necessity, the client-oriented approach dominates everything the school does.

Another dean whose program portfolio included significant degree and nondegree programs highlighted the importance of recruiting suitable faculty. This dean's school aims to recruit the best young faculty straight from graduate school. Nonetheless, an important part of hiring involves making judgments about whether a possible recruit has the potential to be credible at some stage in the future when talking to top-level executives and, further, whether the individual has any interest in developing such credibility.

The requirements for success in the nondegree program market suggest an interesting potential tension in conventional university-based business schools. Although activities such as executive education might seem to present opportunities to generate additional revenue, they also pose problems in terms of incentive structures. For faculty whose career progress depends upon conventional measures of research activity and teaching proficiency, it is not clear what incentives exist to get them involved with nondegree programs.

Income From Investments and From Alumni and Corporate Giving

Data from AACSB (AACSB International Business School Questionnaire, 2011) suggest that investment income can be a significant proportion of the annual budget for some U.S. business schools. For example, assuming a drawdown rate of 5 percent per annum, the AACSB data suggest that one of the U.S. schools in our sample derived nearly 50 percent of its budget from such income streams. Others derived approximately 10 percent or less. Although we might associate the need for investment income mainly with private business schools, the evidence suggests that plenty of state schools have significant endowments.

For non–U.S. schools, investment income tends to be less significant. Most likely this is due to the differences in culture among countries and, in particular, between the United States and elsewhere. For example, data from the 2010–2011 financial statements of the London Business School (London Business School, 2011, p. 2) describing sources of income suggest it derives only a small part of its budget from either investment income or general giving. Other schools (such as the WHU Otto Beisheim School of Management in Germany) have received significant gifts from a key donor who enabled the school to enhance its facilities and expand its activities. Indeed, WHU Dean Michael Frenkel voiced the opinion that the ideal funding model uses tuition to cover operating costs and income from endowments to cover real estate costs.

For those deans (almost all in the United States) who see fund-raising as a significant part of their jobs, our interviews make it clear that they do not handle this crucial task alone. They have substantial support staff (sometimes more than thirty people in the business school alone) to organize contacts with alumni and potential donors to maximum effect. The dean's fund-raising activities involve much travel, which necessitates additional support in the dean's office to cover internal governance. In these cases, one role of business school advisory boards can be to support fund-raising activities. Clearly, raising significant funds requires a significant investment from the start to build up a supportive and highly professional infrastructure.

Overall, our findings make it appear that

- Public or state funding for business education is unlikely to increase.
- MBA and other tuition cannot maintain past rates of increase.
- Labor costs for faculty are likely to continue to rise in real terms (an issue we discuss in the salary trends section following).

These forces will pressure U.S. business schools in particular to look either for other sources of revenue (among which fund-raising could be increasingly important, but so could executive education, MS programs, and so on) or for reductions in cost (such as substituting adjunct or non-tenure-track for regular faculty). The choice will be affected by how costly it is to pursue different courses of action. Such concerns could be increasingly relevant outside the United States as well.

Research's Importance to Business School Business Models

We consider the importance of research not because we regard it as an inherent virtue but because it significantly affects the economics of running a business school. Research activities typically increase the labor costs associated with teaching, which can have knock-on effects elsewhere. Furthermore, given that faculty typically represent an important (if not *the* most important) use of business school revenues, it is valuable to consider what benefits, tangible or intangible, flow from research activity and who is willing to pay for it.

Before discussing this issue, it is worth noting that the U.S. business school scene, as an example, is not dominated by schools that are highly focused on research. Table 3.1 illustrates the distribution of U.S. business schools using the 2000 Carnegie

Table 3.1 Distribution of U.S. Business Schools by Classification, 2001–2012 to 2011–2012

	2001–2002	2002–2003	2003–2004	2004–2005	2005–2006	2006–2007	2007–2008	2008–2009	2009–2010	2010–2011	2011–2012
Research extensive	110	116	121	118	119	120	125	129	126	127	128
Research intensive	67	69	75	75	76	79	79	80	78	80	80
Master's 1 and 2	176	174	202	196	213	224	228	237	235	230	241

Source: AACSB International Business School Questionnaire (2000–2012).

Classification[1] that runs from "research extensive" (business schools located in universities with a high degree of research focus), "research intensive" (business schools located in universities with a medium degree of research focus), and "Master's 1 and 2" (essentially teaching focused), at least in the AACSB universities for which we obtain data (AACSB International Business School Questionnaire, 2000–2012). The table suggests that business schools set in universities with a heavy research focus are not the majority in the United States. Indeed, in general a majority of schools are teaching focused.

Considering Research's Fundamental Desirability—and Who Pays

The deans we interviewed expressed differing views about whether it's desirable to have a complement of academics who are primarily research active. Given the direct implication that these research-active faculty are not full-time educators, the question arises: Who pays for their research time? Among the possible answers:

- The state (as in local or central government) may pay via block grants of one kind or another.
- Charitable giving may pay. This presupposes that a business school receives a predictable amount of private giving.
- Students (from either degree or nondegree programs) may pay. They could do this via higher tuition, through higher student–faculty ratios (meaning that students are taught in larger classes than they otherwise would be), or both. But if purchasers of educational services are to pay for research, the question then arises: What is the link between faculty research and teaching outcomes that justifies this additional cost to students?
- More and more teaching may be done by adjunct or non-tenure-track faculty, allowing research-active faculty to

pursue research. (See the section called "Using Non-Tenure-Track Faculty" for further discussion.)

Justifying Research Activity

Most deans view research activity as desirable; only a small minority are against the presence of conventional research-active faculty. However, the reasons given for employing research-active faculty are highly varied.

One set of deans does not seem to consciously question the level of research activity. Research is what their universities do, and business schools must be a part of the general ethos. One dean said that failing to be research active in his research-focused university would be political suicide for the business school because the other subunits would look down on it.

Nonetheless, another dean expressed dismay that the university president was pressuring the business school to become more research active. Although this pressure was associated with the president's move to generate a higher overall reputation for the university, the dean suggested that the move could change the school's nature. It might shift from a successful, teaching-oriented, regional activity with a well-understood shared mission to a potentially unsuccessful research-active school with a mission that many existing faculty did not share. However, still another dean in a similar situation thought such a move would be good for the business school. The differing views appeared to be based upon the existing faculty's level of acceptance of the strategic change. In the former case, the move to become research active is not well accepted. In the latter case, it is.

A further view, expressed by a number of U.S. and non-U.S. deans, is that if their schools are to rise in the business school rankings they must compete in the research arena. As they see it, to be successfully research active is to publish work in the most prestigious academic journals. Whether the work has any clear-cut relevance to the business world, or enables the school to claim a thought leadership role within the business community, appears to be largely irrelevant.

More generally, a number of deans of non-U.S. business schools in particular suggest that they are moving to a more explicitly research-based strategy because of general reputational issues that they believe are associated with the level of research activity. Here, the outside world can be important. The WHU dean, Michael Frankel, suggested that when faculty members are asked to speak to business audiences, it bolsters a school's general reputation, prestige, and visibility. He added that in his view, when speakers are sought by the outside world, it is unlikely that they will be approached on any basis other than research-related prestige.

It may seem surprising that business schools do not have a stronger view of how research provides thought leadership to the overall business community or at the governmental policy level (as opposed to within the academic community). However, one dean did say that the former is most definitely the overall purpose of the school's research activities. At this institution, it is accepted that junior faculty first have to demonstrate their ability to provide thought leadership within the academic community. But more senior faculty are then expected to start thinking in terms of research questions that matter to both academic and relevant business communities. To this end, a review process for senior academics is in place to support them not only with money but also with, for example, contacts through the school's alumni network. Such an approach is impressive in that it ties research to intended relevance in the overall business community. Nonetheless, a business school's ability to adopt, and to succeed at adopting, this approach might depend heavily upon the school's prestige and resources.

A small minority of deans said they are adamantly against research activity within their schools, at least in the conventional terms of publishing in highly ranked, refereed academic journals. Such deans are interested only in research that helps achieve pedagogical objectives. They believe that a conventional research focus obstructs their schools' missions and strategies, which rely on a highly student-centric focus in everything the school does.

Recruiting Faculty

One implication of a research focus is the need to recruit suitable research-active faculty. At the junior level, recruiting from top PhD programs appears to involve fierce competition not just among U.S. schools but also, increasingly, among non–U.S. schools.

Figure 3.2 illustrates trends in average salaries for new hires in U.S. business schools in the areas of accounting, finance, marketing, and all other disciplines (AACSB International Global Salary Survey, 2000–2012). The first three disciplines typically constitute about 50 percent of U.S. business school hires. The data are also split up into the three types of business schools identified earlier. From the figures, we can observe two stylized facts.

1. There has been a generally upward trend in salaries for new hires in each of the disciplines. In fact, the data suggest that the average annual rate of increase in starting salary is mostly above the average U.S. inflation rate of 2.46 percent for the same period.

2. New hires at business schools in research-extensive universities are getting substantially higher salaries than those at business schools in research-intensive universities. Similarly, new hires at business schools in research-intensive universities generally get substantially higher salaries than new hires at business schools in largely teaching universities. Further, untabulated data suggest that salaries for new hires at the associate and full professor levels display similar characteristics. However, the gap between salaries for new hires at these levels

Figure 3.2 Trends in Average Starting Salaries For New Hires at U.S. Business Schools, by Type of Business School and Subject Areas

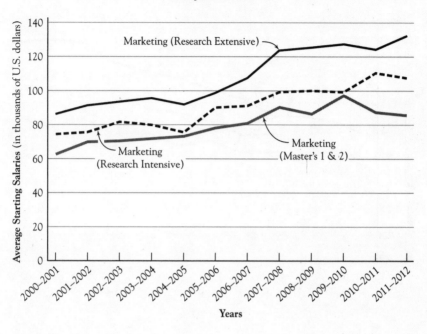

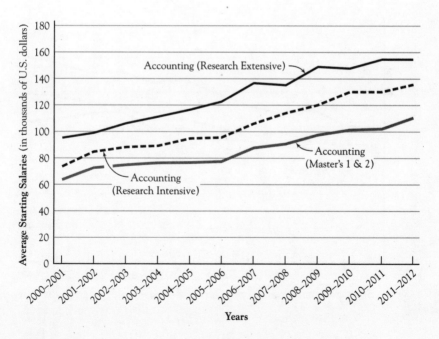

Note: The figures shown in the graphs are in U.S. dollars in thousands.

Source: AACSB International Global Salary Survey (2000–2012).

Figure 3.2 (*Continued*)

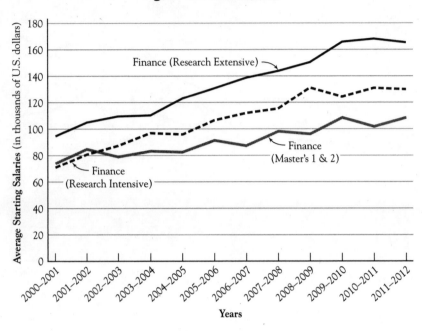

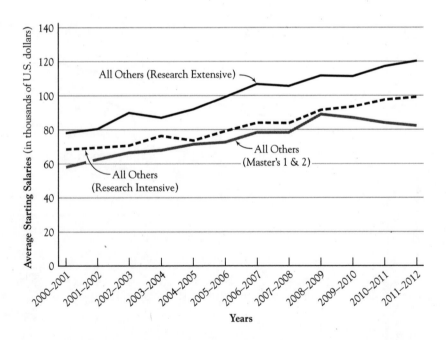

between business schools located in research-extensive universities and others has increased over time and is substantially higher than for newly hired assistant professors.

These effects are not confined to U.S. business schools. Indeed, starting salaries at some non–U.S. schools have also been rising substantially. The phenomenon causes particular difficulties for business schools within universities that have pay scales or that limit the tuition they charge. Such schools are considerably restricted in how they can try to attract suitable faculty to support their research missions.

Using Non-Tenure-Track Faculty

Given that research-active faculty are more expensive than teaching-focused faculty, when a school has a research mission an issue arises concerning the *extent* to which the school pursues the latter. If the school accepts the idea that not every faculty member has to be research active, the possibility arises that the school could hire teachers as non-tenure-track faculty, teaching-only faculty, or adjunct faculty. This can be seen as a way of reducing costs per student.

Table 3.2 shows recent trends in the employment of full-time tenured and tenure-track faculty, full-time non-tenure-track faculty, part-time adjunct faculty, and graduate teaching assistants by U.S. business schools in the different classes of universities (AACSB International. Global Salary Survey, 2000–2012). It appears that the trends differ in the three classes of universities. For business schools in research-extensive universities, the use of full-time tenured and tenure-track faculty has fallen by a little more than 6 percent during eleven years. This drop has been compensated for largely by increased use of full-time, non-tenure-track faculty, together with a smaller increase in part-time adjunct faculty. To a lesser extent, this trend also appears in business

Table 3.2 Percentages of Full-Time and Full-Time Equivalent Faculty at U.S. Business Schools, 2001–2002 to 2011–2012

Doctoral Extensive	2001–2002	2002–2003	2003–2004	2004–2005	2005–2006	2006–2007	2007–2008	2008–2009	2009–2010	2010–2011	2011–2012
Full-time—tenured	49.39%	49.51%	48.73%	47.95%	47.32%	47.76%	45.65%	45.06%	44.97%	45.13%	43.92%
Full-time—tenure-track	19.36%	19.40%	18.92%	19.33%	19.65%	18.58%	18.73%	19.35%	19.38%	19.14%	18.56%
Full-time—non-tenured	16.76%	16.13%	17.11%	17.11%	16.90%	17.97%	18.79%	19.32%	20.19%	20.30%	21.24%
Full-time equivalent—excluding graduate teaching assistants	9.61%	10.24%	10.68%	10.87%	11.14%	11.02%	11.80%	12.13%	11.17%	11.23%	12.05%
Full-time equivalent graduate teaching assistants	4.87%	4.71%	4.56%	4.74%	4.99%	4.68%	5.03%	4.14%	4.30%	4.20%	4.23%

Doctoral Intensive	2001–2002	2002–2003	2003–2004	2004–2005	2005–2006	2006–2007	2007–2008	2008–2009	2009–2010	2010–2011	2011–2012
Full-time tenured	52.01%	50.49%	45.56%	48.41%	48.52%	48.97%	48.71%	47.87%	48.89%	48.42%	48.62%
Full-time—tenure-track	18.95%	19.10%	18.06%	18.52%	18.40%	17.85%	18.31%	17.90%	17.76%	16.82%	17.17%
Full-time non-tenured	15.59%	15.45%	15.66%	16.56%	17.68%	18.02%	17.25%	17.60%	17.53%	18.72%	19.10%

	2001–2002	2002–2003	2003–2004	2004–2005	2005–2006	2006–2007	2007–2008	2008–2009	2009–2010	2010–2011	2011–2012
Full-time equivalent excluding graduate teaching assistants	12.84%	14.25%	19.98%	15.81%	14.55%	14.32%	14.61%	15.21%	14.22%	14.63%	13.54%
Full-time equivalent graduate teaching assistants	0.61%	0.71%	0.74%	0.69%	0.85%	0.83%	1.12%	1.42%	1.60%	1.41%	1.57%
Master's 1 and 2											
Full-time tenured	50.37%	49.31%	50.10%	49.36%	48.66%	51.61%	50.69%	49.16%	47.27%	46.61%	49.00%
Full-time—tenure-track	17.73%	18.71%	18.96%	19.02%	18.44%	19.62%	20.33%	20.88%	19.58%	18.86%	19.21%
Full-time non-tenured	11.22%	10.94%	11.57%	11.31%	11.35%	13.78%	13.33%	13.79%	13.69%	13.90%	13.19%
Full-time equivalent excluding graduate teaching assistants	20.52%	20.91%	19.20%	20.15%	21.35%	14.77%	15.17%	15.65%	18.94%	20.27%	18.11%
Full-time equivalent graduate teaching assistants	0.16%	0.13%	0.17%	0.16%	0.20%	0.21%	0.49%	0.51%	0.52%	0.36%	0.49%

Source: AACSB International Global Salary Survey (2000–2012).

schools in research-intensive universities. But there is no obvious substitution in mainly teaching universities.

Some of the deans we interviewed are at business schools that actively use adjunct faculty. Nonetheless, their explanations for doing so did not relate to saving money as such, even when using adjuncts might also achieve that aim. One explanation related to the opportunity to bring relevance into the classroom—an opportunity that depends partly on location. In this respect it's an advantage to, for example, be near a large number of alumni who work in business sectors of interest to students. Another explanation concerned bringing general relevance to a business school's activities in not only teaching but also research. Still another was that non-research-active faculty are useful when conventional research-active faculty are unsuitable for a particular task, such as executive education.

Assessing the Impact of Research on Teaching and Curricula

One argument for the possible impact of research activities is that they increase teaching quality. This can occur in a number of ways.

- In a given curriculum, a research-active faculty member will have superior knowledge of the theoretical and empirical work that underpins specific business disciplines. As a consequence, the faculty member's explanations will bring greater clarity and depth to the topics studied.
- If a specific curriculum is based on material from, for example, a textbook, research-active faculty can provide valuable updates.
- Research-active faculty will be better at updating the curriculum to reflect both recent advances in the disciplines and changing views on the importance of various aspects of the disciplines.

- When an overall curriculum design involves interaction between disciplines, research-active faculty members will be better able to create links because they have better understandings of the intellectual basis for their own disciplines.

These views, however, need to be set in the context of the incentive structures that research-active academics face. Many individuals enter academic life because they like, and want, to teach. But even though incentive structures do not ignore teaching quality, they do tend to emphasize the quality and quantity of research. As a consequence, it is not clear that all the possible impact that research may have on teaching quality will be seen in practice. It depends on how research-active faculty members view the cost of pursuing better teaching.

Of the four possibilities outlined, the first appears to cost faculty nothing. As a consequence, whether research-active faculty provide clearer and deeper explanations is an empirical issue. Some deans we interviewed argued that this is not the case.

Typically, the other possibilities cost faculty members time that they could spend on research. Therefore, we might expect that many research-active faculty see teaching as something involving sacrificing rather than optimizing. In this respect, one dean observed that curriculum development at his school had been harmed as a consequence of hiring more discipline-based, research-active faculty.

What It Takes to Develop Reputations

A number of the schools whose deans took part in our interviews were founded relatively recently. For example, the Hult International Business School (HIBS) and the Indian School of Business (ISB) started taking students only in the past decade. Both CEIBS and the Said Business School were established in the 1990s, WHU in the 1980s, and IE in the 1970s. Yet all of these schools have achieved international reputations for some or all of their postgraduate programs.

Given that it is possible to establish a reputation in a relatively short time, what lessons can others draw from these schools' experiences? When we talked with their deans, it became clear that each school inherited, or was endowed with, or worked hard to acquire, one or more forms of access to key resources.

Key Resource 1: Student and Labor Markets

Two of the young schools were able to take advantage of underserved markets. Dean Weijong Zhang of CEIBS pointed out that his business education programs could serve the burgeoning labor market of Shanghai. Dean Ajit Rangnekar of ISB noted that his institution could funnel its graduates into the labor markets of fast-growing India. When it came to attracting students, both CEIBS and ISB had the additional advantage of relatively little competition from other business schools in their countries.

Key Resource 2: Quality Faculty

How can a new business school attract suitably qualified faculty to develop and deliver its curriculum? One possibility is to "borrow" such faculty while gradually building up the resident faculty. Dean Rangnekar said that much of the curriculum development and delivery in ISB's early days was provided with the help of Kellogg, Wharton, and the London Business School. As a consequence, ISB was able to tie in with the expertise (and reputation) residing within those institutions at a relatively low cost while building up its market share. Now that its reputation has been established, ISB is looking to hire faculty from the same sources as other top business schools.

Another possibility is to use a preexisting set of faculty. HIBS was built on the foundations of the Arthur D. Little School of Management, which previously existed mainly to provide a business education that focused on the Arthur D. Little client practice. Because this set of faculty was available, HIBS could take advantage of its emphasis on teaching and practical business education while looking to expand into more general degree programs.

Key Resource 3: Capital

In its early years, an emerging business school cannot generally expect to generate sufficient cash flows to fund its growth and development while also building market share.

A number of the young schools in our sample benefited from major outside financing early on. For example, CEIBS was supported by the Chinese government and the European Commission. HIBS is named after Bertil Hult, an educational entrepreneur who funded the early development of the school. The Saïd Business School is named for an early donor. Otto Beisheim, a successful German businessman, provided financial support for the development of WHU.

Key Resource 4: Brand

Only one of the young schools in our sample is university based. The rest have had to develop their own brands and reputations (with the exception of HIBS, which inherited them, at least in terms of an educational approach). However, Dean Peter Tufano of the Saïd Business School is positive that being a part of the University of Oxford brings enormous advantages. Saïd benefits from the attractiveness of the university name to actual and potential stakeholders of the business school; access to resources (including influential and helpful alumni of the overall university and important scholars elsewhere in the university); and the general intellectual traditions of the institution.

Another example of this phenomenon is the Judge Business School, which as a part of the University of Cambridge has also acquired a high reputation in a relatively short period of time. Nonetheless, a number of UK universities—ones that have lesser stature than Oxford and Cambridge but are still highly respectable—have set up business schools in the past twenty years and experienced less success in overall reputation. One conclusion would be that the number of universities that can endow their business schools with a beneficial, ready-made university brand is relatively small.

Key Resource 5: Autonomy

As we just pointed out, the young business schools in our sample, other than Saïd, are freestanding and autonomous.[2] The interviews with the deans of those five schools suggested that the degree of autonomy the schools possessed was, and is, an important part of the schools' development.

This is perhaps not surprising. The job of university presidents, rectors, and vice chancellors is to balance the needs of the numerous elements of their institutions while forwarding the mission of the university overall. Furthermore, universities cannot operate like businesses looking to fund all good opportunities, if only because their access to funding is different from (and more restricted than) businesses'. As a consequence, university budgets will typically be constrained relative to the good investments that could be made. It follows that a business school's need for investment money to, for example, implement a key change in strategy or physical facilities has to be weighed against the investment needs of other parts of the university.

Discussion and Conclusions

It seems clear that, especially in the current climate, research orientation is one of the key factors affecting the business school business model. As corroborated by the external data we examined, in addition to the interviews we conducted, the issue is essentially that research is expensive, especially in the United States, where salaries for research-active faculty are particularly high. Furthermore, as more and more business schools compete to hire PhD graduates from top business schools, finding suitable faculty is increasingly challenging and costly.

This implies that if a business school wants to change its position by improving its prominence in research, it must either be in a position to charge high tuition (whether for degree or nondegree programs) or raise endowment funding, or both. Both actions have their challenges. Charging high tuition typically means having to meet high expectations about standards of teaching, employability, school visibility, and so on. Unfortunately, fulfilling these expectations also adds to the costs of marketing, admissions, placement, alumni relations, and such. In addition, as we discussed earlier, many business schools may have reached a plateau as to the tuition their market will bear.

Similarly, fund-raising does not come cheaply. Success requires considerable skilled and continuous support (usually in the form of a development office), and, undoubtedly, it also adds to management tasks.

Our results also suggest that the mix of activity between degree and nondegree programs can vary, adding to the complexity of faculty hiring and rewards. Unless the business school operates in a privileged position with little competition, the nondegree program market is difficult to compete in and requires highly specialized faculty. Furthermore, faculty who are well trained and hired to be top researchers do not always have the interest or ability to succeed at nondegree program teaching. Additionally, high-level nondegree program activity makes it necessary to take a more client-oriented view across all dimensions. This may mean a complete paradigm shift in some business schools—a shift that may or may not be welcomed by research-oriented faculty.

Much of the complicated physical and human infrastructure that business schools with a high research orientation require is not needed by schools at the low research orientation end of the market. Furthermore, low research orientation schools may be successful at satisfying their stakeholders. In other words, it is perfectly valid for a business school to position itself as highly oriented toward teaching and serving its customers, especially when neither higher tuition nor successful fund-raising opportunities seem feasible. In fact, all but one of the young schools we interviewed started without a high research emphasis. Nonetheless, they were able to rapidly generate high reputations for their educational activities.

In almost all cases, however, the dean is not always the one who determines the degree of research orientation within the business school. If the school is set within a university, the need for a high research orientation can result from an overall ethos the business school simply has to accept. Furthermore, if the university decides it wants to upgrade its research reputation, then the business school will have to follow.

This raises the question of how easy or desirable it is, once a school has been established in one position, to move toward another position. Business school deans must consider how many levers they are allowed to pull in terms of what decisions they have the right to make and what implications concerning budget and delegated decision making they have to face. The move to a new position might have a long payback period, require investment over a long period of time, and, as a consequence, demand much strategic vision, nerve, and organizational patience. Furthermore, the dean will need the tacit approval of existing faculty and support staff. It is not clear how many institutions possess the desirable preconditions for a major strategic change. As a consequence, a business school's ability to substantively change its strategic positioning is likely to depend heavily upon specific aspects of context (such as the university's governance structures and budgeting systems, the dean's influence and negotiating power, and so on).

It is our view that we will see more pronounced polarization among business schools in the not too distant future. A business school with abundant resources (reputation, endowment, location, flexible governance structure, and so on) will be able to occupy, and improve on, a prominent position as a research-oriented institution that satisfies various stakeholders. Another business school that possesses some but not all of the relevant resources yet nevertheless has a strong customer-centric approach will also be able to maintain a clear identity and reputation and succeed at satisfying its stakeholders.

It seems that many business schools intend to improve their position by adopting a higher research orientation and coaxing their faculty, sometimes in an unconstructive manner, to engage in more academic research with the aim of publishing in top journals. However, these business schools often lack the resources or autonomy to respond quickly to changing market needs, and they may suffer from unclear positioning and disillusioned faculty, students, and other stakeholders. Furthermore, it is not clear how much of the relatively new trend toward increased levels of academic research and publication helps students and clients transform their lives by producing knowledge that's relevant to the worlds of business or policy. Perhaps it is time for business schools to collectively assess their roles in business and society.

Summing Up

- The era of continuing tuition increases could be at an end, and it is possible that state funding will be further reduced in many jurisdictions.

- Finding suitable faculty will become even more of a challenge.

- It is not easy for a business school to significantly change its business model and positioning (or to rapidly rise to prominence) unless it can acquire one or more forms of access to key resources.

- The degree of autonomy a business school possesses can be a key factor in achieving success and in changing position.

- Not all business schools should aspire to be top ranked or to improve their reputations by requiring faculty to engage in academic and theoretical research and publish in top academic journals. We believe this is an expensive business model to adopt and that it may not provide the expected payback (such as higher ranking, more and higher-quality students, and so on). Worse, this model could result in a misplaced identity and unclear positioning.

In sum, the choice of a business model, or the consideration of a change in business model, involves a complex analysis of the interrelationships between existing and potential resources, possible aspirations, and constraints on freedom of strategic choice at a particular school. All-purpose magic wands do not exist.

Appendix: The List of Business School Deans Interviewed

U.S. Business Schools

1. Michael J. Ginzberg	American University Kogod School of Business
2. Raghu Tadepalli	Babson College F. W. Olin Graduate School of Business
3. Glenn Hubbard	Columbia Business School
4. Stephen Hodges	Hult International Business School
5. George Plesko	University of Connecticut School of Business
6. Rick L. Andrews	University of Delaware Lerner College of Business & Economics
7. G. "Anand" Anandalingam	University of Maryland Robert H. Smith School of Business

8. Judy D. Olian	UCLA Anderson School of Management
9. Stanley J. Garstka and Rick Antle	Yale School of Management

Asian Business Schools

10. Weijiong Zhang	CEIBS
11. Lin Zhou	Shanghai Jiao Tong University, Antai College
12. Ajit Rangnekar	Indian School of Business

European Business Schools

13. Bernard Ramanantsoa	HEC Paris
14. Santiago Iñiguez de Onzoño	IE Business School
15. Jodi Canals	IESE Business School
16. Dominique V. Turpin	IMD
17. Michael Frenkel	WHU Otto Beisheim School of Management
18. Andrew Likierman	London Business School
19. Peter Tufano	Oxford University Saïd Business School

Notes

1. The Carnegie Classification is a classification of U.S. universities. Over the years, classifications have changed. The classification we use is the one from 2000, in which research universities are classified into two types (doctoral/research universities–extensive; and doctoral/ research universities–intensive), which we refer to as "research extensive" and "research intensive." The other universities in the data provided to us by the AACSB fall into

the Master's Colleges and Universities classifications, of which are two, depending upon the number of master's degrees awarded per year. Details on the Carnegie Classifications past and present can be found at http://www .carnegiefoundation.org/, together with universities belonging to various classifications. It should be noted that the classifications ascribed to U.S. business schools as a consequence of their university affiliation might not describe the degree of research focus of the business schools themselves.

2. The co-signatories, providing institutional guarantees of support, to the agreement founding CEIBS are the EFMD and the Shanghai Jiao Tong University (SJTU). Nonetheless, CEIBS remains autonomous from those two institutions. Further, SJTU contains within it two units operating in the area of postgraduate business education (the Antai School of Economics and Management and the Shanghai Advanced Institute of Finance). Neither of these units enjoys the autonomy possessed by CEIBS.

References

AACSB International (2000–2012). *Global Salary Survey*. Tampa, Fla., 2012.

AACSB International (2000–2012). *Business School Questionnaire*. Tampa, Fla., 2012.

Bossard, J. H. S., & Dewhurst, J. F. *University Education for Business*. Philadelphia: University of Pennsylvania Press, 1931.

Gordon, R. A., & Howell, J. E. *Higher Education for Business*. New York: Columbia University Press, 1959.

Haas School of Business. *Full-Time MBA Cost of Attendance for 2012–13*, n.d. http://www.haas.berkeley.edu/MBA/finaid/costs/index.html

Haas School of Business. *Haas School: MBA Program*, n.d. http://www .haas.berkeley.edu/MBA/allfaqs.html#cost

Harvard Business School. *Cost Summary*, n.d. http://www.hbs.edu/mba/ financial-aid/Pages/cost-summary.aspx

Khurana, R. *From Higher Aims to Hired Hands: The Social Transformation of American Business Schools and the Unfulfilled Promise of Management as a Profession*. Princeton, N.J.: Princeton University Press, 2007.

Levs, M. L. (January 2007). *Thinking MBA? Here's How to Pay For It.* http://
    www.divinecaroline.com/32/25201-thinking-mba-here-s-pay

London Business School. *Financial Statements 2010–2011.* http://www
    .london.edu/assets/documents/theschool/Financial_Statement
    _2011.pdf

Matthews, D. "Keep the Cream, Willetts Tells 'Cash Cow' Business
    Schools." *Times Higher Education,* October 25, 2012. http://www
    .timeshighereducation.co.uk/story.asp?sectioncode=26&storycode
    =421602

"MBA Applications: No Price Too High." *The Economist,* January 8, 2013.
    http://www.economist.com/whichmba/mba-applications-no-price
    -too-high

Nelson, C. "Business Schools Cannot Live by Tuition Alone." *AACSB
    International: Business Education Data and Research Blog,* November
    28, 2012. http://aacsbblogs.typepad.com/dataandresearch/2012/11/
    business-schools-cannot-live-by-tuition-alone.html

Nicas, J., & McWhirter, C. "Universities Feel the Heat Amid Cuts." *Wall
    Street Journal,* Education, June 14, 2012. http://online.wsj.com/
    article/SB10001424052702303734204577466470850370002.html

Porter, L. W., & McKibbin, L. E. *Management Education and Development: Drift
    or Thrust Into the 21st Century?* New York: McGraw-Hill, 1988.

"Purdue University: Krannert School of Management—Full Time MBA
    Profile." *Bloomberg Businessweek,* n.d. http://www.businessweek.com/
    bschools/rankings/full_time_mba_profiles/krannert.html

Steinbock, D. *U.S. Business Schools: Origins, Rankings, Prospects,* March 2005.
    http://www.aka.fi/Tiedostot/Tiedostot/Julkaisut/US%20Business.pdf

4

INTELLECTUAL SIGNATURES

Impact on Relevance and Doctoral Programs

JC Spender
ESADE

Rakesh Khurana
Harvard Business School

Key Topics Covered in This Chapter

- How academic discipline came to shape development of business schools
- Evolution of the intellectual signature at four U.S. doctoral programs
- Rigor versus relevance: reconsidering relationship between problematics and methodologies
- History of business school research methodologies
- Managing doctoral programs effectively to contribute to schools' intellectual signatures

Even though college-level business education has been available in the United States since the late 1800s, its academic quality and business value have remained generally suspect. Likewise, faculty training and selection, and the research conducted by faculty, have long been questioned. As the post–World War II economic boom unfolded and the Cold War set in, there was

131

a palpably urgent national need to put management education onto a stronger footing, more like the professional training in place for architects and lawyers.

In 1959, the Ford Foundation sponsored economists Robert Gordon and James Howell to produce what became a highly influential report on the state of U.S. business education (Gordon & Howell, 1959), and the Carnegie Corporation sponsored a companion report (Pierson & others, 1959). These foundation reports analyzed a variety of issues relating to the poor quality of business education: the schools themselves, their curriculum, faculty and student selection, and their research. The reports' conclusions were similar and the prescriptions unambiguous: If U.S. business schools were to fulfill their mission as professional schools, they needed to recruit and develop a more discipline-oriented faculty, properly trained in social science theory, research, and formal modeling. World War II advances in planning, logistics, and operations research (OR) persuaded many that management had become a science (Smiddy & Naum, 1954). New professional skills needed to be nurtured via new curricula using scientific research methods, fieldwork, and case studies. During the next thirty years, these foundation reports, especially Gordon and Howell's, became the blueprint for schools of business domestically and, eventually, globally.

Three decades later, in 1988, AACSB (then the American Assembly of Collegiate Schools of Business, now the Association to Advance Collegiate Schools of Business) commissioned the first follow-up report since the foundation reforms. It was produced by business school psychologist Lyman W. Porter and international business executive Lawrence McKibbin, a serial business school dean and former president of AACSB (L. W. Porter & McKibbin, 1988). The report was researched in detail and sampled dozens of schools and employers. Its focus was on the same issues the Gordon and Howell report covered—curriculum structure and content, student selection, faculty training, teaching metrics, research, and executive education—

and confirmed the considerable impact of the earlier reports' prescriptions. Many of the report's findings were positive and welcome, but some aspects were unintended and alarming. Specifically, L. W. Porter and McKibbin noted that the pursuit of academic respectability and discipline-oriented reform had mutated and now threatened business schools' relevance. The transformation seemed viciously circular. Many business school faculty were distancing themselves from the problems that managers faced. Instead, they focused on advancing their disciplines, on adding to the academic literature, and on refining their definitions and research problematics. Although the foundation reports certainly intended to promote greater emphasis on the disciplines, they were not intended to persuade business schools against preparing managers to deal with practical problems. Yet that was what was happening.

The tension between business students' needs and faculty members' professional interests increased. At the same time, many business schools were increasingly unsure about their role within the larger university, even as the schools became major university income producers after three decades of rising numbers of undergraduate business and MBA students looking for a practical education.

To respond to these insecurities, many deans recruited prestigious academics to raise their schools' reputations, rewarded them for their academic production, and disregarded their lack of contribution to managerial practice—which further widened the gap between student and faculty interests. Likewise, most of the new management tools that advanced management practice during this period were developed by consulting firms (Jarzabkowski, Giuletti, & Oliveira, 2009; McNamee, 1987). L. W. Porter and McKibbin were especially disturbed by the schools' lack of planning for the future or concern about their economic and social impacts—even though they agreed the schools had improved greatly since the earlier foundation reports and had better facilities and processes. But searching for an appropriate characterization, L. W. Porter and McKibbin labeled the schools *complacent* (L. W. Porter & McKibbin, 1988, p. 81). Despite the doubts of the university's other faculty, business school administrators seemed anxious about neither their institutional viability nor planning improvement.

A second follow-up report by Porter in 1997 showed markedly less complacency and further improvement, although it was accompanied by rising anxiety about the business school's identity and place in the university. Porter noted that the single-curriculum model implicit in the Ford Foundation report had given way to several different models. Although these addressed an expanding variety of audiences, none offered a clear paradigm or concept of management education (L. W. Porter, 1997, p.:8).

Today, more than two decades after the report by L. W. Porter & McKibbin, it is clear that their concerns were not misplaced. Both students and faculty feel that the MBA's value lies more in the connections and credentials students acquire than in its academic content. Getting the credential may make a student more employable, which qualifies it as a personal investment with a reasonable return. However, the credential does not seem to improve managerial performance and may have no measurable organizational or national payoff. Seeing it as no more than a stepping stone to managerial employment feeds a growing cynicism about the role and place of business education generally (Crainer & Dearlove, 1999; Mintzberg, 2004; M. Stewart, 2009).

Meanwhile, managers see the expanding volume of research that business school faculty publish as increasingly trivial and without practical value, and the classroom tension between academics' interests and students' managerial interests grows greater than ever. In short, business schools are now in the grip of the dysfunctional cycle L. W. Porter and McKibbin feared. Most management education scholars and administrators are aware of this. Yet the self-critique that began with Hambrick's notable Academy of Management presidential address in 1993 (Hambrick, 1994) has done little to lessen the oft-noted rigor–relevance concern, even though the critique has been taken up by many others since (Bennis & O'Toole, 2005; Huff, 2000; Pfeffer, 2007; Pfeffer & Fong, 2002).

If the vicious cycle is to be broken and business education is to move in new directions,[1] the effort probably begins with rethinking, once again, the process of faculty selection, preparation, and development. Specifically, rather than presuming that the problems will be solved by reforming the MBA and undergraduate curricula (Datar, Garvin, & Cullen, 2010; Durand & Dameron, 2008; Fragueiro & Thomas, 2011; French & Grey, 1996; Lorange, 2008; Morsing & Sauquet, 2011; O'Connor, 2011; Starkey & Tiratsoo, 2007), there should be a critical examination of the schools' doctoral programs and how they shape faculty and business schools and, by extension, the discipline.

What are the facts? Business school doctoral programs are curiously under-tallied and under-researched, even as the schools that have them trumpet a strategic emphasis on the foundation reports' research-oriented agenda. We do not, it seems, do much research into ourselves or our doings. There are few analyses of business school doctoral programs and not many data about their performance—except that the programs appear to have an approximately 50 percent dropout rate (Luthans, Walker, & Hodgetts, 1969; Mitchell, 2007; Summer & others, 1990). There is little research into where graduates go and how their careers proceed. This is less true of doctoral work in the other professional schools, especially education (Ehrenberg & Kuh, 2009; Gardner, 2009a, 2009b, 2010; Gardner & Mendoza, 2010; Golde & Walker, 2006; Maki & Borkowski, 2006; Newman, Couturier, & Scurry, 2004; Walker, Golde, Jones, Bueschel, & Hutchings, 2008).

Although more facts would be welcome, the real issue is how faculty preparation shapes the development of business schools. There is no effective division of labor—as there is in many other professional disciplines—between "pure" academics researching and moving the discipline forward and "clinical faculty" teaching practice-oriented students. This gives business school doctoral programs mixed objectives as they try to train students both to teach and to produce significant research, which adds to students' stress. Why is this?

In this chapter, we consider doctoral programs' place in the history of business schools and make some comparisons with doctoral programs in other professional schools. Crucial is Porter's 1997 observation that the one-curriculum-fits-all implication of the 1959 foundation reports has given way to a recognition that schools differ in significant ways (L. W. Porter, 1997). AACSB has changed its strategy as well, abandoning its original stance of policing schools to adopt a standard model and instead supporting individual schools' efforts to establish quality programs of their chosen types.

To analyze the variants, we create a fourfold typology, invoking the Weberian notion of ideal type. Although no school conforms fully to any, the differences among types point up a doctoral program's chosen intellectual and pedagogical signature (Olson & Clark, 2009). This then defines the program's institutionalized research methodology, ontology, level of analysis, and pedagogy, thus setting its objectives, structure, and process.

With this typology in hand, we sketch the history of several schools to illuminate the type they chose without getting too deeply into the historical minutiae. We focus on Harvard (HBS), Chicago (Booth), Carnegie Mellon (Tepper), and Yale (School of Management). Each intellectual signature implies:

1. A posture with regard to the social and political context of business education

2. Its sense of disciplinarily legitimated research topics, or problematics

3. Its selection of acceptable research methods, and

4. The agent who benefits from the research conducted (whom we label *the protagonist*)

There is some match between our exemplars and the Ford Foundation's decision in the 1960s to fund five schools as centers of excellence: Harvard, Columbia, Chicago, Stanford, and Carnegie Mellon (Khurana, 2007, p. 250). There is also some connection to the conventional way of assessing faculty performance—research, teaching, and service—and seeing which activity the school emphasizes.[2] The loose notion that management education is intended to benefit managers—which leads to the rigor–relevance discussion—may be obscuring important inter-signature differences. Indeed, managers may have significantly less stake in management education than nonmanagers (students looking for corporate employment) or their employers, or the universities that benefit from the cash flow.

Socialization and the care and feeding of doctoral students are known challenges (Gardner & Mendoza, 2010; Golde, 2008; Nerad & Heggelund, 2008; Nerad & Trzyna, 2008). Students in business school face the additional challenge of negotiating the school's hidden curriculum when the school lacks a clear signature (Hafferty, 2002). Few schools achieve a coherent intellectual signature; MBA students must synthesize microeconomics, ethics, accounting, international business, psychological behaviorism, and so on into coherent practice in ways the discipline and faculty cannot. The lack of a coherent signature prevents PhD students from planning and measuring their progress. Ironically, the heterogeneity of research topics and attitudes is often embedded in a context of almost complete methodological uniformity—the quantitative positivist methodologies so evident in our A-journals.

If business schools' evident rigor-and-relevance issues are to be addressed, the research methods and problematics developed in the post–World War II era must be reconsidered. If schools are to change, doctoral programs will have to be redesigned, publication practices reshaped, and students' range of legitimated activity significantly enlarged. Although an epistemological tension between the academic's pursuit of theoretical generalization and the practitioner's interest in action and specific instances is part and parcel of all professional education, it need not fuel the dysfunctional cycle now apparent in business education.

The foundation reports and the way they were interpreted by the business school community had a principal unintended negative consequence. Positivist scientific methods were not merely adopted—without question a major improvement—but were adopted in such a way that other social science methodologies were made to seem significantly less legitimate. Given that management is a practical art in a highly dynamic and only partially understood context (Knight, 1923), these strictures have proven extremely damaging, especially to our discipline's younger researchers.

Intellectual Signatures at Four Business Schools

Doctoral programs are only a small part of the business school enterprise, yet they are pivotal to the future of management education and to the future of management as a professional discipline (Summer & others, 1990). First, doctoral programs train students to do the research that defines and sustains business schools' academic identity and reputation, both within the university and in the wider world. Second, the programs are now the principal source of business school teachers; practicing managers are not welcome in the classroom.

The programs' research training and research product have come under increasing criticism, as noted already. At the same time, there is growing anxiety about a shortfall in the quantity of doctoral students—that is, whether production is sufficient to meet business schools' expanding needs, even with substantial flow of international students into U.S. programs—as well as about whether the training provided is sufficient to meet students' career needs (AACSB, 2002, 2003, 2005a, 2005b, 2008; Ivory, Miskell, Neely, Shipton, & White, 2007; Joseph, 2004).

But perhaps the most remarkable thing about the programs is how little is known about them, how seldom they are discussed, and how difficult they are to define, measure, and manage (Mitchell, 2007; M. M. Stewart, Williamson, & King Jr., 2008; Summer & others, 1990).[3]

To address this issue we adopt the historian's view and, as already mentioned, trace the evolution of four intellectual signatures. This history helps show which of the many possible directions have been followed. Three of our signature exemplars are the business schools at Harvard, Chicago, and Carnegie Mellon. Each pursued different views of the foundational problematics of management as a discipline and the methods considered legitimate for researching them. The differences were central to the inter-institutional battle to define the profession's high ground (such as the University of Chicago occupies today in the economics profession—though there is no similarly dominant business school today).[4] The evolution of the management discipline as a whole was clearly shaped by these different schools' views, even when we tell the story in terms of the work of individuals such as Herbert Simon, Milton Friedman, Oliver Williamson, or Michael Porter. Indeed, we argue that these individuals were, to a surprising extent, instruments of their schools' intellectual signatures (Wren, 1979). We add Yale's School of Management, founded in 1974, as a fourth exemplar, representing an altogether different intellectual and methodological position.

Harvard Business School

When Harvard Business School was founded in 1908, several undergraduate schools of commerce already existed in the United States (the University of Pennsylvania's Wharton School, established in 1881, was the first), and other institutions offered graduate courses (including Dartmouth College's Amos Tuck School of Administration and Finance, founded in 1900). But HBS's stipulation that entering students possess an undergraduate degree made it the first true *graduate* school of business. Charles W. Eliot, Harvard's then-president, stated that "business in its upper walks has become a highly intellectual calling, requiring knowledge of languages, economics, industrial organization, and commercial law, and wide reading concerning the resources and habits of the different nations" (see Cruikshank, 1987). Eliot's first initiatives after assuming the Harvard presidency in 1869 included raising academic standards at both the medical and law schools. For him, the academic rigor of the new business school would be the mark of its "professional" character.

From its earliest days, the school was what Eliot's successor, Abbott Lawrence Lowell, termed "a delicate experiment." HBS's first dean, Edwin F. Gay, wrestled with the question of what it meant to teach business as a professional discipline. In a 1915 article called "Teaching the Profession of Business at Harvard," Benjamin Baker offered one approach to the problem. "The profession of business cannot be taught from text-books," Baker wrote.

> Actual business problems, as the business executive has to meet and deal with them, are as unlike any purely text-book presentation of them as the sick person calling at the young doctor's office is unlike the "symptoms" in the medical text-book. So, as the young doctor must learn to diagnose by service in the hospitals, the student of the profession of business must learn to recognize and deal with business facts by dealing with actual business situations.

Baker also noted that the "necessary facts and principles of business" remained "largely to be discovered." "Once these facts and their meanings are verified," he concluded, "formulation of business principles, perhaps of 'laws' in the strict sense of that word, will follow; and the profession of business will become truly scientific in spirit and methods" (Baker, 1915, pp. 9–11).

HBS's initial MBA curriculum was made up of accounting, commercial contracts, U.S. economic resources, industrial organization, corporate finance, and banking. Second-year students moved on to railroading, insurance, and municipal administration. In the 1920s, this industry-oriented curriculum was revised into the cross-industry "functional orientation" so widely familiar today—production, finance, marketing, and accounting (Khurana, 2007, p. 260). HBS's doctoral program sputtered into existence in 1922, envisioned as an extension of the MBA program but specifically refashioned toward training business school teachers, because fifty-five schools had written to HBS in the previous year asking for instructors (Cruikshank, 1987, p. 195).

Given the importance that HBS's founders attached to identifying inductively the facts from which principles could be drawn, the doctoral program was organized around fieldwork and the development of rich, detailed cases. Doctoral students were recruited primarily from the school's own MBA program. Their training consisted of one year of coursework made up mostly of required courses. These usually consisted of seminars led by faculty, such as Fritz Roethlisberger and Kenneth Andrews, who were doing research. The curriculum was often composed of readings, mostly books, of classic social science and works on administration. In their second year, students worked under the auspices of a faculty member as a research assistant and usually wrote cases. The third year consisted of independent work by the doctoral student and the development of a dissertation built on extensive fieldwork and case studies on a small number of organizations.

From its founding onward, the Harvard DBA has been a degree for students with strong interests in management practice. Research in the program has been closely related to problems of practical significance, albeit using a variety of disciplines (such as microeconomics, psychology, and sociology) and research methods (such as fieldwork, large sample empirical, and modeling). For a number of years, the DBA program served as the primary recruiting source for HBS faculty. The program was relatively ineffectual until after World War II.[5] But the research accent was always on business's current challenges rather than on developing theory, a strategy reaffirmed several times even into the 1970s (Cruikshank, 1987, p. 280). In their 1959 report for the Ford Foundation, however, Gordon and Howell criticized Harvard's program as especially weak on methods and argued that case studies rarely led to theory. They wrote:

> [Harvard offered] little or no training in research methods other than case preparation. No central body of theory was recognized, nor were there any core fields required of all candidates beyond what was necessary for the MBA. . . . Doctoral training at Carnegie Tech is obviously more oriented toward a sophisticated kind of research training than it is at Harvard, which emphasizes research training much less and preparation for teaching considerably more. (Gordon & Howell, 1959, p. 405)

The HBS program's protagonist, signature, and problematics are clear and central to the school's history and present. The protagonist is the working manager, addressing a complex of real-world problems that can be captured sufficiently only in the case format. The emphasis is to help the aspiring manager control the enterprise (Heaton, 1968; Zeff, 2008, p. 16). The research problematic is not a fully optimal solution; it is the practical or satisficing choice of an appropriate and timely action that will move the firm forward competitively, socially, financially, and so on.

This research problematic was strikingly framed in the questions found in the business policy textbook by Learned, Christensen, Andrews, and Guth (1965). On pages 20 and 21, they write that the business person has to decide for the firm what it (a) might do, (b) can do, (c) wants to do, and (d) should do. These questions were taken almost verbatim from the work of

John R. Commons, whose writings contributed substantially to the industrial organization (IO) tradition that underpinned HBS's intellectual signature and especially informed the work of, for instance, Richard E. Caves and Michael Porter (Commons, 1924, p. 6). As M. Porter makes clear, the focus is on action, with the details of history and context mediating the collection of data and the rigor of mathematical analysis (Spender & Kraaijenbrink, 2011).

The University of Chicago

On February 3, 1894, the University of Chicago faculty approved a plan to found an undergraduate College of Commerce and Politics. Eventually founded in 1898 with a planned budget of $38,500 (of which only $5,800 was approved), the college was made up of little more than a syllabus, which provided a selection of the already-listed university courses. In 1902, the school was allowed to hire a small number of faculty and administrators.

But not until 1910, when J. D. Rockefeller (the founder of the University of Chicago) bequeathed his final $10-million gift to the university, did the school begin to operate independently. In 1916, its name was changed to the College of Commerce and Administration. After undertaking an analysis of all existing business schools, university research bureaus, and schools of public policy, Dean Leon C. Marshall drew up a vision for the school. He focused on the relationship among the various branches of knowledge, commerce, and the larger society. Marshall (1913) wrote:

> In its relation to the community, this college conceives that very considerable existing stores of scientific information in the field of the social sciences should be made more accessible for the furthering progress of society. The college . . . hopes to serve by aiding commercial and industrial development; it hopes equally to serve by assisting in the solution of our pressing political and

social problems. It believes that there is sufficient unity and coherence in the social sciences to justify an attempt to advance all along the line; and it has accordingly placed under one organization the functions which in some institutions are performed by schools or colleges of commerce, the functions which in other institutions are performed by schools for social workers, and the functions which in still other institutions are given over to bureaus of municipal research. (pp. 100–101)

Marshall launched the school's PhD program in 1920. The MBA was first offered in 1935, and the world's first Executive MBA debuted in 1943. The school was renamed School of Business in 1932, then Graduate School of Business in 1959, and then Booth School of Business in 2008.

The Chicago model incorporated specific ideas about the relationship between the social sciences and the problems confronting society. It pursued an intersection of foundational sources of knowledge, methods for answering questions, and a normative stance regarding the ends that such knowledge and methods might serve. The notion of social science in the service of society was no afterthought from the school's public relations department; it went to the heart of the vision of the university, which was known in the 1930s and early 1940s less for its academic excellence than for its charismatic president (and later chancellor), Robert Maynard Hutchins. Although suspicious of professional schools—other than medical and law schools—and thinking that business schools lacked serious academic underpinnings, Hutchins believed in the potential of great ideas to change society. As the university's head, he helped institutionalize the Chicago approach to the social sciences. The approach, articulated by Chicago sociologists in the 1940s, was based on quantitative analysis but engaged a wide variety of intellectual disciplines. Hutchins was committed to academic theorizing but not to theory-less empiricism, and he gave the business school little support.

After retiring in 1951, Hutchins was succeeded by Lawrence Kimpton, a philosopher and skilled administrator who sought to make Chicago the center of empirical social sciences in postwar America. Both ideologically and pragmatically disposed to support the business school, Kimpton backed more efforts to put its research on sounder academic footing. Kimpton appointed as its new dean W. Allen Wallis, a Columbia-trained statistician who had studied in the Chicago economics department during the 1930s.

Back during his time in the economics department, Wallis had begun what would become a lifelong friendship with two fellow students, Milton Friedman and George Stigler; the three would reunite during World War II at the U.S. Navy-sponsored Statistical Research Group at Columbia University. Shortly after the war, partly at Friedman's urging, the University of Chicago recruited Wallis to found a department of statistics, and the Rockefeller Foundation supported its attempts to disseminate new statistical methods into other fields (Olkin, 1991). Together with Associate Dean James Lorie (another Chicago-trained economist), Wallis worked to ensure that the business school would reflect the character of the university. This meant it would be oriented toward higher learning, as opposed to vocational training, and produce first-rate research. The reformed business school would draw faculty from disciplines closely related to business—statistics, accounting, law, and, especially, economics. Wallis controlled hiring and leveraged his considerable academic reputation to recruit like-minded economists and statisticians, being "shrewd and indeed almost ruthless in carrying out his program" (Gordon, 1957). When he became dean in 1956, Wallis hired eighteen faculty members in his first year; several of them went on to become the most prominent economists of their generation.

Within the decade, the school expanded from twenty-one to 112 faculty members. It also significantly increased the size of its doctoral program and number of postdoctoral fellowships. The school saw its doctoral program as a counter to Harvard's case-based program. Grounded in the social sciences, it offered training that could not be acquired simply through careful observation of managers and firms.[6] Its quantitative orientation and emphasis on methodology and statistics was particularly exciting to the Ford Foundation, which saw the program's potential to reshape the development of future business school faculty throughout the nation. Chicago-trained faculty would be able to carry out the type of trickle-down strategy that Ford had formulated, and seeing business research as an applied social science, Chicago actively recruited faculty from the social sciences. Of the seventy faculty members hired after the publication of the Ford Foundation report, 40 percent came from social science departments, principally economics. Another 15 percent came from Chicago's own doctoral program. Within two decades, Chicago's doctoral students would dominate the faculty at the business schools at the University of Rochester, University of California, Los Angeles, and the University of Minnesota.

Today Booth students can receive a PhD in eight areas: accounting, econometrics and statistics, economics, finance, management science, managerial and organizational behavior, marketing, and organizations and markets. Of these, five are grounded in economic theory and methods and share core course requirements with the PhD program in economics. The organizational behavior track and organizations and markets track also require the economics sequence.[7] Dissertations are mostly quantitative, and most are grounded in economic theory. The archive of dissertation proposals and defenses between 2007 and 2012 shows that, of 120 presentations, all used large statistical databases or surveys, or quantitative experimental methods. Sixteen had the title "Essay," a category usually comprising three separate empirical studies, often in the form of a presubmission to a journal. The most common topics are finance and the capital markets, industrial organization studies, behavioral economics, and managerial incentives.

The protagonist, problematic, and intellectual signature of the Chicago approach seem clear. The protagonist is the discipline itself. Researchers are its servants, and their project is to bring mathematical rigor to the social and economic sciences generally and to advance the agenda conceived by Auguste Comte and Émile Durkheim, underpinned by a commitment to efficient markets. The defining function of the firm is to connect and clear the economy's markets efficiently. In sharp contrast to HBS's focus on managerial effectiveness, at the core of the Booth School's multidisciplinary program are quantitative research methods.

Carnegie Mellon's Science of Management

History shows, ironically, that the Chicago school's efforts were probably less influential than those of the business school at Carnegie Mellon University (CMU; known as the Carnegie Institute of Technology from 1912 to 1967). There, several Chicago-trained scholars dramatically reshaped business education by creating a template that would be used by most business school MBA and doctoral programs.

Carnegie's Graduate School of Industrial Administration (GSIA) was founded in 1949 with a $6 million grant from William Larimer Mellon, a member of the powerful Mellon banking family and founder of the Gulf Oil Company. GSIA was intended to "help the growing need in American industry for executives trained in both engineering and management" (Carnegie GSIA, 1952). GSIA would model a new rationalistic approach to business questions, an approach decisively rooted in the most advanced technical methods in the social sciences and deeply suspicious of traditional, practitioner-dominated forms of training.

In contrast to the historical paradigm at Harvard and the economics one at Chicago, Carnegie's approach was grounded in engineering and systems analysis.[8] Yet, because GSIA was relatively marginal to the mainstream of U.S. universities, it enjoyed a degree of intellectual autonomy. It incubated several new approaches to economics and administrative science that had found no place in more prestigious institutions: behavioral economics, modern finance theory, decision theory, and rational expectations theory.

Carnegie's strategy was risky, for the postwar business education field was crowded and dominated by Harvard, Wharton, Stanford, Columbia, and Chicago. The perception of a business school's quality mostly reflected the age, size, and prestige of its host university. Lacking these endowments, GSIA cannily raised its status by gaining the patronage of the Ford Foundation, a rich and powerful organization publicly committed to improving management education. This then propelled GSIA into the inner circle of modern business schools—legitimating its pedagogy, research models, and its faculty. Both the Ford Foundation's 1959 report on business education and the Carnegie Corporation's companion report extolled the application of quantitative analysis to social and economic matters in the manner of World War II operations research.

The reports presumed that a *science of management* was now possible and could be developed rapidly with quantitative methods. It followed that an entirely new breed of researcher was needed and that doctoral students should be trained into quantitative methods rather than into the historical and descriptive methods, such as case studies and company-specific research reports, that most doctoral programs adopted (Backhouse & Fontaine, 2010). The Ford Foundation's James Howell later revealed that, even as early as 1954 (only one year into Ford's foray into business school programs), GSIA was recognized as "the advanced projects laboratory, the R&D group that [Ford] had to find or create; fortunately, it already existed" (Schlossman, Sedlak, & Wechsler, 1987, p. 19). In 1957, in an implicit endorsement of the Carnegie approach, the foundation supported a GSIA-administered seminar titled "New Developments in Business

Administration." Faculty from the other business schools who had received, or were looking to receive, Ford Foundation money were encouraged to attend.

In 1946, George Leland ("Lee") Bach, a Chicago economics PhD, was recruited to chair the Carnegie Tech economics department but became GSIA's founding dean. He promptly hired Herbert Simon. GSIA's doctoral program was designed after the two undertook an extensive survey of business education curricula, students, faculty, and research. They decided the doctoral courses would be taught only by scholars trained in the latest quantitative methods and who would be drawn from established disciplines such as economics, engineering, mathematics, sociology, psychology, and statistics. The GSIA program grounded students in the social sciences and directed their research toward fundamental theory. It also required PhD students to collaborate with faculty on existing research projects rather than to pursue their own ideas (Haskell, 2000).

Bach implemented the GSIA approach with a strong team of research-oriented scholars. The results were impressive. No fewer than eight scholars who taught or were trained at GSIA during the 1950s and '60s eventually won Nobel Prizes in economics—a remarkable feat for such a small, young institution, and a business school to boot.

Even more significant was the distinctive style of research that evolved at GSIA. Carnegie graduates, especially those trained by Herbert Simon and his protégé, Jim March, fanned out to the most prestigious graduate schools to reshape their doctoral and MBA programs. The GSIA model, with crucial Ford Foundation[9] support, was disseminated rapidly through the business school community (Donham, 1954; McNair & Hersum, 1954; Yin, 1981). Almost immediately, other top-tier schools began to hire faculty on the basis of their quantitative research expertise. By 1964, the volume of business school research and the number of newly founded journals that published it began to rise rapidly—a trend that has accelerated. Research and its publication in refereed journals quickly became the profession's measure of academic capability (C. A. Smith, 1962, p. 146; Khurana, 2007).[10]

The protagonist, signature, and problematics of the Carnegie Mellon program[11] are clear. As is the case at Chicago, the protagonist is the discipline rather than the individual manager, the firm, or society at large. But unlike the Chicago case, the faculty project at GSIA was not to model the economy rigorously or provide a comprehensive and intellectually coherent answer to the question "What is the firm?" Rather, the Carnegie intellectual signature embraced the social sciences at large and echoed the multidisciplinary program instituted by Hutchins at Chicago and carried to GSIA by Herbert Simon and others. It provided the background for multidisciplinary milestones such as March and Simon's *Organizations* (1958) and Cyert and March's *Behavioral Theory of the Firm* (1963), books that redefined the boundaries of management theorizing.

It also admitted a methodology that paid great attention to mathematics and modeling, but not to the exclusion of other modes of social science research. In contrast to Chicago's admitting only those aspects of the economy that could be rigorously modeled, the Carnegie signature turns mostly on systems theory. Herbert Simon—along with Chester Barnard and Talcott Parsons—helped introduce systems thinking into organization studies. Notwithstanding his economics Nobel, Simon moved into the CMU psychology department and reoriented his research toward artificial intelligence while turning his back on the Chicago-style economics his GSIA colleagues were doing. Yet GSIA retains the multidisciplinary and systems theory imprint Bach and Simon created; organizational behavior remains an accepted doctoral field.

But the GSIA signature has also been greatly diluted—if not excised—since about the turn of the century. What is now the Tepper School of Business has become increasingly indistinguishable from the Booth School.

Yale School of Management's Focus on Social Improvement

The Yale School of Management (SOM) is the youngest doctoral program we examine. Although a group of Yale alumni had been advocating for a business school since the 1950s, the university did not seriously explore establishing one until Kingman Brewster became university president in 1963 and began arguing that Yale needed to "do more in the social sciences" and to educate "future managers." Brewster sought to connect Yale's historic mission of providing leaders to American society with a threefold focus on the public, private, and nonprofit sectors; these goals, he argued, were deeply intertwined with each other.

The 1976 founding mission of the Yale School of Organization and Management (which changed its name to the School of Management in the 1980s) struck many as ambiguous. The intent was to advance thinking on organizational management through a multidisciplinary focus with strong psychological and sociological elements (as opposed to purely economic ones). But Brewster's vision was that organizations, like individuals, live in association with, interact with, are supported by, and affect and are affected by others. Brewster believed that the school's distinctiveness could be built on graduate programs that took full advantage of the university's distinctive social science strengths.

The school initially offered a master's in public and private management (MPPM) along with PhDs in administrative sciences. For a period, this *was* a distinctive model of doctoral education; it was deeply disciplinary but applied theory to important social, organizational, and managerial problems, particularly where they related to individuals and organizations embedded in a political or public sector context. In addition to standard methodology courses such as statistics, doctoral students were required to take organizational behavior courses, including "Individual Behavior in Organizations" and "Group Behavior in Organizations." Also required was a practicum on organizational consulting; under faculty supervision, doctoral students collaborated with specific clients. Doctoral students also played an important role in the master's program as teaching assistants.

Yale's SOM was the school that perhaps came closest to mirroring the Booth School's intellectual signature, but with the behavioral social sciences, sociology, and psychology at its center rather than Chicago's economics. The individual work of Paul DiMaggio, Clayton Alderfer, and Chris Argyris stand out as examples of the research produced at the school in its early years.

However, Yale's distinctiveness proved unmanageable, showing that the entire business education industry has become institutionalized around other signatures. SOM's economics- and quantitatively oriented professors found themselves in the unusual position of not being the faculty's most powerful, which resulted in strife and division. Continuous infighting destabilized the administrative structure, and from its founding in 1976 until this chapter's publication in 2013, the school has had eleven deans. The Yale alumni magazine described it as the university's "most problem-plagued professional school." In contrast to the economics training students received, their organizational behavior courses were accused of raising uncertainties about their professional identity and of creating "mental disturbance."

In 1988, another newly appointed dean, Michael Levine (a former airline executive and mentee of the corporate takeover artist Frank Lorenzo), dismantled what was widely seen as one of the more innovative and creative research groups in business schools on the grounds it was too "touchy-feely." All six untenured professors in the organizational behavior group were asked to leave. Victor Vroom, one of the school's founding faculty, described it as "an absolute disaster." Some prominent alumni, angered by these heavy-handed actions, began calling it the "School of Disorganization and Mismanagement"; they even hired an airplane to trail a banner calling for Levine's dismissal during the Yale–Harvard football game and during Yale's commencement ceremony.

After Levine stepped down, the school retooled; but the behavioral sciences group never recovered. The group did, however, leave a lasting impact on doctoral programs in business elsewhere, demonstrating that a strong disciplinary orientation could be combined with field methods and action research to produce highly creative management scholarship.

Yale SOM's intellectual signature remains distinctive. The protagonist is society itself. The program seeks to generate social improvement through academic means—of which the most important means is the university's demarcating characteristic, its research methods. The goal is to draw the study of management back into social science generally and political science in particular, more so even than in Hutchins's Chicago tradition. The Yale signature encompasses the political and psychological dimensions of institutional theory that informed the work of Powell and DiMaggio, and it may also reflect the influence of the prestigious Yale Divinity School. The school's difficulties and the later shift from MPPA to MBA show two things: the immiscibility of the social sciences' broader intellectual signature, and the tendency to look inward that characterizes management education's current fabric, dominated as it is by the Booth and GSIA signatures.

The Relationship Between Problematics and Methodologies

In the previous sections, we argued that the leading U.S. business schools have adopted a variety of signatures. Our next objective is to investigate and identify the context within which a school's PhD program is lodged. We use examples to illustrate rather than define the various signatures and make the point that schools are oriented toward different beneficiaries, or protagonists. In the cases described above, these protagonists could be (a) the managers faced with complex and uncertain situations that call for decisive action (HBS); (b) the firms in competitive market

Figure 4.1 Problematics and Methodologies

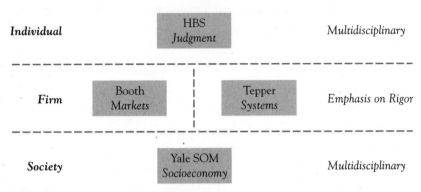

situations that focus on analysis and the exercise of economic rationality (Booth); (c) the firms in competitive market situations that focus on designing and administering economic and technological systems captured in formal models (Tepper); or (d) the manager in a complex and political socioeconomy seeking better policy (Yale SOM) (Figure 4.1).

The different signatures suggest that PhD students at a given institution have to work within their school's specific topic sets, which are the most visible aspects of a school's academic reputation: Chicago works on finance; Harvard works on strategy; Yale works on social policy; and so on. A PhD student whose interests lie in other directions takes on significant added burdens and risks.

We also suggest that the topic sets integrated into a PhD program are associated with the school's signature. This is a more difficult case to make because few academic projects are entirely mono-methodological. But there is no question that economists, for example, are heavily committed to rational choice theorizing, and students pursuing a topic outside of mainstream neoclassical economics (for example, Austrian economics or the economics of intrinsic incentives) have a rougher time (Lawson, 2012).

The methodological narrowness that has overtaken business schools as a result of the signatures developed at, and disseminated by, schools like Booth and Tepper may well be damaging business education by intellectually neutering PhD students. Key here is the concept of *critique*, whereby the purposes for which PhD students are educated are not simply the development of critical thinking skills or as teachers of dogma; rather, the purpose is to develop an understanding that theoretical progress is driven by making a second methodological footing available from which the scholar can critique all others' work (Allais, 1990; Foster, 1968; Lakatos & Musgrave, 1970).

Our present, almost dogmatic, emphasis on positivist methods means that instead of pursuing critically bold intellectual ends, our PhD students are being taught to be risk-avoiding journeymen and contributes to the relevance-and-rigor divide. To understand how this has happened and further grasp the implications, it is useful to glance at the history of business school research methodology.

The Relevance and Rigor Diverge

The widespread adoption of neoclassical ideas and quantitative methods in business schools, instigated by the Ford and Carnegie foundations' reports, accompanied a wider change in attitudes in the post–World War II era about what can be loosely labeled *positivism*. But rather than pursue the Comtean program theorizing social science for the betterment of mankind, postwar social science began to incline toward theorizing for its own sake. Rigorous theory and methods of generating theory began to be valued more than the social or even personal impact of the results (Grant & Mills, 2006). The untethering of research publications from their social consequences made historical methods irrelevant and the Comtean project of problems as the source of method and theory was stood on its head.

In business schools, this meant that instead of having the needs of society or even the corporation drive the choice of research method, the more rigorous and easily applied methods began to drive the choice of research topics. The search for a scientific rigor and objectivity that kept the researchers' views, values, and prejudices out of the conclusions inevitably produced theories that could no longer be readily applied to the human, social, or corporate situation. The rigor and the relevance of management research began to diverge. As theory—rather than the challenges of practice and betterment—became our research target, the disciplines themselves fragmented into subdisciplines and became even more parochial, each with its own journals, standards, and languages. The cross-disciplinary, socially improving notions instituted by Hutchins at Chicago and Simon at GSIA became less tenable, and the problems of balancing them within a school became more difficult (Backhouse & Fontaine, 2010; Khurana & Spender, 2012; Locke, 2008; Simon, 1967).

The funding of business school research also changed after World War II. The foundations, and the Cowles Commission, were the major players in the immediate postwar era, though their impact was softened once government agencies such as the Office of Naval Research and the National Science Foundation became interested in management. Curiously, funding from these other sources did not result in greater emphasis on managerial relevance. Business school researchers moved, instead, toward rigorous microtheory. This research aesthetic preferred positivistic research, to the point that nonpositivistic research methodologies were not only embattled and contested but increasingly delegitimated.

Further fragmentation in business-related research programs was apparent in, for instance, the growing heterogeneity of research topics and projects evident at the Academy of Management, now with twenty-five subdisciplinary divisions. Widening gulfs also separate the research produced by the many accounting associations ([such as the American Accounting Association, American Institute of CPAs [AICPA], and the Institute of Management Accountants) and their journals, versus the research from the American Marketing Association, Society for Business

Ethics, Business History Conference, Journal of International Business, the American Economic Association, Operations Research Society, the American Psychological Association, the Institute of Electrical and Electronics Engineers (IEEE) and Association for Computing Machinery (ACM) for IT faculty, and so on. Note that the members of these societies seldom attend Academy of Management meetings; they inhabit very different academic universes even when co-located in business schools.

Some pushback came from those who, presuming the importance of investigating the human actor's viewpoint, regarded the hermeneutic tradition as equally valuable to the human and social sciences (for example, Alasuutari, 2010; Alvesson & Kärreman, 2011). The argument that the thinking actor's behavior cannot ever be fully explained by a mechanistic analysis of causation goes back millennia, of course. But in the European tradition, the argument can be traced to Giambattista Vico, and thence to Max Weber and *Verstehen*, and thence too to Gestalt psychology and *sense-making* (Berlin, 2000; Weick, 1969).

This more subjective perspective is especially significant in the public sector, where a catch-all objective function such as maximizing profit was neither meaningful nor capable of being operationalized. Yale's SOM, focusing on a broader agenda than the private for-profit sector alone, presupposed a degree of methodological diversity—one that, as we have seen, was sustained only with difficulty and periodic existential crises. At Harvard and elsewhere, business schools—with their narrow focus on the private sector—were institutionally separated from the schools of public administration, with their broader concerns for politics and the public good. Within business schools, the shift toward rational choice theorizing was significantly supported by changes in the national political discourse that began in the late 1970s and early 1980s. In the absence of empirical evaluation by business users, the research generated by business schools was increasingly open to being shaped and judged according to unarticulated political criteria, particularly those of neoliberal-ism (for example, Amadae, 2003; Grant & Mills, 2006; Harvey, 2005; Peck, 2010; and Spector, 2006).

The unintended negative consequences of the foundation reports were—and still are—exacerbated by AACSB's uncritical adoption of the reports' agenda. AACSB's 2002, 2006, and 2008 reports are intellectually and administratively passive, accepting rational choice–driven doctoral preparation without considering either AACSB's own institutional influence or how AACSB might temper the doctoral programs' increasing dysfunctionality.

Hence, it is useful to contrast the situation in schools of management with the situation in schools of accounting—all the more so because AACSB offers them separate accreditation along with separate accreditation to business schools that cover both accounting and management. As the foundation reports were being prepared, schools of accounting were grappling with rebuilding their own educational and research agendas in the wake of the intellectual revolutions of the postwar era (Zeff, 2001, 2003a, 2003b). Although the same critique that has been leveled at management research has been leveled at accounting education (Granoff & Zeff, 2008), it is interesting that in con-trast to AACSB's passivity, accounting's professional bodies established their own discipline-wide research programs and regulatory bodies (Zeff, 2001). The result has been that even though there has been a substantial increase in the number of business school–based accounting research journals and in the volume of articles, schools and departments of accounting have maintained links with professional practitioners, and these links have inhibited the dysfunctional cycle evident in business schools as a whole.

The larger issue, however, is that given that few view research management as a holistic practice, business schools' academic focus has turned to methodological prowess as the only test of academic ability and has made it the core of doctoral programs everywhere. Thus, the challenge is not simply to invent better administrative structures or attend more carefully to the care, feeding, and socialization of doctoral students. The challenge may be the more difficult one of (a) generating a more useful set of problematics and methods and (b) institutionalizing them as the infrastructure within which doctoral students learn the purposes and methods of research. Instead of training students to prepare quantitatively proficient, publishable articles, we would train them to conduct research that contributes to management practice. Instead of rewarding the submission of marginalia to established academic ideas that provide few insights into real-world managerial practice, we must encourage and reward our doctoral students' break with convention and innovate, "to boldly go where none has gone before."

Conclusions and PhD Program Implications

This final section summarizes our analysis of doctoral programs in U.S. business schools. We hope the comments will help business school administrators think about their doctoral programs' place in their schools' strategies and how they might better reinforce each other.

In the business school community, various prescriptions have been offered for the dysfunctional predicament in which schools and faculty now find themselves. Analyses of the widening rigor-and-relevance gap sometimes suggest that doctoral research can be rehabilitated by changing its topics—working on empirical data about management's current concerns rather than debating the scholarly literature (De Rond & Miller, 2005). Thus, some argue that business school research should be co-supervised by management practitioners and academics. We feel that (a) this is no longer viable, given the explosion of topics pursued by the different subdisciplines, and (b) it ignores our deeper methodological predicament.[12]

Still others—including unfortunately, the leadership of AACSB—think that what ails business school doctoral programs is a design problem, a problem that can be solved by restructuring without taking into account the signature of the school in which a program is housed (Khurana & Spender, 2012). The temptations to take the redesign route are considerable. It is easy to write interdisciplinary research and multiple methods into a school's strategic plan, even though they are stubbornly difficult to implement. The background assumption that doctoral education is a coherent product is clearly absurd, especially as it denies the fantastic variety of subdisciplines and topics that are now evident (Ehrenberg & Kuh, 2009; Golde & Walker, 2006; Maki & Borkowski, 2006; Nerad & Heggelund, 2008; Nerad & Trzyna, 2008; Walker & others, 2008). We see the methodology and publishing legitimacy issues as central, because what it ultimately means to be an academic is determined by the research methods underpinning the expert knowledge claimed.

Although we have called the dominant theoretical stance in business schools today "positivist," few social scientists sympathize with the modernist project, or expect that all disciplines might eventually converge into a grand rationality-based socioeconomic theory of everything, as originally envisaged by Comte and pursued by Parsons (Usher, Bryant, & Johnston, 1997). Given pluralism as the postmodern touchstone, PhD-level research is inevitably fragmented in topic and method, and no amount of theory policing can put it back together again (Pfeffer, 1993). Today's doctoral students are extremely unlikely to share the modernist dream, even if it still echoes among the senior academics and academic institutions that shape their research. We note the increasing financial and business press acknowledgment of the destructive impact of rationality-alone thinking, even as this debate is unresolved within our A-journals, in the academy's presidential speeches, and in AACSB's methodologically agnostic passivism. Although *pluralism* may be today's intellectual watchword, that does not mean that doctoral education, faculty development, and research are scattershot.

Effectively managing a contemporary doctoral program so that it contributes significantly to a school's intellectual signature, and thus to both the discipline and the community, begins when the school's administration makes a careful selection of problematics and resolves the many tensions around researching them. These schisms and tensions are plentiful because, despite the obvious methodological hegemony and apparent coherence of positivist research evident in our A-journals, the actual scope of the work appearing in management journals today is staggeringly vast. The work displays a wide variety of methodological positions, research techniques, and topics. The challenge is to render the variety fruitful rather than chaotic.

Although Pfeffer complains that this richness prevents us from advancing to true academic status, the reality is the reverse. Architects such as Frank Lloyd Wright, Michael Graves, and Frank Gehry managed to design everything from buildings to furniture, textiles, postage stamps, and teapots without threatening the integrity of the architectural profession. Instead, their enterprise stretched the twentieth-century notion of architecture into new ways of understanding how design can shape the ways in which people experience their living spaces—the architectural profession's fundamental problematic. Such analysis helps surface the interplay of a profession's history, practices, professional identity, and educational agenda.

The PhD student's choice of problematic—in addition to getting faculty support and mentoring—obviously matters hugely. But the key dimensions are methodological, and given the dimensions' variety in the social and economic sciences, no issue can be more central than how to carefully manage the relationship between methodologies and problematics. Every school's intellectual signature turns on this, and there are alternative configurations; our types represent only four of the ways to cut our disciplinary cake. We argue that the principal determinant of the quality of the student's intellectual experience is the coherence of the school's signature. When the signature lacks coherence, the student is exposed to the internecine faculty wars found in so many schools. Each of the intellectual signatures we identify in Figure 4.1 can be made coherent, but they differ in ways that make it difficult to form a bridge across them—to embrace, for instance, HBS case-oriented synthesizing within a Booth-like theorizing environment. As Porter observed in his second analysis (L. W. Porter, 1997), our discipline has evolved and expanded to the point at which differentiation and granulation have occurred, and there are wide divergences among its different parts.

We can take our analysis a step further by considering the different approaches to the rigor-and-relevance gap that are implicit in the different signatures. There are several positions here. As noted, one is that the rigor-and-relevance gap can be overcome by shifting researchers' attention from problematics defined by the academic literature toward those defined by managers (Gulati, 2007; Hodgkinson & Rousseau, 2009; Rynes, Bartunek, & Daft, 2001; Tushman & O'Reilly, 2007; Tushman, O'Reilly, Fenollosa, Kleinbaum, & McGrath, 2007; Varadarajan, 2003; Walsh, Tushman, Kimberly, Starbuck, & Ashford, 2007; Worrell, 2009). The implication is that the gap arises only from the researcher's inappropriate choice of problematic—perhaps chosen in anticipation of publication ease rather than social value—and has nothing to do with methodological incompatibilities. This is naïve and trivializes the issues, which are problems reinforced by our discipline's uncritical acceptance of triangulation and mixed methods (Jick, 1983; Teddlie & Tashakkori, 2009).

Scholars trained in the European critical tradition—aware, for instance, of the *Methodenstreit* and the discontinuities between the positivist and interpretive positions in the social and economic sciences—are less sanguine than others about the possibilities of bringing them together into a single coherent method (Burrell & Morgan, 1979). These scholars look, instead, for some complementarity between contrasting methods—positivist and interpretive (for example, Andriessen, 2004; Schutz, 1970). Continuing this tradition was a previous generation of American management scholars—such as Thorstein Veblen, Richard Ely, Edwin Gay, and Chester Barnard—many of whom were educated in Europe. As we know, this approach was more or less banished from business schools as the foundation reports were implemented (Khurana, 2007; Khurana & Nohria, 2008; Khurana & Penrice, 2011). Even ignoring the institutionalized challenges to publishing nonpositivist, nonquantitative research of high relevance to managers, such as what appears in the *Harvard Business Review*, the relevance question still hangs over us, given our profession's claim that we are focused on aiding managers.

We believe there is considerable value in recovering and refurbishing the prerationalist tradition in light of today's disciplinary situation, problematics, criticisms, and methodological institutionalization. If this is to happen, it must begin with our schools' doctoral programs.

One illustration can be found in the work of Carl von Clausewitz (Sumida, 2008). His focus was on the actor confronting an uncertain and underspecified situation with an urgent goal in mind. The task is to synthesize an analysis or reasoned support for selecting an action that leads toward achieving the goal with some degree of confidence. This is what defines relevance—being judged relevant to the actor's intentions, a subjective definition. In the positivist tradition, theory seeks to be objective, to escape the subjectivities of the researcher or decision maker. Clausewitz argued that in real-world situations such as battle, no single theory could provide realistically informed confidence. The military actor seeks to grasp a single particular situation in ways that lead to strategic advantage. The theorist, in contrast, seeks what is general about a population of situations, with the residual differences being taken care of in ceteris paribus clauses. Clausewitz argued that theory might well be relevant to an action but was never sufficient to determine it. The responsible actor must grasp the action situation, bringing further specifics to bear and synthesizing everything considered relevant in an act of personal judgment, treating theory as informing rather than determining. Rigor is a statement about the objective quality of the theoretical information and has no direct bearing on the actor's sense of its relevance. In this setting, rigor and relevance are orthogonal—mutually independent.

Herbert Simon's paper on the design of a business school turned on the same distinction between managing on the basis of analysis and on the basis of judgment (Khurana & Spender, 2012, Christensen, Garvin, & Sweet, 1991). Under the conditions of uncertainty and bounded rationality that Simon took to be unavoidable in management practice, judgment is the precursor to action. Analysis and judgment complement each other. Once synthesis is admitted to the school's signature, the problems of designing and managing the signature grows out of achieving a fruitful relationship of analysis and synthesis. Clearly, judgment should be supported by data collection and quantitative analysis to the fullest extent possible. But analysis suffices only under conditions of certainty. Natural sciences presume the underlying logicality, knowability, and thus theorize-ability of the universe. The modernist project from Comte to Durkheim to Coleman was based on similar presumptions about the socioeconomic universe, that it was deeply rational and analyzable using purely rational thought.

Though Simon was a self-declared positivist, he rejected the possibility of this kind of explanation. He presumed that business operated in, and could only exist within, a realm of uncertainty (Spender, 2013). He implied that a business school should help develop students'—and MBA students' especially—powers of judgment and synthesis over and above their powers of analysis. As Simon learned from Barnard, training in executive synthesis rather than computable analysis is how a business school's courses can help create economic value. Thus, value-creating research need not be positioned against positivist research in the sense of a dialectical struggle. Those trained into a broader methodological aesthetic see the two methodologies as mutually supportive and informing. Most empirical research begins with fact finding in a sense-making phase, teasing out some independent and dependent variables before proceeding to the data-intensive work that matches our journals' current quantitative style. The epistemological justification for the transition is brushed under the carpet, an accepted synthesis on which all useful research stands. Likewise, positivist theorists are inclined to overlook the fact that their choice of axioms is a matter of judgment, not scientific truth—despite the Kuhnian paradigm shift as axioms are changed.

Earlier we implied that the coherence of a school's intellectual signature is a key determinant of the intellectual quality of the PhD student's experience. A school's position on the rigor-and-relevance debate is likewise a key metric of its signature. Figure 4.1 can be adapted to illustrate this (as you can see in Figure 4.2). The HBS signature depends on synthesis at the individual level, recalling Commons. The Booth signature eschews synthesis and seeks market-based rigor. The Tepper position is less exclusive but seeks rigorous models that are based on definable systems. The Yale SOM position seeks analysis at a broader level, perhaps institutional, perhaps social.

Figure 4.2 Methodological Signatures and Position on the Rigor–Relevance Debate

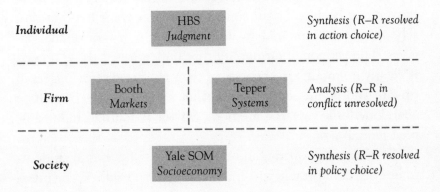

Individual	HBS Judgment		*Synthesis (R–R resolved in action choice)*
Firm	Booth Markets	Tepper Systems	*Analysis (R–R in conflict unresolved)*
Society	Yale SOM Socioeconomy		*Synthesis (R–R resolved in policy choice)*

Summing Up

Doctoral programs are of inestimable value to our schools and disciplinary institutions, and they warrant our most careful attention. They are the gardens in which we nurture and create our discipline's future. At the same time, they are the places where our neglect most seriously damages the futures of our students and our discipline. Rather than tarring doctoral students with the criticisms directed at the business school project as a whole, we should see the students as crucial to how we might take charge of our discipline's evolution.

Without doubt, AACSB and the Academy of Management have roles to play in recognizing the challenges of doctoral education and supporting attention to them. But the point of strategic leverage lies at the school level. Curriculum redesigns, without adequate consideration of the signatures that mark out the discipline's territory, are simply not adequate. Our discipline's methodological institutionalization must evolve from the iron cage of positivist methods; we must shift into training for the academic innovations that might move us closer to helping professionalize management, and not merely management education (Spender, 2007).

Ironically, in spite of the many criticisms of business school research, it may well be that the prospects for path-breaking doctoral-level research—as opposed to rote training in statistical methods as qualification for a position on the teaching ladder—have never been so bright since the postwar era, when business schools were hammered by foundation reports' recommendations. The economic rationality that underpinned those reports is clearly crumbling in the eyes of the public and of managers in private and public sectors. The other social sciences have long abandoned sole research methods. So our A-journals may be its final redoubt.

Training, supporting, and encouraging our doctoral students to be both comfortable within, and to think outside of, the ratio-

nalist box gives them a laissez-passer to reengage creative managerial practices and to break out of the iron cage and into the
new territory implied by the study of entrepreneurship, leadership, and strategy. At work there, the students may well have to
depend on the efforts of a few senior dissident or heterodox academics to start the new journals, e-pubs, and blogs in which they
can publish. But this is an old story about how change happens—
slowly—in academe.

Notes

1. Porter was especially gloomy about this, noting that despite
   the many curriculum and organizational changes in response
   to decreased funding, new technologies, the shift from full-
   timers to adjuncts, the erosion of the tenure system, and to
   increased diversity and product heterogeneity, the doctoral
   programs seemed stuck in a time warp, unchanged since the
   Foundation reports (L. W. Porter, 1997, p. 6).
2. Much of the research and literature on the other professional
   schools converges on the notion of better "socializing" doctoral students into the academic profession. Against this, our
   focus is less on general preparation for a productive and
   satisfying professional career and more on the specific intellectual places they are trained to occupy in our discipline's
   institutional processes.
3. It turns out that, in these respects, business school doctoral
   programs are not significantly different from those in other
   professional schools (Golde & Walker, 2006; Maki &
   Borkowski, 2006). Around the world, doctoral education
   seems to be failing to do what many feel is needed to sustain
   and develop the professional schools, and there is growing
   dissatisfaction among the students too.
4. Even if HBS seems to loom large, the unquestioned dominance it achieved before World War II has now diffused.
   Stanford might claim bragging rights (Augier & March,

2011)—or Wharton (Sass, 1982), the London School of Economics, or INSEAD.

5. Unlike most of the other U.S. business schools, HBS was transformed into a military leadership school during World War II, and one dimension of this transformation was that it learned to provide training in the applied statistics essential to the war machine (Cruikshank, 1987, p. 243). After World War II HBS realigned itself toward the private sector, but applied statistics remained as the research focus went back onto the managerial leadership and industrial economics thinking on which the school was founded (Bok, 1978).

6. Many of Chicago's MBA courses were only slightly watered down versions of the doctoral courses.

7. A solid introductory course (or two-course sequence) in microeconomics, game theory, or behavioral economics (for example, B33101 [Turbo-Micro], ECON30500 [Game Theory], ECON21800 [Experimental Economics], and so on).

8. Carnegie president Robert E. Doherty (who served from 1936 to 1950) had begun to promote research at the institute in the 1930s, and by 1948 Carnegie had a small cohort of doctoral students, principally in engineering and related subjects (Crowther-Heyck, 2006). Mathematics, formal modeling, and statistics were central to the research programs in these disciplines.

9. Bach worked closely with Donald David, a former Harvard Business School dean who had left HBS in 1955 to become chairman of the executive committee of the Ford Foundation, to initiate and prepare the foundation's highly critical report on the parlous state of U.S. business education (Fenton, 2000; Khurana & Penrice, 2011; Khurana & Spender, 2012). Bach and David were also instrumental in shaping the parallel report from the Carnegie Corporation (Gordon & Howell, 1959).

10. These changes within the business school community would not and could not have taken place had complementary changes not also taken place within the other disciplines relatively recently accepted into the university such as economics, psychology, and sociology. Academic professionalization in these disciplines progressed at a rapid pace between the 1880s and World War II (L. W. Porter & McKibbin, 1988). Statistics was being advanced, especially by Karl Pearson, and statistical arguments were becoming central to public and business life (Bledstein, 1978; Larson, 1977; Light, 1983). Computers were also beginning to be accessible. Soon all the social sciences were converging rapidly on the quantitative research methods promoted by the Foundation reports (T. M. Porter, 1986, 1995).

11. The GSIA at Carnegie Mellon was renamed the Tepper School of Business in 2003.

12. A closer look at how we see and use the methods now labeled "qualitative" shows that their practitioners seldom pay much attention to the problematics of hermeneutics and are often simply relabeling positivist methods, dealing with words and textual analysis instead of numbers (Bluhm, Harman, Lee, & Mitchell, 2011; Fragueiro & Thomas, 2011; Gulati, 2007; Lorange, 2005, 2008; Morsing & Sauquet, 2011; Starkey & Tiratsoo, 2007; Van de Ven, 2007). The history of the disciplines admitted into the university shows low tolerance for methodological balance, the *Methodenstreit* being one of the more famous instances of academic distrust and struggle, though the various "faculty wars" in law, economics, and sociology were brutal as well. The story of GSIA, with Simon moving into the Carnegie Mellon psychology department to get out of the way of the school's neoliberal economists, shows how even if interdisciplinary activity was an espoused strategy, it was already difficult to implement in the 1950s, even before the management

discipline was "sharpened up" in response to the foundation-impelled reforms.

References

AACSB. *Management Education at Risk*. St Louis, Mo.: Association to Advance Collegiate Schools Business, 2002.

AACSB. *Sustaining Scholarship in Business Schools*. St Louis, Mo: Association to Advance Collegiate Schools of Business, 2003.

AACSB. *The Business School Rankings Dilemma*. Tampa, Fla.: Association to Advance Collegiate Schools of Business, 2005a.

AACSB. *Why Management Education Matters: Its Impact on Individuals, Organizations, and Society*. Tampa, Fla.: AACSB International, 2005b.

AACSB. *The Impact of Research*. Tampa, Fla.: AACSB International, 2008.

Alasuutari, P. "The Rise and Relevance of Qualitative Research." *International Journal of Social Research Methodology*, 2010, 13(2), 139–155.

Allais, M. "Criticism of the Axioms and Postulates of the American School." In Paul K. Moser (ed.), *Rationality in Action: Contemporary Approaches* (pp. 113–139). Cambridge: Cambridge University Press, 1990.

Alvesson, M., & Kärreman, D. *Qualitative Research and Theory Development: Mystery as Method*. London: Sage, 2011.

Amadae, S. M. *Rationalizing Capitalist Democracy: The Cold War Origins of Rational Choice Liberalism*. Chicago, Ill.: University of Chicago Press, 2003.

Andriessen, D. "Reconciling the Rigor–Relevance Dilemma in Intellectual Capital Research." *Learning Organization*, 2004, 11(4/5), 393–401.

Augier, M., & March, J. G. *The Roots, Rituals, and Rhetorics of Change*. Stanford, Calif.: Stanford University Press, 2011.

Backhouse, R. E., and Fontaine, P. (eds.). *The History of the Social Sciences Since 1945*. Cambridge: Cambridge University Press, 2010.

Baker, B. "Teaching the Profession of Business at Harvard," Supplement to *Official Register of Harvard University*, February 27, 1915, 12(1), Pt. 6, 9–11.

Bennis, W., & O'Toole, J. "How Business Schools Lost Their Way." *Harvard Business Review*, 2005, 83(5), 96–104.

Berlin, I. (2000). *Three Critics of the Enlightenment: Vico, Hamann, Herder*. Princeton N.J.: Princeton University Press, 2000.

Bledstein, B. J. *The Culture of Professionalism: The Middle Class and Higher Education in America*. New York: Norton, 1978.

Bluhm, D. J., Harman, W., Lee, T. W., & Mitchell, T. R. "Qualitative Research in Management: A Decade of Progressions." *Journal of Management Studies*, 2011, 48(8), 1866–1891.

Bok, D. C. *The President's Report 1977–1978*. Cambridge, Mass.: Harvard University, 1978.

Burns, T., & Stalker, G. M. *The Management of Innovation*. London: Tavistock, 1961.

Burrell, G., & Morgan, G. *Sociological Paradigms and Organizational Analysis*. London: Heinemann Educational, 1979.

Carnegie Graduate School of Industrial Administration. "Fact Sheet: Official Dedication," 1952.

Christensen, C. R., Garvin, D. A., & Sweet, A. *Education for Judgment: The Artistry of Discussion Leadership*. Boston, Mass.: Harvard Business School Press, 1991.

Colquitt, J. A., & Zapata-Phelan, C. P. "Trends in Theory Building and Theory Testing: A Five-Decade Study of the Academy of Management Journal." *Academy of Management Journal*, 2007, 50(6), 1281–1303.

Commons, J. R. *The Legal Foundations of Capitalism*. New York: Macmillan, 1924.

Crainer, S., & Dearlove, D. *Gravy Training: Inside the Business of Business Schools*. San Francisco, Calif.: Jossey-Bass, 1999.

Crowther-Heyck, H. "Herbert Simon and the GSIA: Building an Interdisciplinary Community." *Journal of the History of the Behavioral Sciences*, 2006, 42(4), 311–334.

Cruikshank, J. L. *Delicate Experiment: The Harvard Business School, 1908–1945*. Boston, Mass.: Harvard Business School Press, 1987.

Cyert, R. M., & March, J. G. *A Behavioral Theory of the Firm*. Englewood Cliffs, N.J.: Prentice-Hall, 1963.

Datar, S. M., Garvin, D. A. & Cullen, P. G. (2010). *Rethinking the MBA: Business Education at a Crossroads*. Boston, Mass.: Harvard Business Press, 2010.

De Rond, M., & Miller, A. N. "Publish or Perish: Bane or Boon of Academic Life?" *Journal of Management Inquiry*, 2005, 14(4), 321–329.

Donham, W. B. "The Case Method in College Teaching of Social Science." In M. P. McNair & A. Hersum (eds.), *The Case Method at the Harvard Business School* (pp. 244–255). New York: McGraw-Hill, 1954.

Durand, T., & Dameron, S. (eds.). *The Future of Business Schools: Scenarios and Strategies for 2020*. Basingstoke, U.K.: Palgrave Macmillan, 2008.

Ehrenberg, R. G., & Kuh, C. V. (eds.). *Doctoral Education and the Faculty of the Future*. Ithaca, N.Y.: Cornell University Press, 2009.

Fenton, E. *Carnegie-Mellon 1900–2000: A Centennial History*. Pittsburgh, Penna.: Carnegie Mellon University Press, 2000.

Foster, R. "Reflections on Teaching Criticism." *Contemporary Literature*, 1968, 9(3, Modern Criticism), 406–418.

Fragueiro, F., & Thomas, H. *Strategic Leadership in the Business School: Keeping One Step Ahead*. Cambridge: Cambridge University Press, 2011.

French, R., & Grey, C. *Rethinking Management Education*. London: Sage, 1996.

Gardner, S. K. "Conceptualizing Success in Doctoral Education: Perspectives of Faculty in Seven Disciplines." *Review of Higher Education*, 2009a, 32(3), 383–406.

Gardner, S. K. The Development of Doctoral Students: Phases of Challenge and Support: ASHE Higher Education Report. San Francisco, Calif.: Jossey-Bass, 2009b.

Gardner, S. K. "Faculty Perspectives on Doctoral Student Socialization in Five Disciplines." *International Journal of Doctoral Studies*, 2010, 5, 39–53.

Gardner, S. K., & Mendoza, P. (eds.). *On Becoming a Scholar: Socialization and Development in Doctoral Education*. Sterling, Va.: Stylus, 2010.

Golde, C. M. "Applying Lessons From Professional Education to the Preparation of the Professoriate." *New Directions for Teaching and Learning*, 2008, 113(Spring), 17–25.

Golde, C. M., & Walker, G. E. (eds.). *Envisioning the Future of Doctoral Education: Preparing Stewards of the Discipline*. Stanford, Calif.: Carnegie Foundation for the Advancement of Teaching, 2006.

Gordon, R. "Gordon to Chamberlain Memo." November 1957, Ford Foundation Archives, 58, Section IV.

Gordon, R., & Howell, J. *Higher Education for Business*. New York: Columbia University Press, 1959.

Granoff, M. H., & Zeff, S. A. "Research on Accounting Should Learn From the Past." *Chronicle of Higher Education*, 2008, 54(28), p. A34.

Grant, J. D., & Mills, A. J. "The Quiet Americans: Formative Context, the Academy of Management Leadership, and the Management Textbook, 1936–1960." *Management & Organizational History*, 2006, 1(2), 201–224.

Gulati, R. "Tent Poles, Tribalism, and Boundary Spanning: The Rigor-Relevance Debate in Management Research." *Academy of Management Journal*, 2007, 50(4), 775–782.

Hafferty, F. W. "What Medical Students Know About Professionalism." *Mount Sinai Journal of Medicine*, 2002, 69(6), 385–397.

Hambrick, D. C. "1993 Presidential Address: What If the Academy Actually Mattered." *Academy of Management Review*, 1994, 19(1), 11–16.

Harvey, D. *A Brief History of Neoliberalism*. Oxford: Oxford University Press, 2005.

Haskell, T. L. *The Emergence of Professional Social Science: The American Social Science Association and the Nineteenth-Century Crisis of Authority*. Baltimore, Md.: Johns Hopkins University Press, 2000.

Heaton, H. (1968). *A Scholar in Action: Edwin F. Gay*. New York: Greenwood, 1968.

Hodgkinson, G. P., & Rousseau, D. M. "Bridging the Rigour-Relevance Gap in Management Research: It's Already Happening!" *Journal of Management Studies*, 2009, 46(3), 534–546.

Huff, A. S. "1999 Presidential Address: Changes in Organizational Knowledge Production." *Academy of Management Review*, 2000, 25(2), 288–293.

Ivory, C., Miskell, P., Neely, A., Shipton, H., & White, A. *The Future of Business School Faculty*. London: Advanced Institute of Management Research, 2007.

Jarzabkowski, P., Giuletti, M., & Oliveira, B. *Building a Strategy Toolkit: Lessons from Business*. London: Advanced Institute of Management Research, 2009.

Jick, T. D. "Mixing Qualitative and Quantitative Methods: Triangulation in Action." In J. van Maanen (ed.), *Qualitative Methodology* (pp. 135–148). Beverly Hills, Calif.: Sage, 1983.

Joseph, G. W. "Shortage of PhDs? We're Turning Them Away." *BizEd*, 2004, July/August, 54–55.

Khurana, R. *From Higher Aims to Hired Hands: The Social Transformation of American Business Schools and the Unfulfilled Promise of Management as a Profession*. Princeton N.J.: Princeton University Press, 2007.

Khurana, R., & Nohria, N. "It is Time to Make Management a True Profession." *Harvard Business Review*, 2008, 86(10), 70–77.

Khurana, R., & Penrice, D. "Business Education: The American Trajectory." In M. Morsing & A. Sauquet (eds.), *Business Schools and the Contribution to Society* (pp. 3–15). London: Sage, 2011.

Khurana, R., & Spender, J.-C. "Herbert A. Simon on What Ails Business Schools: More Than 'A Problem in Organizational Design.' " *Journal of Management Studies*, 2012, 49(3), 619–639.

Knight, F. H. "Business Management: Science or Art?" *Journal of Business*, 1923, 2(March 4), 5–24.

Kraaijenbrink, J., Spender, J.-C., & Groen, A. "The Resource-Based View: A Review and Assessment of Its Critiques." *Journal of Management*, 2010, 36(1), 349–372.

Lakatos, I., & Musgrave, A. (eds.). *Criticism and the Growth of Knowledge*. Cambridge: Cambridge University Press, 1970.

Larson, M. S. *The Rise of Professionalism: A Sociological Analysis*. Berkeley, Calif.: University of California Press, 1977.

Lawson, T. "Mathematical Modelling and Ideology in the Economics Academy: Competing Explanations for the Failings of the Modern Discipline?" *Economic Thought*, 2012, 1(1), 3–22.

Learned, E. P., Christensen, R., Andrews, K., & Guth, W. *Business Policy: Text and Cases*. Homewood, Ill.: Richard D. Irwin, 1965.

Light, D. W. (1983). "The Development of Professional Schools in America." In K. H. Jarausch (ed.), *The Transformation of Higher Learning*

1860–1930 (pp. 345–365). Chicago, Ill.: University of Chicago Press, 1983.

Locke, Robert R. "Comparing the German and American Systems. Round-table on Business Education. A Consideration of Rakesh Khurana's *From Higher Aims to Hired Hands.*" *Business History Review*, 2008, 82(2), 336–342.

Lorange, P. "Strategy Means Choice: Also for Today's Business School!" *Journal of Management Development*, 2005, 24(9), 783–790.

Lorange, P. *Thought Leadership Meets Business: How Business Schools Can Become More Successful.* Cambridge: Cambridge University Press, 2008.

Luthans, F., Walker, J. W., & Hodgetts, R. M. "Evidence on the Validity of Management Education." *Academy of Management Journal*, 1969, 12(4), 451–457.

Maki, P. L., & Borkowski, N. A. (eds.). *The Assessment of Doctoral Education: Emerging Criteria and New Models for Improving Outcomes.* Sterling, Va.: Stylus, 2006.

March, J. G., & Simon, H. A. *Organizations.* New York: Wiley, 1958.

Marshall, L. C. "The College of Commerce and Administration at the University of Chicago." *Journal of Political Economy*, 1913, 21(2), 97–110.

McNair, M. P., & Hersum, A. (eds.). *The Case Method at the Harvard Business School.* New York: McGraw-Hill, 1954.

McNamee, P. B. *Tools and Techniques for Strategic Management.* Oxford: Pergamon, 1987.

Mintzberg, H. *Managers Not MBAs: A Hard Look at the Soft Practice of Managing and Management Development.* San Francisco, Calif.: Berrett-Koehler, 2004.

Mitchell, T. R. "The Academic Life: Realistic Changes Needed for Business School Students and Faculty." *Academy of Management Learning & Education*, 2007, 6(2), 236–251.

Morsing, M., & Sauquet, A. (eds.). *Business Schools and Their Contribution to Society.* London: Sage, 2011.

Nerad, M., & Heggelund, M. *Towards a Global PhD? Forces and Forms in Doctoral Education Worldwide.* Seattle, Wash.: University of Washington Press, 2008.

Nerad, M., & Trzyna, T. "Conclusion: Globalization and Doctoral Education—Toward a Research Agenda." In M. Nerad & M. Heggelund (eds.), *Towards a Global PhD? Forces and Forms in Doctoral Education Worldwide* (pp. 300–312). Seattle, Wash: University of Washington Press, 2008.

Newman, F., Couturier, L., & Scurry, J. *The Future of Higher Education: Rhetoric, Reality, and the Risks of the Market.* San Francisco, Calif.: Jossey-Bass, 2004.

O'Connor, E. S. *Creating New Knowledge in Management: Appropriating the Field's Lost Foundations.* Stanford, Calif.: Stanford Business Books, 2011.

Olkin, I. "A Conversation With W. Allen Wallis." *Statistical Science*, 1991, 6(2), 121–140.

Olson, K., & Clark, C. M. "A Signature Pedagogy in Doctoral Education: The Leader–Scholar Community." *Educational Researcher*, 2009, 38(3), 216–221.

Peck, J. *Constructions of Neoliberal Reason.* Oxford: Oxford University Press, 2010.

Pfeffer, J. "Barriers to the Advance of Organizational Science: Paradigm Development as a Dependent Variable." *Academy of Management Review*, 1993, 18(4), 599–620.

Pfeffer, J. "What's Right and Still Wrong with Business Schools." *BizEd*, 2007, January/February, 42–49.

Pfeffer, J., & Fong, C. T. "The End of Business Schools? Less Success Than Meets the Eye." *Academy of Management Learning & Education*, 2002, 1(1), 78–95.

Phelan, S., Ferreira, M., & Salvador, R. "The First Twenty Years of the Strategic Management Journal." *Strategic Management Journal*, 2002, 23, 1161–1168.

Pierson, F. C., & others. *The Education of American Businessmen: A Study of University-College Programs in Business Education.* New York: McGraw-Hill, 1959.

Porter, L. W. "A Decade of Change in the Business School: From Complacency to Tomorrow." *Selections*, 1997, 13(2), 1–8.

Porter, L. W., & McKibbin, L. E. *Management Education and Development.* New York: McGraw-Hill, 1988.

Porter, T. M. *The Rise of Statistical Thinking 1820–1900.* Princeton, N.J.: Princeton University Press, 1986.

Porter, T. M. *Trust in Numbers: The Pursuit of Objectivity in Science and Public Life.* Princeton, N.J.: Princeton University Press, 1995.

Rynes, S. L., Bartunek, J. M., & Daft, R. L. "Across the Great Divide: Knowledge Creation and Transfer Between Practitioners and Academics." *Academy of Management Journal*, 2001, 44(2), 340–355.

Sass, S. A. *The Pragmatic Imagination: A History of the Wharton School 1881–1981.* Philadelphia, Penna.: University of Pennsylvania Press, 1982.

Scandura, T. A., & Williams, E. A. "Research Methodology in Management: Current Practices, Trends, and Implications for Future Research." *Academy of Management Journal*, 2000, 43(6), 1248–1264.

Schlossman, S., Sedlak, M., & Wechsler, H. *The "New Look": The Ford Foundation and the Revolution in Business Education.* Los Angeles: Graduate Management Admission Council, 1987.

Schutz, A. "On Concept and Theory Formation in the Social Sciences." In D. M. Emmett & A. McIntyre (eds.), *Sociological Theory and Philosophical Analysis*. New York: Macmillan, 1970.

Simon, H. A. "The Business School: A Problem in Organizational Design." *Journal of Management Studies*, 1967, 4(1), 1–16.

Simons, H. W. *The Rhetorical Turn: Invention and Persuasion in the Conduct of Inquiry*. Chicago, Ill.: University of Chicago Press, 1990.

Smiddy, H. F., & Naum, L. "Evolution of a 'Science of Managing' in America." *Management Science*, 1954, 1(1), 1–31.

Smith, C. A. *Fifty Years of Education for Business at the University of Texas*. Austin, Texas: University of Texas, College of Business Administration Foundation, 1962.

Spector, B. "The Harvard Business Review Goes to War." *Management & Organizational History*, 2006, 1(3), 273–295.

Spender, J.-C. "Crisis Casework for Policy Courses." *Journal of Management Education*, 1983, 8(4), 35–37.

Spender, J.-C. "Management as a Regulated Profession: An Essay." *Journal of Management Inquiry*, 2007, 16(1), 32–42.

Spender, J.-C. "Herbert Alexander Simon: Philosopher of the Organizational Life-World." In M. Witzel & M. Warner (eds.), *Oxford Handbook of Management Thinkers* (pp. 297–357). Oxford: Oxford University Press, 2013. In press.

Spender, J.-C., & Kraaijenbrink, J. "Why Competitive Strategy Succeeds—and With Whom." In R. Huggins & H. Izushi (eds.), *Competition, Competitive Advantage, and Clusters: The Ideas of Michael Porter* (pp. 33–55). Oxford: Oxford University Press, 2011.

Starkey, K., & Tiratsoo, N. *The Business School and the Bottom Line*. Cambridge: Cambridge University Press, 2007.

Stewart, M. *The Management Myth: Why the Experts Keep Getting It Wrong*. New York: Norton, 2009.

Stewart, M. M., Williamson, I. O., & King Jr., J. E. "Who Wants to Be a Business PhD? Exploring the Minority Entry Into the Faculty 'Pipeline.' " *Academy of Management Learning & Education*, 2008, 7(1), 42–55.

Sumida, J. T. *Decoding Clausewitz: A New Approach to On War*. Lawrence, Kan.: University Press of Kansas, 2008.

Summer, C. E., Bettis, R. A., Duhaime, I. H., Grant, J. H., Hambrick, D. C., Snow, C. C., & others. "Doctoral Education in the Field of Business Policy and Strategy." *Journal of Management*, 1990, 16(2), 361–398.

Teddlie, C., & Tashakkori, A. *Foundations of Mixed Methods Research*. Thousand Oaks, Calif.: Sage, 2009.

Teece, D. J., Pisano, G., & Shuen, A. "Dynamic Capabilities and Strategic Management." *Strategic Management Journal*, 1997, 18(7), 509–533.

Tushman, M. L., & O'Reilly, C. A. "Research and Relevance: Implications for a Pasteur's Quadrant for Doctoral Programs and Faculty Development." *Academy of Management Journal*, 2007, 50(4), 76–774.

Tushman, M. L., O'Reilly, C. A., Fenollosa, A., Kleinbaum, A. M., & McGrath, D. "Relevance and Rigor: Executive Education as a Lever in Shaping Practice and Research." *Academy of Management Learning & Education*, 2007, 6(3), 345–362.

Usher, R., Bryant, I., & Johnston, R. *Adult Education and the Postmodern Challenge: Learning Beyond the Limits*. London: Routledge, 1997.

Van de Ven, A. H. *Engaged Scholarship: A Guide for Organizational and Social Research*. Oxford: Oxford University Press, 2007.

Van Fleet, D. D. & Wren, D. A. "Teaching History in Business Schools: 1982–2003." *Academy of Management Learning & Education*, 2005, 4(1), 44–56.

Varadarajan, P. R. "Musing on Relevance and Rigor of Scholarly Research in Marketing." *Journal of the Academy of Marketing Science*, 2003, 31(4), 368–376.

Walker, G. E., Golde, C. M., Jones, L., Bueschel, A. C., & Hutchings, P. *The Formation of Scholars: Rethinking Doctoral Education for the Twenty-First Century*. Stanford, Calif.: Carnegie Foundation for the Advancement of Teaching, 2008.

Walsh, J. P., Tushman, M. L., Kimberly, J. R., Starbuck, B., & Ashford, S. "On the Relationship Between Research and Practice." *Journal of Management Inquiry*, 2007, 16(2), 128–154.

Weick, K. E. *Social Psychology of Organizing*. Reading, Mass.: Addison-Wesley, 1969.

Worrell, D. L. "Assessing Business Scholarship: The Difficulties in Moving Beyond the Rigor–Relevance Paradigm Trap." *Academy of Management Learning & Education*, 2009, 8(1), 127–130.

Wren, D. A. *The Evolution of Management Thought* (2nd ed.). New York: Wiley, 1979.

Yin, R. K. "The Case Study Crisis: Some Answers." *Administrative Science Quarterly*, 1981, 26, 58–65.

Zeff, S. A. "The Work of the Special Committee on Research Program." *Accounting Historians' Journal*, 2001, 28(2), 141–186.

Zeff, S. A. "How the US Accounting Profession Got Where It Is Today: Part 1." *Accounting Historians Journal*, 2003a, 17(3), 189–205.

Zeff, S. A. "How the US Accounting Profession Got Where It Is Today: Part 2." *Accounting Historians Journal*, 2003b, 17(4), 267–286.

Zeff, S. A. "The Contribution of the Harvard Business School to Management Control, 1908–1980." *Journal of Management Accounting Research*, 2008, 20(Special Issue), 175–208.

5

CURRICULUM MATTERS

Toward a More Holistic Graduate Management Education

Sara L. Rynes
University of Iowa

Jean M. Bartunek
Boston College

We thank Erich Dierdorff, Sarah Gardial, Nancy Hauserman, and Jeff Ringuest for comments on earlier drafts of this chapter.

Key Topics Covered in This Chapter

- Why curricular choices are important
- Content of the typical graduate management core curriculum
- Imbalance between core curricula and needs of employers and other constituents
- Role of extra- or co-curricular activities in graduate management programs
- Challenges and opportunities in curricular design

It is hard to think of any aspect of management education that is more important than the curriculum. Critics point to the prototypical MBA curriculum as a central reason that graduates display lax ethics; weak interpersonal, teamwork, and leadership skills; limited awareness of global issues; rampant materialism; and little concern for others (Ferraro, Pfeffer, & Sutton, 2005; Ghoshal, 2005; Leavitt, 1989; Mintzberg, 2004; Pfeffer & Fong, 2002). At the same time, curricular offerings are major drivers of student satisfaction; curriculum relevance is the main predictor of full-time MBA students' satisfaction when they graduate; and comprehensiveness is the main predictor of part-time students' satisfaction (GMAC, 2011). Curricular choices are also important to the future of business schools themselves. Navarro (2008, p. 121) argues that in an environment of sharply increasing competition among business schools and other purveyors of management education, curricular innovation may be the only way for schools without "powerful brand names and top-ten rankings" to survive.

The editors of this volume initially challenged us to answer this question: How can schools ensure that their curriculum program (content, structure, and activities) aligns with the needs and demands of managers and organizations? However, given the long-standing criticisms of MBA education (for example, Leavitt, 1989; L. W. Porter & McKibbin, 1988), we have broadened the range of stakeholders to include students and the broader society.

Throughout our investigation, we consider a relatively narrow scope of the term *curriculum*, focusing mainly on required or core coursework within graduate management education. Although a broad view would also include overall sequencing of courses, program duration, ratio of required-to-elective courses, overall purpose, and pedagogy, these issues will not receive much attention due to space limitations and the desire to avoid overlap with other chapters. In addition, we focus more heavily on full-time, on-campus MBA programs because far more research has been done on these programs than on part-time, online, executive, or specialized master's programs; we discuss these programs only as appropriate.

Our chapter is organized as follows. First, we describe the courses most frequently contained in the core (that is, required) curriculum. Next, we evaluate how closely the typical core curriculum maps onto the principal competencies required by managerial jobs, particularly on five competency areas. Within each area, we first document the current state, including deficiencies or excesses, and then describe recent trends and some exemplary approaches to addressing deficiencies. We then briefly discuss the role of extra- or co-curricular activities in enhancing graduate management education. Finally, we explore other challenges and opportunities in MBA programs, speculate about the future, and conclude with four key takeaways.

What Do MBA Programs Teach Now?

Like most previous examinations of management curricula, this one begins by focusing on required, or core, coursework. The curricular core is crucial for several reasons:

- The required curriculum sends a strong signal, particularly to students, about what a school believes to be essential knowledge for graduates to master (Rubin & Dierdorff, 2011).
- The structure of a program's core curriculum at least partially reflects its strategy regarding other programs (Navarro, 2008; Segev, Raveh, & Farjoun, 1999).
- When evaluated across multiple programs, the generalized core curriculum suggests the extent to which a field's required body of knowledge reflects a profession (Khurana, 2007; Trank & Rynes, 2003).

In the earliest study reviewed here, Segev and colleagues (1999) examined the 1993 core curricula of the top twenty-five ranked full-time MBA programs. They found that all but one or two required courses in finance, financial accounting, marketing, microeconomics, operations, and organizational behavior (OB) or management.

A second study by Navarro (2008) drew on information from school websites of the top fifty MBA programs in the United States. He reported that the typical MBA program consists primarily of functional and analytical offerings, with the following courses offered in 88 percent to 100 percent of top programs: corporate finance, marketing, financial accounting, operations, managerial economics, and quantitative analysis. However, Navarro found that soft-skill courses (OB, general management, leadership, human resource management) and courses reflecting ethics, social responsibility, and globalization were less prominent.

The most recent study (MBA Roundtable [MBAR], 2012) obtained data from 168 graduate management programs that had revised their core curricula between 2009 and 2011. Table 5.1 shows the percent of those programs that required various courses or content areas in the MBA core.[1] As the table indicates, more than 80 percent of both U.S. and non–U.S. programs required these seven courses: marketing, finance, strategy, management or OB, financial accounting, operations, and managerial accounting (MBAR, 2012).

The final column of Table 5.1 displays findings from Rubin and Dierdorff's (2009) study of 373 AACSB-accredited MBA programs. Because Rubin and Dierdorff obtained their data from program websites rather than program directors' self-reports, they found lower percentages of course coverage than in the MBAR survey. This was particularly true for topics that were most frequently integrated into other courses rather than taught as standalone courses in the MBAR study (for example, ethics, social responsibility, and entrepreneurship). However, the differentials may also reflect the fact that the MBAR data were collected three to four years later than Rubin and Dierdorff's. Thus, Rubin and Dierdorff's (2009) figures and MBAR's (2012) figures prob-

Table 5.1 Courses Required in MBA Core in U.S. and Non–U.S. Programs

Course	MBA Roundtable (2012)[a] All Respondents (N = 168)	MBA Roundtable U.S.- Based (N = 125)	MBA Roundtable Outside U.S. (N = 43)	Rubin & Dierdorff (2009) (N = 373)
Marketing	99%	99%	100%	87%
Finance	96%	98%	93%	90%
Strategy	94%	95%	91%	67%
Management/ Organizational behavior	93%	92%	98%	68%
Financial accounting	88%	90%	81%	96%[b]
Operations	84%	84%	84%	62%
Managerial accounting	83%	84%	81%	96%[b]
Quantitative methods/ Statistics	83%	87%	72%	56%[d]
Microeconomics	76%	78%	72%	68%[c]
Leadership	71%	69%	79%	30%
Macro Economics	69%	66%	77%	68%[c]
Ethics	68%	70%	60%	30%
International business	61%	63%	53%	25%
Information technology	55%	58%	44%	64%

(Continued)

Table 5.1 (Continued)

Course	MBA Roundtable (2012)[a] All Respondents (N = 168)	MBA Roundtable U.S.- Based (N = 125)	MBA Roundtable Outside U.S. (N = 43)	Rubin & Dierdorff (2009) (N = 373)
Business law	36%	42%	16%	40%
Corporate social responsibility	35%	26%	63%	30% [d]
Entrepreneurship	32%	22%	58%	4%
Project management	19%	18%	23%	2%
Geoeconomics/Geostrategy	13%	10%	19%	n/a

Note: Programs represented in the first three columns were determined via self-selection of program administrators from the broader MBA Roundtable membership. Programs represented in the last column reflect 373 AACSB-accredited institutions in 2007–2008. In addition, data for the first three columns come from self-reports of program administrators, while data in the last column come from program websites. These different methodologies introduce different sources of bias into reported estimates, particularly in areas (such as leadership, ethics, social desirability) where there is a strong element of social desirability.

[a] Respondents were restricted to those who reported some change in core curricula over the past three years. The specific question asked was "Which of the following subject areas are included in the core or required content for this MBA program?"

[b] Financial and/or managerial accounting; distinction not made.

[c] Macro- and/or microeconomics; distinction not made.

[d] Ethics and/or corporate social responsibility; almost always taught together; and about 60 percent were also paired with business law or policy (i.e., there were very few stand-alone courses for either topic).

Sources: MBA Roundtable *Curriculum Innovation Survey*, 2012. Adapted with permission of MBA Roundtable; Rubin, R. S., & Dierdorff, E. C., 2009; unpublished table acquired from the authors. Adapted with permission of authors.

ably serve as lower and upper bounds, respectively, of content coverage in MBA core curricula.

A final study by Datar, Garvin, and Cullen (2010) focused on eleven of the most elite (all private) business schools, such as Harvard, Stanford, Wharton, Yale, and INSEAD. Their results were highly similar to those from the preceding studies, with the primary core consisting mostly of eight functional and analytical courses: financial accounting, finance with a capital markets emphasis, microeconomics, marketing, operations, strategy, OB/leadership, and decision sciences or statistics.

In summary, the five studies suggest that there is a high degree of consistency into the primary core, which consists mostly of functional and analytic courses.

This conclusion leads us to a discussion of the following question: How well does the core MBA curriculum match the requirements of managerial jobs, recruiters' statements about what they are seeking in applicants, recent graduates' self-assessments of how well their programs prepared them for employment, and the views of deans, program directors, and other faculty members? Generally speaking, our analysis shows that there is a strong emphasis (perhaps overemphasis) on functional and quantitative/analytical courses, and an underemphasis on the other four areas: leadership and interpersonal skills; decision making and problem solving; ethics and social responsibility; and globalization.

How Well Do Core Requirements Match Stakeholder Needs?

The most formal comparison of MBA core curricula to managerial job requirements was conducted in the previously mentioned study by Rubin and Dierdorff (2009). To succinctly characterize the core curricula of these programs, the authors sorted nearly 3,600 core courses into six empirically derived behavioral competencies required by management jobs. These competencies (in order of importance as assessed by 8,633 managerial job incumbents) were

1. Managing decision-making processes
2. Managing human capital
3. Managing strategy and innovation
4. Managing the task environment
5. Managing administration and control, and
6. Managing logistics and technology

Using information from program websites, two raters matched each of 3,594 core courses into one of these six competencies. Table 5.2 shows the extent of imbalance between the importance of each competency to managerial job performance and the average number of core courses devoted to it across the 373 programs. As the table shows, the number of courses devoted to

Table 5.2 Number of Course Offerings by Managerial Competency

Competency Category	0 Courses	1 Course	2 or More Courses	3 or More Courses
Managing decision-making processes	28.7%	52.3%	19.0%	3.5%
Managing human capital	6.4%	64.9%	28.7%	2.4%
Managing strategy and innovation	31.4%	55.5%	13.1%	1.9%
Managing the task environment	4.0%	26.3%	69.7%	27.1%
Managing administration and control	2.1%	11.0%	86.9%	48.0%
Managing logistics and technology	13.9%	41.3%	44.8%	6.2%

N = 373 schools.

Source: Data from Rubin, R. S. & Dierdorff, E. C., 2009, p. 215.

decision-making processes and to human capital management are both less than their importance in managerial jobs would seem to merit. But, the opposite is true for courses relating to administration/control and management of the task environment (Rubin & Dierdorff, 2009, p. 215). Other studies have also concluded that there is an imbalance between core management curricula and the demands of various constituents, as described following.

Functional, Quantitative, and Analytical Knowledge and Skills

Current State. The most consistent finding from the five studies reviewed is that the overwhelming majority of the required management core consists of functional, quantitative, and analytical courses. Rubin and Dierdorff's (2009) analysis showed that the managerial competency most attended to in MBA programs is *managing administration and control,* exemplified by such courses as managerial accounting, financial analysis, corporate finance, cost analysis, and business law. Nearly 87 percent of the 373 programs the researchers analyzed required at least two of these courses, and 48 percent required three or more.

The second most represented managerial competency is *managing the task environment,* exemplified by such courses as macroeconomic policy, managerial economics, globalization, international economics, and marketing. Nearly 70 percent of programs required two such courses, while 27 percent required three or more.

For comparison purposes, fewer than 30 percent of programs required two or more courses in *managing human capital competency,* while a miniscule 2.4 percent required three or more.

Trends and Innovations. Given that functional, quantitative, and analytical courses dominate most management core curricula, a central question is whether the number of such courses should be reduced. Many observers of MBA programs have argued that they should. One concern is that rather than covering the broad practice of management, MBA programs have moved toward being specialized training grounds for specific business functions (Mintzberg, 2004; Rubin & Dierdorff, 2009). A second concern is that the heavy focus on functional coursework provides little true professional education, which would also focus on skills, values, and a code of ethics (for example, Khurana, 2007; Trank & Rynes, 2003).

The most serious concern, however, is that the dominance of functional and analytical coursework—particularly in finance and economics—may be creating a student worldview that makes short-sighted, selfish, and even unethical behavior more likely among MBA graduates (for example, Bebchuk & Fried, 2004; Ferraro, Pfeffer, & Sutton, 2005; Ghoshal, 2005; Giacalone & Thompson, 2005; Wang, Malhotra, & Murnighan, 2011).

On the basis of these concerns, several influential critics have argued for a reduction in the number of finance and economics courses in management programs. Others, however, have seen this as an unrealistic option and have focused instead on adding more balance or counterweight to them. This is the probably the more pragmatic option, for a variety of reasons:

○ The most highly desired and best-paying jobs for MBA graduates are in finance (Carruthers & Kim, 2011; Ho, 2009). Placing students in high-paying positions generates multiple spinoff benefits for business schools, including generous donations from the finance industry, higher media rankings, and greater ease of recruiting future students.

○ The vast majority of MBA students seek their initial postgraduation jobs in functional areas rather than in management. Even after the financial crash of 2008, 31 percent of graduating full-time MBA students still sought jobs in finance or accounting, as compared with 25 percent in marketing/sales, 21 percent in consulting, and 10 percent in management (GMAC, 2010). Although many of these functionally oriented graduates will eventually assume management positions, they are likely to be selected for their first jobs primarily on the basis of technical rather than managerial knowledge and skills (GMAC, 2012; Rynes, Trank, Lawson, & Ilies, 2003).

○ Finally, jobs in virtually all functional areas continue to become ever more technically sophisticated, so much so that certain areas of investment banking are now often filled by engineering, math, and physics graduates rather than business students (Carruthers & Kim, 2011). Thus, cutting back on functional and technical coursework is likely to be an unattractive option for many business schools.

However, there *is* a rather widespread call for other types of courses and co-curricular activities that would make graduate management programs more holistic and balanced. We turn now to a discussion of several areas where there is widespread agreement about the need for more coursework, different types of coursework, or both. In each area, we first summarize the nature of the deficiencies and then describe innovations to address them.

Leadership, Human Capital Management, and Interpersonal Skills

Current State. Rubin & Dierdorff's (2011) literature review clearly demonstrates that recruiters, alumni, current managers, and business school deans and faculty *all* believe that people management skills are crucial elements of managerial jobs. For example, interpersonal skills were ranked first of fifteen knowledge, skills, and abilities (KSAs) in terms of value to alumni in their current jobs (GMAC, 2009). In addition, leadership was the most frequently mentioned attribute sought by recruiters in the GMAC *Corporate Recruiters Survey* (2012). Managing human resources was ranked as the second most important managerial competency by more than 8,600 managers in Rubin & Dierdorff (2009). The Rubin and Dierdorff (2011) follow-up study showed that business school deans, administrators, and faculty also place a high value on these competencies.

Despite this widespread agreement about the importance of human capital competencies, studies of management curricula consistently show that they are underemphasized in most programs. In the GMAC *Global Management Education Graduate Survey* (2011), for example, nearly 5,000 graduating students reported learning less about how to manage people than about how to manage strategy and innovation, decision-making processes, or the task environment. Similarly, Rubin and Dierdorff (2009) found that while the vast majority of programs require at least two courses directed toward administration and control (87 percent) and managing the task environment (70 percent), only 29 percent require more than one course related to managing human capital. Unfortunately, the practical implication of having only a single required course about human capital is that skill development is usually given short shrift relative to mastering knowledge (Brown, Charlier, Rynes, & Hosmanek, 2012). This is an important deficiency in light of GMAC's (2009) survey showing that managers perceive interpersonal *skills* as considerably more important for on-the-job success than interpersonal or behavioral *knowledge*.

Trends and Innovations. On the bright side, there is evidence that having two or more human capital courses appears to be a best practice, at least in the common parlance of being what the best schools do. For example, Brown and colleagues (2012) found that 56 percent of programs that were ranked in at least one major media ranking required two such courses, while only 24 percent of unranked programs did. Similarly, Datar and colleagues (2010) found that eight of the eleven very elite MBA programs they studied required more than one human capital-related course.

Moreover, recent data suggest that attempts to respond to deficiencies in human capital competencies are fairly widespread. The MBAR (2009) report on curriculum innovation revealed that an increase in core content related to leadership was the single most frequent change (49 percent of responding programs) between 2005 and 2009. A 2011 follow-up study indicated that an additional 30 percent of programs had increased leadership coverage in the core and another 31 percent in elective offerings (MBAR, 2012). Additionally, MBAR's *2011 Leadership Assessment Survey* found that half of respondents' programs had added funding for leadership development ($1,832 per student on average; $3,326 in the most expensive programs; MBAR, 2011).

What kinds of specific changes are being made in programs that have increased their emphasis on leadership? In general, they are providing more opportunities for students to practice leadership (that is, to build skills through doing), to enable personal growth and self-discovery by reflecting on values and goals, or both. An excellent example of the first approach appears in Benjamin and O'Reilly's (2011) description of creating a leadership mind-set at Stanford by focusing on the types of early career transitions recent graduates most often face and giving students practice in preparing for them. Another impressive example comes from Texas Tech, where entering MBA students are evaluated for leadership skills using an assessment center; they then take a required experiential leadership course followed by a second assessment. A five-year study of how effectively the course improved leadership skills showed very positive results (Hoover, Giambatista, Sorenson, & Bommer, 2010). Georgia State and DePaul also evaluate students' leadership skills via assessment centers. Still other schools provide leadership practice through capstone leadership courses. For example, the University of Virginia's Darden School of Business requires an intensive capstone course involving service learning that assists nonprofits not only with strategy and planning but also with financial support generated through entrepreneurial student ventures (James, 2011).

In the category of personal growth and self-discovery, INSEAD makes an intensive effort to help students accelerate their personal development during its ten-month program. It provides up to twenty hours of psychotherapy to help students integrate their formal learning with personal learning about their values, preferences, and decision styles (Petriglieri, Wood, & Petriglieri, 2011). Other schools use personal development methods modeled on programs developed at the Center for Creative Leadership (CCL; Datar & others, 2010, pp. 217–238). Consistent with CCL approaches, MBAR's 2011 *Leadership Assessment Survey* found that 40 percent of responding programs offer professional coaching programs (73 percent for executive programs), 29 percent require individualized development plans (45 percent for executive programs), and 24 percent use peer coaching (32 percent for full-time programs; MBAR, 2011).[2] However, use of psychological assessment or 360-degree feedback instruments is relatively rare (less than 30 percent), except at elite schools and in executive MBA programs. Among those that use assessments, by far the most commonly used instrument is the Myers-Briggs Type Indicator (MBTI; 83 percent), despite academic concerns about its lack of demonstrated content and predictive ability (Druckman & Bjork, 1991).

Finally, Stanford has done several things that other schools could emulate to enhance the emphasis on leadership and people management skills. Stanford has not only added multiple courses dealing explicitly with leadership, it has also changed the sequencing of its curriculum. The first quarter is loaded with leadership and management courses (for example, ethics in management, leadership labs, managerial skills, managing groups and teams, organizational behavior, strategic leadership) and only one functional course (financial accounting). In addition, the motto on Stanford's admissions webpage (and the introductory message from its dean) is "Principled Leadership for a Life of

Meaning and Impact." Given the convincing research on applicant–organization fit (for example, Cable & Judge, 1996), it is likely that emphasizing a higher purpose and sequencing courses to emphasize leadership rather than finance would have an impact not only on student attitudes and learning but also on the type of individuals who apply to management programs in the first place (Schneider, 1987).

Decision Making and Problem Solving

Current State. Employers have lodged a variety of complaints about MBA graduates' decision-making and problem-solving skills (Datar & others, 2010; Ghoshal, 2005; Khurana, 2007). One concern is that graduates are not creative or innovative enough in their thinking. Employers worry that students have been taught to analyze via conventional, standardized methodologies that do not yield competitive advantage or help organizations prepare for the future. A second concern is that graduates do not have enough critical thinking and argumentation skills. A third is that students are trained to analyze highly structured problems (that is, via cases) with little missing or ambiguous information, which leaves them unprepared to solve or even identify unstructured problems.

An additional set of complaints has been lodged by a subset of faculty who are critical of the dominant methods in which business schools teach decision making. These critics argue that students must be taught more about the limitations of abstract economic and financial models and assumptions as well as about the need to understand the sometimes positive roles of regulation, responsibility to constituents other than shareholders, and more rigorous risk management (Datar & others, 2010; Ferraro & others, 2005; Ghoshal, 2005; Rubin & Dierdorff, 2011). A recent internal GMAC survey of 740 management faculty members revealed that they perceive a clear need to improve students' abilities to make sound decisions, discern patterns, and combine verbal and quantitative reasoning to solve problems. This feedback was sufficiently strong to cause GMAC to add a new integrated reasoning section to the GMAT exam in 2012. (See http://www.mba.com/the-gmat/interactive-map-test/find -out-whats-changing.aspx; GMAC, 2013).

Beyond the criticisms leveled here, the previously mentioned study by Rubin and Dierdorff (2009) found that "managing decision-making processes" showed the largest discrepancy between the proportion of required courses that cover the subject and its importance as evaluated by practicing managers. Specifically, even though practicing managers indicated that managing decision processes was the single most important managerial competency, MBA programs tended to offer the second lowest percentage of related core courses (9.6 percent). Rubin and Dierdorff's study also showed a large negative discrepancy between the proportion of core coursework directed toward strategy and innovation (8.9 percent) relative to the importance of these skills as managerial competencies (see Table 3 and Figure 1 in Rubin & Dierdorff, 2009, pp. 214–15).

In contrast to these criticisms and concerns, graduating students appear to have a very different notion of their decision-making and strategy and innovation skills. Specifically, recent graduates rated their "improvement in knowledge, skills, and abilities" in both decision making and strategy and innovation as 4.3 on a 5-point scale. Out of fifteen categories, they rated this second only to their increase in knowledge of general business functions (see Figure 16 in GMAC, 2010, p. 21). In other words, graduating students feel that the top three areas in which they have learned the most are general business functions, decision making, and managing strategy and innovation.

Putting these four sources of information together, we have a paradox: Employers, faculty surveys, and analyses of curricula all suggest that decision-making processes and strategy/innovation are undertaught in MBA programs. But graduating students believe these are among their top three areas of learning! How do we explain this discrepancy?

Although our explanation is necessarily tentative, we believe that the discrepancy is caused by different mental models of what decision making and strategy/innovation mean to MBA students versus to employers and critics of management curricula. Specifically, we speculate that because financial models and calculation of return on investment are the primary bases for making decisions in business schools, students believe they are well equipped to make complex decisions. However, those who hire them and faculty who evaluate their decision-making capabilities in courses other than finance believe otherwise. Specifically, employers believe that MBAs do not think outside the box in ways that create competitive advantage (Datar & others, 2010), and faculty members worry that students are learning how to make decisions based almost exclusively on short-term financial analyses in the service of shareholders alone. Still others worry that graduates do not know how to solve unstructured problems, given the emphasis on formal models and case discussions in which any necessary structuring has already taken place (Liang & Wang, 2004; Swiercz & Ross, 2003).

Trends and Innovations. Fortunately, many programs have been working to remedy perceived deficiencies in decision making and problem solving. One of the most popular attempts to increase creative thinking and innovation is based on *"human-centered design,"* or *design thinking*. Pedagogically, design thinking courses focus on multifunctional teams, rapid prototyping, fast failure, and learning by doing as opposed to learning via theory and abstract thinking. Although courses on design thinking originated in engineering departments, they are now moving into both full-time and executive programs at such schools as the University of Virginia's Darden, the University of Toronto's Rotman, Carnegie Mellon's Tepper, Johns Hopkins's Carey, and

ESADE. Good examples of design thinking can be seen on an *ABC Nightline* segment showing how the design firm IDEO used design thinking to produce a revolutionary new shopping cart. (See http://www.youtube.com/watch?v=M66ZU2PCIcM; *ABC Nightline*). Several TED Talks videos illustrate other human-centered IDEO projects (for example, http://www.ted .com/talks/david_kelley_on_human_centered_design.html; TED Talks, 2007).[3]

A second area of decision-making innovation focuses on *critical thinking*. A fairly wide variety of courses fall under the rubric of critical thinking. These include Stanford's Critical Ana-lytical Thinking course (Datar & others, 2010); Rotman's two integrative thinking courses (http://www.iedp.com/University_Toronto_Rotman/Integrative-Thinking); MIT's Systems Think-ing program (http://sdm.mit.edu/education/systems-thinking .html); Harvard's Leadership and Corporate Accountability course (Datar & others, 2010); and many courses that also fall under the heading of ethics and corporate social responsibility (CSR; see next section).

A third set of innovations focuses on learning to *solve unstruc-tured problems* via involvement in complex, broadly scoped con-sulting projects. One of the best-known projects of this sort is the Multidisciplinary Action Project (MAP) at the University of Michigan's Ross School of Business (Datar & others, 2010; http://www.bus.umich.edu/MAP/Dev/WhatisMAP.htm). The MAP takes place for seven weeks at the end of the first year and is the students' sole activity for that period of time. Ross seeks "complex projects in ambiguous contexts that require stu-dents to identify problems, navigate organizational politics, and formulate multidisciplinary solutions" (Datar & others, 2010, p. 151). Recent projects have involved designing market entry strategies in new countries, assessing the feasibility of renewable energy solutions, and determining appropriate business strategies in the face of pending legislation. The Tippie College of Business in Iowa provides similar cross-functional projects through its

Business Solutions Center, but on a different time schedule: Teams of first-year students conduct seventeen-week projects that require ten hours of student time per week.

Ethics and Corporate Social Responsibility

Current State. With increasing frequency, we have seen corporate and market collapses tied at least in part to ethical and legal breaches by graduates of prominent MBA programs (for example, Lewis, 1989; McLean & Elkind, 2003; Johnson & Kwak, 2010). As a result, concerns have emerged about the role of business schools in fostering lax ethics and limited concern for social welfare (Aspen Institute, 2008; Schneider, 2002; Swanson, 2004). Although some deans and faculty have argued that management curricula bear little responsibility for corporate scandals and egregious legal and ethical violations, others believe that the normative dominance of neoliberal economics and investor capitalism in most business schools is directly implicated in these outcomes (Ferraro & others, 2005; Ghoshal, 2005; Giacalone & Thompson, 2005; Ho, 2009; Khurana, 2007).

Surveys conducted by the Aspen Institute in both 2002 and 2007 showed that the longer MBA students stay in business school, the more likely they are to lose their idealism and the less confident they feel that their business education will help them confront values conflicts on the job (Aspen Institute, 2008; Schneider, 2002). For example, in Aspen's 2007 survey, 55 percent of MBAs who had just started their programs strongly agreed that they had "opportunities to practice ethical/responsible decision making as part of their MBA"; however, this dropped to 41 percent for those about to graduate (Aspen Institute, 2008). Similarly, the majority of 2007 students felt that employers hiring at their schools strongly valued functional area (68 percent) and industry experience (53 percent); but only 8 percent believed they placed a high value on awareness of social issues and 5 percent on experience in government, nonprofit, or volunteer work.

Why might this erosion of student confidence regarding ethics and values be taking place? To answer this question, it helps to examine the extent to which MBA curricula currently require courses on such topics. By gathering and combining results across four studies, we see that somewhere between 25 percent and 40 percent of programs appear to require core courses to include ethics, corporate social responsibility, or both, with higher percentages obtained in studies using more elite samples (Dierdorff & Rubin, 2009; Evans & Marcal, 2005; Evans, Trevino, & Weaver, 2006; Navarro, 2008). Higher figures were reported in MBAR's *2012 Curricular Innovation Study* (65 percent for ethics and 35 percent for CSR); but the self-selection of study participants and self-reporting of program data are likely to inflate results compared to studies that use more complete sampling and objective, rather than self-reported, data (MBAR, 2012).

Several studies have also investigated factors associated with a greater likelihood of requiring ethics instruction. Evans and Marcal (2003) and Evans and others (2006) both found that the prevalence of ethics courses was higher in religiously affiliated schools rather than public schools. A similar religious-versus-public school result was reported at the undergraduate level by Rutherford, Parks, Cavazos, and White (2012), who also found that required ethics courses were more likely to be found in schools with female deans, deans with management backgrounds, and schools with lower financial endowments. These authors concluded that "the primary drivers appear to be the values of the school and the college's leadership. . . . If schools genuinely care about business ethics, they will find the resources needed to provide the course to their students" (Rutherford & others, 2012, p. 183).

Many faculty members and researchers have made forceful arguments in favor of additional coursework in ethics and CSR (for example, Rasche, Gilbert, & Schedel, in press; Rutherford

& others, 2012; Swanson, 2004; Swanson & Fisher, 2011). However, there are differences of opinion about the best way to do this. One point of contention is whether additional courses should be required of all students as part of the core or offered as electives. A second issue is whether this type of material should be taught in a stand-alone course or integrated into one or more functional courses (for example, a session or two on ethical issues in marketing, ethical issues in finance, and so on). Many (probably most) proponents of stronger ethics instruction would like to see both approaches—a required stand-alone course for all students, supplemented by integrating the topic into most or all functional courses. However, this rarely happens at present.

After considering the various arguments, our view is that at least with respect to ethics (leaving aside corporate social responsibility for the moment), a stand-alone course should be required of all students. Failure to include ethics in the required core transmits a message to students that this is not really a central business issue (for example, Swanson, 2004; Rubin & Dierdorff, 2009). Given the cataclysmic effects that unethical behaviors have had on the world economy and people's livelihoods, the idea that ethics is not central to business is simply untenable (Adler, 2002; Khurana, 2007; Rutherford & others, 2012). Further, failing to require an ethics course means that only students who are already convinced of its value are likely to seek an ethics elective (Dean & Jolly, 2012), which may then have the unintended negative effect of labeling such students as "soft."

Another very important consideration is that ethics is a challenging subject to teach. Discussions of ethical dilemmas often surface deeply felt differences in individuals' beliefs and values. As such, instructors need considerable classroom facilitation skills to create a safe environment for all students—not just the most aggressive ones—to explore and express their views. In addition, teaching ethics involves far more than posing a challenging situation and having students express their opinions. Rather, ethics is "part of a 2,000-year-old moral tradition of

Western philosophy" (Swanson, 2004, p. 49) whose principles cannot be absorbed in quick pre-lecture preparation as part of a functional course in some other area (such as marketing). Furthermore, ethics is not simply a body of knowledge but also a set of reasoning skills that students must attain through practice in specific, rather than abstract, contexts (Badaracco, 1997).

Indeed, one of the persistent challenges of teaching ethics is helping students to realize when they are being confronted with an ethical dilemma. This is much more complex than most people believe. Although the common notion of organizational wrongdoing is that it is committed by a few bad apples, such as Enron's Jeffrey Skilling or Kidder Peabody's Joseph Jett, in reality much organizational wrongdoing results from highly normalized activities that have become rationalized, institutionalized, and taken for granted by most members of an organization (Anand, Ashforth, & Joshi, 2005; Grind, 2012; Ho, 2009; Palmer, 2012). In addition, there are many ethical issues that do not involve wrongdoing at all, but rather consist of complex multistakeholder dilemmas in which it is impossible to meet everyone's legitimate interests (Badaracco, 1997).

Given these daunting complexities, it should not be surprising that many faculty members express a fear of teaching ethics (Dean & Beggs, 2006) or that many deans believe there is a shortage of people qualified to teach it (Evans & Weiss, 2008). As such, attempts to integrate ethics into one or more functional courses (the position that AACSB has favored since its 1991 shift to a mission-based approach) runs the risk that instructors will either avoid it altogether or botch the job (Rasche & others, in press; Rutherford & others, 2012; Swanson, 2004). In addition, studies show that when ethics instruction is infused rather than taught in stand-alone courses, it is less likely to be covered in finance and accounting (the functional areas associated with the most consequential ethical meltdowns) than in areas such as management and marketing (Hansen, Moosmayer, Bode, & Schrader, 2007; Nicholson & DeMoss, 2009; Rasche & others, in press).

Finally, CSR is frequently addressed via co-curricular activities such as service learning. For example, in the Carroll School of Management at Boston College, full-time MBA students are required to provide several hours of service to the community by, for example, mentoring or tutoring in underserved communities or providing pro bono professional services to local nonprofit organizations.

Ethics, however, is rarely addressed except via voluntary promulgation of an ethics oath or occasional ethics case competitions. Following the initiative of a number of Harvard Business School students, for example, graduates of several MBA programs have begun taking the MBA oath (Anderson & Escher, 2010). This is a voluntary pledge for graduating and current MBAs to "create value responsibly and ethically." (See http://mbaoath.org/.)

Trends and Innovations. One of the most important developments in this area has been the emergence and spread of the "Giving Voice to Values" (GVV) curriculum. This approach to teaching values was developed with financial support from the Aspen Institute, the Yale School of Management, and Babson College (Gentile, 2010). The framework can be taught either in stand-alone ethics classes or as part of functional area courses. Similar to Stanford's approach to leadership development described earlier (Benjamin & O'Reilly, 2011), the GVV curriculum is tailored to the types of ethical dilemmas that are most likely to confront employees in the early phases of their careers; it focuses on practice and self-reflection as well as knowing. GVV has been piloted in more than 140 educational settings on six continents. (See http://www.givingvoicetovalues.com.)

A very different approach focuses on the fact that "ethical failures don't occur at random. . . . They result from numerous biases that exacerbate distractions from ethical consequences" (Fisman & Galinsky, 2012, p. 2). For example, experiments have shown that the mathematical tools generally taught to students in business schools cause them to unthinkingly make decisions based solely on maximizing profits. However, when data and analytic tools are presented in other ways, students take a broader range of factors into consideration. Similarly, research has shown that signing a pledge of honesty *before* filling out a legal form leads to less misreported data than signing at the end (as is done with tax filings, for example). This has led some schools (such as Harvard and Northwestern) to teach principles of process design that are less likely to lead to unthinking ethical lapses (see Fisman & Galinsky, 2012; for a similar approach applied to a wider range of issues, see Thaler & Sunstein, 2009).

Globalization

Current State. Rubin and Dierdorff (2009) found that only 25 percent of programs required a core course in international business (IB) in 2007–2008. In contrast, 63 percent of U.S.-based respondents to the 2012 MBAR's *Curricula Innovation Study* indicated that international business was a required content area (either as a core course or infused into functional areas), with higher percentages in executive (78 percent) than in full-time MBA programs (54 percent). Moreover, 81 percent of recent graduating students indicated that they had received instruction in international business (IB); see Table 5, GMAC, 2011, p. 18), although it should be noted that there were ten content areas ranked above IB in terms of coverage. Once again, differences across studies are probably attributable to both timing and method, with Rubin and Dierdorff's (2009) study coming earlier than the others and its methodology being more conservative. There is little doubt, however, that business schools are more interested in expanding coverage of global issues than they used to be (MBAR, 2012). AACSB is also placing more emphasis on globalization in its certification standards (AACSB, 2012).

It is also clear that U.S. schools lag behind European ones in globalism. For example, the top five U.S. schools (based on the

2012 *Financial Times* ranking) have only 41 percent international faculty, while the top five European schools average 75 percent. Regarding international students, the respective percentages are 41 percent and 91 percent (*Financial Times*, 2012). One reason that U.S. schools tend to lag in globalization is that when recruiting students U.S. recruiters do not yet place a very high priority on international experience, cross-cultural sensitivity, or foreign language skills. For example, the GMAC 2012 *Corporate Recruiters' Survey* findings list the top five qualifications recruiters look for in hiring managerial and professional talent. This survey found that international experience was a top-five qualification for 45 percent of European and 32 percent of Asian-Pacific recruiters, but only 7 percent of U.S. recruiters. Foreign language capabilities were important to 48 percent of European and 38 percent of Asian-Pacific recruiters, but only 10 percent of U.S. recruiters (see Figure 15, GMAC, 2012, p. 23). The greater interest that European and Asian recruiters and business schools show in global issues means that European schools are likely to be better bets than U.S.-based schools for students who want to take jobs in either Europe or Asia. For example, in 2006, 52 percent of INSEAD graduates took jobs in Western Europe, and 20 percent took jobs in Asia (Datar & others, 2010).

Trends and Innovations. However, a number of U.S.-based schools have pursued cross-national alliances to supplement their global curricula, particularly at the executive education level. In fact, four of the top-ten ranked executive MBA programs in the *Financial Times* 2011 rankings were joint international programs, such as the number one collaboration between Kellogg and Hong Kong University of Science and Technology (http://www.petersons.com/graduate-schools/mba-program-global-perspectives.aspx; *Financial Times*, 2011). These collaborations allow schools to share faculty, use distance education, and arrange field trips to other locations as part of their standard executive education. A less involved (and hence more common) method of incorporating globalism into the curriculum is to provide short trips to other countries, visiting international businesses and business schools in the process.

Extracurricular or Co-curricular Enhancements

Given employers' growing expectations of MBA graduates and the pressures from students to restrict both costs and time spent away from employment, many programs use co-curricular activities to supplement or fill gaps in curricula. There is clear evidence that some co-curricular activities are important enhancements to students' employability at graduation. A recent survey (see Figure 14, GMAC, 2011, p. 17) showed a variety of relationships between graduating students' ($n \sim 5,000$) receiving job offers and their participation in various extracurricular activities. For example, students who participated in case competitions were 32 percent more likely to have received an offer at the time of the survey than those who did not. Comparable figures for other activities include participation in leadership programs (30 percent); mentor programs (28 percent); internships (26 percent); student government (20 percent); community service organizations (18 percent); and volunteer activities (17 percent). Indeed, the sometimes close linkage between co-curricular activities and employment has caused some deans to complain of "a steady erosion of student interest in, and commitment to, academics per se" (Datar & others, 2010, p. 81). At one school that has tracked the number of hours spent in (or preparing for) classes, the number of hours fell from forty-five hours in 1975 to thirty hours in 2003–2004.

A variety of types of co-curricular activities—business plan and case competitions, career development, and consulting projects—are available (and sometimes required) at a majority of MBA programs worldwide, particularly in full-time programs (see Table 5.3; also MBAR, 2012). Table 5.3 suggests that one co-curricular activity—career development—is required in

Table 5.3 Co-curricular Offerings in MBA Programs

Type of Activity		Part-Time MBA (N = 94)	Full-Time MBA (N = 97)	Executive MBA (N = 63)	U.S. Based (N = 207)	Outside U.S. (N = 47)
Business plan competition	Required	7%	4%	8%	4%	17%
	Optional	64%	87%	49%	71%	62%
Career development	Required	16%	64%	13%	30%	47%
	Optional	78%	35%	79%	66%	45%
Case competitions	Required	5%	13%	8%	8%	15%
	Optional	62%	78%	48%	63%	70%
Community outreach	Required	6%	15%	8%	10%	13%
	Optional	68%	76%	51%	70%	53%
Consulting projects	Required	18%	29%	29%	21%	43%
	Optional	60%	67%	29%	58%	40%

Source: From MBA Roundtable *Curricular Innovation Survey,* 2012. Figures do not add to 100 percent because the categories "not offered" and "don't know" have been omitted for ease of interpretation.

approximately two-thirds of full-time MBA programs and nearly half of programs located outside the United States. Consulting projects are another co-curricular activity required by a sizable percentage of graduate management programs, particularly outside the United States (43 percent).

A perusal of the websites of a large number of MBA programs accredited by AACSB suggests that most programs include at least some co-curricular activities. In most instances, co-curricular activities are located entirely within particular universities and programs. However, some organizations (such as Net Impact and Toastmasters) have chapters in multiple universities. In addition, competitions for best case analyses and best business plans routinely take place across multiple universities. For example, the Global Social Venture Competition (GSVC) is an innovative collaboration among six business schools on three continents. The competition aims to foster a new generation of business leaders who value improved social outcomes as well as the profit potential of business.

A comparison of several highly ranked programs and AACSB-accredited but unranked programs suggests that the extent to which school websites explicitly described co-curricular activities as part of the student experience distinguishes ranked from unranked schools. Specifically, a scan of the websites of seventeen accredited and highly ranked MBA programs revealed that 100 percent of them described co-curricular activities, often in the dozens. In contrast, a scan of seventeen unranked but AACSB-accredited programs revealed that only 36 percent included any description of co-curricular activities, and in most cases the number of activities was relatively small. Thus, one difference between highly ranked and unranked MBA programs appears to be the availability of offerings that help supplement the curriculum in developing various types of knowledge, skills, and social connections. The number of co-curricular activities is also greater in full-time programs.

Challenges and Opportunities in Formulating Curricula

In this section, we discuss several issues that business schools face when attempting to devise the best possible curricula. In our discussion, we distinguish MBA programs (full-time, part-time, and executive) from specialized master's programs (for example, in finance, accounting, or design thinking). This is because we believe that *all* of the five competencies discussed in preceding sections should be adequately addressed in programs that grant the MBA degree. To do otherwise is to risk the MBA brand— both in individual programs and as a whole—by producing graduates who are not prepared to competently and ethically handle the many people- and values-oriented challenges they will confront on the job.

Specialized master's programs serve a different purpose. They are designed to produce not general managers but rather technical specialists capable of applying the most up-to-date methods and technologies. As Datar and others indicate (2010), some employers are already bypassing MBAs in favor of programs that focus more explicitly on mathematical and technical analyses, including programs outside of business schools entirely. These specialized master's degrees can meet a need within some markets, but they should not be confused with the MBA brand and its broader set of competencies.

Given the broader mission of MBA programs, one preeminent challenge for administrators is to determine how best to develop the full range of managerial competencies in ways that are appropriate to their own settings. Our earlier discussions of trends and innovations suggest a number of inventive ways to integrate leadership, interpersonal, decision-making, problem-solving, and ethical reasoning skills with more functional or analytical knowledge and skills. These ways include interdisciplinary consulting projects, capstone courses, summer internships, career development and planning modules, service learning projects, and a wide variety of co-curricular activities such as career clubs and affinity groups, case competitions, and international alliances or exchanges. Planners can develop grids that indicate which competencies—both knowledge and skill based—are covered by required coursework and then plan ways to meet any revealed gaps via electives, internships, capstones, or co-curriculars.

Such a planning approach can also help address the increasing time and cost constraints confronting business schools and affecting both students and employers. These constraints have been exacerbated by the growth of specialized master's programs, corporate universities, online MBAs, one-year MBA programs in Europe and Asia, and consulting firms focused on leadership development (Dierdorff & Rubin, 2009; DiMeglio, 2007; Gerdes, 2005; McGrath, 2007). In light of this increasing competition, becoming as efficient as possible in covering all important competencies could provide MBA programs with a significant competitive advantage and might allow schools to shorten two-year MBA programs to three semesters (or perhaps make them even shorter). Although most one-year MBA programs typically short-circuit leadership, ethics, and interpersonal skills, this need not be the case (as with INSEAD; see Petriglieri & others, 2011). Programs might also become more time and cost efficient by employing large-lecture online technologies for courses that are primarily knowledge based (such as economics, finance, and accounting), while reserving smaller and more resource-intensive pedagogies for courses intended to develop critical thinking abilities, analyses of ethical dilemmas, and interpersonal competencies.

Of course, the extent to which the preceding actions will translate into competitive advantage depends on the existence of high-quality information about the strengths and weaknesses of alternative programs. One of the most effective ways for programs to advertise their distinctive competencies is through their websites. A high-quality website enables outside constituents to determine what is distinctive about a program, especially with respect to the competencies discussed in this chapter. In particular, programs that work hard to inculcate the full range of competencies necessary for management to become a true profession (Khurana, 2007; Trank & Rynes, 2003) should be easily distinguishable on their websites from those that do not. Similarly, programs that focus heavily on finance should be distinguishable from those that focus on marketing, health care, or general management.

Another challenge that nearly all schools face, regardless of their quality, is the considerable diversity of incoming students. Even at the highest-ranked schools, which can expect all new entrants to be quite accomplished, the precise nature of those accomplishments varies widely. Some students have undergraduate degrees in business and Wall Street experience; and others come from liberal arts programs and early careers in nonprofits. Schools with abundant resources (such as Stanford) have responded to these challenges by offering core courses at varying levels of difficulty. Other schools waive students out of courses they had as undergraduates, freeing more time for electives. Regardless of the methods the school chooses, ensuring that all competencies are adequately addressed depends to some extent on understanding the competencies students bring with them and on having tools that help administrators map individual student skills onto the same competencies used in planning curricula.

A final curricular challenge pertains to the fact that many critics of MBA programs (and many students and faculty as well) would like to see business schools attract and educate more students who are willing to use their business education in the service of nonprofits, social enterprise, or public service (for example, Grant, 2012; Lawrence, Phillips, & Tracey, 2012; Porter & Kramer, 2011; Prahalad, 2010; Yunus, Kuckul, Terjesen, Bacq, & Griffiths, 2012). At present, many business schools do not encourage these vocations or the competencies on which they particularly depend (such as ethics, CSR, critical thinking, and multistakeholder decision making); after all, placing students in lower-paying sectors of the economy hurts the schools' performance in rankings that focus heavily on student placements and starting salaries. (This last criterion also limits emphasis on entrepreneurship in many business school curricula.) Thus, not only do many students enter finance and consulting of their own volition because of the high financial rewards, but they are also encouraged to do so by their programs for the same reason (Ho, 2009). As a result, the number of students who go into less well-paying sectors that might address the broader needs of society is severely restricted in most programs.

Tackling this very important issue will require changes not only in curricula but also in the way that MBA programs are accredited, evaluated, and ranked. At present, the priority that program rankings place on graduate salaries and the minimal emphasis that AASCB accreditation places on ethics and CSR reinforce many of criticisms we laid out at the beginning of this chapter. Business schools need to emphasize additional outcomes—such as placements in social enterprises, nonprofits, or government or founding entrepreneurial ventures—to support broader and longer-term objectives. (See Chapter Eight by Rubin and Morgeson in this volume.)

Final Thoughts on More Effective Curricula

To summarize our findings and translate them into usable takeaways, we offer the following observations and recommendations. At least five competencies should be taught in all MBA programs:

1. Functional and quantitative/analytical knowledge and skills
2. Leadership, human capital management, and interpersonal skills

3. Decision making and problem solving
4. Ethics and corporate social responsibility, and
5. Globalization

There is a fairly strong research consensus that, from the employers' point of view, the two areas most in need of curricular enhancement are leadership and management of human capital and decision making or problem solving. Non–U.S. employers also expect greater emphasis on global and cross-cultural competencies. From a broader societal perspective, there is also a need to enhance ethical, multistakeholder, and CSR-related decision-making capabilities.

Research suggests that most MBA programs cover functional and analytical skills adequately. However, this may not be the case for two market niches: ones in which employers want technical specialists who are not particularly expected to move into general management; and in high-end financial, accounting, design, or IT firms that require state-of-the-art technical skills as well as upper-management potential. The first niche may be best filled by specialized master's programs. The latter may be served either by the most elite MBA programs, which have adequate resources to address both technical and leadership competencies at the highest levels, or by joint degree programs among management and IT, engineering, or design. Graduates of specialized master's programs who show managerial promise might subsequently be steered toward executive MBAs.

There is great pressure on business schools to educate students more quickly and cost effectively. A key challenge is to determine how to develop all the core competencies necessary to ensure that management will be practiced as a true profession, even under time and cost constraints. We suggest that program leaders develop planning grids to map core curricula onto all desired competency areas and then fill the remaining gaps with electives, capstones, consulting projects, and co-curricular activities. For career-planning purposes, career counselors and students might use similar grids to map individual student knowledge and skills against the needed competencies.

Multiple constituents are calling for business schools to produce students with more global, prosocial, and longer-term views. At present, such efforts are hampered by the low value placed on them by many employers and by evaluation and ranking systems. However, many students are very interested in applying their business skills to prosocial purposes; this means that businesses are increasingly likely to find that emphasizing social responsibility provides them with a competitive advantage when recruiting students.

To encourage further shifts in this direction, we need to see modifications to accreditation and ranking systems so we can move beyond student selectivity, placements, and graduate salaries as measures of program effectiveness. What if we do not address these broader issues? Our failure may act as a brake on attempts to rebalance curricula to be more holistic, focus on multiple stakeholders, and move our schools and our students in directions that benefit society.

Notes

1. The reason for talking about both "courses" and "content areas" is that several of the subjects listed in Table 5.1 often were not taught in stand-alone courses, but rather were integrated or "infused" into one or more courses. The most commonly infused topics were corporate social responsibility (51 percent infused rather than stand-alone), entrepreneurship (42 percent infused), ethics (38 percent infused), and project management (38 percent infused). Of course, when content is reported to be infused across multiple courses, there is always some question about the extent to which integration or infusion is actually occurring (for example, Swanson, 2004).

2. This is almost certainly not a representative sample, but rather is likely to over-represent programs that are doing the most with respect to leadership development.

3. For an excellent qualitative study of the processes and benefits of the design thinking process, see Sutton and Hargadon (1996).

References

AACSB. *AACSB Business Standards 2012 Update.* http://www.aacsb.edu/accreditation/standards/

ABC *Nightline.* "The Deep Dive: IDEO Shopping Cart." First broadcast on July 13, 1999. http://www.youtube.com/watch?v=M66ZU2PCIcM

Adler, P. S. "Corporate Scandals: It's Time for Reflection in Business Schools." *Academy of Management Executive,* 2002, 16, 148–149.

Anand, V., Ashforth, B. E., & Joshi, M. "Business as Usual: The Acceptance and Perpetuation of Corruption in Organizations." *Academy of Management Executive,* 2005, 19, 9–23.

Anderson, M., & Escher, P. *The MBA Oath: Setting a Higher Standard for Business Leaders.* New York: Portfolio, 2010.

Aspen Institute. *Where Will They Lead? Business Student Attitudes About Business and Society.* Aspen, Colo.: Aspen Institute Center for Business Education, 2008.

Badaracco, J. L., Jr. *Defining Moments: When Managers Must Choose Between Right and Right.* Boston, Mass.: Harvard Business School Press, 1997.

Bebchuk, L., & Fried, J. *Pay Without Performance: The Unfulfilled Promise of Executive Compensation.* Cambridge, Mass.: Harvard University Press, 2004.

Benjamin, B., & O'Reilly, C. "Becoming a Leader: Early Career Challenges Faced by MBA Graduates." *Academy of Management Learning & Education,* 2011, 10, 452–472. DOI: 10.5465/amle.2011.0002.

Brown, K. G., Charlier, S. D., Rynes, S. L., & Hosmanek, A. "What Do We Teach in Organizational Behavior? An Analysis of MBA Syllabi." *Journal of Management Education* (in press).

Cable, D. M., & Judge, T. A. "Person-Organization Fit, Job Choice Decisions, and Organizational Entry." *Organizational Behavior and Human Decision Processes,* 1996, 67, 294–311.

Carruthers, B. G., & Kim, J-C. "The Sociology of Finance." *Annual Review of Sociology,* 2011, 37, 239–259.

Datar, S. M., Garvin, D. A. & Cullen, P. G. *Rethinking the MBA: Business Education at a Crossroads.* Boston, Mass.: Harvard Business Press, 2010.

Dean, K. L., & Beggs, J. M. "University Professors and Teaching Ethics: Conceptualizations and Expectations." *Journal of Management Education*, 2006, 30, 15–44.

Dean, K. L., & Jolly, J. P. "Student Identity, Disengagement, and Learning." *Academy of Management Learning & Education*, 2012, 11, 228–243.

Dierdorff, E. C., & Rubin, R. S. *The Relevance, Requirements, and Ramifications of Specialized MBA Programs*. Technical report submitted to the Management Education Research Institute of the Graduate Management Admissions Council, McLean, Va., 2009.

DiMeglio, F. "Specialized MBAs Grow in Number." *Business Week*, July 20, 2007, p. 28.

Druckman, D., & Bjork, R. A. (eds.). *In the Mind's Eye: Enhancing Human Performance*. Washington, D.C.: National Academy Press, 1991.

Evans, F. J., & Marcal, L. E. "Educating for Ethics: Business Deans' Perspectives." *Business and Society Review*, 2005, 110(3), 233–248.

Evans, F. J., & Weiss, E. J. "Views on the importance of ethics in business education." In D. L. Swanson & D. G. Fisher (eds.), *Toward Assessing Business Ethics Education* (pp. 43–66). Charlotte, N.C.: IAP, 2008.

Evans, J. M., Trevino, L. K., & Weaver, G. R. "Who's in the Ethics Driver's Seat? Factors Influencing Ethics in the MBA Curriculum." *Academy of Management Learning & Education*, 2006, 5, 278–293.

Ferraro, F., Pfeffer, J., & Sutton, R. I. "Economics Language and Assumptions: How Theories Can Become Self-Fulfilling." *Academy of Management Review*, 2005, 30, 8–24.

Financial Times. http://rankings.ft.com/businessschoolrankings/emba-rankings-2011

Financial Times. http://rankings.ft.com/exportranking/global-mba-rankings-2012/pdf

Fisman, R., & Galinsky, A. "We Need a New Way to Teach Ethics to Business School Students." *Slate*, September. 4, 2012, pp. 1–4. http://www.slate.com/articles/business/the_dismal_science/2012/09/business_school_and_ethics_can_we_train_mbas_to_do_the_right_thing_.html

Gentile, M. C. *Giving Voice to Values: How to Speak Your Mind When You Know What's Right*. New Haven, Conn.: Yale University Press, 2010.

Gerdes, L. "B-Schools With a Niche." *Business Week*, September 5, 2005, pp. 70–72.

Ghoshal, S. "Bad Management Theories Are Destroying Good Management Practices." *Academy of Management Learning & Education*, 2005, 4, 75–91.

Giacalone, R. A., & Thompson, K. R. "Business Ethics and Social Responsibility Education: Shifting the Worldview." *Academy of Management Learning & Education*, 2005, 5, 266–277.

GMAC. *2009 Alumni Perspectives Survey Report*. McLean, Va.: Graduate Management Admissions Council, 2009.

GMAC. *2010 Global Management Education Graduate Survey Report*. McLean, Va.: Graduate Management Admissions Council, 2010.

GMAC. *2011 Global Management Education Graduate Survey Report*. Reston, Va.: Graduate Management Admissions Council, 2011.

GMAC. *2012 Corporate Recruiters Survey Report*. Reston, Va.: Graduate Management Admissions Council, 2012.

GMAC. "The New Integrated Reasoning Section and Why It Matters." January 2013. http://www.mba.com/the-gmat/interactive-map-test/find-out-whats-changing.aspx

Grant, A. M. "Giving Time, Time After Time: Work Design and Sustained Employee Participation in Corporate Volunteering." *Academy of Management Review*, 2012, 37, 589–615.

Grind, K. *The Lost Bank: The Story of Washington Mutual, the Biggest Bank Failure in American History*. New York: Simon & Schuster, 2012.

Hansen, U., Moosmayer, D., Bode, M. & Schrader, U. *Values at Work: Business Professors' Influence on Corporate Values*. Berlin: Logos, 2007.

Ho, K. *Liquidated: An Ethnography of Wall Street*. Durham, N.C.: Duke University Press, 2009.

Hoover, J. D., Giambatista, R. C., Sorenson, R. L., & Bommer, W. H. "Assessing the Effectiveness of Whole Person Learning Pedagogy in Skill Acquisition." *Academy of Management Learning & Education*, 2010, 9, 192–203.

James, E. H. "Learning to Lead While Giving Back: An MBA Capstone Leadership Experience." *MBA Innovation*, 2011, Summer, 17–19.

Johnson, S., & Kwak, J. *13 Bankers: The Wall Street Takeover and the Next Financial Meltdown*. New York: Pantheon, 2010.

Khurana, R. *From Higher Aims to Hired Hands*. Princeton, N.J.: Princeton University Press, 2007.

Lawrence, T., Phillips, N., & Tracey, P. "Educating Social Entrepreneurs and Social Innovators." *Academy of Management Education & Learning*, 2012, 11, 319–323.

Leavitt, H. J. "Educating Our MBAs: On Teaching What We Haven't Taught." *California Management Review*, 1989, 31(3), 38–50.

Lewis, M. *Liar's Poker*. New York: Norton, 1989.

Liang, N. & Wang, J. "Implicit Mental Models in Teaching Cases: An Empirical Study of Popular MBA Cases in the United States and China." *Academy of Management Learning & Education*, 2004, 3, 397–413.

MBAR. *2009 Curricular Innovation Trends Comprehensive Report*. Bloomington, Minn.: MBA Roundtable, 2009.

MBAR. *Leadership Assessment Survey*. Bloomington, Minn.: MBA Roundtable, 2011.

MBAR. *2012 Curricular Innovation Study.* Bloomington, Minn.: MBA Round-table, 2012.

McGrath, R. G. "No Longer a Step-Child: How the Management Field Can Come Into Its Own." *Academy of Management Review,* 2007, 50, 1365–1378.

McLean, B. & Elkind, P. *The Smartest Guys in the Room: The Amazing Rise and Scandalous Fall of Enron.* London: Portfolio, 2003.

Mintzberg, H. *Managers Not MBAs: A Hard Look at the Soft Practice of Managing and Management Development.* San Francisco, Calif.: Berrett-Koehler, 2004.

Navarro, P. "The MBA Core Curricula of Top-Ranked U.S. Business Schools: A Study in Failure?" *Academy of Management Learning & Education,* 2008, 7, 108–123. DOI: 10.5465/AMLE.2008.31413868

Nicholson, C.Y., & DeMoss, M. "Teaching Ethics and Social Responsibility: An Evaluation of Undergraduate Business Education at the Discipline Level." *Journal of Education for Business,* 2009, 84, 213–218.

Palmer, D. *Normal Organizational Wrongdoing: A Critical Analysis of Theories of Misconduct in and of Organizations.* New York: Oxford University Press, 2012.

Petriglieri, G., Wood, J. D., & Petriglieri, J. L. "Up Close and Personal: Building Foundations for Leaders' Development Through the Personalization of Management Learning." *Academy of Management Learning & Education,* 2011, 10, 430–450.

Pfeffer, J. & Fong, C. "The End of Business Schools? Less Success Than Meets the Eye." *Academy of Management Learning & Education,* 2002, 1, 78–95. DOI: 10.5465/AMLE.2002.7373679

Porter, L. W., & McKibbin, L. E. *Management Education and Development: Drift or Thrust into the 21st Century?* New York: McGraw Hill, 1988.

Porter, M. E., & Kramer, M. R. "Creating Shared Value." *Harvard Business Review,* 2011, 89 (1/2), 62–77.

Prahalad, C. K. *The Fortune at the Bottom of the Pyramid: Eradicating Poverty Through Profits.* Upper Saddle River, N.J.: Pearson Education, 2010.

Rasche, A., Gilbert, D. U., & Schedel, I. "Cross-Disciplinary Ethics Education in MBA Programs: Rhetoric or Reality?" Forthcoming in *Academy of Management Learning & Education* (in press).

Rubin, R.S., & Dierdorff, E. C. "How Relevant Is the MBA? Assessing the Alignment of Required Curricula and Required Managerial Competencies." *Academy of Management Learning & Education,* 2009, 8, 208–224. DOI: 10.5465/AMLE.2009.41788843

Rubin, R. S., & Dierdorff, E. C. "On the Road to Abilene: Time to Manage Agreement About BA Curricular Relevance." *Academy of Management Learning & Education,* 2011, 10, 148–161.

Rutherford, M. A., Parks, L., Cavazos, D. E., & White, C. D. "Business Ethics as a Required Course: Investigating the Factors Impacting the Decision to Require Ethics in the Undergraduate Business Core Curriculum." *Academy of Management Learning & Education*, 2012, 11, 174–186.

Rynes, S. L., Trank, C. Q., Lawson, A. M., & Ilies, R. "Behavioral Coursework in Business Education: Growing Evidence of a Legitimacy Crisis." *Academy of Management Learning & Education*, 2003, 2, 269–283. DOI:10.5465/AMLE.2003.10932135

Schneider, B. "The People Make the Place." *Personnel Psychology*, 1987, 40, 437–453.

Schneider, M. "Learning to Put Ethics Last." *Business Week*, March 10, 2002. http://www.businessweek.com/stories/2002-03-10/learning-to-put-ethics-last

Segev, E., Raveh, A., & Farjoun, M. "Conceptual Maps of the Leading MBA Programs in the United States: Core Courses, Concentration Areas, and the Ranking of the School." *Strategic Management Journal*, 1999, 20, 549–56.

Spence, M. "Signaling in Retrospect and the Informational Structure of Markets." *American Economic Review*, 2002, 92, 434–459.

Sutton, R. I., & Hargadon, A. "Brainstorming Groups in Context: Effectiveness in a Product Design Firm." *Administrative Science Quarterly*, 1996, 41, 685–718.

Swanson, D. L. "The Buck Stops Here: Why Universities Must Reclaim Business Ethics Education." *Journal of Academic Ethics*, 2004, 2, 43–61.

Swanson, D. L., & Fisher, D. *Got Ethics? Toward Assessing Business Ethics Education.* Charlotte, N.C.: Information Age, 2011.

Swiercz, P. M., & Ross, K. T. "Rational, Human, Political, and Symbolic Text in Harvard Business School Cases: A Study of Structure and Content." *Journal of Management Education*, 2003, 27, 407–430.

TED Talks. "David Kelley on Human Centered Design." May 2007. http://www.ted.com/talks/david_kelley_on_human_centered_design.html

Thaler, R. H., & Sunstein, C. R. *Nudge: Improving Decisions About Health, Wealth, and Happiness.* London: Penguin Books, 2009.

Trank, C. Q., & Rynes, S. L. "Who Moved Our Cheese? Reclaiming Professionalism in Business Education." *Academy of Management Learning & Education*, 2003, 2, 189–205.

Wang, L., Malhotra, D. & Murnighan, J. K. "Economics Education and Greed." *Academy of Management Learning & Education*, 2011, 10, 643–660.

Yunus, M., Kuckel, J., Terjesen, S., Bacq, S. & Griffiths, M. "Social Business Education: An Interview With Nobel Laureate Muhammad Yunus." *Academy of Management Learning & Education*, 2012, 11, 453–462.

6

OVERLOOKED AND UNAPPRECIATED

What Research Tells Us About How Teaching Must Change

Kenneth G. Brown
University of Iowa

J. Ben Arbaugh
University of Wisconsin Oshkosh

George Hrivnak
Bond University

Amy Kenworthy
Bond University

Key Topics Covered in This Chapter

- Why faculty knowledge of general principles of teaching and learning fosters better educational outcomes for students
- Core learning process and outcome theories that all teaching faculty should know
- Recommendations for schools to advance student learning in graduate management education
- Recommendations for effective delivery of online and blended learning opportunities
- Recommendations for effective experiential learning methods

Scholarly critiques of graduate management programs primarily target content and curriculum. But what if it is *how* faculty teach as much as *what* is taught that hinders the success of these programs and their graduates? As we identify new skills that our graduates will need to thrive in the global work environment, how can we ensure that they possess those skills? The answer, we believe, is that business school faculty and administrators can foster their students' success by giving teaching and learning more significance and putting associated research findings into practice.

As simple as these proposals may sound, research on learning does not seem to have permeated university teaching, let alone teaching in graduate management programs. As Halpern and Hakel (2003) have argued, "It would be difficult to design an educational model that is more at odds with current research on human cognition than the one that is used in most colleges and universities" (p. 38). Since this statement was written, the pace of learning-related research has accelerated and moved well beyond the bounds of cognitive psychology.

Numerous journals, conferences, and newsletters have synthesized best practices in university teaching; one noteworthy example is the *Teaching Professor* newsletter and conference. In his popular book *What the Best College Teachers Do* (2004), Ken Bain presented the results of his analysis of outstanding college teachers and argued for a set of general practices. Many journals specific to graduate management education now publish research about learning business-related knowledge and skills. These journals include *Academy of Management Learning and Education*, *Decision Sciences Journal of Innovative Education*, *Journal of Accounting Education*, *Journal of Financial Education*, *Journal of Education for Business*, *Journal of Management Education*, and *Journal of Marketing Education*. A search for the keyword MBA in these journals reveals that the total number of articles more than doubled from 2002 to 2012.

One approach to making better use of research findings is to synthesize them into best practice recommendations for teaching graduate management students. Although this would be useful, we believe that best practice claims can be overstated and misleading, perhaps even detrimental, when fostering the success of any one program. Instead, in this chapter we offer a flexible framework and broad-based recommendations that are all consistent with the current scholarship of teaching and learning (SOTL). By advancing broad recommendations, we acknowledge that different business schools have different programs (as Hay notes in this volume) and that these program features should influence both what and, to some degree, how students learn. Moreover, we recognize that finance, accounting, operations, marketing, information systems, and general management require that students learn different types of knowledge, which suggests that no one teaching approach should dominate across courses. Of course, we also appreciate that learners' characteristics influence the process and outcomes of learning. So when the profile of the typical student at one business school differs from the profile at another, teaching methods may not work equally well in both settings. Consequently, the teaching practices that work well for a course in a highly selective program preparing management consultants may not work in a regional program preparing marketing specialists.

Our framework and recommendations begin with the foundational work by Shulman (1987). Shulman argued that at a minimum, effective teachers possess content knowledge, pedagogical knowledge, and, at the intersection between the two, pedagogical content knowledge (PCK).[1] *Content knowledge* refers to an understanding of the material to be taught. When business schools hire corporate finance researchers to teach corporate finance, they are relying on content expertise to guide course staffing decisions. *Pedagogical knowledge* is an understanding of general principles of teaching and learning and, as we argue here, is generally underappreciated in business schools.

The intersection of these two areas of knowledge offers what many consider to be the greatest contribution of this framework (Mishra & Koehler, 2006). *Pedagogical content knowledge* is an explicit recognition that effective teachers understand ways in which they can teach particular topics most effectively, including through effective analogies, illustrations, examples, demonstrations, and practice activities. The PCK concept acknowledges that teachers develop expertise within a particular content domain that allows them to effectively foster learning. Additionally, Mishra and Koehler (2006) proposed another form of knowledge: technological knowledge. We return to this concept in our section on online and blended learning environments.

Most would agree that the first area of Shulman's categorization, content knowledge, is the dominant driver of university faculty selection, promotion, and rewards, at least at large research universities. Faculty who publish more in their content domain, and those who are recognized internationally as experts within a particular area, are widely considered by deans and other administrators to be the most desirable faculty to attract and retain. Yet there is little evidence to suggest that content experts, and in particular those who publish more, possess pedagogical knowledge and PCK. One cross-disciplinary review of studies on research and teaching proficiency revealed a near-zero relationship (Lewicki & Bailey, 2009; see also the Hattie & Marsh, 1996, meta-analysis). So when business schools recruit, promote, and reward content experts, they are doing little, if anything, to improve the quality of teaching and learning.

Given this chapter's broad scope, our focus is primarily on pedagogical knowledge—that is, what teachers should know about learning and teaching. We begin by examining foundational learning theories as well as more recent work that we believe faculty should use as guides to teaching decisions. Then we consider how business schools could manage their faculties to ensure that they possess high levels of pedagogical and other related forms of knowledge. Finally, we provide more specific recommendations in two important areas: online and blended delivery, and experiential learning. The underlying belief guiding this chapter's focus is that increased faculty knowledge, driven by changes in business school policy and practices, will improve students' learning in ways that foster success after graduation.

What Is Learning?

Across disciplines in business schools, *learning* is a term used to cover a broad variety of topics, including processes and outcomes of individuals, organizations, and machines. For purposes of this chapter, we focus on human learning as a psychological process that results in a relatively enduring change in what a person thinks or does. More formally we adopt this definition:

> Learning is a multidimensional process that results in relatively enduring change in a person or persons, and consequently how that person or persons will perceive the world and reciprocally respond to its affordances physically, psychologically, and socially. (Alexander, Schallert, & Reynolds, 2009, p. 186)

The critical features of this definition are the emphasis on change and the assertion that learning is not just about action but also perception, thought, and social identity. Many learning theories are congruent with this definition and can guide decisions about teaching. In the coming paragraphs, we review four taxonomies of learning outcomes before we turn to four process-oriented theories.

Learning Outcomes

Taxonomic frameworks that identify various dimensions or types of learning outcomes abound. In the next paragraphs, we note some implications of four taxonomies for management education: Bloom's Revised Taxonomy, Gagné's Learned Capabilities, the Taxonomy of Learning Outcomes, and Aristotelian Ethics. Table 6.1 provides a summary of these taxonomies along with

Table 6.1 Learning Outcome Taxonomies and Related Observations

Theory	Representative Citation	Dimensions of Learning	Observations
Bloom's Revised Taxonomy	Anderson & Krathwohl (2001), *A Taxonomy for Learning, Teaching, and Assessing: A Revision of Bloom's Taxonomy of Educational Objectives.*	Cognitive processes (remembering, understanding, applying, analyzing, evaluating, and creating) and types of knowledge (factual, conceptual, procedural, and metacognitive) Affective (receiving, responding, valuing, organizing, and internalizing) Psychomotor	Bloom's taxonomy, in its revised form, has both the better known "cognitive process" outcomes and the recently added "types of knowledge," which are largely consistent with other learning taxonomies. Affective and psychomotor domains are studied much less frequently than cognitive. Connections between the cognitive and affective domains are asserted but have been infrequently studied.
Gagné's Learning Capabilities	Gagné (1984), "Learning Outcomes and Their Effects: Useful Categories of Human Performance."	Verbal information Intellectual skill Cognitive strategy Attitude Motor skill	Cognitive capabilities can be subdivided into verbal information, intellectual skill, and cognitive strategy. Cognitive strategy includes metacognition, which can be learned and can aid further learning.

Taxonomy of Learning Outcomes	Kraiger, Ford, & Salas (1993), "Application of Cognitive, Skill-Based, and Affective Theories of Learning Outcomes to New Methods of Training Evaluation."	Cognitive Affective Skills based	Affective domain, including attitudinal and motivational outcomes, continues to be understudied.
Aristotelian Ethics	Chia (2009), "The Nature of Knowledge and Knowing in the Context of Management Learning, Education, and Development."	Episteme Techné Phronesis	Episteme includes explicit, universal propositions that other taxonomies would label factual and conceptual knowledge. Techné is knowledge oriented toward creation or production, akin to skills. Phronesis is a unique concept capturing personal and holistic expertise, gained from experience and difficult to codify; it is neglected in management education and should be given greater attention.

observations about them. The following narrative focuses on implications for graduate management education.

Teaching is seldom assessed by measures of student learning, although this is a controversial trend in U.S. secondary education (Weldon, 2011). Instead, faculty efforts related to learning and teaching are often examined through ratings provided by their students. These measures do not correlate highly with actual learning outcomes, although there is certainly debate on this topic (Clayton, 2009), and there is legitimate concern that the fact that students like a course may not translate into their learning from it. To alleviate concerns about liking, one evaluation method asks students, "How much did you learn in this class?" rather than "How much did you like this class?" Unfortunately, research suggests that self-assessments of learning consistently correlate more highly with other measures of liking and student motivation than with objective measures of learning (Sitzmann, Ely, Brown, & Bauer, 2010). This does not render self-assessments useless, but it does mean that students' reports of how much they learn are heavily colored by their enjoyment of a course. If we measure and manage according to this standard alone, we risk increasing enjoyment rather than learning.

If we want to assess faculty teaching via learning outcomes, such outcomes should be measured directly, by assessing what students know and are capable of doing at the conclusion of their courses and program. In this regard, the taxonomic frameworks are quite useful and show a high degree of overlap. They each acknowledge that verbal information (remembered and understood) is an important dimension of learning. They also agree that more complex cognitive processes, like learning strategies and metacognition, are valuable and can be measured.

Perhaps most noteworthy is what we do not do with regard to these learning outcomes. In general, we do not measure (at least not directly or intentionally) affective outcomes, including motivation, attitudes, and identity. This seems to be a major oversight, given that an implicit goal of most curricula is to help students see the importance of associated content, such as (in the context of finance) the time value of money and (in context of organizational behavior) the usefulness of certain types of goals. That students can answer questions on this material (cognitive outcome of verbal knowledge) does not necessarily help us know whether students believe the material is useful and important (affective outcomes) and will use it unprompted in the future because it is part of their identity (internalization or phronesis).

To some faculty, measuring affective outcomes seems incongruent with what they perceive to be their role as expert sources of content knowledge. These faculty believe that presenting the material should be enough. But what if, at the program level, we believe our students will be more effective employees and managers if they hold certain beliefs and attitudes? Then we should set these as learning goals, explore ways to persuade students in those directions, and assess our effectiveness with explicit measurement strategies.

One particularly useful affective outcome is motivation (Kraiger, Ford, & Salas, 1993). Motivational concepts such as self-efficacy, self-set goals, and persistence have been identified as powerful predictors of learning and subsequent performance (Bandura, 1997; Sitzmann & Ely, 2011). Self-efficacy, defined as a person's confidence that he or she can successfully carry out a course of action in a specific domain, would not seem to be a problem for MBA students. Indeed, to many MBA instructors, students often seem overconfident about their abilities. But if we accept that domain specificity is critical, then overall confidence or specific confidence in analytical ability is not management education's primary concern. Our concern should be that students have self-efficacy for performing the less analytical and more interpersonal demands of their work. Students who are better at doing financial analysis may shy away from efforts to thoughtfully manage others in part because of low confidence in their interpersonal abilities. Acknowledging the importance of self-efficacy opens the door to concrete research-driven practices that foster its development, including (not surprisingly) more opportunities for practice (Bandura, 1997). And, to the extent that faculty seek to encourage phronesis, or practical wisdom, they must put students in real situations that demand the development of not just new skills but also a new understanding of their identities and relationships with others. This is precisely what some experiential learning activities attempt to do; we pick up that discussion later in the chapter.

Learning Processes

Learning is a process, but it is neither a single faceted nor simple one. As a result, there are many different theories about how learning occurs. In Table 6.2, we present four that we believe all faculty should consider as part of their instructional design and teaching. These four learning theories offer a variety of different ways to think about learning. No one theory is complete, but taken together, they offer a number of counterintuitive teaching suggestions that do not appear in mainstream graduate education. These suggestions include deliberate behavior modeling, using worked examples, shifting the emphasis and complexity of cases over time, attempting to form associations to foster the development of particular attitudes, and supporting the development of communities of practice. Although a detailed discussion of these theories is beyond the scope of this chapter, the citations included in the table provide exemplary references for each.

A useful illustration of an approach that blends theories is the framework for teaching social entrepreneurs that has been presented by Kickul, Janssen-Selvaudrai, and Griffiths (2012). Drawing on social learning and situated learning theories, they propose introducing intra-university and community resources to support pedagogical themes within this area. When these resources and supports are blended, the researchers argue, students gain appropriate knowledge and skill and also develop

Table 6.2 Learning Process Theories and Related Observations

Theory	Representative Citation	Key Processes	Observations
Social Learning Theory	Bandura (1986), *Social Foundations of Thought and Action*.	Four processes: attention, retention, reproduction, and motivation.	Basis for behavioral modeling, which has been documented to be highly effective at boosting skills.
Cognitive Load Theory	Paas, Renkl, & Sweller (2003), "Cognitive Load Theory and Instructional Design: Recent Developments."	Working memory capacity limits what can learned; reductions in extraneous cognitive load benefit learning.	Extraneous load is often created by presenting too much information at once; using worked examples during early learning stages has been shown to aid learning.
Associative-Propositional Evaluation	Gawronski & Bodenhausen (2006), "Associative and Propositional Processes in Evaluation: An Integrative Review of Implicit and Explicit Attitude Change."	Implicit and explicit attitudes both predict behavior and are not always highly related; change of each can occur in a variety of different ways.	Changing student attitudes may require attention to both explicit (expressed and influence via propositional reasoning) and implicit attitudes (expressed and influenced via associative connections).
Situated Learning	Lave & Wenger (1991), *Situated Learning: Legitimate Peripheral Participation*.	Learning is social and context dependent; learners move from peripheral to core participation in communities of practice.	Suggests that personal identity and social relationships are central to learning.

self-efficacy for social entrepreneurship. Although this approach has not yet been systematically assessed for its affects on student learning, the approach's logic shows the potential for blending different theories to guide teaching decisions. We believe that these ideas, presented by Kickul and others (2012), have broad applicability and could be used to teach many skill sets, not just entrepreneurship.

What Can Business Schools Do to Improve Learning Outcomes?

A logical path to improving student learning outcomes would get faculty involved in broad-based participation in and dissemination of the scholarship of teaching and learning. However, this is not yet occurring. Many business schools do not encourage their faculty to conduct and publish this type of research, and not just because of bias within business schools. The *Financial Times* Global MBA ranking uses a faculty research index that counts publications in forty-five academic and practitioner journals. None of the journals on this list are educational in focus. (See "45 Journals Used in FT Research Rank, 2012.)

Compared to other professional schools—and specifically medicine and engineering—business schools pay meager attention, resources, and respect to educational research. In these other professions, educational research is the subject of numerous conferences and journals, many of them quite prestigious (*Academic Medicine* and *Journal of Engineering Education*, for example). Grant-funding opportunities are also vastly different. Although the Graduate Management Admission Council (GMAC) Management Education Research Institute provides grants to management faculty, it is one of the only sources for such funding in management. In contrast, in the United States both medical and engineering education is funded by federal granting agencies, including the National Science Foundation and the National Institutes of Health. There is some evidence that management education research is maturing (see Rynes &

Brown, 2011), but it remains far behind its equivalents in the fields of medical and engineering education.

Raising the status of management education scholarship, and increasing its application to daily teaching in business schools, are not simple endeavors. It requires change both within and outside business schools. For purposes of this chapter, we focus on activities that deans and program directors can undertake to increase their faculty members' knowledge of this type of scholarship. Drawing on frameworks of human resource management, we also consider the various processes that go into hiring, socializing, and otherwise shaping faculty knowledge and behavior. In addition, we briefly consider how the ways in which business schools are run can influence what students learn. Table 6.3 summarizes these recommendations.

Table 6.3 Recommendations for Increasing Levels of Pedagogical and Pedagogical Content Knowledge Among Faculty

Category	Recommendations
Selection	Have faculty applicants give two job talks: one to assess content knowledge (research-related expertise) and the other to assess pedagogical and pedagogical content knowledge.
Training	Offer developmental opportunities for faculty and graduate students that leverage existing resources within the college and university. Encourage observation, reflection, and discussion.
Rewards	Offer awards and grants that encourage scholarly activity related to teaching and learning, including but not limited to learning new techniques, examining their effects on students, and publishing the results.
Redesign	Encourage the development of shared resources that reflect the best ideas from a particular group of faculty teaching similar courses. Codify, where possible, in syllabi and other teaching materials.
Management practices	Examine management practices routinely to determine whether policies and practices reinforce the learning outcomes in courses and curriculum.

Selection

The process of staffing courses in business schools, whether by full-time or adjunct faculty, begins with recruitment and selection. Schools seeking to hire faculty with more pedagogical experience and pedagogical content knowledge could require them for application for faculty positions and test for them during the selection process. This does, in fact, occur in some teaching-oriented colleges, where faculty applicants give two talks: a research talk to faculty and a teaching talk to students through which the applicant teaches part of a class session. This approach is fundamentally sound, as the underlying knowledge bases for a research talk (content knowledge) are not entirely the same as for a teaching talk (pedagogical and PCK). Although a research talk would help identify major flaws in presentation style, it would not help distinguish candidates with more expertise in conducting a case discussion or explaining a concept.

Training Faculty to Be More Effective

Once hired, a business school can provide faculty with opportunities to gain teaching-related knowledge; doctoral students benefit from such training as well. Given the powerful effect that observation has on learning, developmental activities should not be limited to outside speakers or talks about research findings. Instead, the activities should involve systematic observation, reflection, and discussion among faculty.

However, faculty development activities, as they are called, are unevenly practiced across business schools. Some schools, like Harvard and Columbia, have centers that offer training on pedagogy. In contrast, some schools do not even have standing teaching committees, let alone dedicated resources for faculty to learn more about teaching. For the latter types of schools, it is worthwhile to investigate the many universities with teaching and learning centers that offer workshops and consultations to help build pedagogical knowledge. (For one list, visit http://www.hofstra.edu/faculty/ctse/ctse_links.cfm.)

If a school's management faculty are not actively involved with a particular center, there may appear to be limited developmental opportunities to build PCK. However, there may be opportunities based on content overlap with other disciplines. For example, faculty who teach psychology and sociology may have knowledge of how to teach management and marketing concepts, and faculty who teach statistics, actuarial sciences, and applied mathematics may have knowledge of how to teach business statistics and analytics.

Rewarding Efforts to Improve

As noted earlier, available research does not suggest a relationship between research productivity and teaching proficiency. Thus, providing faculty with rewards and promotions based on research alone does nothing to improve the quality of teaching. The solution some scholars propose, consistent with the suggestions of Ernest Boyer about multiple forms of scholarship (Boyer, 1990), is to reward different types of scholarship, including the scholarship of discovery (traditional scholarship) and the scholarship of teaching and learning. This does not mean offering teaching awards based on students' ratings; such a practice encourages happy students first and learning second. Instead, faculty members should be recognized for actively experimenting with and learning from their teaching-related practice. That is, schools should encourage scholarly efforts to improve teaching. To be scholarly, the efforts must be made public, they should be reviewed and critiqued by peers, and they must influence other scholars (Glassick, 2000).

Rewards could take the form of grants to pay not just for costs but also for the time that faculty must take away from other obligations. But to truly encourage scholarship, grants should be awarded for documentation and dissemination rather than for activity alone. It should not be enough to attend a workshop; faculty members should document and share how the workshop altered their approach to teaching and improved their students' learning outcomes.

Redesigning Teaching Resources

When faculty begin to teach, they often make heavy use of materials that are already in use by their peers or provided by a publisher. The quality of these materials is an open question. In our general experience, materials other faculty pass along are highly variable, and materials publishers provide are often of poor quality.

Faculty in a particular college might be better served by working together to draw on their best work and create their own set of shared resources. Resources can include not just syllabi but also examples, sample problems, cases, and illustrations conveyed in teaching notes. Faculty members are sometimes reluctant to share this information, which they may see as their intellectual property. In such cases, faculty members can enter into mutual agreements to share materials only for teaching purposes and then work together to develop these materials. Of course, such collaborations are much more likely to be successful when the school's selection and rewards practice has already fostered a community of faculty interested in improving students' learning outcomes.

Management of Hidden Curriculum

Research indicates that much of what is learned is never formally taught. Bransford and colleagues (2006) wrote, "Across both live, face-to-face interactions and [technology-] mediated interactions, the common conclusion is that people can learn patterned regularities without intending to do so and sometimes without being able to describe the patterns they have learned" (p. 211). These authors conclude that this type of learning is natural and has major implications for educational practices.

What regularities do our graduate students observe in and out of their classrooms? Certainly they discern the dynamics of power, but it is likely that they also perceive how decisions are made and what priorities are observed. If a school is primarily led by finance faculty and decisions are generally made behind closed doors without input, then students may implicitly learn that this is who holds power and how decisions should be made. Like all educational institutions, business schools have a hidden curriculum that, despite never being formally taught, may still have very real consequences for students (Snyder, 1973).

In 2007 the United Nations launched an initiative to develop and advance management principles consistent with the UN's Global Compact for human rights. Called "Principles for Responsible Management Education" (PRME), the initiative asks all educational organizations to endorse this statement: "We understand that our own organisational practices should serve as examples of the values and attitudes we convey to our students" (http://www.unpreme.org/the-6-principles/index.php). This initiative speaks to issues related to human rights and sustainability, so it focuses primarily on management practices related to human capital (How are faculty and staff treated?) and physical capital (How are energy use and waste managed?) (United Nations, 2012.)

Business schools that recognize hidden curricula and wish to abide by this PRME principle should ensure fair personnel processes and decisions and continually examine ways to be better stewards of environmental resources. Doing so will encourage students to develop beliefs consistent with management curricula that should recognize the importance of ethics and human rights. (See Rynes & Bartunek, this volume.)

What's Next for Graduate Management Education?

Hay (this volume) notes that one major choice point for MBA programs is the type of technology they will employ to deliver instruction. Supporting the importance of this choice, the biggest trend in both higher education and workplace training is online delivery (Brown & Sitzmann, 2011). An equally important trend, driven in part by criticisms of MBA curricula (such as Mintzberg, 2004), has been to increase the use of experiential education, including simulation and fieldwork. We discuss research on each of these topics in turn and present additional recommendations in the sections that follow.

Online and Blended Education

One of the most noticeable trends in education today is the use of technology to deliver instruction, whether entirely online or as a blend between face-to-face and online components. Online delivery has many potential benefits, including easy access for remote students, reduced cost to students and the hosting institution, the convenience of reduced travel, and potential scalability.

These benefits appear to be a major driver behind the development of massive open online courses (MOOCs). As their name implies, MOOCs are free courses offered online to all comers; in some cases, enrollments have topped 30,000. There are now enough of these courses that an integration and review website, Coursetalk.com (http://coursetalk.com), has been launched; as of January 2013 it lists more than 300 courses from more than forty universities, hosted by eight providers.

In spite of thriving online MBA programs offered by schools accredited by the Association to Advance Collegiate Schools of Business (AACSB), such as Indiana University, University of Maryland University College, and the University of Florida, skepticism persists about the viability of delivering graduate management education via the Internet (Redpath, 2012). As Redpath (2012) notes, such attitudes may be influenced by a lack of awareness of the volume of research on online and blended management education. Lack of awareness of research is a criticism that is also increasingly leveled against MOOCs (Bujak,

Baker, DeMillo, & Sandulli, 2012; Parry, 2011). One MOOC innovator, Udacity's Sebastian Thrun, confessed ignorance of this literature when he first designed his course. Subsequently, he has come around to profess admiration for the efforts of earlier online educators and scholars (Young, 2012). The buzz around MOOCs in the academic popular press sounds similar to calls about online learning's potential back in the 1990s (for examples, see Dede, 1991; Ives & Jarvenpaa, 1996). However, we see this as further support for Redpath's (2012) contention that business school faculty and administrators remain largely unaware of the volume (and history) of scholarship in this area.

Because of the explosive growth of the technology-mediated business and management education literature during the past decade (Arbaugh, 2010a; Arbaugh, Godfrey, Johnson, Leisen Pollack, Niendorf, & Wresch, 2009; Sitzmann, Kraiger, Stewart, & Wisher, 2006), we can identify characteristics that are commonly associated with successful online delivery of graduate management education. These characteristics are summarized as recommendations in Table 6.4.

Interactions. An emerging extension of situated learning theory is the Community of Inquiry (COI) framework. Garrison,

Table 6.4   Recommendations for Online and Blended Learning

Category	Recommendations
Interaction	Provide opportunities for peers and instructors to interact online, and at least a few times face to face. Balance the roles of disseminator and facilitator as called for by the content being taught.
Organization	Ensure opportunities for interaction, balancing instructor information/dissemination with participant interaction. Use a variety of activities and ongoing group projects.
Blended Learning	Add online activities for face-to-face students to allow for additional practice opportunities. Provide encouragement and support for participation in these opportunities.

Anderson, and Archer's (2000) COI framework provides a process-oriented, comprehensive theoretical model that contends that higher-order learning outcomes result from interactions that create social, cognitive, and teaching presence. Research indicates that each of these dimensions is related to perceived student learning (Arbaugh, 2013).

Social presence is often considered the starting point of the framework (Garrison & Cleveland-Innes, 2005; Akyol & Garrison, 2008). In the context of online teaching and learning, the definition of social presence has evolved to indicate the degree to which learners feel socially and emotionally connected with others in an online environment (Gunawardena & Zittle, 1997; Richardson & Swan, 2003).

Cognitive presence describes the extent to which learners are able to construct and confirm meaning through sustained reflection and discourse. Drawing from Dewey's notion of scientific inquiry, Garrison, Anderson, and Archer (2001) argue that cognitive presence in online learning is developed through a four-phase process. These phases are

1. A triggering event, through which some issue or problem is identified for further inquiry
2. Exploration, when learners investigate the issue both individually and corporately
3. Integration, when learners construct meaning and generate potential solutions from the ideas developed during exploration, and finally
4. Resolution, when learners select and apply the newly gained knowledge to educational contexts or workplace settings

Teaching presence is, ultimately, the organizing element of COI—the design, facilitation, and direction of cognitive and social processes that lead to realizing personally meaningful and educationally worthwhile learning outcomes (Garrison & Cleveland-Innes, 2005). Teaching presence has been conceptualized as having three components:

1. Instructional design and organization
2. Facilitating discourse, and
3. Direct instruction (Anderson, Rourke, Garrison, & Archer, 2001)

Recent research on the COI using business courses as part of their research samples suggests that teaching presence predicts and influences the extent to which the other types of presence will occur in online courses (Arbaugh, 2007; Ke, 2010; Shea & Bidjerano, 2009). Similar research indicates that to make online learning effective, instructors must play the roles of both disseminator and facilitator (Arbaugh, 2010b; Arbaugh & Hwang, 2006; Ke, 2010; Shea & Bidjerano, 2009), although more recent evidence suggests that the relative importance of these roles may vary by course topic (Arbaugh, 2013).

Organization. To date, course design issues in online graduate management education have received limited attention. However, research does suggest that a primary design factor in effective graduate courses involves organizing for a balance between instructor information dissemination and participant activity. This concept has received empirical support from studies such as Arbaugh and Benbunan-Fich's (2006), which found that online MBA courses were most strongly associated with learning and satisfaction when they were designed on instructor-based content dissemination and group-based learning activities.

A balance between instructor- and student-centered activities is perceptible in the MBA@UNC program at the University of North Carolina's Kenan-Flagler Business School. For each course, approximately two and a half hours a week of asynchronous content from videotaped lectures and cases is accentuated with ninety minutes a week of synchronous interaction with an instructor and twelve to fifteen students via live video chats (Byrne, 2012). The importance of group-based interaction at the graduate level suggests several design features: the use of student groups that have continuity (Hodgson & Reynolds, 2005; Williams, Duray, & Reddy, 2006); an established body of knowledge from which to structure group activities (Benbunan-Fich & Arbaugh, 2006); and a variety of types of assignments (Arbaugh & Rau, 2007).

Blended Learning. Initial research suggests encouraging results for incorporating, or blending, online learning activities into traditional face-to-face classes. Introducing online elements or exercises has shown positive results in numerous studies at the MBA level (Chen & Jones, 2007; Webb, Gill, & Poe, 2005). Online graduate management education often accomplishes such blending via residencies that are interspersed through the program, such as those offered by Indiana's Kelley Direct and the University of Florida's Hough Graduate School of Business. Residencies give the programs opportunities to incorporate socialization rituals, develop student teams, foster case analysis discussions, and cultivate social presence for subsequent online activities.

The benefits of blended instruction in management education include increased confidence about working in virtual project teams (Olson-Buchanan, Rechner, Sanchez, & Schmidtke, 2007); the learner's increased control of the educational experience (Klein, Noe, & Wang, 2006); and enhanced communication skills (Eveleth & Baker-Eveleth, 2003). Initial research has also identified characteristics that influence successful blending, including faculty-driven rather than administration-driven blending initiatives (Alavi & Gallupe, 2003); student peer encouragement (Martins & Kellermanns, 2004); perceived usefulness of course management systems for accessing content (Martins & Kellermanns, 2004); experiential learning exercises

(Proserpio & Gioia, 2007); and adequate technical and administrative support (Alavi & Gallupe, 2003).

Experiential Methods

Experiential learning is one of the most widely used theoretical and practical approaches in management education (A. Y. Kolb & D. A. Kolb, 2009). Simply stated, experiential learning takes place through doing—reflecting on direct experience to construct new knowledge, skills, and attitudes. Although there are a number of theories, D. A. Kolb's (1984) Experiential Learning Theory (ELT) has been the dominant paradigm in the management education domain for more than three decades. Consistent with the theories discussed earlier and based on the constructivist scholarship of John Dewey, Kurt Lewin, Jean Piaget, Carl Rogers, and others, ELT views all learning as relearning—an ongoing reconstruction of the meaning of experience involving a continuous back-and-forth between action and reflection and thinking and feeling. This experience involves the interaction between the learner and his or her environment (Kolb, 1984).

Instructors using an experiential approach strive to create a scenario that facilitates learning. For example, *case studies*—a longtime staple of management education popularized by Harvard Business School (for example, Christensen & Hansen, 1987)—are experiential in that they provide structured situations to develop decision making, critical thinking, problem solving, and related skills.

Another example that uses a slightly different format and medium is the Leadership in Focus video case series produced by Stanford's Center for Leadership Development and Research. The series's goal was to create a leadership mind-set in students through practice and reflection (Benjamin & O'Reilly, 2011; see also Conger & Benjamin, 1999). Leadership in Focus uses real career challenges (for example, role transitions, launching a new initiative, dealing with a personal setback) garnered from recent graduates now employed in managerial positions. The first video's initial two to three minutes are played up to the point at which the graduate has explained the problem he or she confronted; afterward the video is paused to give students time to discuss what action they would take. Then, the next two to three minutes of the video play and describe what the informant did in the situation—without revealing how well it worked. This is followed by additional class discussion, role-playing, or both. Finally, the remainder of the video is played and the informant describes how the problem was resolved and what he or she learned from the experience. The videos are used in conjunction with evidence-based content about leadership and organizational behavior so that principles and action are constantly cross-referenced. This method—starting with the teaching of principles, practicing with cases, reviewing and extending principles, and then practicing again—has long been used successfully in negotiation classes (Lewicki, 1997; Lowenstein, Thompson, & Gentner, 2003).

Similarly, *games, simulations, and role-plays* allow instructors to provide realistic scenarios designed to elicit specific learning outcomes. Because they provide shared experience as a basis for student learning, such exercises are common instructional features in organizational behavior, negotiations, leadership, and similar courses with an interpersonal or soft-skills focus. More recently, developers and instructional designers have been looking for ways to leverage information technology to further enhance the functionality and effectiveness of these methods. For example, *Change Management: Power and Influence* (Judge & Hill, 2010) is a ninety-minute, single-player online simulation with four different scenarios based on the level of the player's organizational role and whether the main driver for change is internal or external. On the basis of existing change management literature, players are challenged to build a guiding coalition in the organization by wielding nearly a dozen different influence techniques. In the first eighteen months after its publication, the simulation had been used by 285 professors and more than 14,500 students in 102 universities.

Individual and group projects are another category of experiential activity that can provide dynamic, problem-based learning opportunities in a real-world setting (DeFillippi & Milter, 2009). Service learning and student consulting projects are two of the more popular types of instructional activities in this category. Service learning is particularly interesting for its potential to influence student values, ethical behavior, and social awareness (Kenworthy-U'Ren, 2008; Yorio & Ye, 2012). Generally speaking, properly designed group projects can provide a realistic context in which students can practice and develop their leadership, teamwork, conflict management, and other interpersonal skills.

Not surprisingly, group projects are a common feature of management and program capstone courses. A recently launched initiative at the University of Virginia's Darden School of Business exemplifies this trend. The capstone is an intensive week-long, two-pronged program during the last week of the first-year curriculum. The 2011 inaugural cohort involved twelve-student teams, each designing and running a business venture during the week to raise money for a local nonprofit organization. The other prong involved five class sections of sixty students each partnering with a local nonprofit. Each section was tasked with developing a business plan for its nonprofit that included developing a compelling purpose statement; providing a rigorous assessment of the magnitude and scope of the problem being addressed; assessing how the organization can or should help with this problem; and outlining a proposed local, national, or global policy to deal with the problem. Students turned over the money from their entrepreneurial ventures to the five partnering organizations and presented their business plans to Darden faculty, staff, and media, as well as to directors and staff from the nonprofits (James, 2011). Typical of a well-designed service learning project, Darden students both increased their leadership skills and their sensitivity to community needs while providing tangible benefits to community partners.

Last, *internships* and *practicums* are common, sometimes required, features of many full-time MBA programs. They are another category of experiential learning, as they provide an authentic opportunity for students to apply and test what they have learned. For many two-year graduate business programs, these experiences are typically scheduled between the first and second years. The work experience provides students with invaluable development opportunities to apply what they have learned and, in many cases, explore career opportunities with potential employers. The experience also provides employers with an effective way to thoroughly evaluate potential new hires; a source of talented, motivated, and low-cost labor; and a strengthened relationship with the business school.

Facilitating Experiential Learning

Despite the increasing prevalence of these and other experiential methods, the unfortunate truth is that too often most faculty members teach the way that they were taught: through lectures or other similar approaches. Although the results have not always been ideal, this reality is evidence of two things: the power of observational learning highlighted by social learning theory, and the lack of formal training that doctoral students receive in general pedagogical and content pedagogical knowledge.

Drawing on the theory and evidence reviewed earlier, we offer several recommendations to help faculty and program administrators facilitate an experiential learning approach. It should be noted, however, that although this is not an exhaustive list; the principles presented here are interdependent and are not meant to be selected and implemented in a piecemeal fashion. The overall effectiveness of such an approach depends on careful and balanced consideration of several factors that are discussed following and summarized in Table 6.5.

Table 6.5 Recommendations for Experiential Learning

Category	Recommendations
Alignment	Select instructional methods that align with desired learning goal (that is, cognitive, behavioral, or affective).
Variety	Vary method and context of instruction to facilitate long-term retention and transfer.
Sequencing	Offer a guiding framework to foster and sustain motivation to learn. Choose a sequencing model that best suits what is to be learned.
Reflection	Engage learners in critical reflection, challenging them to continue applying and experimenting.

Striving for Alignment. The notion that different learning goals require different instructional approaches has become a fundamental tenet of modern learning theory (Bransford, Brown, & Cocking, 2000; Gagné, 1984, 1985). Similarly, there is reason to believe that experiential methods may vary in efficacy with respect to certain categories of learning goals (such as affective, behavioral, and cognitive). For example, in a meta-review, Yorio and Ye (2012) found that service learning projects had positive effects on student cognitive development, social awareness, and personal awareness. Although more evidence of service learning's effects on skill and attitudinal outcomes is still needed, the review does provide compelling evidence that this particular experiential approach is useful for achieving cognitive learning outcomes.

As Social Learning Theory and Experiential Learning Theory suggest, if we want to teach skills and behaviors, we need to show, model, and allow students to practice these behaviors in a variety of situations. Simulations, role-plays, group projects, and similar experiential methods are much better suited for these types of learning goals, but they typically take more time and can have the limitations we noted earlier. One possibility emerging from continued technological advances is an increasing number of lectures that can be recorded as digital video and watched repeatedly by learners at their convenience. If students can acquire basic conceptual knowledge in a course this way, it could free up valuable class time for integrating experiential learning activities.

Introducing Variety. The second recommendation stresses the importance of multiplicity. Varying learning conditions, using different cognitive processes, and applying knowledge, skills, and attitudes in different ways and in different settings makes learning and in some cases, teaching, more difficult. But ultimately it leads to more effective outcomes (Bransford & others, 2000; Halpern & Hakel, 2003).

In terms of Social Learning Theory, variety supports learning retention through varied repetition, and it encourages learning reproduction by helping learners identify the salient factors and conditions that warrant recalling knowledge or demonstrating a specified behavior. A review of simulation studies (Sitzmann, 2011) provided compelling support for the effectiveness of simulation to learning. However, the study also concluded that a simulation was more effective when it actively (as opposed to passively) conveyed course content and when it supplemented other instructional methods (as opposed to when it was the only method).

In terms of context, the importance of similarity between the learning and its application is a long-established principle in research on transfer of learning—a principle supported by the theories discussed earlier in the chapter. Although placing knowledge in context is important for initial learning, the learner must be able to achieve some abstract understanding of the underlying principles to be able to generalize to new situations (Bransford & others, 2000). Introducing learners to multiple contexts over time while also emphasizing the development of metacognitive skills is believed to enhance learning transfer and improve its generalizability.

Choosing Appropriate Sequencing Strategies. Our third suggestion is to sequence learning activities according to student needs. We know from motivation research that experiences that are challenging, but not too challenging, are optimal for making students work most persistently at the highest level of effort (Locke & Latham, 2002). Vygotsky's (1978) notion of a zone of proximal development (ZPD) is arguably the earliest articulation of the notion that learners have an identifiable range of developmental challenge. Cognitive Load Theory and the educational concept of scaffolding are but two more recent examples of this fundamental idea's theoretical adaptation. From a practical standpoint, this relates to the common instructional challenge of how to structure what students are to learn. There are numerous schools of thought on this matter, and we cannot provide a single generalizable rule of thumb for every case. As an illustration of the difference in sequencing strategies, Gagné's (1985) hierarchical sequencing recommends a bottom-up approach, moving from specific details and gradually building up to the generalities. Alternatively, Ausubel's (1963) strategy is a top-down sequence in which an organizing framework is presented first, followed by increasingly more detailed ideas.

So what recommendation can we offer here? As suggested earlier, one strategy is to use worked examples to tax a learner's germane cognitive capacity as much as possible. Of course, this presupposes that the instructor has used various assessments to understand the limits of each student. It further suggests the need for continued assessment to gauge students' individual progression through the stages of learning. Ultimately, the purpose behind all the sequencing strategies is to ensure that learners can approach a topic or learning objective in a systematic way and learn effectively. Thus, the answer is to select the sequencing strategy that best meets the needs of the subject matter, the intended learners, the learning and transfer contexts, and the instructors' experience of the students (Rothwell & Kazanas, 2003).

Encouraging Reflection. Finally, we remind those who would use an experiential approach of an old adage: Experience alone is a poor teacher. In experiential learning, reflection is a critical developmental process that allows learning to take place (Merriam, 2008). This is consistent with the more recent taxonomies of learning that emphasize metacognitive skills and self-regulatory processes as cognitive learning outcomes. Acquiring these particular cognitive skills makes it possible for students to learn more from subsequent experience. Along with sense-making, self-assessment, self-regulation, and other metacognitive processes, teaching practices such as experiential learning that emphasize the development of these metacognitive skills have been shown to increase the degree to which students transfer their learning to new settings and events (Bransford & others, 2000).

Indeed, schools such as INSEAD have gone so far as to offer a Personal Development Elective (PDE) that gives students the opportunity to work with a psychotherapist while going through its intensive ten-month program. The PDE consists of twenty personal, one-hour sessions with a psychotherapist whom the student chooses from a pool of twenty therapists. An intensive qualitative study of differences among those who chose the PDE and those who did not showed that nonparticipants tended to describe what they had learned during the program mostly in terms of abstract knowledge and professional skills. In contrast, students who went through PDE reported an additional layer of learning that encompassed three categories of outcomes: "self awareness, self management, and experiences of integration related to revisiting their life narratives" (Petriglieri, Wood, & Petriglieri, 2011, pp. 438–439). We realize that most schools will not be able to devote the same magnitude of resources to student self-reflection that INSEAD does. Nevertheless, the careful conceptualization and detailed study of INSEAD's program provides a model for other schools to emulate at a less intensive level.

What Are the Benefits of Taking Learning Seriously?

The concept of advancing the importance of learning in MBA programs is not entirely novel. In fact, it is reflected in the emphasis that accrediting bodies like the Association to Advance Collegiate Schools of Business, the European Quality Improvement System (EQUIS), and the Association of MBA (AMBA) place on learning goals and assurance of learning. Moreover, these agencies recognize that the choices instructors make in the classroom influence learning outcomes. For example, AACSB's 2012 accrediting standards discuss learning and argue that "passive learning should not be the sole, or primary, model for collegiate business education" (AACSB, 2012, p. 31). A subsequent section of the standards emphasizes the essential role of faculty–student interaction, which can take the form of opportunities for student questions, feedback, and discussion (p. 39). These suggestions are positive and useful, not to mention fully consistent with our review here. But they are a bit too broad to provide specific guidance to faculty who are teaching a particular course.

Similarly, AACSB standards are useful but do not provide the concrete ideas about learning and teaching that faculty need to increase how much their students learn. This is true because faculty must develop pedagogical knowledge and PCK over time while they learn to be better teachers. In this chapter, we presented a few theories of learning outcomes and process and then provided a cursory examination of the SOTL literature and literature specifically relevant to major trends in MBA education. We contend that these theories and literatures are underused, and we need to change how business schools select, train, reward, and support faculty to increase the prevalence of PCK among business school faculty. With these increases, business schools should get better and better at obtaining the learning outcomes they seek from their students.

There is another noteworthy benefit to having faculty with a stronger knowledge base related to teaching and learning: This allows programs to make better use of limited resources. If, for example, faculty can discern a way to help students understand, calculate, and believe in the time value of money in 20 percent less time, then faculty can spend fewer hours on that topic (and students who have mastered the concept will be able to appreciate the value of their reduced learning time). In lieu of extra work on that topic, students can engage in experiential activities that let them apply the concept in various settings. Moreover, faculty can engage in other activities, whether research oriented or teaching related. From the perspective of a dean or program director, testing learning outcomes and actively experimenting with different teaching approaches raises the possibility of discovering more efficient ways of teaching that result in the same learning outcomes.

There are, of course, challenges associated with emphasizing teaching and learning. Encouraging faculty to spend time advancing their teaching and publishing in journals that are not listed in rankings like the *Financial Times* may reduce time spent on more traditional scholarship and thus reduce the institution's research profile. Whether this *would* occur is an open question. It could be that creating a better balance between faculty members' content and pedagogical knowledge would instead help build a more vibrant learning community among faculty. And in some colleges, it could be that opportunities to study teaching and learning would help revitalize the careers of faculty who have burned out or lost interest in traditional research.

Looking to the future, we believe it would be beneficial if business schools, and associated stakeholders, made a stronger investment in management education scholarship. Ongoing research can help develop context-specific guidelines for faculty engaged with graduate management education. This research is slowly but surely building the various forms of knowledge that Shulman advocated. Of course, Shulman's premise was that teaching should be a profession with a knowledge base. Unfortunately, in its current state, the business school professoriate is part of a profession that does not generally place much value on any form of knowledge beyond content knowledge.

In this chapter, we have offered specific recommendations for how business schools might follow the lead of some schools and other disciplines that are advancing teaching and learning. We have also presented specific suggestions for how current trends in management education—online and experiential activities— can be made more effective. If faculty members, guided and supported by their administrators, take their professional role as teachers more seriously, then students will benefit during their program by learning more, and after graduation by showing off even greater knowledge and skill—and perhaps even greater wisdom.

Summing Up

- Faculty who possess knowledge of content, pedagogy, pedagogical content, and technological pedagogical content should be better able to create fruitful learning processes for, and foster desired learning outcomes with, their students.

- Existing theory on learning processes and outcomes (that is, pedagogical knowledge) offers a number of implications for what faculty should do and measure to improve learning.

- Business schools that seek to advance learning should consider their own management practices and alter them in ways that encourage acquiring and developing faculty with relevant knowledge and motivation to teach effectively.

- Online and blended delivery is becoming increasingly common, and it can be better designed and delivered if theory and research are used as guides.

- Experiential learning is considered critical to graduate management education, and it can also be more effective if theory and research are used as guides.

> If we are to take learning seriously, we must profess teaching, and take our profession as teachers seriously.

—Lee Shulman, 1999

Note

1. Shulman argued for a longer list of knowledge areas, but those lists changed slightly over time, and no consensus has emerged on what would be a complete list (Mishra & Koehler, 2006). As a separate point regarding terminology, some learning scholars prefer to use the term *andragogy* to refer to theory and practice related to adult learning. In this chapter we use the term *pedagogical* to maintain consistency with Shulman.

References

AACSB. "Business Accreditation Standards." 2012. http://www.aacsb.edu/accreditation/business/standards/participants/intent.asp

Akyol, Z., & Garrison, D. R. "The Development of a Community of Inquiry Over Time in an Online Course: Understanding the Progression and Integration of Social, Cognitive and Teaching Presence." *Journal of Asynchronous Learning Networks*, 2008, 12(3), 3–22.

Alavi, M., & Gallupe, R. B. "Using Information Technology in Learning: Case Studies in Business and Management Education Programs." *Academy of Management Learning and Education*, 2003, 2, 139–153.

Alexander, P. A., Schallert, D. L., & Reynolds, R. E. "What Is Learning Anyway? A Topographical Perspective Reconsidered." *Educational Psychology*, 2009, 44, 176–192.

Anderson, L., & Krathwohl, D. A. *Taxonomy for Learning, Teaching and Assessing: A Revision of Bloom's Taxonomy of Educational Objectives*. New York: Longman, 2001.

Anderson, T., Rourke, L., Garrison, D. R., & Archer, W. "Assessing Teaching Presence in a Computer Conferencing Context." *Journal of Asynchronous Learning Networks*, 2001, 5(2), 1–17.

Arbaugh, J. B. "An Empirical Verification of the Community of Inquiry Framework." *Journal of Asynchronous Learning Networks*, 2007, 11(1), 73–85.

Arbaugh, J. B. "Does the Community of Inquiry Framework Predict Outcomes in Online MBA Courses?" *International Review of Research in Open and Distance Learning*, 2008, 9, 1–21.

Arbaugh, J. B. "Do Undergraduates and MBAs Differ Online? Initial Conclusions from the Literature." *Journal of Leadership and Organizational Studies*, 2010a, 17(2), 129–142.

Arbaugh, J. B. *Online and Blended Business Education for the 21st Century: Current Research and Future Directions.* Oxford, UK: Chandos, 2010b.

Arbaugh, J. B. "Does Academic Discipline Moderate COI-Course Outcome Relationships in Online MBA Courses?" *The Internet and Higher Education*, 2013, 16(2), 16–28.

Arbaugh, J. B., & Benbunan-Fich, R. "An Investigation of Epistemological and Social Dimensions of Teaching in Online Learning Environments." *Academy of Management Learning & Education*, 2006, 5, 435–447.

Arbaugh, J. B., Godfrey, M. R., Johnson, M., Leisen Pollack, B., Niendorf, B., & Wresch, W. "Research in Online and Blended Learning in the Business Disciplines: Key Findings and Possible Future Directions." *The Internet and Higher Education*, 2009, 12(2), 71–87.

Arbaugh, J. B., & Hwang, A. "Does 'Teaching Presence' Exist in Online MBA Courses?" *The Internet and Higher Education*, 2006, 9(1), 9–21.

Arbaugh, J. B., & Rau, B. L. "A Study of Disciplinary, Structural, and Behavioral Effects on Course Outcomes in Online MBA Courses." *Decision Sciences Journal of Innovative Education*, 2007, 5, 65–95.

Ausubel, D. *The Psychology of Meaningful Verbal Learning.* New York: Grune & Stratton, 1963.

Bain, K. *What the Best College Teachers Do.* Cambridge, Mass.: Harvard University Press, 2004.

Bandura, A. *Social Foundations of Thought and Action.* Englewood Cliffs, N.J.: Prentice-Hall, 1986.

Bandura, A. *Self-Efficacy: The Exercise of Control.* New York: W. H. Freeman, 1997.

Benbunan-Fich, R., & Arbaugh, J. B. "Separating the Effects of Knowledge Construction and Group Collaboration in Web-Based Courses." *Information & Management*, 2006, 43, 778–793.

Benjamin, B., & O'Reilly, C. "Becoming a Leader: Early Career Challenges Faced by MBA Graduates." *Academy of Management Learning & Education*, 2011, 10, 452–472.

Boyer, E. L. *Scholarship Reconsidered: Priorities of the Professoriate.* Princeton, N.J.: Carnegie Foundation for the Advancement of Teaching, 1990.

Bransford, J. D., Brown, A. L., & Cocking, R. R. (eds.). *How People Learn: Brain, Mind, Experience, and School* (exp. ed.). Washington, D.C.: National Academy Press, 2000.

Bransford, J. D., Stevens, R., Schwartz, D., Meltzoff, A. N., Pea, R., Roschelle, J., Vye, N., Kuhl, P. K., Bell, P., Barron, B., Reeves, B., & Sabelli, N. "Learning Theories and Education: Toward a Decade of Synergy." In P. A. Alexander & P. H. Winne (eds.), *Handbook of Educational Psychology* (2nd ed., pp. 209–244). Washington, D.C.: American Psychological Association, 2006.

Brown, K. G., & Sitzmann, T. "Training and Employee Development for Improved Performance." In S. Zedeck (ed.), *Handbook of Industrial and Organizational Psychology* (Vol. 2, pp. 469–503). Washington, D.C.: American Psychological Association, 2011.

Bujak, K. R., Baker, P.M.A., DeMillo, R., & Sandulli, F. D. "The Evolving University: Beyond Disruptive Change and Institutional Innovation." Paper presented at the XXII World Congress of Political Science, Madrid, Spain, July 8, 2012.

Byrne, J. A. "UNC Brings Rarity to Online MBA Programs: Credibility." March 23, 2012. http://management.fortune.cnn.com/2012/03/23/unc-online-mba/

Chen, C. C., & Jones, K. T. "Blended Learning vs. Traditional Classroom Settings: Assessing Effectiveness and Student Perceptions in an MBA Accounting Course." *Journal of Educators Online*, 2007, 4(1), 1–15.

Chia, R. "The Nature of Knowledge and Knowing in the Context of Management Learning, Education, and Development." In S. J. Armstrong & C. V. Fukami (eds.), *Handbook of Management, Learning, Education, and Development* (pp. 25–41). Thousand Oaks, Calif.: Sage, 2009.

Christensen, C. R., & Hansen, A. J. *Teaching and the Case Method.* Boston, Mass.: Harvard Business School Press, 1987.

Clayton, D. E. "Student Evaluations of Teaching: Are They Related to What Students Learn?" *Journal of Marketing Education*, 2009, 31, 16–30.

Conger, J. A., & Benjamin, B. *Building Leaders: How Successful Companies Develop the Next Generation.* San Francisco: Jossey-Bass, 1999.

Dede, C. J. "Emerging Technologies: Impacts on Distance Learning." *Annals of the American Academy of Political & Social Science* (pp. 146–158). Beverly Hills, Calif.: Sage, 1991.

DeFillippi, R., & Milter, R. G. "Problem-Based and Project-Based Learning Approaches: Applying Knowledge to Authentic Situations." In S. J. Armstrong & C. V. Fukami (eds.), *The SAGE Handbook of Management *Learning, Education and Development* (pp. 344–363). Thousand Oaks, Calif.: Sage, 2009.

Eveleth, D. M., & Baker-Eveleth, L. J. "Developing Dialogue Skill: A Qualitative Investigation of an On-Line Collaboration in a Team Management Course." *Journal of Education for Business*, 2003, 78, 228–233.

"45 Journals Used in FT Research Rank." *Financial Times*, February 22, 2012. http://www.ft.com/intl/cms/s/2/3405a512-5cbb-11e1-8f1f-00144fea bdc0.html#axzz2IAgeJFeI

Gagné, R. M. "Learning Outcomes and Their Effects: Useful Categories of Human Performance." *American Psychologist*, 1984, 39(4), 377–385.

Gagné, R. M. *The Conditions of Learning and Theory of Instruction* (4th ed.). New York: Holt, Rinehart & Winston, 1985.

Garrison, D. R., Anderson, T., & Archer, W. "Critical Inquiry in a Text-Based Environment: Computer Conferencing in Higher Education." *The Internet and Higher Education*, 2000, 2(2–3), 87–105.

Garrison, D. R., Anderson, T., & Archer, W. "Critical Thinking, Cognitive Presence and Computer Conferencing in Distance Education." *American Journal of Distance Education*, 2001, 15(1), 7–23.

Garrison, D. R., & Cleveland-Innes, M. "Facilitating Cognitive Presence in Online Learning: Interaction Is Not Enough." *American Journal of Distance Education*, 2005, 19(3), 133–148.

Gawronski, B., & Bodenhausen, G. V. "Associative and Propositional Processes in Evaluation: An Integrative Review of Implicit and Explicit Attitude Change." *Psychological Bulletin*, 2006, 132(5), 692–731.

Glassick, C. E. "Boyer's Expanded Definition of scholarship, the Standards for Assessing Scholarship, and the Elusiveness of the Scholarship of Teaching. *Academic Medicine*, 2000, 75, 877–880.

Gunawardena, C. N., & Zittle, F. J. "Social Presence as a Predictor of Satisfaction Within a Computer-Mediated Conferencing Environment." *American Journal of Distance Education*, 1997, 11(3), 8–26.

Halpern, D. F., & Hakel, M. D. "Applying the Science of Learning to the University and Beyond." *Change*, 2003, 35(4), 36–41.

Hattie, J., & Marsh, H. W. "The Relationship Between Research and Teaching: A Meta-Analysis." *Review of Educational Research*, 1996, 66, 507–542.

Hodgson, V., & Reynolds, M. "Consensus, Difference and 'Multiple Communities' in Networked Learning." *Studies in Higher Education*, 2005, 30(1), 11–24.

Ives, B., & Jarvenpaa, S.L. "Will the Internet Revolutionize Business Education and Research?" *Sloan Management Review*, 1996, 37(3), 33–41.

James, E. H. "Learning to Lead While Giving Back: An MBA Capstone Leadership Experience." *MBA Innovation*, 2011, Summer, 17–19.

Judge, W. Q., & Hill, L. A. *Change Management: Power and Influence.* Boston: Harvard Business School, 2010.

Ke, F. "Examining Online Teaching, Cognitive, and Social Presence for Adult Students." *Computers & Education,* 2010, 55, 808–820.

Kenworthy-U'Ren, A. "A Decade of Service-Learning: A Review of the Field Ten Years after JOBE's Seminal Special Issue." *Journal of Business Ethics,* 2008, 81, 811–822.

Kickul, J., Janssen-Selvaudrai, C., & Griffiths, M. D. "A Blended Value Framework for Educating the Next Cadre of Social Entrepreneurs." *Academy of Management Learning & Education,* 2012, 11, 479–493.

Klein, H. J., Noe, R. A., & Wang, C. "Motivation to Learn and Course Outcomes: The Impact of Delivery Mode, Learning Goal Orientation, and Perceived Barriers and Enablers." *Personnel Psychology,* 2006, 59, 665–702.

Kolb, A. Y., & Kolb, D. A. "Experiential Learning Theory: A Dynamic, Holistic Approach to Management Learning, Education, and Development." In S. J. Armstrong & C. V. Fukami (eds.), *The SAGE Handbook of Management Education, Learning, and Development* (pp. 42–68). Thousand Oaks, Calif.: Sage, 2009.

Kolb, D. A. *Experiential Learning.* Englewood Cliffs, N.J.: Prentice Hall, 1984.

Kraiger, K., Ford, J. K., & Salas, E. "Application of Cognitive, Skill-Based, and Affective Theories of Learning Outcomes to New Methods of Training Evaluation." *Journal of Applied Psychology,* 1993, 78(2), 311–328.

Lave, J., & Wenger, E. *Situated Learning: Legitimate Peripheral Participation.* Cambridge: Cambridge University Press, 1991.

Lewicki, R., & Bailey, J. B. "The Research-Teaching Nexus: Tensions and Opportunities." In S. J. Armstrong & C. V. Fukami (eds.), *The SAGE Handbook of Management Learning, Education and Development* (pp. 385–402). Thousand Oaks, Calif.: Sage, 2009.

Lewicki, R. J. "Teaching Negotiations in Business Schools: The State of the Practice." *Negotiation Journal,* 1997, 13, 253–269.

Lewis, L. H., & Williams, C. J. "Experiential Learning: Past and Present." *New Directions for Adult and Continuing Education,* 1994, 62, 5–16.

Locke, E. A., & Latham, G. P. "Building a Practically Useful Theory of Goal Setting and Task Motivation." *American Psychologist,* 2002, 57(9), 705.

Lowenstein, J., Thompson, L., & Gentner, D. "Analogical Learning in Negotiation Teams: Comparing Cases Promotes Learning and Transfer." *Academy of Management Learning & Education,* 2003, 2, 119–127.

Martins, L., & Kellermanns, F. W. "Student Acceptance of a Web-Based Course Management System." *Academy of Management Learning & Education,* 2004, 3, 7–26.

Merriam, S. B. "Adult Learning Theory for the Twenty-First Century." *New Directions for Adult & Continuing Education*, 2008, 119, 93–98.

Mintzberg, H. *Managers Not MBAs: A Hard Look at the Soft Practice of Managing and Management Development*. San Francisco, Calif.: Berrett-Koehler, 2004.

Mishra, P., & Koehler, M. J. "Technological Pedagogical Content Knowledge: A New Framework for Teacher Knowledge." *Teachers College Record*, 2006, 108, 1017–1054.

Olson-Buchanan, J. B., Rechner, P. L., Sanchez, R. J., & Schmidtke, J. M. "Using Virtual Teams in a Management Principles Course." *Education + Training*, 2007, 49, 408–423.

Paas, F., Renkl, A., & Sweller, J. "Cognitive Load Theory and Instructional Design: Recent Developments." *Educational Psychologist*, 2003, 38, 1–4.

Parry, D. "Mobile Perspectives: On Teaching Mobile Literacy." *Educause Review*, 2011, 46(2), 14–16.

Petriglieri, G., Wood, J. D., & Petriglieri, J. L. "Up Close and Personal: Building Foundations for Leaders' Development Through the Personalization of Management Learning." *Academy of Management Learning & Education*, 2011, 10, 430–450.

Proserpio, L., & Gioia, D. A. "Teaching the Virtual Generation." *Academy of Management Learning & Education*, 2007, 6, 69–80.

Redpath, L. "Confronting the Bias Against On-Line Learning in Management Education." *Academy of Management Learning & Education*, 2012, 11, 125–140.

Richardson, J. C., & Swan, K. "Examining Social Presence in Online Courses in Relation to Students' Perceived Learning and Satisfaction." *Journal of Asynchronous Learning Networks*, 2003, 7(1). http://www.aln.org/publications/jaln/v7n1/index.asp

Rothwell, W. J., & Kazanas, H. C. *Mastering the Instructional Design Process* (3rd ed.). San Francisco, Calif.: Pfeiffer, 2003.

Rynes, S. L., & Brown, K. G. "Where Are We in the 'Long March to Legitimacy?' Assessing the Legitimacy of scholarship in Management Learning and Education." *Academy of Management Learning & Education*, 2011, 10, 561–582.

Shea, P., & Bidjerano, T. "Community of Inquiry as a Theoretical Framework to Foster 'Epistemic Engagement' and 'Cognitive Presence' in Online Education." *Computers and Education*, 2009, 52, 543–553.

Shulman, L. "Knowledge and Teaching: Foundations of the New Reform." *Harvard Educational Review*, 1987, 57, 1–22.

Shulman, L. "Taking Learning Seriously." *Change*, 1999, 31(4), 10–17.

Sitzmann, T. "A Meta-Analytic Examination of the Instructional Effectiveness of Computer-Based Simulation Games." *Personnel Psychology*, 2011, 64, 489–528.

Sitzmann, T., & Ely, K. "A Meta-Analysis of Self-Regulated Learning in Work-Related Training and Educational Attainment: What We Know and Where We Need to Go." *Psychological Bulletin*, 2011, 137, 421–442.

Sitzmann, T., Ely, K., Brown, K. G., & Bauer, K. N. "Self-Assessment of Knowledge: A Cognitive Learning or Affective Measure?" *Academy of Management Learning & Education*, 2010, 9, 169–191.

Sitzmann, T., Kraiger, K., Stewart, D., & Wisher, R. "The Comparative Effectiveness of Web-Based and Classroom Instruction: A Meta-analysis." *Personnel Psychology*, 2006, 59, 623–664.

Snyder, B. R. *The Hidden Curriculum.* Cambridge, Mass.: MIT Press, 1973.

United Nations. 2012. *The 6 Principles for Responsible Management Education.* http://www.unprme.org/the-6-principles/index.php

Vygotsky, L. S. *Mind in Society: The Development of Higher Psychological Processes.* Cambridge, Mass.: Harvard University Press, 1978.

Webb, H. W., Gill, G., & Poe, G. "Teaching With the Case Method Online: Pure Versus Hybrid Approaches." *Decision Sciences Journal of Innovative Education*, 2005, 3, 223–250.

Weldon, T. "Does Merit Pay for Teachers Have Merit? Pros and Cons of New Models for Teacher Compensation." The Knowledge Center, Council of State Governments. November 7, 2011. http://knowledgecenter.csg.org/kc/content/capitol-research-does-merit-pay-teachers-have-merit-pros-and-cons-new-models-teacher-compensation

Williams, E. A., Duray, R., & Reddy, V. 2006. "Teamwork Orientation, Group Cohesiveness, and Student Learning: A Study of the Use of Teams in Online Distance Education." *Journal of Management Education*, 2006, 30, 592–616.

Yorio, P. L., & Ye, F. "A Meta-analysis on the Effects of Service-Learning on the Social, Personal, and Cognitive Outcomes of Learning." *Academy of Management Learning & Education*, 2012, 11, 9–27.

Young, J. R. "At Conference, Leaders of 'Traditional' Online Learning Meet Upstart Free Providers." *Chronicle of Higher Education* (Wired Campus blog). October 11, 2012. http://chronicle.com/blogs/wiredcampus/at-conference-leaders-of-traditional-online-learning-meet-upstart-free-providers/40426?cid=wc&utm_source=wc&utm_medium=en

7

STUDENT ENGAGEMENT: SELECTION, MANAGEMENT, AND OUTCOMES

Daniel C. Feldman
University of Georgia

Key Topics Covered in This Chapter

- Common assumptions about student engagement
- Multidimensional nature of student engagement
- Creating more engaging environments for MBA students
- Situational factors determining levels of student engagement
- Relationship of student engagement to MBA program outcomes
- Matching student aspirations and profiles with MBA program goals

The question is one that's been repeatedly discussed among business school deans, MBA directors, career services professionals, student affairs staff, and alumni: How can we engage students more fully in the MBA program experience? The question itself, however, makes at least four assumptions about the nature of MBA student engagement:

1. There is widespread consensus among business school stakeholders about the activities in which MBA students should be most engaged.

2. MBA programs have it largely within their power to create highly engaging environments.

3. Students generally want to be highly engaged in the MBA program experience.

4. MBA student engagement is positively related to desired program outcomes, such as cognitive learning, professional development, and placement.

This chapter addresses each of these assumptions in turn. In the first section, we highlight the conflicts among stakeholders about the activities in which they want MBA students to be engaged. Faculty members would like the primary target of that engagement to be acquisition of cognitive knowledge and skills. The student affairs staff would like students to participate in professional development and extracurricular activities. Many business school deans, MBA directors, and career services professionals want them to concentrate on the employment search so that a high percentage will obtain high-paying jobs by the time they graduate. Because of all these conflicting views, most MBA students receive mixed signals about where their priorities should lie.

In the second section of the chapter, we highlight the situational factors that are most likely to lead to (or detract from) student engagement. As all the chapters in this volume discuss, business schools can use a variety of strategies to enhance the MBA student experience, from revising the nature of the curriculum to altering the types and quality of available career services. At the same time, it is important to understand that business schools cannot force MBA students to fully engage in program activities; situational pulls and pushes influence them.

Further, these countervailing forces are set in motion not only by different groups of stakeholders within business schools but also by family members and friends who feel they also have legitimate claims on MBA students' time. As Seashore has noted, "Partners, children, and intimate friends are often confused, angered, or envious in the face of an intrusive and elusive "crazy" program that has stolen their dear one away. . . . It can be a depressing experience to realize that changes in one's own life-style create powerful waves in the systems of which one is a part" (Seashore, 1975, p. 2).

In the third section, we address the broader question of what students want. We observe that numerous MBA students do not desire to be deeply engaged in some of the activities key stakeholder groups see as critical (Debnath, Tandon, & Pointer, 2007). For example, the work of Beier and Kanfer (2010) and Noe, Tews, and Dachner (2010) highlight that personality differences help explain why some students are more engageable than others. Consequently, input processes (recruitment and admissions) may be as important as throughput processes (classroom education and career management services) in driving MBA student engagement.

In the fourth section, we consider whether student engagement is related to MBA programs' desired outcomes, including performance in the classroom, professional development outside the classroom, and job-hunting success. We suggest here that MBA students' psychological engagement in their coursework is positively related to how MBA students feel about their programs (Noe & others, 2010) and how much knowledge and skill they acquire (Kahn, 1990). There is some indirect evidence, at least, that participating in extracurricular activities and professional development opportunities helps power job-hunting success (GMAC, 2011). However, even though student engagement in the classroom is positively correlated with engagement in career planning (Boswell, Zimmerman, & Swider, 2012; Kenny,

Blustein, Haase, Jackson, & Perry, 2006), the research suggests that students' engagement in their own career development drives their engagement in classroom learning, not vice versa.

In the last section of the chapter, we review the implications of our arguments for the strategies MBA programs use to engage their students. As we suggest, it is important for MBA programs to be more selective and deliberative about the activities in which they try to engage their students. Moreover, rather than asking how we can increase MBA student engagement as a goal in and of itself, perhaps we should be asking whether MBA students are as engaged as they want or need to be.

The Multidimensional Nature of Student Engagement

In this chapter, we focus on MBA students for two main reasons. First, they are the largest segment of the graduate business school population; second, the majority of research on student engagement in graduate business schools has been conducted in the context of MBA education. Nonetheless, much of the material here is also germane to other graduate programs in business schools (such as master's of accountancy, marketing research, mathematical finance, and human resource management).

Although the term *student engagement* has been widely used in academia, there is no widespread agreement about what it means in practice. In the literature on education and training, the traditional focus of engagement research has been on motivation and how to energize students to acquire greater cognitive knowledge (Chen & Klimoski, 2007). To that end, this line of research has mainly examined how to alter the behavior of the instructor, information delivery mode, program structure, and learning context to encourage student learning (Goldstein, 1974). In recent years, engagement research has shifted from a focus on the instructor to a focus on the learner (Kraiger & Ford, 2007; Noe & others, 2010). Researchers are now paying greater attention to student activation and the role learners play in self-motivating and self-directing their own educations (Brint, Cantwell, & Hannerman, 2008).

In the organizational sciences literature, it has been harder to pin down precisely what scholars mean when they talk about engagement. In early work on this topic, Kahn (1990, p. 694) defines engagement as "the harnessing of organization members' selves to their work roles; in engagement, people express themselves physically, cognitively, and emotionally during role performances." Maslach, Schaufeli, and Leiter (2001) conceptualize engagement as a psychological state characterized by energy, involvement, and efficacy, while Salanova, Augt, and Peiro (2005) characterize it as encompassing vigor (high levels of energy), dedication (high levels of enthusiasm and pride), and absorption (high levels of involvement in the task itself).

Each research stream identifies energy and involvement as key elements of student engagement, yet they differ in the importance they attribute to different agents (the instructors versus the students) and the scope of the engagement. For example, the industrial psychology and educational psychology tradition has taken as its main focus student engagement in cognitive learning, whereas the organizational sciences literature has broadened its focus to include the commitment of affective, emotional, and physical resources to the school experience, too.

For the purposes of this chapter, we define MBA student engagement as the amount of time, energy, and enthusiasm students devote to acquiring new skills and knowledge, participating in professional self-development and extracurricular activities, and self-directing their job search. This definition captures the student-as-agent view of engagement in more recent research on the topic while at the same time broadening the focus of graduate business school students' engagement to activities outside the classroom.

Most notably, the scope of MBA student engagement extends beyond classroom learning to include nonclassroom and non-school-based activities. As the GMAC 2011 Global

Management Education Graduate Survey suggests, there are numerous dimensions along which MBA students assess the value of their programs: faculty, admissions, fellow students, program structure, curriculum, program management, student services, and career services (GMAC, 2011). To discuss engagement only in the context of classroom learning without examining engagement in nonclassroom settings does a disservice to the nature of the MBA student experience.

Further, this definition highlights that students' engagement in one valued activity is likely to occur at the expense of engagement in some other activity (Hobfoll, 1989). Certainly, all the recent research in cognitive psychology has led to the conclusion that individuals have only limited amounts of psychological energy and cognitive attention (Kahneman, 2011; Pinker, 2002). Consequently, the energy and attention students put into any one task come at the expense of the energy and attention they could potentially put into other tasks (Lavie, 2010). In fact, when Salanova and others (2005) measured absorption in their conceptualization of engagement, they used such scale items as "When I'm working, I forget everything else around me." Almost by definition, then, high levels of engagement in one arena mean lower levels of engagement in others (Schacter, 2001).

It is not surprising, then, that important stakeholders find themselves in a battle for MBA students' time and enthusiasm. One of the consequences of these conflicting pulls and pushes on MBA students is "brownouts" in their engagement; at any one point in time, a significant segment of the student population is disengaged from some activity deemed essential by at least one important stakeholder group (Feldman, 2005). Indeed, as Mintzberg (2004) noted in his critique of graduate business education, MBA students are often frenetically engaged in too many activities. The unfortunate result, he argues, is that students have little "white space" in which they can integrate the material they are exposed to in class or reflect upon the important career decisions they are in the process of making.

Creating More Engaging Environments

In this section of the chapter, we consider how MBA programs can modify program content and program structure to enhance student engagement. The following list is not exhaustive; indeed, several other chapters in this volume go into more detail about some of these issues (such as curriculum redesign and instructional delivery). Nonetheless, the issues discussed here are representative of the ongoing conversations among faculty members, deans, MBA program administrators, and staff about how to increase MBA student engagement. These situational factors are organized around the targets of engagement: increasing cognitive knowledge and skills, increasing professional development and extracurricular activity, and improving job placement.

Increasing Cognitive Knowledge and Skills

Faculty. Without question, faculty members play a major role in engagement in cognitive learning, both in terms of their teaching prowess in the classroom and the quality of their informal interactions with students outside the classroom (Umbach & Wawrzynski, 2005). For this reason, it is increasingly common to give MBA teaching assignments to non-tenure-track lecturers hired for their teaching effectiveness or to "professionally qualified" executives with significant managerial experience.

At the same time, the pressure on tenure-track faculty to produce research is increasing—and in many cases, teaching MBAs is not seen as a research-friendly assignment (Armstrong, 1995; Boyer, 1990; Fairweather, 2002; Marsh & Hattie, 2002). Consequently, placing greater responsibility for MBA instruction on lecturers, adjuncts, and executives seems on its face to be a reasonable strategy.

If some tenure-track faculty members are either unwilling or unable to provide the quality of instruction MBA students demand, then deans and MBA program administrators are justified in looking outside their ranks for talented instructors. No one really questions whether this strategy is wrong in any absolute sense; indeed, in some situations, there are simply no feasible alternatives.

Rather, the issue is whether MBA programs are importing faculty too frequently and creating unintended negative consequences by doing so. Interestingly, GMAC's Global Graduate Survey (2011, p. 21) highlights that the trend line for executive MBA students' satisfaction with faculty has declined since 2007—a time period that coincides with an increase in imported faculty in executive MBA programs. This finding is also consistent with the research of Trieschmann, Dennis, Northcraft, and Niemi (2000), who found a positive correlation between MBA student performance and the proportion of full professors teaching in their programs.

One possible explanation for this downward trend is that executive MBA students are especially sensitive to status differences among faculty and feel disrespected when they are not taught by their home institution's "best and brightest." Another possibility is that imported faculty members are not as readily available to MBA students outside of class, and thus the level of one-on-one engagement is lower; Kuh (2001) found significant positive correlations between amount of faculty contact and amount of student effort and learning. Yet a third possibility is that faculty outsourcing has led to a decline in the seriousness of classroom learning. Although there is not a great deal of systematic, cross-university research on this point, there is considerable anecdotal evidence that these lecturers and executives are easier graders—leaving many tenure-track faculty wondering if the key to being a good MBA teacher is providing less rigor and more infotainment. As Peter Vail notes, "'The entertainment factor' has skyrocketed . . . but I don't think it has enhanced the quality of what is being presented very much. In fact, I would say that as we have sought to make our graphics more 'professional' and our 'platform skills' more stylish, we have had to trivialize content" (Vail, 1989, p. 000F).

At a minimum, such findings and observations suggest we take a close second look at how extensively (rather than whether) we should use nonaffiliated faculty in MBA programs.

Curriculum. This is the second key factor in enhancing MBA students' engagement in cognitive learning. As the GMAC Global Graduate Survey suggests, "Curriculum is universally important in driving overall value for each [MBA] program type" (2011, p. 22). With the exception of executive MBA students, who have experienced a decline in satisfaction with their curricula since 2007, a large majority of MBA students view their educations in a positive light. Several other key findings about curriculum emerge from the literature on MBA student engagement as well.

○ A significant disconnect seems to be emerging between the content of many MBA programs' curricula and the skills potential employers require in the real world (Pfeffer & Fong, 2002; Rubin & Dierdorff, 2009).

○ Several schools have been able to better align MBA curricula with the key managerial competencies employers desire by changing the nature of their pedagogy. These changes have included increasing the amount of experiential learning (Boyatzis, Stubbs, & Taylor, 2002; Kolb & Kolb, 2005), decreasing the amount of attention given to jargon and memorization (Pfeffer & Sutton, 2000), and increasing the instructional skills of the faculty themselves (Umbach & Wawrzynski, 2005).

○ Increased use of technology does not necessarily increase MBA student engagement in learning (Arbaugh, 2002). Greater use of technology may help already effective instructors engage MBA students even further, but it does not compensate for otherwise ineffective instructors. Indeed, in many business classes today, faculty ban laptops because MBA students are too readily distracted by e-mail and too tempted to multitask during class.

Two other current issues warrant mention, too.

1. The jury is still out on whether integrative courses (the "anti-silo" curricula) are more or less effective than traditional coursework. Proponents of their own school's curriculum redesign provide anecdotal evidence on such programs' positive effects (compare Boyatzis & others, 2002; Mintzberg, 2004), but cross-university data are not available on this point. A recent article by Rubin and Dierdorff (2011) suggests that the content of the material delivered, rather than the level of cross-course integration or method of delivery, is the most critical contributor to the acquisition of cognitive knowledge and skill.

2. MBA faculty seem to be disproportionately involved in redesigning core curricula, but the chains of electives that prepare students for the job market in their functional areas seem to receive less attention. As a result, in many schools, these electives need considerable updating in light of major changes in the external environment (Friga, Bettis, & Sullivan, 2003).

Although grade distributions among MBA students have long exhibited an inflationary tendency, it is now open to question what level of competence, if any, an MBA degree conveys. As J. Scott Armstrong notes, "In today's prestigious business schools, students have to demonstrate competence to get in, but not to get out. Every student who wants to (and who avoids financial and emotional distress) will graduate. . . . Less than one percent of the students fail any given course, on average. . . . The probability of failing more than one course is almost zero. In effect, business schools have developed elaborate and expensive grading systems to ensure that even the least competent and the least interested get credit" (Armstrong, 1995, p. 104).

Increasing Professional Development

The manifest (or stated) function of extracurricular professional development is to strengthen students' skills as leaders and managers. However, participating in these opportunities serves an important latent function as well: increasing the students' likelihood of receiving job offers upon graduation. The GMAC 2011 Global Graduates Survey data suggest that participating in case competitions increases the likelihood of a job offer by 32 percent, and internships increase that likelihood by 26 percent (GMAC, 2011, p. 16).

The targets of engagement in professional development activities seem to fluctuate from school to school and over time. In some contexts, it appears that professional development refers to building competence in soft skills, such as leadership, communication, and teamwork. In other cases, the issue under discussion appears to be the school's responsiveness to the business community's concerns about MBA education. In yet other cases, it appears that professional development refers to involvement in extracurricular activities, such as membership in student clubs, attending presentations by guest speakers, taking roles in the MBA student association, or helping out in recruiting new students. Indeed, in some cases, the goals of engagement in professional development activities include several or all of the above activities. We address each of these perspectives on professional development in turn.

Developing Soft Skills in Coursework. Some pedagogical techniques are clearly more effective than others in helping students develop leadership, communication, and teamwork skills. Although not many studies have compared different pedagogical techniques within business schools specifically, there is evidence from the broader field of educational psychology that students learn such skills more readily through case analyses, in-class discussions, presentations, and hands-on practice than by listening to lectures. In particular, these pedagogical approaches appear to be more effective in grabbing students' attention and helping them apply theoretical knowledge to real-world situations (Arbaugh, 2002; Boyatzis & Saatcioglu, 2008; Debnath & others, 2007; Kolb & Kolb, 2005).

Perhaps the knottier problem here is how to ensure that MBA students actually develop soft skills (Burke & Hutchins, 2007; Burke & Saks, 2009). Virtually everybody agrees that these skills are important, but it is harder to coordinate efforts to develop these skills and to measure the efforts' success. Some schools implicitly assume that the management faculty will take the lead; other MBA programs outsource these skill-building activities to external consultants; in still other cases, MBA programs try to use integrative team meetings among MBA faculty to achieve this goal. The diffusion of responsibility and accountability in this area is a daunting problem.

Incorporating Feedback From the Business Community. Faculty express some natural—and arguably healthy—skepticism regarding the feedback they receive from businesses about deficiencies in MBA students' competencies (Porter & McKibbin, 1988; Rubin & Dierdorff, 2009). The reason some tension might be healthy is that each group, left to its own devices, might design a curriculum that would widely miss the mark. Business leaders tend to be more swayed by fads that shift quickly and fail to build a solid foundation for lifelong learning. At the same time, faculty members tend to be very influenced by (a) what they themselves were taught as students and (b) current theoretical debates in their own disciplines. Not surprisingly, the content of several MBA courses can become divorced from the real world over time (Gioia & Corley, 2002).

Indeed, by professional training, faculty members are taught to accept no claims without evidence and without the appropriate caveats. In contrast, business leaders are more prone to predicting the next big thing with exuberant overconfidence. Although there is little empirical research on best practices for integrating feedback from the business community into the curriculum, it could be argued that the dean (or an MBA director with faculty rank) might be in the best position to separate the wheat from the chaff in dealing with suggestions from businesses. Without some filtering, faculty are unlikely to accept or incorporate recommendations from the business community—especially since curriculum redesign is one of the few areas in which faculty still hold the ultimate power.

Increasing Involvement in Extracurricular Activity. The underlying principle about active engagement in the classroom applies to the domain of extracurricular activity as well—namely, that MBA students can develop better leadership, communication, and teamwork skills by practicing those skills outside of the classroom, too. As noted earlier, though, MBA students have heavy and often conflicting demands on their time. Whether to devote time to extracurricular activities is a decision only students can make; they can justify it only if the perceived benefits outweigh perceived costs. Two situational factors, in particular, seem to impede such involvement.

1. *The overchoice phenomenon* (Kahneman, 2011). One of the pitfalls MBA programs sometimes fall into is carpet-bombing students with extracurricular opportunities. The hope is that if programs offer a wide enough range of options, every student will find at least one activity of interest. The downside, of course, is that students are often overwhelmed by the number of choices (Feldman & Whitcomb, 2005). In some cases, students end up surfing from activity to activity without developing deep ties (or skills) in any. In smaller MBA

programs, another problem is that students are bombarded with requests to attend every outside speaker so there will be a good showing, but some attendees end up feeling like seat-fillers rather than engaged participants. Moreover, attending talks by outside speakers is not so different from attending faculty lectures; there is no evidence that attendance develops soft skills. Thus, in the area of variety of extracurricular activities, less might mean more.

2. *Family demands* (Carlson, Kacmar, & Williams, 2000; Greenhaus & Beutell, 1985). MBA students who are single or have no children may have more free time to participate in extracurricular activities. They are likely to have fewer fixed demands on their time outside of school or be better able to integrate extracurricular activities into their social lives. However, for MBA students who are single parents or are married with children, the hurdle for involvement is much higher. Their time demands outside of class are both greater and less flexible; one cannot put off picking children up from day care until a club meeting is over at 7:00 p.m.

Interestingly, directors of part-time MBA programs and executive MBA programs are highly aware that their students have less desire to be totally immersed in MBA activities and structure their programs accordingly. In part-time programs, extracurricular and job-hunting activities are clearly less central to the mission, particularly since the vast majority of these students are working full time and fewer than 25 percent are looking for jobs upon graduation (GMAC, 2011). However, in full-time day MBA programs, the reigning assumption seems to be that students should be fully immersed (or as immersed as possible) in activities that program administrators and faculty view as critical. Although faculty and administrators are intellectually aware that full-time day MBA students have lives outside of school, all too often those competing interests are not taken into account when planning activities. As full-time MBA programs strive to admit older, more experienced students, the traditional model of engaging students in extracurricular activities during evenings and weekends will continue to decline in effectiveness.

Enhancing Motivation and Skill in Job Hunting

The third target of student engagement is job placement. The GMAC 2011 Global Graduate Survey data certainly suggest that full-time day MBA students are motivated to return to graduate school to obtain better jobs, either in terms of fit or salary. On average, upon graduation these students expected a 38 percent increase in salary and a 44 percent increase in job responsibilities. Although only 10 percent of executive MBA and 14 percent of part-time MBA students sought jobs upon graduation, 78 percent of students in two-year full-time programs and 68 percent of students in one-year full-time programs were seeking new job opportunities (GMAC, 2011, p. 4). Rankings of MBA programs by such publications as *Bloomberg Businessweek* and *U.S. News & World Report* also give substantial weight to placement, especially average starting salaries and percentages of students placed by time of graduation (or three months thereafter). Thus, it is not surprising that deans, program administrators, and program staff all have incentives to pump up the volume about placement. MBA programs have tried to address job search activity both directly (by trying to find job opportunities for students) and indirectly (by increasing students' motivation and skill in job hunting).

Locating Job Opportunities for Students. In the 1970s and 1980s, it was not uncommon for business schools to have "placement offices" whose stated (or presumed) purpose was to find jobs for graduating MBA students (Porter & McKibbin, 1988). As the size of MBA programs exploded in the 1980s and 1990s, that model of dealing with placement broke down. In part, the number of specialized staff needed to find hundreds of jobs became prohibitively expensive. In addition, the existence of such offices had some unintended negative consequences on student motivation and expectations. When MBA program staff members were accountable for finding students jobs, students' sense of entitlement to high-paying jobs in highly desirable industries (such as management consulting or investment banking) escalated as student motivation to find jobs for themselves declined.

Obviously, large or urban business schools continue to run on-campus interview schedules for companies that plan to hire graduating MBA students. But for schools that are smaller, less readily accessible to recruiters, or both, there are still some program-level activities that help MBA students engage more directly with potential employers. For example, some schools have set up alumni events so students can network with potential employers. In other cases, schools have organized trips for groups of MBA students to targeted locations (such as New York City) so that graduates can interview for jobs. Some MBA programs run career fairs or other events to bring recruiters to campus for shorter periods of time, and other programs use outside speakers to connect students to particularly desirable employers. An increasingly popular way to directly connect students to full-time jobs is via summer internships between the first and second years of school. In this case, program administrators hope that a high percentage of summer interns will be able to convert their positions into full-time jobs (Taylor, 1988).

Increasing Students' Skill and Motivation in Job Hunting. Over the past twenty years, the emphasis in most MBA programs has shifted from finding jobs for students to equipping students with the skills to find jobs for themselves. Placement offices have been supplanted by "career services centers," which are charged with providing students with career counseling, résumé preparation, mock interviews, and job leads as they come in. These career service centers are now also charged with increasing students' motivation to land good jobs by graduation.

Virtually every major MBA program now has a portfolio of career services to address topics that include dressing for success, résumé preparation, interview training, networking, and negotiation skills. Although the quality of these training programs varies, one would be hard-pressed to argue that MBA programs have failed to provide graduating MBA students with the necessary skills to job hunt—especially since MBA programs generally limit admissions to students who have already had some experience in the labor market.

Interestingly, though, while the GMAC 2011 Global Graduates Survey data suggest that satisfaction with career services has risen from 2007 to 2011 (with roughly 50 percent of graduates now rating those services as outstanding or excellent), students' satisfaction with this component of the MBA experience has generally lagged behind their satisfaction with faculty, fellow students, and admissions (GMAC, 2011). The tepid labor market in the United States and Europe since 2008 has, of course, adversely affected students' perceptions of the placement opportunities available to them. The recent downturn in macroeconomic conditions, however, has highlighted three career services areas that have long been in need of improvement.

1. *Ongoing struggles with class scheduling* as employers' demands to interview students at their pleasure conflict with faculty demands that students attend class regularly. Some boundaries and enforcement mechanisms need to be set to keep all four sets of actors—employers, students, program staff, and faculty—in some sort of equilibrium, imperfect though it may be.

2. *Silos among development, alumni affairs, and career services.* These staffs often hoard information, leads, and contacts, with the result that MBA students do not get as much (or the right kind of) access to job leads because of counterproductive conflicts among staff groups. In some cases, at least, schools need to create an overarching corporate

relations unit or make some other structural changes to resolve these conflicting incentives.

3. *Excessive reliance on interest inventories and self-assessment exercises* to get students headed in the right direction—despite overwhelming evidence that self-assessments are often inaccurate (Feldman, 2002a; Feldman & Whitcomb, 2005). An additional problem is that most MBA career services staff members come from positions as corporate recruiters, headhunters, or executives; rarely have they had any formal, or even informal, training in counseling. It is not surprising, then, that many of these staff members have trouble digging beneath the surface of students' placement problems. Further, in an era in which affirming self-esteem has taken higher priority than giving honest feedback, MBA students are rarely confronted about their unrealistic job expectations or self-assessments. When students with a 3.0 GPA and little relevant work experience say that their goal is hedge fund management, they are rarely told that the probability of attaining such a position asymptotically approaches zero. Rather, the typical response is more likely to be an upbeat "Let's see what we can do to make that happen!"

How might MBA programs better focus their students' attention and energy on job hunting? Several tactics stand out. First, the research suggests that students who search for jobs on the basis of their *skills* rather than their *interests* are more likely to succeed. Second, getting 360-degree feedback from peers, supervisors, and subordinates on their last jobs may provide greater insight into a student's strengths and weakness (and help develop better action planning for improvement) than self-assessment inventories do. Third, too much energy is being put into identifying students' wants rather than the trade-offs MBA graduates are willing to make in accepting job offers (Feldman, 2002b).

In fact, when MBA students are asked what they are looking for in a job (compare GMAC, 2011), it is not surprising that they mention such attributes as a career path with a lot of growth, a corporate culture consistent with their values, a job with a great deal of autonomy, an employer with a positive financial future, and a pleasant work environment. Indeed, who wouldn't want a job with all these attributes? From a counseling perspective, however, simply identifying these desirable attributes is not especially helpful because rarely does such a perfect job come along. Moreover, in most studies of MBA student job choice decisions, graduates do not mention high salary as one of their top selection criteria—strong evidence that students have a social desirability response bias when responding to self-assessment instruments (Arnold & Feldman, 1981). Thus, a useful alternative to these interest inventories is Schein's Career Anchor Survey (1990), which is geared to helping students identify the trade-offs they are willing to make among imperfect alternatives. This survey also has the advantage of having been developed and validated specifically for MBA students (Feldman & Bolino, 1997).

Differences Across Students in Ability and Willingness to Engage

As the previous section highlights, the implicit assumption underlying most of the research in this area is that the MBA program itself has a major impact on how engaged students will be. This traditional focus on MBA programs' power to foster engagement is consistent with traditional research on student engagement, which assumes that engagement is driven top down rather than bottom up (Noe & others, 2010). However, the literature from educational and social psychology paints a very different scenario. This perspective suggests that student engagement is a function not only of the school context but also of the characteristics of the students themselves (Noe & others, 2010). That is, there are certain attributes individuals bring to MBA programs that make some of them more "engageable" than others.

Moreover, these individual differences may interact with situational differences to affect students' levels of engagement. In other words, different groups of students will be easier to engage in some activities than others. For example, it might be easier to get students who are very high on cognitive ability but low on extraversion to engage fully in classroom learning, but easier to get students who are lower on cognitive ability but very high on extraversion to fully engage in job-hunting activities (Boswell & others, 2012). In this third section, then, we identify four groups of individual-level differences that affect students' likelihood of engagement—personality variables, demographic status, educational background, and career indecision—and the implications of these individual differences for recruitment and admissions.

Personality Traits

Since the late 1980s, there has been an extensive, indeed exhaustive, study of personality traits that facilitate success in school and work settings. Although this chapter's aim is not to comprehensively review that literature, there are several personality traits that are particularly germane to MBA education (Noe & others, 2010).

1. *Proactivity personality*: individuals' predisposition to set goals for themselves and take personal responsibility for overcoming obstacles to those goals (compare Macey & Schneider, 2008). A core theme that runs through the engagement literature is that much of that engagement has to be bottom up and student driven. Proactive students do not wait for someone else to take the initiative to address their concerns about curriculum or placement. Rather, they view themselves as active agents who are responsible for managing their own educations and careers. As a result, they exert more energy in excelling in the classroom and landing desirable jobs.

The research on core self-evaluations (referring to individuals' self-esteem, generalized self-efficacy, emotional stability, and locus of control) yields very similar findings (Erez & Judge, 2001; Judge & Hurst, 2008).

2. *Positive affectivity:* the predisposition to respond to situations in a positive light and to enter new situations expecting the best (Costa, McRae, & Zonderman, 1987). Positive affectivity is a driver of career success in two ways. First, it helps students network more effectively; subordinates who are high on positive affectivity are viewed as easier to lead than those who are high on negative affectivity. Second, students who are high on positive affectivity tend to be more psychologically hardy; that is, they are less likely to fall into downward spirals when faced with negative feedback or setbacks. As a result, positive affectivity helps students weather the inevitable disappointments they will face while job hunting (Maslach & others, 2001).

3. *Extraversion:* the level of an individual's outgoingness, ease in initiating conversations, and comfort in speaking in public (Barrick & Mount, 1991). Extraversion helps MBA students engage in program activities in a variety of ways. For example, students who are high on extraversion are more likely to become involved in professional development and extracurricular and job-hunting activities; they are also less likely to face those activities with dread or apprehension. In addition, extraverts do better in job interviews, tend to get promoted more quickly, and perform more effectively in leadership roles.

4. *Conscientiousness:* individuals' level of organization, attention to detail, need for closure, and drive to results (Digman, 1989). In classroom learning, especially, conscientiousness is closely related to performance because it helps students complete tasks in a timely, professional way. Further, high levels of organization and attention to detail help

students juggle coursework, extracurricular activities, job hunting, and family demands.

As this discussion suggests, individual differences may vary in their relevance to driving engagement in different spheres of activity. For instance, positive affectivity and extraversion are likely to facilitate engagement in extracurricular activities and job hunting, but the traits are unlikely to have much impact on cognitive learning. In contrast, conscientiousness is likely to enhance engagement in cognitive learning and job hunting, but it may have little impact on engagement in extracurricular activities.

Demographic Variables

In studies of undergraduate student engagement, major differences have been found based on individuals' gender, race, and enrollment in private versus public universities (Hu & Kuh, 2002). However, in the GMAC 2011 Global Graduates Survey, the only demographic variable that stands out as particularly important is age. Across a variety of dimensions, students who are twenty-four to thirty appear to be most satisfied with their MBA programs (GMAC, 2011). On the basis of GMAC survey data alone, it is not possible to know with certainty why this group of students seems to derive the most benefit from MBA programs, but research from related areas provides some clues.

The research on career stages and life stages suggests that there are normative expectations about when individuals should hit key benchmarks in their professional and personal lives (Dalton, Thompson, & Price, 1977; Feldman, 1988). In general, that line of research suggests that individuals are most comfortable in apprentice roles while in their twenties but chafe if they do not achieve much more independence as they turn thirty. Since participation in MBA programs involves some curtailing of independence and conforming to others' expectations, it is not surprising that students who are thirty or older struggle more frequently against MBA program structure. In addition, students who are in full-time MBA programs in their thirties and forties are out of sync with the traditional managerial labor market. As a result of this lack of synchronicity, older full-time students are making bigger sacrifices to come back to school yet may face greater age discrimination in the job market upon graduation. The literature in labor economics, too, suggests that there are penalties in the labor market for "career disorderliness" (Kilty & Behling, 1985). For these reasons, it is not surprising that out-of-sync older students gravitate more frequently to entrepreneurial ventures, where career paths are more fluid and flexible (Feldman, 1988, 2002b).

Undergraduate Educational Background

Over the years, the pendulum of business school preferences has shifted back and forth between trying to cater to the needs of MBA students *with* undergraduate degrees in business (Mintzberg, 2004) and to those with undergraduate degrees *outside of* business (Whyte, 1957). When MBA degrees first became popular after World War II, the major focus was on training students who had little undergraduate business education to become managers. Today, in many MBA programs, business undergraduates make up a large percentage of the entering class. Besides presenting a challenge to MBA faculty, the diversity of students' educational backgrounds has implications for student engagement. Students with undergraduate business degrees will have additional discretionary time to engage in extracurricular activities and job hunting because more of their graduate classwork will be familiar. In contrast, MBA students with undergraduate degrees outside of business will have to engage more in coursework because they have lower knowledge bases.

Career Indecision

A related issue is students' levels of career indecision (Feldman & Whitcomb, 2005). Recruiters and admissions officers fervently hope that entrants into their MBA programs already have some fairly well-defined career goals and will use their time in graduate school to pursue activities aligned with those goals. However, applicants to MBA programs are no different from job applicants in general: They are frequently skillful at interviewing and writing essays that show a greater sense of purpose than they actually possess. As a result, numerous MBA students enroll to *find* their vocation rather than *pursue* it (Feldman, 2002a, 2002b). This phenomenon is more likely to occur with entrants who are younger, have less relevant work experience, have non-business undergraduate degrees, or all three. But career indecision is not limited to students with this profile.

Students with high levels of career indecision are especially unlikely to be engaged in critical MBA program activities. Engagement implies depth of interest and involvement. However, students who have a great deal of career indecision are more prone to sample a wide variety of activities in less depth. Writing about undecided young adults, Allan Bloom (1987) observes that such students are free to be anything at all, but see no reason to be anything in particular. Thus, the time demands of exploring lots of different career paths constrain undecided students' ability to engage in any one activity too deeply.

Recruitment and Admissions

It is clear, then, that the types of individuals recruited and admitted into MBA programs influence both the aggregate level of student engagement and the specific activities in which students will be most heavily engaged. For example, if schools select students largely on the basis of GPA and GMAT scores, entrants will be more likely to focus on their academic coursework. In contrast, if schools select on the basis of years of related work experience, entrants are more likely to focus on job-hunting activities. Younger students who enter the program with high levels of career indecision or few years of relevant work experience might engage in greater networking and professional development activity in order to discover the right career paths, while MBA students who were undergraduates at the same institution are more likely to become engaged as participants in extracurricular activities.

In short, many of the challenges MBA programs face in engaging students are due to misalignment between admissions criteria and program goals. Rather than trying to force students to engage in activities program staff view as desirable, MBA programs might be better off selecting students whom they can readily engage in the activities that already fit their programs' core missions and strategic goals. Indeed, the work of Van Maanen and Barley (1984) suggests that elite business schools tend to recruit heavily from a small subset of undergraduate institutions and then place their graduates in a small subset of corporations. In doing so, these business schools help ensure that the students they admit will be more engaged in what their MBA programs have to offer and will be more satisfied with their likely placement options. In other words, these students are easier to engage because the "chains of socialization" are more tightly aligned and soldered (Van Maanen, 1984).

Outcomes of MBA Student Engagement

The last issue we consider here is whether MBA student engagement does, in fact, lead to more desirable outcomes such as greater cognitive learning, better professional development, and more successful placement. As we show, the links between student engagement and these outcomes, while positive, are not as strong as frequently assumed. In addition, the causal direction of those relationships is sometimes surprising.

The Value of an MBA Degree

For many faculty and students, the conversation about student engagement has been inextricably linked to the conversation about the value of the MBA degree itself (Zhao, Truell, Alexander, & Hill, 2006). The multiple critiques of MBA education generally echo the assessment of Pfeffer and Fong: "less success than meets the eye" (2002, p. 78).

It is worth noting, though, that students' perceptions of their own engagement diverge from faculty perceptions of students' engagement. The 2011 GMAC Global Graduates Survey data suggest that 92 percent of graduating business school students rated their experience in MBA programs as outstanding (38 percent), excellent (36 percent), or good (19 percent; GMAC, 2011, pp. 20–22). Further, surveys of students' reactions to MBA education suggest that they attribute much of their career success to the knowledge they acquired, the connections they made, and the employment opportunities that opened up to them in MBA programs (compare Baruch & Peiperl, 2000).

Unfortunately, it is hard to draw conclusions about the reliability and validity of these claims—on either side of the issue—because of inadequate research designs and data collection methodologies. As research in cognitive psychology makes clear, individuals engage in cognitive dissonance reduction to justify the decisions they have already made (Pinker, 2002; Schacter, 2001). Having invested two or three years (and tens of thousands of dollars) in obtaining an MBA degree, graduates are more inclined to report that their sacrifice was worth it than to admit they made a gargantuan mistake. Further, even in studies that compare MBA graduates to similarly employed managers without MBA degrees (for example, Baruch & Peiperl, 2000), there are plausible alternative explanations for why MBA graduates went farther and faster than their non–MBA counterparts. Specifically, students admitted into MBA programs, as a group, are likely to have stronger academic backgrounds, career focus, or both than students who do not pursue MBA degrees. In addition, an MBA degree serves a signaling function in the labor market; there is a presumption (whether true or false) that MBA graduates have some skills that non–MBA graduates do not. Consequently, MBA graduates may have a self-fulfilling prophecy working in their favor (Eden, 1984). Because employers may see MBA graduates in a more favorable light, these graduates may receive greater opportunities for professional development or advancement regardless of what they learned in graduate school.

The Value of Engagement

The next logical question is whether highly engaged MBA students obtain more desirable outcomes than their less engaged colleagues. There are several consistent answers—and at least one surprising finding—in this area.

In the area of knowledge acquisition, the evidence is quite consistent that engagement accelerates the cognitive learning process for MBA students (Arbaugh, 2000; Boyatzis & Saaticioglu, 2008; Boyatzis, Stubbs, & Taylor, 2002; Debnath & others, 2007). These studies find that MBA students who are highly engaged invest more time in cognitive learning, are more motivated to learn, and are more attentive to classroom instruction and educational materials. It is important to note, though, that the presumed intervening or explanatory variables (such as actual time studied or level of intrinsic motivation) are usually not measured in these studies (Hu & Kuh, 2002).

Evidence on the effects of MBA student engagement on professional development and extracurricular activity is scanter. One of the weaknesses of the student engagement literature is that levels of student engagement have been inferred from students' levels of activity in a variety of areas. However, engagement is usually not measured in terms of those students' independently observable characteristics (Kuh, 2003). This strategy for defining engagement can lead to a troubling tautology, namely, if engagement is defined in terms of students' level of activity, how can we assert that engaged students participate more fully in those activities? For example, Hu and Kuh (2002) identify ten types of engaged students (such as "grind," "socializer," and "recreator"), but such types are defined by profiles of students' activities rather than by independent measures of student motivation, enthusiasm, and focus.

The GMAC Global Graduates Survey (2011, p. 17) does link participation in extracurricular activities to a higher likelihood of receiving job offers, and here the data do provide some evidence that student engagement is correlated with likelihood of receiving such offers. The GMAC data indicate that the likelihood of receiving a job offer goes up by 10 percent for students who participate in multicultural events but as much as 30 percent for students participating in extracurricular leadership programs. These data suggest that involvement in skill-based activities has greater payoff in initial employment than do more socially oriented activities. Even within the realm of extracurricular activities, then, there is a hierarchy of benefits from different types of student engagement.

One of the most surprising findings in this literature concerns the presumed causal arrow between engagement in the classroom and engagement in career development. Much of the literature in this area has assumed that engagement in school activities leads to greater engagement in career development activities (compare Fredericks, Blumenfeld, & Paris, 2004). However, Kenny and others (2006) and Lapan (2004) present some convincing longitudinal evidence that the causal arrow actually works in reverse. In fact, these studies found that higher levels of engagement in career development lead to greater engagement in school work, not vice versa. Although these studies have not been conducted with MBA students in particular, their implications for MBA programs are quite clear:

1. Career-undecided MBA students will benefit less from their educations than those who enter the programs with greater career focus.

2. Getting students engaged in classwork to engage them more fully in job searching is likely to be less successful than admitting students who are already highly engaged in their career development.

Conclusion: Focusing on What Truly Matters

Engaging students in their graduate management education has become a more important goal for business school deans, program directors, career services and student affairs professionals, and faculty. But the evidence suggests that some of the implicit assumptions underlying the conversation about engagement are tenuous at best. In particular, it is difficult, if not impossible, to fully engage MBA students in all the activities that program administrators, staff, and faculty deem essential components of the MBA experience. There are situational constraints that make it hard for MBA programs to engage students as much as faculty and administrators would like, and there are situational constraints that make it hard for MBA students to engage as fully as they would like.

Moreover, there are major differences among MBA students in their ability and willingness to engage in program activities, and MBA programs cannot change these stable individual differences in a matter of a few months.

Finally, although student engagement does appear to have a positive impact on cognitive learning in MBA programs, the relationship between engagement in the classroom and engagement in job hunting may be the opposite of what is frequently assumed. Specifically, rather than engagement in the classroom leading to engagement in job hunting, it is more likely that high levels of engagement in developing one's career leads MBA students to engage more fully in classroom learning.

Where do we go from here?

First, setting "increase student engagement" as an overall program goal may not be productive. Instead, business school deans and program directors should first decide which outcomes they most care about and then align curriculum and other program activities to ensure that those specific outcomes are achieved. As Mintzberg (2004) rightly observed, keeping students busy is not a desirable goal in and of itself; indeed, keeping students too busy interferes with deep learning and strategic thinking about their careers. The struggle for students' attention among different groups of stakeholders only leads to unpredictable brownouts of student energy that prove frustrating for all.

Second, there are numerous strategies that graduate business programs can use to increase student engagement. The range includes redesigning curriculum, experimenting with new pedagogy, investing more heavily in developing talented instructors from the tenure-track faculty, focusing on a smaller but more meaningful set of extracurricular activities, and providing students with more realistic feedback even if such feedback is discomfiting. At the same time, massive shifts of resources to MBA programs and away from undergraduate, doctoral, and other master's programs can lead to even greater disillusionment and opposition from business school faculty. More thoughtful allocation of resources *within* MBA programs should precede the transfer of funds *out of* other degree programs and academic units. The fact that MBA program demands have to be balanced with the demands of other programs should be stated explicitly, and administrative actions should be consistent with that philosophy. In the long run, knee-jerk reactions to address every student complaint or concern erode faculty investment in MBA education.

Third, much is to be gained by paying greater attention to the profile of the entering class beyond the metrics of various business school rankings. Students gravitate to activities that they already do well and try to avoid ones in which they are less successful (Feldman, 2002b; Seashore, 1975). If the goal of the program is to achieve better placement, then program staff must pay greater attention to discerning whether applicants do, in fact, possess both some sort of career focus and the personal attributes (such as conscientiousness and extraversion) to succeed in critical program activities. Without doubt, it is easier to teach and place students who are highly self-motivated and self-directed. At the same time, motivation can take students only so far if they lack commensurate ability and the requisite dispositional attributes to succeed (Feldman, 2002b; Feldman & Bolino, 1997; Schein, 1990).

In the final analysis, the ultimate goal of graduate management education is not to engage students as much as possible. In fact, the differences in how full-time MBA programs, part-time evening programs, and executive MBA programs are structured give proof to the argument that deans and MBA directors know how to modulate the level of desired engagement according to how much time and energy different groups of students can draw upon.

Thus, rather than asking how we can increase graduate students' engagement, perhaps we should be asking instead: Are MBA students as engaged as they want and need to be?

Summing Up

○ Graduate business students' capacity to be engaged is finite; increasing student engagement in one type of activity (such as coursework, extracurricular activity, or job hunting) is attainable only at the expense of their involvement in another activity.

○ Increasing student engagement may not be a productive program goal in and of itself because keeping graduate management students too busy interferes with how well they integrate what they have learned and how strategically they plan their careers.

○ Involvement in extracurricular activities does, in fact, help students obtain jobs, but business schools often undermine the potential benefits of these activities by carpet-bombing students with too many choices and scheduling extracurricular activities at inconvenient hours. As a result, students end up surfing from activity to activity without developing deep skills or deep network ties.

○ Much of the literature on student engagement has assumed that engagement in school activities leads to greater engagement in career development activities. However, the evidence is much more compelling that the causal relationship works in the opposite direction. That is, students who are highly engaged in their own career development are more likely to become engaged in their school activities.

○ Rather than expending enormous energy trying to engage students in activities that program directors deem essential, graduate business schools would be better served by admitting applicants whose own preferences and aspirations fit the strategic goals of the program.

References

Arbaugh, J. B. "How Classroom Environment and Student Engagement Affect Learning in Internet-Based MBA Courses." *Business Communication Quarterly*, 2000, 63, 9–26.

Arbaugh, J. B. "Managing the On-Line Classroom: A Study of Technological and Behavioral Characteristics of Web-Based MBA Courses." *Journal of High Technology Management Research*, 2002, 13, 203–223.

Armstrong, J. S. "The Devil's Advocate Responds to an MBA Student's Claim That Research Harms Learning." *Journal of Marketing*, 1995, 59, 101–106.

Arnold, H. J., & Feldman, D. C. "Social Desirability Response Bias in Self-Report Choice Situations." *Academy of Management Journal*, 1981, 24, 377–385.

Barrick, M. R., & Mount, M. K. "The Big Five Personality Dimensions and Job Performance: A Meta-analysis." *Personnel Psychology*, 1991, 44, 1–26.

Baruch, Y., & Peiperl, M. "The Impact of an MBA on Graduate Careers." *Human Resource Management Journal*, 2000, 10, 69–90.

Beier, M. E., & Kanfer, R. "Motivation in Training and Development: A Phase Perspective." In S.W.J. Kozlowski & E. Salas (eds.), *Learning, Training, and Development in Organizations* (pp. 65–98). New York: Routledge, 2010.

Bloom, A. *The Closing of the American Mind.* New York: Simon & Schuster, 1987.

Boswell, W. R., Zimmerman, R. D., & Swider, B. W. "Employee Job Search: Toward an Understanding of Job Search Context and Search Objectives." *Journal of Management*, 2012, 38, 129–163.

Boyatzis, R. E., & Saatcioglu, A. "A 20-Year View of Trying to Develop Emotional, Social, and Cognitive Intelligence Competencies in Graduate Management Education." *Journal of Management Development*, 2008, 27, 92–108.

Boyatzis, R. E., Stubbs, E. C., & Taylor, S. N. "Learning Cognitive and Emotional Intelligence Competencies Through Graduate Management Education." *Academy of Management Learning & Education*, 2002, 1, 150–162.

Boyer, E. L. *Scholarship Reconsidered: Priorities of the Professoriate.* Princeton, N.J.: The Carnegie Foundation for the Advancement of Teaching, 1990.

Brint, S., Cantwell, A. M., & Hannerman, R. A. *Two Cultures: Undergraduate Academic Engagement.* Berkeley, Calif.: Center for Studies in Higher Education, University of California at Berkeley, 2008. http://escholarship.org/uc/item/53g8521z

Burke, L. A., & Hutchins, H. "Training Transfer: An Integrative Review." *Human Resource Development Review*, 2007, 6, 263–296.

Burke, L. A., & Saks, A. M. "Accountability in Transfer of Training: Adapting Schlenker's Model of Responsibility to a Persistent but Solvable Problem." *Human Resource Development Review*, 2009, 9, 382–402.

Carlson, D. S., Kacmar, K. M., & Williams, L. J. "Construction and Initial Validation of a Multi- Dimensional Measure of Work–Family Conflict." *Journal of Vocational Behavior*, 2000, 56, 249–276.

Chen, G., & Klimoski, R. "Training and Development of Human Resources at Work: Is the State of Our Science Strong?" *Human Resource Management Review*, 2007, 17, 180–190.

Costa, P. T., Jr., McCrae, R. R., & Zonderman, A. B. "Environmental and Dispositional Influences on Well-Being. Longitudinal Follow-Up of an American National Sample." *British Journal of Psychology*, 1987, 78, 299–306.

Dalton, G. W., Thompson, P. H., & Price, K. L. "The Four Stages of Professional Careers: A New Look at Performance by Professionals." *Organizational Dynamics*, 1977, 6, 19–42.

Debnath, S. C., Tandon, S., & Pointer, L. V. "Designing Business School Courses to Promote Student Motivation: An Application of the Job Characteristics Model." *Journal of Management Education*, 2007, 20, 1–20.

Digman, J. M. "Five Robust Trait Dimensions: Development, Stability, and Utility." *Journal of Personality*, 1989, 57, 195–214.

Eden, D. "Self-Fulfilling Prophecy as a Management Tool: Harnessing Pygmalion." *Academy of Management Review*, 1984, 9, 64–73.

Erez, A., & Judge, T. A. "Relationships of Core Self-Evaluations to Goal Setting, Motivation, and Performance." *Journal of Applied Psychology*, 2001, 86, 1270–1279.

Fairweather, J. "The Mythologies of Faculty Productivity: Implications for Institutional Policy and Decision Making." *Journal of Higher Education*, 2002, 73, 26–48.

Feldman, D. C. *Managing Careers in Organizations.* Glenview, Ill.: Scott, Foresman, 1988.

Feldman, D. C. "When You Come to a Fork in the Road, Take it: Vocational Choices and Career Indecision of Teenagers and Young Adults." In D. C. Feldman (ed.), *Work Careers: A Developmental Perspective* (pp. 93–125). San Francisco, Calif.: Jossey-Bass, 2002a.

Feldman, D. C. "Stability in the Midst of Change." In D. C. Feldman (ed.), *Work Careers: A Developmental Perspective* (pp. 1–26). San Francisco, Calif.: Jossey-Bass, 2002b.

Feldman, D. C. "The Food's No Good and They Don't Give Us Enough: Reflections on Henry Mintzberg's *Managers Not MBAs*." *Academy of Management Learning and Education*, 2005, 4, 217–220.

Feldman, D. C., & Bolino, M. C. "Careers Within Careers: Reconceptualizing the Nature of Career Anchors and Their Consequences." *Human Resource Management Review*, 1997, 6, 89–112.

Feldman, D. C., & Whitcomb, K. M. "The Effects of Framing Vocational Choices on Young Adults' Sets of Career Options." *Career Development International*, 2005, 10, 7–25.

Fredericks, J., Blumenfeld, P. C., & Paris, A. H. "School Engagement: Potential of the Concept, State of the Evidence." *Review of Educational Research*, 2004, 74, 59–109.

Friga, P. N., Bettis, R. A., & Sullivan, R. S. "Changes in Graduate Management Education and New Business School Strategies for the 21st Century." *Academy of Management Learning and Education*, 2003, 2, 233–249.

Gioia, D. A., & Corley, K. G. "Being Good Versus Looking Good: Business School Rankings and the Circean Transformation From Substance to Image." *Academy of Management Learning & Education*, 2002, 1, 107–120.

GMAC. *2011 Global Management Education Graduate Survey*. Reston, Va.: Graduation Management Admission Council, 2011.

Goldstein, I. L. *Training: Program Development and Evaluation*. Monterey, Calif.: Brooks Cole, 1974.

Greenhaus, J. H., & Beutell, N. J. "Sources of Conflict Between Work and Family Roles." *Academy of Management Review*, 1985, 10, 76–88.

Hobfoll, S. E. "Conservation of Resources: A New Attempt at Conceptualizing Stress." *American Psychologist*, 1989, 44, 513–524.

Hu, S., & Kuh, G. D. "Being (Dis)Engaged in Educationally Purposeful Activities: The Influences of Student and Institutional Characteristics." *Research in Higher Education*, 2002, 43, 555–575.

Judge, T. A., & Hurst, C. "How the Rich (and Happy) Get Richer (and Happier): Relationship of Core Self-Evaluations to Trajectories in Attaining Work Success." *Journal of Applied Psychology*, 2008, 93, 849–863.

Kahn, W. A. "Psychological Conditions of Personal Engagement and Disengagement at Work." *Academy of Management Journal*, 1990, 33, 692–724.

Kahneman, D. *Thinking, Fast and Slow*. New York: Farrar, Straus, and Giroux, 2011.

Kenny, M. E., Blustein, D. L., Haase, R. F., Jackson, J., & Perry, J. C. "Setting the Stage: Career Development and the Student Engagement Process." *Journal of Counseling Psychology*, 2006, 53, 272–279.

Kilty, K. M., & Behling, J. H. "Predicting the Retirement Intentions and Attitudes of Professional Workers. *Journal of Gerontology*, 1985, 40, 219–227.

Kolb, A. Y., & Kolb, D. A. "Learning Styles and Learning Spaces: Enhancing Experiential Learning in Higher Education." *Academy of Management Learning and Education*, 2005, 4, 193–212.

Kraiger, K., & Ford, J. K. "The Expanding Role of Workplace Training: Themes and Trends Influencing Training Research and Practice." In L. Koopes (ed.), *Historical Perspectives on Industrial and Organizational Psychology* (pp. 281–309). Mahwah, N.J.: Lawrence Erlbaum, 2007.

Kuh, G. D. "Assessing What Really Matters to Student Learning: Inside the National Survey of Study Engagement." *Change*, 2001, 33, 10–17.

Kuh, G. D. "What We're Learning About Student Engagement From NSSE: Benchmarks for Effective Educational Practices." *Change*, 2003, 35, 24–32.

Lapan, R. T. *Career Development Across the K–16 Years: Bridging the Present to Satisfying and Successful Futures*. Alexandria, Va.: American Counseling Association, 2004.

Lavie, N. "Attention, Distraction, and Cognitive Control Under Load." *Current Directions in Psychological Science*, 2010, 19, 143–148.

Macey, W. H., & Schneider, B. "The Meaning of Employee Engagement." *Industrial and Organizational Psychology: Perspectives on Science and Practice*, 2008, 1, 3–30.

Marsh, H. W., & Hattie, J. "The Relation Between Research Productivity and Teaching Effectiveness: Complementary, Antagonistic, or Independent Constructs?" *Journal of Higher Education*, 2002, 73, 604–641.

Maslach, C., Schaufeli, W. B., & Leiter, M. P. "Job Burnout." *Annual Review of Psychology*, 2001, 52, 397–422.

Mintzberg, H. *Managers Not MBAs: A Hard Look at the Soft Practice of Managing and Management Development*. San Francisco, Calif.: Berrett-Koehler, 2004.

Noe, R. A., Tews, M. J., & Dachner, A. M. "Learner Engagement: A New Perspective for Enhancing Our Understanding of Learner Motivation and Workplace Learning." *Academy of Management Annals*, 2010, 4, 279–315.

Pfeffer, J., & Fong, C. T. "The End of Business Schools? Less Success Than Meets the Eye." *Academy of Management Learning & Education*, 2002, 1, 78–95.

Pfeffer, J., & Sutton, R. I. *The Knowing-Doing Gap*. Boston, Mass.: Harvard Business School Press, 2000.

Pinker, S. *The Blank Slate*. New York: Viking Press, 2002.

Porter, L., & McKibbin, L. *Management Education and Development: Drift or Thrust Into the 21st Century*. New York: McGraw-Hill, 1988.

Rubin, R. S., & Dierdorff, E. C. "How Relevant Is the MBA? Assessing the Alignment of Required Curricula and Required Managerial Competencies." *Academy of Management Learning & Education*, 2009, 8, 208–224.

Rubin, R. S., & Dierdorff, E. C. "On the Road to Abilene: Time to Manage Agreement About MBA Curricular Relevance." *Academy of Management Learning & Education*, 2011, 10, 148–161.

Salanova, M., Augt, S., & Piero, J. M. "Linking Organizational Resources and Work Engagement to Employee Performance and Customer Loyalty: The Mediation of Service Climate." *Journal of Applied Psychology*, 2005, 90, 1217–1217.

Schacter, D. L. *The Seven Sins of Memory*. Boston, Mass.: Houghton Mifflin, 2001.

Schein, E. A. *Career Anchors: Discovering Your Real Values*. San Diego, Calif.: Pfeiffer, 1990.

Seashore, C. "In Grave Danger of Growing." *Social Change: Ideas and Applications*, 1975, 5, 1–4.

Taylor, M. S. "The Effects of College Internships on Individual Participants." *Journal of Applied Psychology*, 1988, 73, 393–401.

Trieschmann, J. S., Dennis, A. R., Northcraft, G. B., & Niemi, A. W., Jr. "Serving Multiple Constituencies in Business Schools: MBA Program Versus Research Performance." *Academy of Management Journal*, 2000, 43, 1130–1141.

Umbach, P. D., & Wawrzynski, M. R. "Faculty Do Matter: The Role of College Faculty in Student Learning and Engagement. *Research in Higher Education*, 2005, 46, 153–184.

Vail, P. *Managing as a Performing Art: New Ideas for a World of Chaotic Change.* San Francisco, Calif.: Jossey-Bass, 1989.

Van Maanen, J. "Doing New Things in Old Ways: The Chains of Socialization." In J. L. Bess (ed.), *College and University Organization* (pp. 211–247). New York: New York University Press, 1984.

Van Maanen, J., & Barley, S. R. "Occupational Communities: Culture and Control in Organizations." In B. M. Staw (ed.), *Research in Organizations* (Vol. 6, pp. 287–365). Greenwich, Conn.: JAI, 1984.

Whyte, W. H., Jr. *The Organization Man.* New York: Anchor Books, 1957.

Zhao, J. J., Truell, A. D., Alexander, M. W., & Hill, I. B. "Less Success Than Meets the Eye? The Impact of MBA Education on Graduates' Careers." *Journal of Education for Business*, 2006 (May/June), 261–268.

8

RECLAIMING QUALITY IN GRADUATE MANAGEMENT EDUCATION

Robert S. Rubin
DePaul University

Frederick P. Morgeson
Michigan State University

Key Topics Covered in This Chapter

- Overview of existing quality systems and their impact on business school stakeholders
- Description of research that offers a new comprehensive model of graduate management education program quality
- Discussion of the central advantages of adopting a new quality rating system as an alternative to current quality measures
- Recommendations for using the quality model to improve program quality within and across business schools

Despite substantial criticism since the turn of the century and the economic downturn that started in 2008, graduate management programs continue to thrive. They represent the central, most profitable, and most visible offerings in a business school's portfolio of programs. Indeed, as of 2009, master's degrees in business accounted for approximately 26 percent of the total master's degrees conferred, second only to degrees in education

(U.S. Census Bureau, 2011). Given this success, business schools now offer a broad range of degree "products," including specialized MBA degrees, joint degrees, and highly specific master's programs (Dierdorff & Rubin, 2009). As programs have proliferated and student choices have expanded, both institutions and consumers have shown an increased desire to evaluate and differentiate graduate management programs in terms of their overall educational or academic quality (Basken, 2012; Dierdorff & Rubin, 2009). This business school trend follows a broader movement in higher education in which institutional stakeholders (such as students, recruiters, and government) increasingly demand evidence of educational achievement and program quality (Basken, 2012; Cabrera, Colbeck, & Terenzini, 2001). That is, stakeholders peering into the ivory tower appear less willing to rely on an institution's vague promises of academic quality or proxy measures of success, such as graduation rates.

For example, in a controversial 2006 report commissioned by U.S. Secretary of Education Margaret Spellings, the Commission on the Future of Higher Education asserted that "there is inadequate transparency and accountability for measuring institutional performance, which is more and more necessary to maintaining public trust in higher education" (U.S. Department of Education, 2006, p. 13). In response, recent reports have reaffirmed a movement toward one of the commission's key recommendations, namely, to create a national college database that would track student learning and outcomes and allow for institution-by-institution comparisons (National Research Council, 2012). As educational costs continue to soar, stakeholders (including the government) are placing more pressure on institutions to prove that they fulfill their central educational missions.

This movement toward increased accountability for quality appears to be particularly important for external stakeholders, such as students and employers, who are the primary consumers of data about business schools' academic quality. As these business school outsiders make enrollment or recruitment decisions, they draw, logically enough, upon existing signals of educational quality—indicators that are often imperfect or incomplete (Spence, 1973). Thus, students, recruiters, and others seek out information they believe will provide the most credible signals about quality to inform their education-related decisions. Indeed, years of institutional research by GMAC have consistently found that program quality and reputation are among the most important, if not *the* most important, factors driving application decisions (GMAC, 2012b). Similarly, employers routinely cite student quality as the most important factor behind deciding to actively recruit from a given institution (GMAC, 2012a). Not surprisingly, then, demand for credible program quality data remains high (Rubin, Dierdorff, & Morgeson, 2011).

For numerous reasons, however, determining the credibility of information about program quality is complicated. As decades of educational research have demonstrated, consensus remains elusive. Studies assessing graduate program quality are routinely met with criticism and "have been a matter of controversy since the first one was published in 1925" (DiBiasio, Girves, & Poland, 1982, p. 99). Indeed, regardless of the approach, most studies of academic quality have serious limitations (Tan, 1992). For example, one approach has been to use "objective" indicators, such as faculty research productivity, financial resources, library holdings, and student selectivity, as measures of quality. This approach has been criticized for its inability to capture interrelationships among the quality indicators (that is, the indicators' relative importance).

Another approach falls under the general rubric of reputational studies, which focus heavily on judgments of alumni and external raters (such as employers, deans, and so on). This approach suffers from biases related to the inherent problems involved in asking alumni to rate their own schools and external raters to judge programs with which they are wholly unfamiliar (Lawrence & Green, 1980).

Still another, the "quantitative correlate" approach, seeks to understand quality by examining factors that relate to quality; it often uses reputation as the starting point, thereby infusing the aforementioned biases. For example, researchers might study the top twenty-five schools and try to understand factors they have in common.

The concept of quality is multidimensional and often oversimplified. A comprehensive understanding of quality requires, at a minimum, a full examination of both educational processes and outcomes (UNICEF, 2000). For example, the notion of academic quality represents elements of both merit and worth, whereby level of attainment and utility of such attainment are to be considered simultaneously (Kuh, 1981).

Even existing quality frameworks rarely distinguish between relative and absolute approaches to evaluation (UNESCO, 2005). Thus, although some approaches capture quality against a standard (such as accreditation), other approaches measure quality by comparing institutions (for example, through media rankings) without regard to a particular level of achievement. Overall, a fair reading of the academic quality literature might conclude that ". . . in the absence of a theory of quality, it has been difficult to select the best-suited variables or combinations of variables for measuring quality" (Tan, 1992, p. 206).

Not surprisingly, then, the existing literature consists of a disparate collection of studies that lacks comprehensive or integrative frameworks. Curiously, even though they are often at odds, both the academic literature and existing quality systems, such as media rankings, have been largely concerned with how to *measure* quality rather than clearly defining the meaning or nature of quality. Yet, fundamental to any valid measurement system is a full explanation of the concepts being evaluated.

In this chapter, we advance the conversation about quality by suggesting that current systems are imperfect measures of graduate school quality. In using the term *quality* we simply mean the extent to which a product or service manages to fulfill the purposes it was designed for (Certo & Certo, 2009). We first offer a brief review of the two most-consumed signals of quality: accreditation and media rankings. From an understanding of their limitations, we then develop a more comprehensive and robust conceptualization of graduate management education quality. This conceptualization, which depicts management education quality as highly multidimensional, leads to a recommendation for developing a rating system as the only legitimate way to index graduate management quality. Before we get to that recommendation, however, we first set the stage, because current quality systems have become part of the fabric of business schools' existence.

Current Conceptualizations of Program Quality

Although the most resourceful stakeholders may find some useful information in the academic literature or by scouring individual program websites, it appears that most people are looking for heuristics they can use to more easily signal quality and compare one institution to another. Here we discuss two that are widely used.

Accreditation

Two prominent accreditation bodies are AACSB International (the Association to Advance Collegiate Schools of Business) or EQUIS (the European Quality Improvement System). By obtaining accreditation from AACSB, for example, institutions attempt to send a clear message that their programs uphold the highest level of educational quality against an absolute set of standards and values. Accordingly, the preamble of the AACSB accreditation guidelines notes unequivocally that "accreditation focuses on the quality of education. Standards set demanding but realistic thresholds, challenge educators to pursue continuous improvement, and guide improvement in education programs"

(AACSB, 2010, p. 3). Given accreditation's commitment to quality and stated intentions, it is not surprising that accreditation is one of a few areas prospective students cite as being important to their enrollment decisions (GMAC, 2008). Further, AACSB accreditation is usually an additional endorsement beyond a university-wide accreditation (by, for example, the North Central Association of Colleges and Schools). As a result, institutions holding this additional seal of approval ought to stand out as being of higher quality than those who haven't received it.

Nevertheless, since 1996, the number of institutions attaining AACSB accreditation has grown by more than 75 percent to 570 as of 2009 (Francisco, Noland, & Sinclair, 2008) and to more than 640 schools as of late 2012. One reason for this growth is the reliance on the "mission-driven" philosophy that encourages "diverse paths to achieving high quality in management education" (AACSB, 2010, p. 4). By affording programs this diversity, AACSB allows for substantial variation in requirements and student experiences across MBA programs. Practically speaking, this means that curriculum decisions regarding required coursework are not predetermined by the accrediting body but rather seen as part of a broader "business model" for accomplishing a school's primary stated mission.

In this sense, AACSB does not certify that the MBA, for example, carries a highly particular set of requirements but rather that the manner in which business schools pursue their variations on the degree is accomplished within certain quality parameters. As a measure of quality, then, AACSB accreditation verifies a baseline standard beyond which it's likely that substantial variation in program quality exists among accredited institutions. Despite such a seal of approval, however, few stakeholders are willing to treat all of the roughly 640 AACSB-accredited business schools as equivalent in terms of overall program quality. As such, because accreditation represents quality in an absolute and not relative sense, it rarely provides enough information to enable individuals to differentiate among business schools.

Media Rankings

Perhaps the most accessible signal of educational quality is communicated not by institutional oversight bodies but by media rankings (for example, *Bloomberg Businessweek*). Unlike accreditation, media rankings provide signals about *relative* levels of quality, with higher rankings intended to represent higher levels of quality compared with lower rankings. Since the 1990s a critical examination has taken place in the literature about the value of media rankings as indicators of educational quality (Elsbach & Kramer, 1996; Morgeson & Nahrgang, 2008; Safon, 2007; Trank & Rynes, 2003; Zemsky, 2008). Regardless of one's opinion of rankings, two conclusions are not in dispute:

1. *Rankings matter.* Rankings are clearly very important to a wide range of business school stakeholders. Ranked schools (and their students) enjoy significant advantages, including increased recruitment and placement activities, enhanced alumni donations, and increases in applicant quality (Argenti, 2000; Corley & Gioia, 2000; Gioia & Corley, 2002). Such advantages are so highly sought that sustaining their positions (or attempting to break into rankings) is thought to "dominate business schools' thought and action" (Gioia & Corley, 2002, p. 108) and focus schools on initiatives to "look good" rather than "be good" (Policano, 2005).

2. *Rankings are here to stay.* Despite a flurry of criticism, business school stakeholders continue to look to rankings to differentiate program quality; as a result, there are at least four major ranking publications (DeNisi, 2008). One of the purported advantages of media rankings reflects the conventional wisdom that business schools cannot be trusted to provide credible or objective information about quality; they

require an independent or objective third party. Less known to the general public, however, are the numerous studies suggesting that rankings are anything but objective indicators. Instead, they represent a relatively narrow focus on institutional reputation rather than a broad assessment of academic quality, even in the most liberal sense (Morgeson & Nahrgang, 2008). Thus, although it is clear that not all business school administrators embrace media rankings (Policano, 2005; Zemsky, 2008), rankings have created a system in which "playing the rankings game" is seen as a requirement (Corley & Gioia, 2000). Given the public's thirst for such information and business schools' continuing participation, media rankings are unlikely to go away anytime soon.

What If We Focus on Quality Instead?

There is an undeniable sense that across all areas of higher education, building a comprehensive understanding of academic quality has been difficult, unproductive, and largely dictated by external bodies that can maintain an "air of objectivity." One central reason for this failure to comprehensively define and measure quality is the sheer complexity of such an undertaking. Indeed, at the heart of this challenge is an issue endemic to all existing quality measurement systems, namely, that they suffer from the so-called "criterion problem" (Thorndike, 1949).[1] The criterion problem refers specifically to the inherent "difficulties involved in the process of conceptualizing and measuring" concepts or performance indicators that are clearly multidimensional in nature (Austin & Villanova, 1992, p. 836). For example, anyone who has ever had his or her job performance evaluated by a manager or supervisor knows how common it is for one's boss to overemphasize certain performance factors while ignoring or underemphasizing others. Thus, the real challenge in accurately capturing a multidimensional concept such as quality is

Figure 8.1 The Criterion Problem

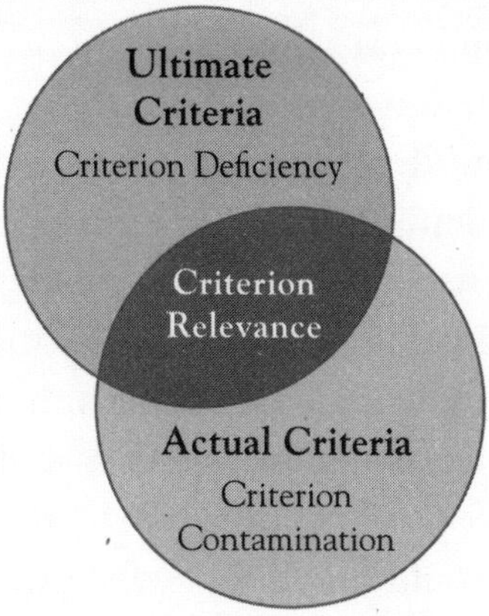

Source: Thorndike, 1949.

that it is an "ultimate criterion," representing an abstraction that can only be approximated because it represents everything that ultimately defines quality.

Because the ultimate criterion is entirely conceptual, one must develop actual criteria to approximate the ultimate criterion. For example, nearly all educational institutions rely heavily on grades, which represent an approximation of individual learning. Ideally, one hopes the actual criteria overlap significantly with the ultimate criterion (resulting in "criterion relevance"). But often criteria are deficient or contaminated (see Figure 8.1; Thorndike, 1949). *Criterion deficiency* refers to a failure to include important criteria that are present in the ultimate criterion; an example of criterion deficiency is rankings that omit measures of student learning. *Criterion contamination* occurs when criteria are included but are largely unrelated to the ultimate criterion, such as the extent to which a school is located in an urban or rural area. Both deficiency and contamination are problematic because together they distort a full understanding of the ultimate criterion (Brogden & Taylor, 1950). Simply put, "if we are measuring the wrong thing, it will not help us to measure it better" (Wherry,

1957, p. 5). It is in this spirit that we set about to systematically define what constitutes MBA program quality, assess the content of that quality model, and refine it.

More specifically, given the high stakes involved in MBA programs (that is, university profit centers, return on investment expectations of students, primary recruiting for employers, and so forth), we argue that it is time for academics to move from simply criticizing existing systems to creating meaningful alternatives. One meaningful and viable alternative to existing quality representations would be to develop a *rating system* of MBA program quality. We are certainly not the first to suggest that moving to ratings would broadly improve the measurement and objective reality of program quality. For example, Morgeson and Nahrgang (2008) noted that adopting a rating system would "make the differences explicit to consumers. . . . Schools that are not significantly different in terms of ratings can then be treated as functionally equivalent in terms of quality" (p. 39). Similarly, in a report from an AACSB task force on issues in graduate management education, the committee's first of four recommendations is to "label MBA rankings accurately" and "convert from rankings to ratings" (AACSB, 2005, p. 10); the report notes that "deans have always believed that rankings measures do not accurately reflect quality of business education" (AACSB, 2005, p. 7). Further, robust rating systems are rather common in education (in, for example, Carnegie classifications) and throughout industry (as in, for example, Standard & Poor's credit-worthiness ratings and *Consumer Reports'* ratings of product quality). This suggests that stakeholders are not averse to rating systems and would likely embrace such an approach.

Although there is ubiquitous agreement among academics that ratings are superior to rankings, far less agreement exists about what criteria such ratings might use. Put simply, creating any meaningful new system first requires a complete understanding of the essential criteria that constitute academic quality in MBA programs. To date, no one has undertaken such an expansive view of MBA program quality, and it remains unspecified in the literature.

Our research offers a comprehensive consideration of MBA quality that can serve as the foundation for such a system. We chose to focus on MBA program quality because of the substantial work that has examined MBA programs already and because they are typically the most prominent business school programs. Given the focus of most graduate management education programs in schools of business, however, the resulting model is likely to be highly generalizable across programs.

Building and Validating a Quality Content Model

Following the best practices in criterion development efforts that the social sciences commonly use, we conducted the research across three broad phases. We summarize our research method in Exhibit 8.1. (For more details, see Rubin, Dierdorff, and Morgeson, 2011). The results of the first phase of research produced an initial content model that includes twenty-four dimensions organized into nine broader meta-dimensions. The number of

Exhibit 8.1 Research Method to Develop and Validate the Program Quality Model

Phase 1: Develop Preliminary Program Quality Model (PQM)

We extensively reviewed the academic literature pertaining to issues of educational quality spanning multiple disciplinary areas, including general business, management, marketing, higher education, and so forth. We extracted from identified sources any definitions, aspects, and/or facets that were described as indicative of educational quality in general. After excluding sources that did not explicitly discuss criteria related to quality in education, we identified a total of 48 usable and unique sources, resulting in a total of 314 quality criteria. These criteria served as the initial input for a PQM.

Phase 2: Conduct a Content Analysis

We conducted a content analysis of the 314 quality criteria via a Q-sort technique by two of the principal investigators, which yielded tentative criteria clusters that were subsequently titled. That is, all of the quality criteria were printed on note cards and then subsequently sorted (grouped) into conceptually similar clusters by two principal researchers[*] The aim of this Q-sort was to iteratively produce a more parsimonious description of collected quality criteria. Following the Q-sort, tentative "titles" for each of the criteria clusters were generated. An independent review of the Q-sort results by the third principal investigator was then conducted. Here, potential misclassifications were identified and discussed among the three investigators and subsequently reclassified. Clusters were further sorted into meta-categories to enhance interpretability and organization of the preliminary program quality model. Finally, we identified and convened a panel of sixteen subject matter experts (SMEs) in total for focus groups and subsequent surveying (Stewart, Shamdasani, & Rook, 2007, p. 54). The major goals of SME review were to gain general background information about what constitutes quality in graduate management education, learn how the SME panel discussed the notion of quality (that is, the context of the discussion), and obtain reactions and/or revisions to the initial PQM.

Phase 3: Collect Supplemental Content Validity Evidence and Reactions

Survey methodology was used to gather quantitative data in this phase. SME panel participants from Phase 2 were the focal respondents. Conventional procedures for collecting content-related validity were followed (Lawshe, 1975) whereby SMEs rated how "essential" each of the twenty-four dimensions of the PQM were. Specifically, SMEs were asked, "Please indicate how

*Along with the chapter authors, Erich Dierdorff of DePaul University also served as a principle project researcher.

essential each of the following factors are in creating a high-quality MBA program." Ratings were made using a three-point scale of "unnecessary," "somewhat essential," and "essential." All dimensions were presented with definitions and examples to facilitate interpretation.

In addition, seventy policy-makers from AACSB-accredited business schools were surveyed to judge the importance of each PQM dimension to MBA program quality, the degree to which each was currently emphasized at their institution, the relative utility of each in maximizing quality, and general reactions toward ranking and rating systems for assessing quality.

dimensions belonging to each of the meta-dimensions range from zero (requires no further explication at the dimension level) to five (contains multiple dimensions). Exhibit 8.2 provides the names of each meta-dimension, corresponding dimensions, definitions, and examples. We refer to this resulting content model as the Program Quality Model or PQM.

Subject matter experts (SMEs) were asked to rate the "essentiality" of each of the twenty-four dimensions of the PQM. Table 8.1 shows the percentage endorsements across the rating categories for each PQM dimension. Each of the twenty-four dimensions received no less than 86.7 percent endorsement of "somewhat essential" or "essential." For half of the dimensions, 100 percent of the SMEs indicated "somewhat essential" or "essential." These results suggest that the PQM is comprehensive in scope and contains little redundancy in capturing the essence of MBA program quality.

We next sought to collect reactions to the PQM from the SMEs and seventy policy-makers (that is, MBA program directors, associate deans, and deans) across several topical areas related to the PQM, as well as obtaining other general reactions

Exhibit 8.2 MBA Quality Dimension, Definitions, and Examples

Metadimension and Definition		Dimensions	Definition (Features)
1. **Curriculum:** The overall quality of the courses of study provided by the program/institution	1.1	Content	Degree of relevance of the learning content presented in the courses of study that constitute the curriculum (for example, relevance to managerial work, practicality, mix of program's courses)
	1.2	Delivery	Specific manner in which the learning content is presented to students (for example, experiential learning, online or distance learning)
	1.3	Program structure	Specific manner with which the courses of study within the curriculum are arranged to constitute the program as a whole (for example, program length, sequence of required courses)
2. **Faculty:** The overall quality of teaching personnel within the program/institution	2.1	Qualifications	The educational and professional backgrounds of faculty that impinge on their ability to effectively impart practical and relevant knowledge to students (for example, educational background of faculty)
	2.2	Research	Degree to which faculty are involved in activities that make intellectual contributions to the knowledge base of the field (for example, research productivity, quality, impact on practice)
	2.3	Teaching	Extent to which faculty provide high-quality learning experiences for students that facilitate the acquisition and retention of relevant knowledge and skills (for example, preparation, facilitation)

	2.4	Overall quality	Overall perceptions of faculty performance (for example, faculty/student perceptions)
3. Placement: The overall quality of career-related programmatic opportunities for students	3.1	Alumni network	Breadth of alumni resources available to students (for example, networking opportunities)
	3.2	Career services	Extent to which services or mechanisms are made available to students regarding career guidance, placement, and development (for example, resume building, recruitment coordination)
	3.3	Corporate and community relations	Extent to which the program/institution has and actively develops relationships with organizations in its community (for example, community outreach activities, local business relationships)
4. Reputation: The extent to which the program/institution is recognized by external stakeholders as being of high quality or merit		None	
5. Student learning and outcomes: The extent to which students acquire relevant knowledge and skills and attain associated career outcomes	5.1	Personal competency development	Training effectiveness of specific competencies required for students to effectively function in their resulting careers (for example, alignment of competency development in target careers)

(Continued)

Metadimension and Definition	Dimensions		Definition (Features)
	5.2	Student career consequences	Impact of program/institution membership (including development experiences and earned credentials) on nonmonetary career outcomes (for example, career options, job mobility)
	5.3	Student economic outcomes	Impact of program/institution membership (including development experiences and earned credentials) on monetary outcomes (for example, starting salaries, salary increases)
	5.4	Learning outcome assessment	Extent to which the program/institution achieves its educational objectives (for example, degree completion rates, learning goal achievement)
6. Institutional resources: The overall quality of resources available to the program/institution and its constituents	6.1	Facilities	Presence of physical and technological infrastructure that facilitates program/institution functioning (for example, library resources, level of classroom technology)
	6.2	Financial resources	Amount of monetary funds available to the program/institution for maintaining and enhancing functioning (for example, endowments, donations)
	6.3	Investment in faculty	Extent to which resources are available and devoted to faculty for facilitating and enhancing faculty activities (for example, research funding, support for development)
	6.4	Tuition and fees	Monetary contributions made by students to the program/institution

6.5	Student support services	Extent to which resources are available and devoted to facilitating and enhancing student activities (for example, academic support, student services office)
7. Program/Institution climate: The overall educational context, consisting of prevailing values, attitudes, and norms within the program/institution		
7.1	Diversity	Extent to which diversity is valued by the program/institution, in addition to the extent that this value is reflected in program/institution personnel and the student population (for example, demographic heterogeneity, international faculty)
7.2	Educational environment	Extent to which program/institution characteristics facilitate student educational development and reflect a value for learning/education (for example, faculty involvement, student interaction)
8. Program student composition: The overall makeup and corresponding quality of the student population with respect to academic achievement and professional experiences	None	
9. Strategic focus: The overall quality of the articulated mission of the program/institution and corresponding strategic planning and positioning with respect to achieving the mission	None	

Table 8.1 Essentiality Ratings of PQM Dimensions by Subject Matter Experts

Dimensions	Unnecessary	Somewhat Essential	Essential
Curriculum			
Curriculum content	0.0%	13.3%	86.7%
Curriculum delivery	13.3%	26.7%	60.0%
Program structure	0.0%	53.3%	46.7%
Faculty			
Faculty qualifications	0.0%	40.0%	60.0%
Faculty research	13.3%	60.0%	26.7%
Faculty teaching	0.0%	0.0%	100.0%
Overall faculty quality	0.0%	26.7%	73.3%
Placement			
Alumni network	0.0%	73.3%	26.7%
Career service	0.0%	20.0%	80.0%
Corporate and community relations	6.7%	60.0%	33.3%
Reputation	6.7%	53.3%	40.0%
Student Learning and Outcomes			
Student personal competency Development	0.0%	53.3%	46.7%
Student career consequences	6.7%	53.3%	40.0%
Student economic outcomes	6.7%	86.7%	6.7%
Student learning outcome assessment	13.3%	33.3%	53.3%
Institutional Resources			
Program/Institution facilities	0.0%	73.3%	26.7%
Program/Institution financial resources	0.0%	66.7%	33.3%
Program/Institution investment in Faculty	6.7%	40.0%	53.3%
Program/Institution tuition and fees	0.0%	73.3%	26.7%
Program/Institution student support Services	6.7%	46.7%	46.7%

Table 8.1 (*Continued*)

Dimensions	Unnecessary	Somewhat Essential	Essential
Program/Institution Climate			
Diversity	6.7%	73.3%	20.0%
Educational environment	0.0%	33.3%	66.7%
Program Student Composition	6.7%	60.0%	33.3%
Strategic Focus	13.3%	26.7%	60.0%

Note: A total of sixteen SMEs completed the ratings. Interrater reliability was in the acceptable range (intraclass correlation [ICC] = .69 across all dimensions).

to issues of assessing MBA program quality (such as media rankings). For each of the twenty-four PQM dimensions, SMEs were asked to "indicate the degree to which each of the following factors is readily changeable or malleable for most MBA programs. In other words, to what extent are the following factors under the control of most MBA programs?" The mean controllability rating across all twenty-four dimensions was 3.54 (SD = .588), suggesting at a broad level that business schools can affect the dimensions of the PQM.

However, closer inspection showed there was considerable variation in controllability ratings across the dimensions. Figure 8.2 shows the mean ratings of controllability for each PQM dimension. As the figure shows, among the most malleable aspects of MBA program quality are the dimensions falling under the Curriculum metadimension; among the least malleable were the Reputation and Career/Economic Outcomes metadimension.

At a more general level, both SMEs and policy-makers were asked to evaluate the relative importance of the metadimensions to overall MBA program quality by placing the dimensions in rank order in terms of their impact on improving overall quality. Table 8.2 shows the percentage of SMEs and policy-makers who ranked each metadimension in the top four positions (that is, with ranks of 1, 2, 3, or 4). The metadimension of curriculum

Figure 8.2 SME Controllability Ratings of Quality Dimensions

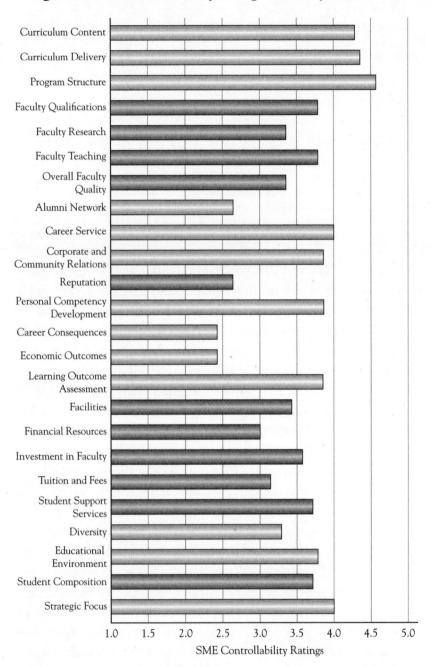

Note: For purposes of clarity, the dimensions are grouped by the nine metadimensions of the PQM. Responses are based upon a 5-point scale in which 1 = not at all controllable, 3 = somewhat controllable, and 5 = completely controllable.

Table 8.2 Percentage Endorsing Metadimension as Important to MBA Program Quality

Metadimension	Subject Matter Experts	Policy-Makers	Average
Curriculum	93%	75%	84%
Faculty	85%	79%	82%
Student learning and outcomes	79%	74%	77%
Placement	57%	53%	55%
Strategic focus	43%	37%	40%
Student composition	21%	34%	27%
Reputation	14%	29%	22%
Institutional resources	14%	19%	17%

received the greatest number of top rankings (that is, ranks of 1); reputation and institutional resources did not receive any top rankings.

Finally, policy-makers responded to survey items that asked about media rankings as well as general reactions to assessing MBA program quality. Table 8.3 provides these items and associated findings. As shown, policy-makers held generally unfavorable views of media rankings' accuracy and meaningfulness (items 4–6). Yet, at the same time, policy-makers responded that there is institutional pressure to use and attend to such media rankings (items 1–3). Policy-makers had positive reactions to using a rating system to depict MBA program quality and thought it was important for business school stakeholders to have program-level information from a procedurally transparent system (items 7–10).

Implications for Assessing Quality

Although substantial evidence derides the reliance on reputation-based indices of quality, scholarship has been slow to offer meaningful alternatives. We think the PQM described here provides

Table 8.3 Policy-Maker Reactions and Attitudes Toward Quality Assessment

Question	M	SD	% Top 2
1. At my school we pay close attention to MBA program media rankings.	3.99	1.04	72.9%
2. My dean frequently discusses his or her concerns about "the competition" (that is, other MBA programs).	3.54	1.05	54.3%
3. Moving up, breaking into, or maintaining our position in a major media ranking is a top priority to my dean.	3.74	1.07	68.6%
4. Program quality differs greatly between schools that are ranked and schools that are not ranked.	2.94	1.04	34.3%
5. Media rankings provide a good measure of the overall quality of an MBA program.	2.23	0.91	8.6%
6. Media rankings are a valid tool to quickly delineate "the best from the rest."	2.41	0.99	15.7%
7. I believe a rating system would add value beyond a ranking system.	3.86	1.05	70.0%
8. Business school stakeholders deserve to know specific information about what a program is doing or not doing.	4.29	0.57	92.9%
9. It would be useful to business school stakeholders to be able to compare one school to another on a set of standardized criteria.	4.20	0.87	85.7%
10. It is important that a rating system is transparent in its data collection procedures.	4.69	0.50	95.7%

Note: Items rated on a 5-point scale (1 = strongly disagree, 3 = neither agree nor disagree, 5 = strongly agree). "% Top 2" represents percentage of responses in the "agree" and "strongly agree" categories.

a necessary first step in offering meaningful alternatives in at least three ways:

1. MBA program quality is multidimensional in nature, and criterion development efforts must seek to identify criteria that are fully representative or cover the full breadth of the quality content domain.

2. To capture the complex multidimensionality of quality, one must examine the phenomenon from multiple perspectives. This necessarily involves input from multiple stakeholders.

3. As with all criteria development efforts, the resulting content model is not likely to be perfectly comprehensive. Thus, the primary goal in criterion development must not be to declare "game over" with respect to understanding quality but to make progress toward improving the accuracy with which we make such approximations.

Comparisons to Current Quality Systems

What stands out most from the derivation of our PQM is that it reflects the considerable multidimensionality undoubtedly present in MBA academic quality. Some dimensions of the model are reflected in other existing systems, such as accreditation standards, because these systems were used as initial input in our criterion development efforts. Yet, our model provides unique elements not represented by existing systems and helps to overcome problems associated with criterion deficiency.

For example, compared to the dimensions contained in our model, the *Bloomberg Businessweek* and *Financial Times* full-time MBA rankings both appear to be deficient in how well they represent MBA quality. They capture roughly 38 percent and 42 percent, respectively, of the PQM dimensions (that is, approximately nine to ten of twenty-four dimensions). Similarly, *U.S. News & World Report* rankings capture only four of the twenty-four quality dimensions. The striking implication is that although these outlets clearly assess some aspects of quality, none of them sufficiently covers the dimensions we uncovered when examining the broad array of quality sources. This highlights one of the key problems with media rankings. Although they purport to comprehensively assess quality, they clearly do not function as advertised because they under-represent or omit entire categories of key quality factors.

At the same time, if stakeholders want to know about a few dimensions, such as student economic outcomes (that is, starting salaries), rankings appear to provide this information sufficiently, albeit for only a very small number of institutions. However, it is one thing to include this information in rankings and omit other critical factors; it is another to give such outcomes disproportional weight. As Gladwell (2011) notes, media rankings do not provide comprehensive views of educational quality but rather make definitive decisions for consumers regarding which educational values or ideals should or should not be important to them when considering a particular institution.

For example, when media rankings assign close to 50 percent of the ranking score to economic outcomes (as in the *Financial Times*) and give virtually no consideration to student learning, the rankings communicate and prioritize a clear set of values regarding what (in their views) should be the ultimate purpose of graduate management education. Because rankings "enshrine very particular ideologies" (Gladwell, 2011, p. 74), stakeholders who hope to use media rankings as credible and definitive signals of MBA program quality should be clear about what the rankings represent to avoid overinterpreting the nature and meaning of such information.

Our results add to substantial and growing concerns about the veracity and usefulness of media rankings in stakeholder decision making. Given the great deficiency in quality content coupled with empirical evidence of the rankings' insufficiency, one might logically surmise that media outlets would be eager to improve their products' accuracy. As Policano (2007) describes, however, the media outlets may have motives beyond the primary task of determining MBA program quality:

> When you recognize the misperceptions that rankings can cause, you would imagine that the media would want to correct this deficiency. But they don't. And why they don't became apparent to me during a conversation that I had with the editor of one of the rankings publications. Basically, I suggested rating, not

ranking, schools. Of course, there would be less change from one year to the next and thus less perceived news associated with any newly released rating and, thus, less public interest. But ratings would provide a more accurate portrayal of the relative quality of programs. The editor responded emphatically they would never adopt any change that would decrease circulation. An interesting response—profits above accuracy. It certainly doesn't seem that, in the rankings game, prospective students are winners. (p. 46)

In contrast to media rankings, accreditation standards from EQUIS and AACSB appear to be substantially more complete in their coverage of the quality dimensions. For example, the AACSB standards cover roughly twelve dimensions, and EQUIS approximately seventeen. Of course, the point of accreditation is to deal primarily with the inputs and process of educational interventions, whereas our model includes inputs, throughputs, and outputs of quality. Although we did not specify relationships among our metadimensions, a high-level examination of the metadimensions reveals this classic open systems framework (Katz & Kahn, 1978). That is, the metadimensions of strategic focus, program student composition, and institutional resources likely represent the major sources of input quality. Curriculum, faculty, program/institution climate, personal competency development and learning, and some aspects of placement (such as career services and community relationships) represent the primary sources of throughput or process quality. Reputation, economic outcomes, and alumni network represent the key sources of output quality. Thus, our quality model could reasonably be used as a diagnostic lens for examining these important program design elements (inputs-throughputs-outputs) to prescribe interventions to improve quality in any given area (see Figure 8.3; Recommendation 1 later in the chapter).

Not All Quality Dimensions Are Equal

Beyond recommending overall improvements in sufficiency over existing quality sources, our SMEs strongly suggested that

Figure 8.3 PQM Represented as an Open Systems Model

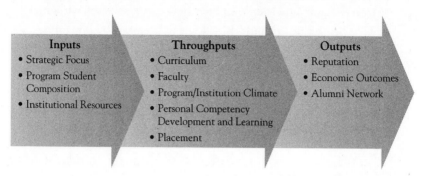

Inputs
- Strategic Focus
- Program Student Composition
- Institutional Resources

Throughputs
- Curriculum
- Faculty
- Program/Institution Climate
- Personal Competency Development and Learning
- Placement

Outputs
- Reputation
- Economic Outcomes
- Alumni Network

although all twenty-four dimensions are important to quality, they are not all equally important. These experts placed the highest importance on quality dimensions such as faculty teaching, curriculum content, and student learning, and the least importance on student economic outcomes, program/institution facilities, and alumni network. One might rightly argue that experts whose life's work is devoted to such concerns would be biased. However, the subject matter experts' views of quality were strongly corroborated by our sample of MBA program directors, whose successful performance is often determined by far less idealistic pursuits. Such pursuits include the number of "butts in seats," placements, and student economic outcomes (areas to which policy-makers did in fact assign more weight than did academic SMEs). Demonstrating the primary importance of teaching and learning, however, one subject matter expert remarked, "Education is largely about the teachers. Does anyone argue that your child's third grade teacher is not the most important element in his or her third grade education? Other things matter, of course, but if you want a great MBA, you need a great faculty that engages students."

The focus on teaching and learning is perhaps not surprising when one considers these are areas in which business schools have considerable control. Yet, an analysis of the dimensions most heavily weighted in media rankings, for instance, shows substantial importance given to the very dimensions that our experts suggest are out of business schools' direct control, namely, alumni networks, reputation, student economic and career outcomes. The implication, of course, is that if quality involves things that cannot be changed, there is simply no use in pursuing activities to attempt to improve them. As one subject matter expert explained, this is a reality of living in a rankings-dominated world:

> "The quality of the program should focus on what we can do, which is facilitating learning. If the students are gaining knowledge and skill, then we are doing our job. All else supports that goal, and flows from it. Of course, that sets aside the reality that some firms hire on reputation, which means that student economic outcomes (placement) are influenced by things outside the control of current leaders and teachers. I think the best we can do is acknowledge this is true, but then focus on what b-schools *can do* to ensure learning."

To reiterate, the PQM presented here does include quality outcomes. But, as the expert view presented exemplifies, quality outcomes are less meaningful when critical educational process components are ignored.

Why Is It So Hard to Adopt a Program Quality Content Model?

Focusing stakeholders on all dimensions of quality beyond reputation and student economic outcomes is not without difficulties. In fact, our data show just how hard this can be. For example, policy-makers rated the quality dimensions of curriculum content, faculty teaching, and overall faculty quality as highly important. However, when asked how much emphasis these areas receive in their respective programs, policy-makers rated each substantially lower. One reason for this misalignment might be the continual shadow of media rankings, which emphasize outcomes over process. For example, although our policy-maker sample strongly rejected the notion that media rankings provide "good measures" of overall quality, 73 percent reported that their institutions pay close attention to the rankings (see Table 8.2). Despite the convincing evidence that breaking into the rankings is an extremely rare occurrence for never-before-ranked institutions (Morgeson & Nahrgang, 2008), schools that believe they are on the cusp are likely to ignore many of the aspects of quality uncovered in our model in favor of focusing on the criteria the rankings weight most heavily. In doing so, these institutions divert critical resources from the central mission of business schools—to inculcate knowledge and skills about the science and practice of management (Khurana, 2007; Mintzberg, 2004; Rubin & Dierdorff, 2009). Paradoxically, one major benefit to schools that are unranked in major media-ranking publications (and whose prospects are low for breaking in) is that they may feel freer to focus on the full breadth of quality dimensions. As Policano (2005) described it, before the major rankings emerged in the late 1980s

> business school deans could actually focus on improving quality in their schools' educational offerings. Discussions about strategic marketing were confined mostly to the marketing curriculum. PR firms were hired by business, not business schools. Many business schools had sufficient facilities, but few buildings had marble floors, soaring atriums, or plush carpeting. Public university tuition was affordable for most students, and even the top MBA programs were accessible to students with high potential but low GMAT scores. (p. 26)

The point is that even the most well-intentioned and mission-focused business schools have been subjected to what Khurana (2007) calls "the tyranny of rankings." This must contribute in some form to the schools' inability to align what they know to be important in terms of quality with their actual program practices. In this way, chasing media rankings pushes business schools away from their core mission—to educate. Although business schools clearly differ in their view of their primary pursuits (Palmer & Short, 2008), we doubt that *any* business school would say that its central mission is to help students make more money.

The result then is an absurd reinforcing cycle: Ranked schools promote aspects of quality from the very limited criteria media rankings capture, and lower-ranked institutions seek to emulate these "leading business schools" who "lead" due to activities that make up a very small slice of the overall quality pie. Even when academic researchers seek to understand quality, they, too, tend to limit their examination to these leading institutions and reinforce the perceived validity of the rankings (for example, Datar, Garvin, & Cullen, 2010; Navarro, 2008).

Thus, despite their associated dysfunction, rankings single-handedly own the quality space and remain resilient in the face of such critiques. This resiliency is due, in part, to that "air of objectivity" that a third party can provide. For instance, media publication editors often callously dismiss even evidence-based criticisms from the Academy of Management as being baseless and motivated by self-interest (see Lavelle, 2008).[2] Portraying the academy as out of touch and hiding behind the ivory tower with respect to quality is at the heart of the media rankings' original intentions. Historically, the rankings were meant to respond to what many believed was the complacency and self-satisfaction that business school administration and faculty developed in the 1980s (see Porter & McKibbon, 1989). Khurana (2007) agrees that one benefit of media rankings is that they have played a "salutary role by focusing [business schools] on their external environment" (p. 342). Therefore, media rankings have in fact achieved their original intent of creating a market in which students and corporations can have data on which to base their application or employment decisions.

In principle, we strongly believe in the usefulness and legitimacy of independent ranking systems. Such systems avoid the appearance of bias and often have mechanisms to buffer potential conflicts of interest. At the same time, we reject systems that refuse to change in the face of substantial, credible evidence regarding their veracity. Regardless of their humble beginnings and despite overwhelming evidence suggesting rankings' inherent problems, media-ranking organizations appear to have absolutely no interest in devoting resources to improved systems (DeAngelo, DeAngelo, & Zimmerman, 2005). Ironically, the very organizations that derided business schools for their apathy and that claim responsibility for upholding a system that encourages business schools to "do better" are themselves unwilling to engage in serious continuous improvement.

Yet, the successes of media rankings are informative in at least one way. They highlight stakeholders' ongoing desire for information about program quality. Indeed, more than any other factor, an institution's quality and reputation are rated by MBA applicants as the most important criteria when selecting schools (GMAC, 2010). Thus, in media-ranking organizations' attempt to deflect legitimate criticism and forestall meaningful change, the real losers are not the business schools that did not make the top twenty but the innumerable stakeholders who make consequential life decisions on the results of a deeply flawed system.

Toward a Better Quality System

As we have said, the time is now for business schools, policymakers, and academics alike to stop critiquing and start creating a new way forward. In doing so, we must start by acknowledging that the advent of business school rankings and their continued popularity are due in part to a long historical lack of transparency and a business-as-usual approach to graduate management education. Further, we must acknowledge stakeholders' continuing desire for information that can help signal quality and provide useful demarcations of various program elements. With this in mind, the next stage of assessing MBA program quality should involve developing a rating system based upon the PQM described here and toward the creation of a comprehensive program quality index. Such a system would offer several unique advantages over media rankings, including (a) clearer depiction of multidimensionality; (b) specific representation of differences and similarities; (c) enhanced transparency, and (d) increased focus on education. Next, we briefly discuss each advantage.

Clearer Depiction of Multidimensionality

First and foremost with respect to content, our model appropriately depicts the clear multidimensionality present in the abstraction known as "quality." Put simply, the key advantage of a rating system is that it would depict program *quality profiles* that stakeholders could use to evaluate the full breadth of quality. Moreover, schools that are not substantially different in these ratings could be treated as functionally equivalent in quality.

At the same time, depicting quality profiles could also allow individuals to weight each quality dimension according to their own unique needs or perspectives. End users could query a rating system to address their particular needs, such as when recruiters are interested in programs with high-quality international internships or applicants want programs that emphasize the development of team skills. For instance, in Figure 8.4 we show how a rating system could provide unique information within and among institutions. In this simplified example, a prospective student truly interested in student learning might select School A given the institution's strength in this area; a student more concerned with economic outcomes might select School B. In both cases, the inherent trade-offs involved in choosing one institution over another would be readily apparent and allow users to weight and prioritize their own quality imperatives.

Figure 8.4 Example of a Quality Dimension Profile Comparison on the Metadimension of Student Outcomes

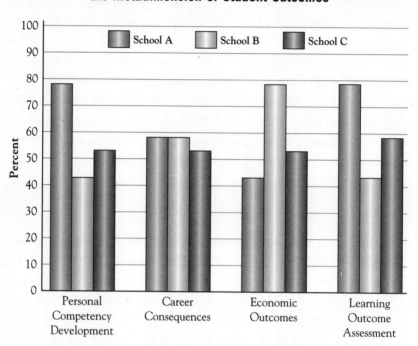

Specific Representation of Differences and Similarities

One misconception about rating systems is that they group too many schools together and therefore do not show meaningful differences. We think this concern represents a half-truth. Because rating systems have the potential to treat large groupings of institutions as functionally equivalent, they almost always do so in the recognition that any differences presented should be valid and not manufactured.

In comparison, rankings suffer from methodological concerns that obscure meaningful performance differences (Murphy & Cleveland, 1995). These concerns include the inability to communicate the magnitude of the differences among schools, arbitrary weighting of different criteria (Policano, 2007), reliance on limited, convenient, and potentially biased data sources, and a highly subjective sampling (Morgeson & Nahrgang, 2008). For example, ranked institutions are often separated by less than one point on total criteria scores (Morgeson & Nahrgang, 2008). In a rating system, school data would more clearly highlight the differences across quality criteria while taking certain baseline information into account. Rating systems allow for both broad classifications of programs that meet certain minimal requirements (such as accreditation) and specific classifications on criteria that show how those programs go *beyond* such requirements (such as clear evidence of student learning). In other words, ratings are by nature compensatory, meaning that the quality dimensions programs choose to emphasize would be more clearly depicted.

Enhanced Transparency

Because rating systems are not limited to an arbitrary "best set" of institutions, stakeholders would be able to see how widely MBA programs vary. This promotes a transparency that is not present today in discussions of quality. No longer would debates be structured around whether a school ranked thirty-first is really worse than the school ranked twenty-seventh; rather, the ratings would allow information to surface regarding differences and similarities.

A rating system would promote transparency further by showing changes over time on quality dimensions that institutions are trying to improve. In contrast, when a school moves up in a ranking, it is often difficult to determine exactly how and why the school "improved." As mentioned earlier, as of this writing, AACSB accredits programs at more than 640 schools of business. On the surface, of course, media rankings make it appear as if all of these institutions had been studied to arrive at the "top" one hundred, fifty, or thirty business schools. As Morgeson and Nahrgang (2008) found, in the three decades *Business Week* has ranked institutions, only thirty-five unique institutions have ever appeared on the top-thirty list. Under a rating system, all institutions that want to be included and rated could be if they so chose, thereby giving stakeholders a real sense of how their local programs would compare to other more nationally or internationally focused institutions.

Finally, transparency is enhanced by rating systems in which data are sourced for multiple stakeholders and through multiple methods. Because ratings would need to capture a wide range of quality information, they would not be limited to self-reported surveys from recruiters and students; rather, they would involve a broader set of institutions, faculty, and policy-makers. Such data collection efforts would necessitate open access to information and allow any individual or institution to use the data to study how the rating system could be continually improved.

Increased Focus on Education

A rating system would likely help reduce the dysfunctional behavior involved when institutions chase or manipulate the most heavily weighted criteria in rankings. Indeed, anecdotes abound regarding all-too-common efforts to game reports of student GMAT scores, internship placements, prior work experience, and so forth. Underscoring the magnitude of the dysfunction that rankings encourage by placing so much weight on so few criteria, Emory University recently acknowledged a decade-long misrepresentation of high school SAT and ACT scores reported to the *U.S. News* rankings (Supiano, 2012), and a similar admission of misreporting of GMAT scores was made by Tulane University administrators (Morse, 2013).

Because ratings are not limited to a small number of narrow criteria, institutions may be more empowered to pursue their strengths and educational missions knowing that their efforts and improvements would be clearer in a rating system. Under media rankings, institutions that place a strong emphasis on, for instance, teaching are not "rewarded" or given credit compared to institutions that pursue a high degree of research output. Thus, rating systems would encourage schools to pursue improvements in many domains that are currently undervalued or ignored by institutions that are heavily involved in playing the rankings game.

Acting Today to Improve Quality Tomorrow

By now, the reader may be frustrated with this chapter's some-what idealistic tone, perhaps including a lack of attention to the on-the-ground realities of most business schools. After all, even though most policy-makers can agree that media rankings are deficient, to date no reasonable alternative exists. Further, although a rating system may sound good in theory, the barriers to putting one in place may seem too daunting, particularly from the perspective of individual schools caught squarely in the rank-ings game.

We suggest that changing the current state may not be as difficult as it appears. The responsibility most definitely starts with institutional leaders who can act now to change their fates in the near term and at the local level. Toward this end, we next offer a few critical recommendations to advance the quality agenda in graduate management education. That said, we fully acknowledge that any action that takes away from the substantial status quo–preserving forces and moves toward improved assess-ment and management of quality is likely to inflict a bit of pain.

Recommendation 1: Use the PQM as an Assessment and Management Tool

It is often said that all politics are local. Similarly, we would contend that regardless of the national or international trends, participation in rankings, or institutional resources, nothing should stand in the way of a business school adopting a broader perspective on educational quality in its own institution. Start with the mission statement and ask stakeholders salient quality-related questions from the PQM. For example, under curriculum, key questions might include,

- "Is our curriculum aligned with what is required for future managers to be successful?"
- "Do we deliver curriculum in a way that engages and promotes optimal learning?"
- "Have we structured the program in a way that encourages or maximizes opportunities to learn?"

Take time to operationalize metrics in each of the model's categories for one's own institution, not relative to others. Here again, asking self-study questions such as "What do we mean when we say, 'quality teaching' and how will we measure it?" or "What is meant by a "'strong alumni network'" and how do we most appropriately measure it?" is likely to lead to the development of unique quality indicators.

Using the model as a guide, an institution can use metrics to create an internal dashboard or performance scorecard to actively track improvements alongside other more traditional key indicators such as revenue, enrollments, and so forth (which of course fall under "institutional resources" in the PQM). As noted, one critical component to making the content model come alive as an assessment and management tool is to get as many people involved as possible who can shape the meaning and nature of the metrics identified and collected. As Figure 8.3 and our data suggest, institutions may benefit from focusing their efforts more closely on important educational throughputs, all of which can be prioritized at the local level. Reach out to and include all major business school stakeholders, including faculty, students, alumni, employers, administrators, community members, and local government.

Recommendation 2: Build Learning Communities or Communities of Practice

In their study regarding the stability of *Bloomberg Businessweek* rankings, Morgeson and Nahrgang (2008) demonstrate that the average correlation between the *Businessweek* lists from ranking year to year is .82. Compare this with an average correlation of .30 for the rankings of NCAA basketball teams from the Associated Press polls tracked over the same time period as the *Bloomberg Businessweek* rankings. The striking implication is that ". . . when a ranking system is based on observable, head-to-head performance, they will exhibit considerable variability over time" because ". . . there is an agreed upon performance criteria . . . that produces clear winners and losers" (Morgeson & Nahrgang, 2008, p. 38). Despite this evidence, much of the success of media ranking has relied on logic that suggests business schools are engaged in heated "head-to-head" competition, much like corporate giants Pepsi and Coke or Costco and Sam's Club, fighting for every percentage of market share they can grab. Ironically, this notion has been propagated by substantial literature produced by the AACSB and others that essentially argues that business schools need to make unique "value propositions" to their primary customers, namely, students (Khurana, 2007). This type of thinking effectively ignores the simple fact that all higher education institutions essentially share the same primary mission: education. Similarly, all business schools share the common purpose of educating managers for future managerial and professional roles in organizations (Rubin & Dierdorff, 2011).

Given that business schools are not really competitors in the true sense of the word and that they share a strong common purpose, we encourage schools to adopt a stance of cooperation rather than competition with respect to quality. One way to promote such cooperation is to create "communities of practice" "that are naturally aligned around critical common characteristics about their programs, such as student composition (for example, part-time MBAs), funding sources (private versus public), and so forth.[3] Although such groups currently exist for purposes of sharing information (for example, AACSB affinity groups), we imagine more robust partnerships being created. Such groups could pool resources, operationalize the most critical quality content criteria from the PQM, and agree to a set of guidelines for sharing information and using such information to improve quality. For example, DePaul University is directing the formation of a new center dedicated to furthering knowledge about quality in part-time graduate management education with the goal of sharing extensive information on different quality dimensions on a yearly basis (http://www.parttimeexcellence.org). Given that no program is perfect with respect to quality, deans may find that such cooperative efforts will help them to further their strengths while improving upon quality challenges that do not equal the standards of others in their communities of practice.

Recommendation 3: Participate in the Construction of a Rating System

Beyond using the PQM at the local level to assess, track, and improve quality in graduate management programs, we strongly encourage all interested institutions to begin conversations with well-suited third parties who could begin to shape and develop a national and international rating system. Pursuing a viable rating system requires additional work on at least two major fronts. First, future research is required to further validate the PQM by understanding the interrelationships among the dimensions. This requires data representing each dimension that would allow researchers to understand the amount of unique variance in overall quality each dimension contributes. Further, work remains to establish a more parsimonious set of metrics as well as isolate metrics that are most representative of the quality dimension to which they pertain. This work also requires the explication of data sources and determination of what sources (for example, student reports, standardized measures, and so forth) best capture the meaning and nature of a given dimension. Undoubtedly, multiple perspectives and sources would contribute to the most robust measurement system.

To be certain, concerns over data are a substantial challenge to the development of a rating system, so much so that it represents a key barrier to creating a new system. Yet, we were curious regarding just how difficult it might be to generate metrics that could reasonably capture the essence of PQM using more objective and direct measures. We put together a small research team to generate an initial listing of dimension-level metrics and then rate each metric generated on its (a) *objectivity* (outcome based versus judgmental), (b) *level of practicality* (high, medium, low), and (c) *degree of discriminability* (high, medium, low), or the extent to which variance between schools is likely. A total of 420 nonredundant dimension-level metrics were generated, with an average of 17.5 sample metrics for each dimension (see Table 8.4). Overall, approximately 62 percent of the generated metrics were deemed objective in nature, 49 percent as highly practical to measure and collect, and 42 percent as providing high variance across different MBA programs ("high discriminability"). Based on this evidence, we believe that with a serious effort and institutional buy-in, developing a set of metrics to populate a quality ratings system is feasible.

Second, beyond additional metric generation and validation efforts, additional work is required with respect to implementation. This effort involves developing a data collection protocol along with extensive buy-in from schools, stakeholders, and other interested parties (for example, AACSB or GMAC). As successful rating systems like Standard & Poor's credit ratings demonstrate, the utility of a rating system depends greatly on the cooperation of myriad institutions and stakeholders. Ideally, such a system would involve the leadership of an existing or newly formed nonprofit that would seek only to provide high-quality

Table 8.4 Descriptive Statistics for Sample Metrics by PQM Dimension

Metadimension	Dimension	f	Objective	Practicality			Discriminability		
				High	Medium	Low	High	Medium	Low
Curriculum	Curriculum content	17	24%	30%	35%	35%	24%	52%	24%
	Curriculum delivery	15	47%	53%	40%	7%	20%	67%	13%
	Program structure	13	77%	77%	23%	0%	31%	46%	23%
Faculty	Faculty qualifications	29	58%	17%	73%	10%	34%	66%	0%
	Faculty research	21	95%	5%	95%	0%	71%	29%	0%
	Faculty teaching	11	18%	64%	36%	0%	27%	55%	18%
	Overall faculty quality	16	44%	44%	38%	18%	44%	50%	6%
Placement	Alumni network	22	68%	27%	55%	18%	23%	68%	9%
	Career service	21	67%	57%	33%	10%	33%	62%	5%
	Corporate and community relations	23	78%	43%	57%	0%	52%	39%	9%
Reputation	Reputation	14	50%	57%	36%	7%	4%	29%	29%
Student learning and outcomes	Student personal competency development	5	20%	20%	60%	20%	0%	100%	0%
	Student career consequences	18	61%	0%	67%	33%	39%	61%	0%

	Student economic outcomes	11	100%	9%	73%	18%	64%	36%	0%
	Student learning outcome assessment	16	62%	38%	44%	18%	12%	63%	25%
Institutional resources	Program/Institution facilities	27	74%	74%	26%	0%	67%	33%	0%
	Program/Institution financial resources	24	83%	88%	12%	0%	46%	46%	8%
	Program/Institution investment in faculty	21	86%	80%	10%	10%	38%	57%	5%
	Program/Institution tuition and fees	14	93%	93%	7%	0%	50%	36%	14%
	Program/Institution student support services	15	80%	80%	20%	0%	47%	47%	6%
Program/ Institution climate	Diversity climate	18	61%	72%	28%	0%	78%	17%	5%
	Educational environment	17	70%	47%	41%	12%	23%	65%	12%
Program student composition	Program student composition	19	58%	69%	26%	5%	37%	53%	10%
Strategic focus	Strategic focus	13	8%	8%	84%	8%	54%	23%	23%

information to stakeholders and not become beset with potential conflicts of interest spurred by profit motives associated with selling magazines or driving Internet traffic.

Recommendation 4: Stop Playing the Victim—Reclaim Quality

Finally, we want to challenge business school leaders, particularly business school deans and their peers in highly ranked institutions, to recognize the power they have to perpetuate the current state as well as the power to create a new way forward. Rather than lament that the rankings have taken control of quality assessment and concede that the "rankings game" must be played; simply stop playing. This can be done in a number of ways.

First, use collective power to insist that if *Bloomberg Businessweek* and others want to continue with rankings that they must demonstrate efforts to overcome their rankings' greatest flaws. At the most basic level this most certainly includes actions to broaden the criteria set, efforts to collect data from multiple sources, expansion of institutional participants to all who wished to be considered, and increasing the transparency to consumers regarding the nature of rankings, namely, the obscuring of meaningful differences among institutions.

Second, if media-ranking organizations show no interest in improving, then deans can make the collective decision to no longer supply data and to prohibit their students from responding to surveys while they are enrolled. Yet, this must be a collective effort. As we have seen in the recent past, even when high-profile institutions like Wharton and Harvard decided not to provide *Bloomberg Businessweek* with data regarding starting salaries, *Bloomberg Businessweek* continued to rank them despite the absence of direct data (DeAngelo & others, 2005). The message of this action was clear: a list without Wharton or Harvard in the top twenty was not likely to be seen as a credible list. However, as Zimmerman (2001) noted more than a decade ago, a strong and unanimous effort could effectively shut down the major rankings: "If just a few university presidents at our most prestigious business schools (based on BW rankings) convened and stopped their deans from disclosing to BW the names of their graduating MBA students, then the BW survey would lose much of its credibility. Once a few universities joined forces, more would follow" (p. 21).

Even with such actions, media rankings are not likely to simply exit the stage. In that regard, prominent deans and senior business school leaders can play an educational role, helping the broader media and business community understand the limitations rankings have as measures of academic quality or, for that matter, as a proxy for their students' capabilities. A single "open letter" with the signatures of the institutions current highly ranked by *Bloomberg Businessweek* and published in the *Wall Street Journal* or other mainstream outlet would send a strong signal that it is time for a change. We are not naïve, of course. We recognize that when a dean at a prestigious institution discredits a media ranking, there is a fear that it would be interpreted as a statement about the inferiority of the institution. Yet, we think this is generally a false fear. As Morgeson and Nahrgang (2008) showed, none of the initial set of ranked institutions from *Bloomberg Businessweek*'s first ranking in 1988 has ever fallen out of the ranking. It is safe to say that these schools are likely to enjoy the positive halo of such rankings for decades to come.

Final Thoughts on Reclaiming Control

The time has clearly come for the academic community to move beyond mere criticisms of media rankings as indicators of MBA program quality. We sought to begin this movement by more systematically developing the criterion space surrounding program quality. It is clear from our findings that developing and refining a quality content model is indeed feasible.

Moreover, there is clear consensus from multiple academic stakeholders (scholars and policy-makers) that the identified dimensions adequately represent quality in graduate management education and that media rankings fall substantially short. We firmly believe it is no longer viable to stand on the sidelines while inadequate systems dictate conversations about what values are most important to the quality of graduate management education.

Instead, it is time to take accountability seriously and apply the philosophy of rigorous and evidence-based decision making that we so often espouse in our schools of business. Put simply, we can—and we should—reclaim control of quality in graduate management education, restore it to its rightful place, and regain the positive outlook of our collective futures.

Summing Up

- Business school stakeholders deserve relevant, useful information about program quality and how programs differ in this regard.

- It is important to recognize the complexity and multidimensionality that exist in program quality and the serious deficiency in current systems such as media rankings.

- Business schools can use the Program Quality Model (PQM) as a basis for diagnosing their programs' level of quality.

- Business schools can improve quality in their own programs if they prioritize efforts by collecting data and tracking model dimensions deemed most critical to program quality. These dimensions include faculty teaching, curriculum content, and student learning.

- School leaders should participate in the creation of an alternative rating system based upon broad operationalization of the PQM. A viable alternative to rankings that can create a comprehensive quality index is within reach.

- It is possible for business schools to use personal and institutional power to engage others in a process of rethinking, retooling, and reclaiming the measurement of quality in graduate management education.

Notes

1. Although the term *criterion* has been used in multiple ways, here *criterion* refers to a "basis for a judgment or qualitative comparison" (English & English, 1958).
2. In response to Morgeson and Narhgang's (2008) study of *Bloomberg Businessweek* ranking stability, a *Businessweek* editor published an article remarking, "Somehow these critiques of our rankings never come from schools at the top of the list" (Lavelle, 2008). Of course, critics have long resided among ranked schools. For instance, Khurana (2007), a Harvard professor, documents a host of systemic problems originating from *Businessweek*'s "top" schools.
3. By "communities of practice," we mean "social systems of shared resources by which groups organize and coordinate their activities, mutual relationships, and interpretations of the world" (Wenger, 1998, p. 13). For a practical explication, see Wenger, McDermott, and Snyder, (2002).

References

AACSB. *The Business School Rankings Dilemma*. A Report from a Task Force of AACSB International's Committee on Issues in Management Education. Tampa, Fla.: Association to Advance Collegiate Schools of Business, 2005.

AACSB. *Eligibility Procedures and Accreditation Standards for Business Accreditation*. Tampa, Fla.: Association to Advance Collegiate Schools of Business, January 2010.

Argenti, P. "Branding B-Schools: Reputation Management for MBA Programs." *Corporate Reputation Review*, 2000, 2, 171–178.

Austin. J. T., & Villanova, P. "The Criterion Problem: 1917–1992." *Journal of Applied Psychology*, 1992, 77, 836–874.

Basken, P. "Quest for College Accountability Produces Demand for Yet More Student Data." *Chronicle of Higher Education*, May 17, 2012. http://chronicle.com

Brogden, H. E., & Taylor, E. K. "The Theory of Classification of Criterion Bias." *Educational and Psychological Measurement*, 1950, 10, 159–186.

Cabrera, A. F., Colbeck, C. L., & Terenzini, P. T. "Developing Performance Indicators for Assessing Classroom Teaching Practices and Student Learning." *Research in Higher Education*, 2001, 42, 327–352.

Certo, S. C. & Certo, S. T., *Modern Management: Concepts and Skills* (11th ed.). Upper Saddle River, N.J.: Prentice Hall, 2009

Corley, K. G., & Gioia, D. A. "The Rankings Game: Managing Business School Reputation." *Corporate Reputation Review*, 2000, 4, 319–333.

Datar, S. M., Garvin, D. A., & Cullen, P. G. *Rethinking the MBA: Business Education at a Crossroads*. Boston, Mass.: Harvard Business Press, 2010.

DeAngelo, H., DeAngelo, L., & Zimmerman, J. L. "What's Really Wrong With U.S. Business Schools?" Social Science Research Network (SSRN). July 2005. http://ssrn.com/abstract=766404.

DeNisi, A. S. "Rain, Snow, and Sleet Are Just Different Types of Precipitation." *Academy of Management Perspectives*, 2008, 22, 15–17.

DiBiasio, D. A., Girves, J. E., & Poland, W. "Assessing Quality in Graduate Programs: An Internal Quality Indicator." *Research in Higher Education*, 1982, 16, 99–114.

Dierdorff, E. C., & Rubin, R. S. *The Relevance, Requirements, and Ramifications of Specialized MBA Programs*. Technical report submitted to Graduate Management Admission Council. McLean, Va.: GMAC, Management Education Research Institute, 2009.

Elsbach, K. D., & Kramer, R. M. "Members' Responses to Organizational Identity Threats: Encountering and Countering the *BusinessWeek* Rankings." *Administrative Science Quarterly*, 1996, 41, 442–476.

English, H. B., & English, A. C. *A Comprehensive Dictionary of Psychological and Psychoanalytic Terms*. New York: Longmans, Green & Company, 1958.

EQUIS. *EQUIS Standards and Criteria*. Brussels, Belgium: European Quality Improvement System, January 2010.

Francisco, W., Noland, T. G., & Sinclair, D. "AACSB Accreditation: Symbol of Excellence or March Toward Mediocrity?" *Journal of College Teaching & Learning*, 2008, 5, 25–30.

Gioia, D. A., & Corley, K. G. "Being Good Versus Looking Good: Business School Rankings and the Circean transformation From Substance to Image." *Academy of Management Learning & Education*, 2002, 1, 107–120.

Gladwell, M. "The Order of Things: What College Rankings Really Tell Us." *The New Yorker*, February 14, 2011, pp. 68–75.

GMAC. *2008 mba.com Registrants Survey Report*. McLean, Va.: Graduate Management Admission Council, 2008.

GMAC. *2010 mba.com Prospective Students Survey Report*. McLean, Va.: Graduate Management Admission Council, 2010.

GMAC. *2012 Corporate Recruiters Survey Report*. Reston, Va.: Graduate Management Admission Council, 2012a.

GMAC. *2012 mba.com Prospective Students Survey Report*. Reston, Va.: Graduate Management admission Council, 2012b.

Katz, D., & Kahn, R. L. *The Social Psychology of Organizations* (2nd ed.). New York: Wiley, 1978.

Khurana, R. *From Higher Aims to Hired Hands: The Social Transformation of American Business Schools and Unfulfilled Promise of Management as a Profession*. Princeton, N.J.: Princeton University Press, 2007.

Kuh, G. D. Indices of *Quality* in the *Undergraduate Experience*. AAHE/ERIC, Research Report, 4. Washington, D.C.: American Association for Higher Education, 1981.

Lavelle, L. "In Defense of *BusinessWeek*'s MBA Rankings." October 23, 2008. http://www.businessweek.com

Lawrence, J. K., & Green, K. C. *A Question of Quality: The Higher Education Ratings Game*. AAHE/ERIC Higher Education Research Report 5. Washington, D.C.: American Association for Higher Education, 1980.

Lawshe, C. H. "A Quantitative Approach to Content Validity." *Personnel Psychology*, 1975, 28, 563–575.

Mintzberg, H. *Managers Not MBAs: A Hard Look at the Soft Practice of Managing and Management Development*. San Francisco, Calif: Berrett-Koehler, 2004.

Morgeson, F. P., & Nahrgang, J. D. "Same as It Ever Was: Recognizing Stability in the Business Week Rankings." *Academy of Management Learning & Education*, 2008, 7, 26–41.

Morse, R. "Tulane Freeman School of Business Misrepresented Some Admissions Data." *U.S. News & World Report*. December 20, 2012. http://www.usnews.com/education/blogs/college-rankings-blog/2012/12/20/tulane-freeman-school-of-business-misreported-some-admissions-data

Murphy, K. R., & Cleveland, J. N. *Understanding Performance Appraisal: Social, Organizational and Goal-Based Perspectives*. Thousand Oaks, Calif.: Sage, 1995.

Muchinsky, P. M. *Psychology Applied to Work*. Pacific Grove, Calif.: Brooks Cole, 1997.

National Research Council. *Improving Measurement of Productivity in Higher Education* . Washington, D.C.: National Academies Press, 2012.

Navarro, P. "The MBA Core Curricula of Top-Ranked U.S. Business Schools: A Study in Failure?" *Academy of Management Learning & Education*, 2008, 7, 108–123.

Palmer, T. B., & Short, J. C. "Mission Statements in U.S. Colleges of Business: An Empirical Examination of Their Content with Linkages to Configurations and Performance." *Academy of Management Learning & Education*, 2008, 7, 454–470.

Pfeffer, J., & Fong, C. T. "The End of Business Schools? Less Success Than Meets the Eye." *Academy of Management Learning & Education*, 2002, 1, 78–95.

Policano, A. J. "What Price Rankings?" *BizEd*, September/October 2005, pp. 26–33.

Policano, A. J. "The Rankings Game: And the Winner Is . . ." *Journal of Management Development*, 2007, 26, 43–48.

Porter, L., & McKibbin, L. *Management Education and Development: Drift or Thrust Into the 21st Century*. New York: McGraw Hill, 1988.

Rubin, R. S., & Dierdorff, E. C. "How Relevant Is the MBA? Assessing the Alignment of Required MBA Curricula and Required Managerial Competencies." *Academy of Management Learning & Education*, 2009, 8, 208–224.

Rubin, R. S., & Dierdorff, E. C. "On the Road to Abilene: Time to Manage Agreement About MBA Curricular Relevance." *Academy of Management Learning & Education*, 2011, 10, 148–161.

Rubin, R. S., Dierdorff, E. C., & Morgeson, F. P. *(Re)Defining MBA Program Quality: Toward a Comprehensive Model*. Technical report submitted to Graduate Management Admission Council. Reston, Va.: GMAC, Management Education Research Institute, 2011.

Rubin, R. S., & Martell, K. "Assessment and Accreditation in Business Schools." In S. Armstrong & C. Fukami (eds.), *Handbook of Management Learning, Education and Development* (pp. 364–383). Thousand Oaks, Calif.: Sage, 2009.

Safon, V. "Factors That Influence Recruiters' Choice of B-Schools and Their MBA Graduates: Evidence and Implications for B-Schools." *Academy of Management Learning & Education*, 2007, 6, 217–233.

Spence, M. "Job Market Signaling." *Quarterly Journal of Economics*, 1973, 87, 355–374.

Stewart, D. W., Shamdasani, P. N., & Rook, D. W. *Focus Groups Theory and Practice* (2nd ed.). Thousand Oaks, Calif.: Sage, 2007.

Supiano, B. "Emory U. Intentionally Misreported Admissions Data, Investigation Finds." *Chronicle of Higher Education*, August 17, 2012. http://chronicle.com

Tan, D. L. "The Assessment of Quality in Higher Education: A Critical Review of the Literature and Research." *Research in Higher Education*, 1986, 24, 223–265.

Tan, D. L. "A Multivariate Approach to the Assessment of Quality." *Research in Higher Education*, 1992, 33, 205–226.

Thorndike, R. L. *Personnel Selection.* New York: Wiley, 1949.

Trank, C. Q., & Rynes, S. L. "Who Moved Our Cheese? Reclaiming Professionalism in Business Education." *Academy of Management Learning & Education*, 2003, 2, 189–206.

UNESCO (United Nations Educational, Scientific, and Cultural Organization). *Education for All: The Quality Imperative.* Paris, France: UNESCO, 2005.

UNICEF. *Defining Quality in Education.* New York: United Nations Children's Fund, 2000.

U.S. Census Bureau. *Statistical Abstract of the United States: 2012* (131st ed.). Washington, D.C.: U.S. Department of Commerce, 2011. http://www.census.gov/compendia/statab/

U.S. Department of Education. *A Test of Leadership: Charting the Future of U.S. Higher Education.* Washington, D.C.: U.S. Department of Education, 2006.

Wenger, E. *Communities of Practice: Learning, Meaning, and Identity.* Boston, Mass.: Cambridge University Press, 1998.

Wenger, E., McDermott, R., & Snyder, W. *Cultivating Communities of Practice: A Guide to Managing Knowledge.* Boston, Mass: Harvard Business School Press, 2002.

Wherry, R. J. "The Past and Future of Criterion Evaluation." *Personnel Psychology*, 1957, 10, 1–5.

Zemsky, R. "The Rain Man Cometh—Again." *Academy of Management Perspectives*, 2008, 22, 5–14.

Zimmerman, J. L. "Can American Business Schools Survive?" Simon School of Business Working Paper No. FR 01–16. September 5, 2001. http://papers.ssrn.com/abstract=283112

EPILOGUE

Erich C. Dierdorff
DePaul University

Brooks C. Holtom
Georgetown University

With their harsh criticisms of business school research, teaching, and students, the reports by the Ford Foundation (Gordon & Howell, 1959) and Carnegie Foundation (Pierson & others, 1959) had a profound influence on graduate management education (Klimoski & Amos, 2012). Not only did the reports express concerns about content, but they also raised issues about delivery. Moreover, Gordon and Howell contended that "research in business schools needs to become more analytical, to develop a more solid theoretical underpinning, and utilize a more sophisticated methodology" (p. 439).

Business schools took the message to heart. They invested heavily in the research enterprise and sought scholars who were "qualified" as evidenced by PhDs in the social sciences (such as economics, psychology, or sociology). Unfortunately, as Spender and Khurana argue vigorously in Chapter Four of this volume, these professors were "distancing themselves from the problems that managers faced. . . . Instead they focused on advancing their disciplines . . . ". One outcome of these changes was the implicit choice of a strong intellectual signature, with the majority of schools adopting Carnegie Mellon University's approach.

Overall, the foundation reports became the blueprint for schools to follow, which they did almost religiously.

In the years that followed, business schools expanded dramatically in number and in overall enrollment. The MBA degree gained respect. To assess the changes that took place over the twenty-five years after the Ford and Carnegie reports, Porter and McKibbin engaged in an extensive data collection effort in 1984. Their state-of-the-profession report (Porter & McKibbin, 1988) revealed considerable progress and optimism about the future. This apparent success notwithstanding, they recommended continued improvements, many of which focused on curriculum (such as building soft skills, integrating international perspectives, increasing cross functional approaches through capstone courses, and so on.). Again, business schools dutifully followed many of these prescriptions. Schools benchmarked the curricula of the "leaders," or top-ranked schools; copied their formulas; and did their best to implement what these schools were doing. This led, naturally, to the considerable homogeneity that we observe in graduate management education today.

An important theme running through this book is that much has changed since Porter and McKibbin (1988) shared their findings. Indeed, there is evidence that the pace of change is accelerating (Klimoski & Amos, 2012). Moreover, as outlined in the Introduction, a number of large challenges are converging, such as shifts in technology, changing applicant demographics, financial pressures, new competitors, and changing demands from society. For these reasons, we believe that graduate management education is at yet another inflection point. The purpose of this volume is to speak to the challenges and provide deans and other business school leaders with ideas about how to *create their own unique signatures*. To this end, business schools must consider their distinctive missions and strengths in order to adapt and thrive.

The chapters in this volume speak to the diverse ways in which schools can meet the challenges confronting graduate management education. In the following paragraphs we organize insights from the chapters around the nine metadimensions that constitute the Program Quality Model that Rubin and Morgeson present in Chapter Eight. We use this organization because the model represents a comprehensive view of the various interrelated components that schools must leverage to improve graduate management education. In addition, this organization promotes interpretability and a parsimonious discussion of the many insights offered across the volume's eight chapters.

Program Quality Metadimensions

Strategic Focus

Two overall features are critical to the long-term health of graduate management education: the overall quality of each institution's articulated mission, and each institution's corresponding *strategic planning and positioning* with respect to achieving this mission. As is clear from Hay in Chapter Two and other authors, such as Kang and Stark in Chapter Three, there is no singular way to be a successful business school. This assertion marks a departure from the past, when strong, normative statements guided the field and resulted in considerable uniform improvements. Today, instead, each school needs to develop a strategy and plan that reflect its own specific aspirations and environment. As Hay contends in Chapter Two, this strategy must start by articulating whom the school will serve. To thrive, schools must carefully choose the degree students, executive education participants, employers, and other communities they will serve so that it will be possible to meet the needs of these various stakeholders. Equally important, schools must decide whom they will *not* serve. These decisions drive all others.

Once a school has settled the question of whom to serve, it can follow the insightful points Hay makes regarding which program development strategies to pursue. To be successful, innovations must:

- Be aligned with the school's core mission
- Protect markets in which the school has reached excellence or distinctiveness
- Build on the school's existing competence
- Foster and leverage interdependence (within each school), and
- Provide additional opportunities for learning (via cross-institutional collaborations, for example)

Finally, a number of authors have suggested that not all business schools should aspire to be top ranked, nor should they pursue the current normative path that involves improving reputation by requiring faculty to publish theoretical and highly stylized research in a narrow set of journals (Kang and Stark, and Spender and Khurana, Chapters Three and Four). This latter path is not only an expensive one that may fail to provide the expected payback (such as higher rankings and better students). The path may also lead to long-term financial commitments (such as senior, tenured professors with low teaching loads) that make adapting to new opportunities difficult. In a fast-changing world, these can be debilitating disadvantages.

Institutional Resources

Included among the *institutional resources,* or overall quality of resources, available to a program or institution and its constituents are the following: facilities (such as library resources and classroom technology); financial resources (such as endowments, donations, and fees from students); investments in faculty (such as research funding and support for development); and student support services (such as academic support and a student services office). Because these resources are all tied to financial models, this volume's authors focus primarily on the financial aspect of the enterprise and the diverse ways in which schools may be started and funded.

One of the fundamental challenges facing the leaders of a new school or one that aspires to ascend is breaking through the substantial inertia in the current rankings system. As Rubin and Morgeson note in Chapter Eight, only thirty-five schools have ever been ranked in the top-thirty *Bloomberg Businessweek* list. Thus, as Hay explains in Chapter Two, to compete effectively a new school must have either a very different value proposition or strong financial backing from government or other sponsors. One model Hay offers is the French government's support of the development of a graduate management institution, INSEAD. Another model is private enterprise's launch of the Moscow School of Management SKOLKOVO, the European School of Management and Technology (ESMT), and the Indian School of Business (ISB). Yet another example comes from the government of Singapore, which established the Finance Scholarship Programme to build up a critical mass of specialists in targeted fields that would contribute to the long-term growth of Singapore as a national finance center.

A second fundamental institutional resource challenge arises from the set of relationships a business school must navigate when it is part of a larger university, as is most often the case. A school may have a high degree of autonomy when, for example, the dean has almost total control over revenues and expenses. However, other schools may be much more tightly controlled by the central university administration. In the former case, it is not unusual to find business schools pursuing possibilities to create new revenues and acting quite entrepreneurially; in the latter case, the lack of incentives makes programmatic growth less likely.

As Hay explains in Chapter Two, some schools have responded to the challenges associated with being part of an established university by making efforts to become quasi-independent. He cites the example of the London Business School, where he is a faculty member. Although it is accountable to the University of London for academic standards and relies on it for degree-granting powers, London Business School is relatively independent for purposes of finances and management. Still another model exists in Germany, where state funding of higher education is relatively stable. However, even in a more stable context, there are increases in entrepreneurial programmatic activity.

Faculty

When we consider the *faculty* dimension, we focus on the overall quality of teaching and research personnel within a program or institution. Our authors highlight a number of critical challenges business school leaders face when seeking to attract, develop, and retain the right mix of faculty to achieve their schools' objectives. The first challenge relates to the widely held perception that to build a school's reputation, faculty must publish high-quality research. Because the most prestigious journals are highly specialized, a second challenge is that faculty are encouraged to focus on increasingly narrow topics. Yet, this trend is at odds with the employers' and students' demands for greater applicability in what business schools teach. The third challenge focuses on the way new scholars are prepared, given that doctoral seminar instructors' primary focus is on research production.

As Spender and Khurana note in Chapter Four, by 1964 the number of academic journals and the amount of published research had begun to rise rapidly, and this trend has accelerated. The number of articles published in what are considered top-tier journals is seen as a major indicator—if not *the* major indictor— of academic capability. Yet, whether this research has any clear relevance to the business world or enables a school to claim thought leadership is rarely considered. Publications in what are called "practitioner-oriented" outlets are generally ignored or minimized for purposes of promotion and tenure. Engagements with executives and media activities are considered service to the school, lumped in with committee membership and attendance at faculty meetings.

We are grateful that the authors included in this volume offer a number of prescriptions for addressing these challenges. As Hay notes in Chapter Two, one of the key decisions a school's leadership team must make concerns the relative importance of research and teaching in each subject area. This decision then determines the proportion of programs to be delivered by tenure-track faculty, management practice faculty, adjuncts, and visitors. The choices leaders make regarding the relative mix of degree programs and executive education will further affect the mix of faculty. For example, in response to clients' demands for programs that address key challenges in their own organizations, many schools that focus on executive education use nonfaculty to develop and lead specific programs.

Central to any reform of graduate management education is the development of new faculty. As Spender and Khurana explain in Chapter Four, if schools are to address the rigor-and-relevance issues, they must reconsider dominant research methods and problematics. Instead of being exclusively focused on and trained to produce quantitatively proficient articles, doctoral students must be trained to research issues of central importance to real-world managerial practice. They would then enlarge the range of valued output from these investigations and be rewarded for their ability to disseminate their findings to a broad audience rather than a narrow academic community. Finally, as Brown, Arbaugh, Hrivnak, and Kenworthy discuss in Chapter Six, new faculty would be selected not only on the basis of their disciplinary content knowledge but also on their pedagogical content knowledge, and this understanding would translate into more fruitful learning outcomes for students.

Curriculum

Ensuring high-quality *curriculum* spans the topical content of graduate management education as well as the manner with which it is structured and delivered. Several authors note the importance of this quality dimension. In Chapter Five, Rynes and Bartunek remind us that the content of coursework is the sine qua non of our educational identity. In Chapter Six, Brown and colleagues add to this point by contending that how we deliver our content is equally critical to success. In Chapter One, Dierdorff, Nayden, Jain, and Jain further argue that enhancing the future value of graduate management education depends upon increasing its current effectiveness in promoting learning and competence.

Authors also outline the multiple challenges that institutions must address when facing curricular innovation and change. Summarizing the findings from multiple studies, in Chapter Five Rynes and Bartunek paint a clear picture of the misalignment of curricular content with managerial reality. They go on to state that such misalignment gives rise to the challenge of increasing curricular emphasis in four key domains: leadership and interpersonal skills; decision making and problem solving; ethics and social responsibility; and globalization. With regard to curriculum delivery, Brown and colleagues in Chapter Six discuss the relevance of a substantial body of existing evidence on effective learning practices. Yet, these authors point to the striking underutilization of this evidence-based knowledge when institutions and faculty design and implement programs and courses. In Chapter Two, Hay expresses a challenge that overlays these content and delivery concerns when he notes, "A school can answer this question only after it has decided whom it serves."

Our authors outline a number of suggestions for confronting these curriculum challenges. To address underemphasized competencies, in Chapter Five Rynes and Bartunek discuss a variety of curricular and co-curricular approaches, such as interdisciplinary consulting projects, capstone courses, career development modules, service learning projects, case competitions, and international alliances or exchanges. With regard to co-curricular options, in Chapter Seven Feldman warns that their use is likely to yield diminishing returns as students begin to devote too much time, effort, and attention to these demands at the expense of their regular coursework. Both Rynes and Bartunek in Chapter Five and Brown and colleagues in Chapter Six further suggest that programs could become more efficient and effective if they aligned the type of desired learning (knowledge or skill based) with the most appropriate technique. For instance, programs could use large-scale online technologies to deliver courses such as finance and accounting, which are primarily knowledge based. Then they could use smaller, more resource-intensive approaches such as behavioral modeling, role plays, and simulations for more skill-based courses focused on critical thinking skills and interpersonal competencies. Brown and colleagues in Chapter Six further exemplify the utility of using evidence-based design principles to improve both traditional instructional methods (such as experiential learning) and more contemporary methods (such as online and blended learning). Given how central curriculum is to the value of graduate management education, it is abundantly clear from our authors' recommendation that we must bring to bear the convincing body of evidence to enhance both the curricular relevance and instructional effectiveness of our current approaches.

Student Composition

Student composition refers to the overall makeup and corresponding quality of the student population with respect to academic achievement and professional experiences. As Feldman notes in Chapter Seven, many challenges that graduate management programs face originate in misaligned admissions criteria and program goals. Rather than expending energy encouraging students to engage in activities the school deems important, graduate programs would be "better off selecting students whom they can readily engage in the activities that fit their programs' core missions and strategic goals." This has been demonstrated in the research revealing a compelling causal relationship that students who are highly engaged in their own career development are much more likely to engage in their school activities (Feldman, Chapter Seven).

Similarly, we can gain a number of insights from the psychological literature on individual differences. In Chapter Seven, Feldman specifically identifies four promising personality variables:

1. *Proactive personality*. As Feldman writes, "Proactive students do not wait for someone else to take the initiative to address their concerns about curriculum or placement. Rather, they view themselves as active agents who are responsible for managing their own educations and careers. As a result, they exert more energy in excelling in the classroom and landing desirable jobs."

2. *Positive affectivity*. This helps students network more effectively. We also know that subordinates who are high on positive affectivity are viewed as easier to lead than those who are high on negative affectivity. Further, students who are high on positive affectivity tend to be more psychologically robust and deal with disappointment effectively.

3. *Extraversion*. This variable involves how outgoing students are, how easily they initiate conversations, and how comfortable they are when speaking in public. "Students who are high on extraversion are more likely to become involved in professional development, extracurricular activities, and job-hunting activities. . . ." They also do better in job interviews, tend to get promoted more quickly, and perform more effectively in leadership roles.

4. *Conscientiousness*. This is an individual's level of organization, attention to detail, need for closure, and drive to results, all of which are related to performance because they help students complete their tasks in a timely, professional way.

In sum, much is known about personality factors that could contribute to graduate management student success. Yet historical approaches to admissions may have overemphasized quantitative measures. If schools desire different student outcomes, it is clearly time to consider revising student composition inputs.

Student Learning and Outcomes and Program/Institutional Climate

The dimension of *student learning and outcomes* reflects the extent to which students acquire relevant knowledge and skills and attain associated career and economic outcomes; the dimension of *program/institutional climate* refers to a school's overall educational context (its prevailing values, attitudes, and norms). At the outset of this book in Chapter One, Dierdorff and colleagues build a compelling case for a host of benefits that accrue to individuals pursuing graduate management education, including positive economic, competence, performance, and career-related consequences. We discuss student learning and program climate together because these metadimensions of quality exert reciprocal relationships and, as Rubin and Morgeson point out in Chapter Eight, they are the products of other quality dimensions such as curriculum, faculty, and institutional resources. In this way, many of the same challenges and recommendations suggested for other more antecedent (or input) dimensions are also pertinent for student learning and program climate. These recommendations include balancing curriculum content, designing program delivery to leverage evidence from the science of learning, improving PhD selection and training to promote more effective future faculty, engaging students, and so forth.

Our authors note some additional challenges and recommendations for student learning and program climate as well. In Chapter Eight, Rubin and Morgeson specifically call attention to the strong influence of media rankings, which substantially overemphasize economic outcomes and underemphasize student

learning. Such an unbalanced focus communicates and priori-
tizes a clear set of values about what should be the ultimate
purpose of graduate management education. The consequence of
this pressure, they argue, is that business schools are distracted
from their core mission: learning. It is interesting to note that
the overemphasis on economic outcomes may lead to additional
challenges if tuition continues to rise and, as some evidence suggests, there is stagnation in the salary growth attributed to the
MBA (Simon, 2013).

In terms of career-related challenges, both Rynes and Bartunek and Feldman (in Chapters Five and Seven) discuss the
difficulties that arise from the fact that graduate management
education must simultaneously be relevant to particular careers
and provide guidance to students who need to figure out what
careers they want to pursue. Feldman further notes that this dual
focus requires highly engaged students, and he also contends that
the optimal level of engagement is unclear and students may
already be stretched too thin. With this in mind, he argues that
the more relevant question is not how to maximize student
engagement. Rather, it is whether students are as engaged as they
want and need to be.

In Chapter Six Brown and colleagues admonish business
schools to hire and develop faculty who have both the motivation and capability to teach effectively. Addressing the challenges associated with student learning and program climate
requires myriad tactics, such as those discussed in the chapters
on curriculum, faculty, and student engagement. Yet, it is safe to
say that meeting these challenges requires broadening our view
of both the purpose of graduate management education and the
factors that will have an impact on its overall quality.

Placement

In discussing *placement*, we consider the overall quality of career-
related programmatic opportunities available to students. Indica-

tors of quality include the breadth of alumni resources (such as networking opportunities); the extent to which the school provides services or mechanisms related to career guidance, placement, and development (such as résumé building and recruitment coordination); and the extent to which the institution actively develops relationships with organizations in its community (through community outreach activities, local business relationships, and so on). The chapters in this volume raise two central issues: the challenge of placing more students when programs are expanded, and the extent of the school's responsibility to place students.

There are foreseeable, but not always anticipated, challenges that arise when schools in search of additional revenue expand program size or variety. First is that although one of the easiest ways to grow enrollment is to relax admissions standards, doing so may make it harder to place students after graduation. Thus, a preferable route may be to follow the examples of CEIBS and ISB, which identified and exploited fast-growing labor markets in Shanghai and Hyderabad that have excess demand for graduate-level business students.

Another challenge involves shaping student expectations about roles and responsibilities related to placement. As Feldman notes in Chapter Seven, since the 1990s most schools have renamed their placement offices as career services centers and charged the latter with providing career counseling, résumé preparation, mock interviews, and job postings. Schools can improve on these efforts by harnessing existing research findings. For example, first we know that students who search for jobs based on their skills are much more successful than those who search based on their interests. Second, beyond providing students with this insight, schools can do more to facilitate involvement in activities that are skill-based rather than socially oriented—whether in the classroom or in extracurriculars. Third, getting comprehensive feedback (such as multisource ratings or 360-degree surveys) from students' previous jobs can also provide them with more insights than interest inventories into their strengths and weaknesses. Finally, in saturated markets, it is more useful for students to understand the tradeoffs graduates are willing to make than to focus on their wants.

Reputation

The *reputation* dimension examines the extent to which external stakeholders recognize a program or institution as being of high quality or merit. Being viewed as highly reputable comes with significant benefits, including increased attractiveness to potential students, higher-quality applicants, increased recruitment, better placement of graduates, greater alumni or corporate donations, and so forth. Due in part to these numerous advantages, schools expend substantial resources on building recognizable and respectable reputations. Yet, as Kang and Stark conclude from their examination of a variety of different schools in Chapter Three, endowing an institution with a ready-made, reputable brand is difficult in general and very rare for young institutions in particular. In Chapter Two, Hay points out that an underlying issue relates to how schools determine the key elements of their activities, such as relative emphasis on research or teaching, which can shape schools' effectiveness and ensuing reputations.

Several authors discuss other issues pertaining to reputation. Taken collectively, the attention paid to reputation does not seem problematic. The problem instead is on what stakeholders are actually basing their perceptions of reputation. It is clear that media rankings are the primary source of influence on stakeholder perceptions. Authors express multiple concerns regarding the focus on media rankings. For example, in Chapter Five Rynes and Bartunek point out that because rankings emphasize graduates' starting salaries, there are significant costs associated with placing students in lower-paying sectors of the economy, such as government organizations, nonprofits, social entrepreneurial ventures, and so forth. Yet, rankings matter and are not going away.

In the most comprehensive examination of what constitutes quality in graduate management educational to date, in Chapter Eight Rubin and Morgeson clearly show two things about media rankings: they are highly deficient in the dimensions they use to indicate quality, and they emphasize outcome-related quality factors (such as placement and salary) over process-related quality factors (such as student learning, faculty, and so on). These authors discuss a host of dysfunctional behavior that comes with playing the rankings game and directly challenge business schools to "reclaim control of quality in graduate management education." Toward this end, they lay out a specific call to action that would create an alternative to media rankings—that is, the comprehensive Program Quality model. The purpose of the model is to more comprehensively and validly capture quality in graduate management education.

Across this volume's chapters, we are reminded that reputation and its consequences are important both to specific schools and to graduate management education as a whole. In this sense, the message is clear: Improving the efficacy and quality of what we do as schools of business will, by necessity, require collective action.

Disrupting Current Models of Graduate Management Education

What the chapters make particularly clear is that the status quo will no longer sustain the value of graduate management education. Reinforcing the urgent need for change is the past decade of piercing criticism, both inside and outside the academy, directed toward the MBA, the flagship program for most business schools. To be sure, change necessitates a fresh look at the current models of graduate management education with the specific intent of creating innovative ways to address the multitude of pressures this book outlines. Yet, innovative change can be challenging. It requires disrupting the commonly held beliefs that inhibit productive revision. To succeed in our collective endeavor, business schools must face the facts this volume describes and use the evidence to create more effective, efficient, and sustainable models of graduate management education.

Critical to such evidence-driven efforts is the recognition of the many half-truths that permeate current thinking and preclude meaningful renovation. These half-truths serve as obstacles to change because they possess just enough truth to remain pervasive without being completely accurate or generalizable. As Pfeffer and Sutton (2006a) remarked, "Even greater damage is done by beliefs that are partly right and apply at certain times, but when treated as completely true and applied in full force to every decision and every action, undermine performance" (p. 25). With this warning in mind, we present is a list of seven half-truths that impede the way forward for graduate management education. This list is by no means exhaustive. Rather, it condenses the many misperceptions that have been exposed by the evidence presented in the preceding chapters. In each case, we first acknowledge the kernel of truth that maintains belief in the accuracy of each half-truth. Then we briefly outline the reasons for each fallacy, pointing the reader to other pertinent chapters in this volume as well as additional scholarship in the broader literature.

Half-Truth 1: Management Is Not a Profession

Certainly there are challenges involved in viewing management as a profession, with some arguing that the role of the manager is "inherently general, variable, and indefinable" (Barker, 2010, p. 58). Indeed, there is significant variety in the types of managerial roles in the broader workforce. For example, the U.S. Department of Labor formally recognizes more than sixty-five distinct management occupations spanning a dozen industries. It is also accurate that management has not yet reached the hallmarks of true professions, such as law and medicine (Khurana, 2007).

However, as Dierdorff and others describe in detail in this volume, more than fifty years of research offer convincing evidence that a common set of competencies underlies all managerial work. Moreover, there is substantial commonality in the broad knowledge domains already taught within graduate management education. Finally, as Spender and Khurana and Rynes and Bartunek write in this volume, there is a strong need to inculcate students with professionalized ideals, such as service to others and the social compact of business (see also Khurana, 2007; Khurana & Nohria, 2008; Podolny, 2009; and Trank & Rynes, 2003). Thus, the time is now to confront this half-truth and fulfill the promise of professionalism in graduate management education. Failing to act ensures that we will see further fragmentation in a field that most already see as "professional" only in the very loosest terms.

Half-Truth 2: Reputation Equates to Educational Quality

Reputation does carry with it very real consequences. Indeed, elite institutions that enjoy superior reputations generally possess more resources, are more selective with regard to faculty and students, and foster greater employment and economic outcomes for their graduates (Gioia & Corley, 2002; Pfeffer & Fong, 2002). In Chapter Eight, Rubin and Morgeson also note that indicators of reputation are largely gleaned from media rankings, which do reflect some important dimensions of educational quality.

However, there are several reasons to expose this half-truth as fallacy. For example:

- In their chapter, Rubin and Morgeson present convincing evidence that educational quality is made up of a host of characteristics that media rankings simply do not reflect.

- Other evidence suggests that there is very little movement in or out of rankings, and there is very little that schools can do to affect their ranking (see Morgeson & Nahrgang, 2008).

- The assumption that top-tier schools have the best faculty is highly questionable (see Bennis & O'Toole, 2005).

- Building institutional reputation on traditional models (such as the research-intensive model) is not necessarily the most effective tactic and represents only one aspect of educational quality. In Chapter Four, Spender and Khurana point out that such an approach has historically emphasized quantitative and economic philosophies that have serious drawbacks, such as less relevance to management practice. In Chapter Three, Kang and Stark provide examples of institutions (such as Hult International Business School) that have built notable reputations without emphasizing the research-intensive model.

In the end, decades of narrowly constructing the meaning of educational quality have created a dysfunctional system that ties reputation to media rankings, irrespective of the rankings' meaning and measurement. The evidence presented in this volume suggests that although a few institutions benefit from the status quo, the vast majority of business school stakeholders are not well served by today's overly circumscribed concept of quality.

Half-Truth 3: Learning Technology *Is* Innovation

It is true that learning technology will continue to have a profound influence on the accessibility, efficiency, and effectiveness of learning in general. In addition, burgeoning empirical literature supports the effectiveness of technology-based instruction, such as online and blended learning and simulation-based learning (Brown & Sitzmann, 2011; Sitzmann, 2011). Yet, it is absolutely essential to recognize that technology pertains to *how* learning is delivered, not *what* is delivered. Put simply, delivery is secondary to content (O'Toole, 2009; Rubin & Dierdorff, 2011).

To believe this half-truth is to be seduced by the notion that we can improve the quality of graduate management education simply by investing in better learning technology. Although technology might improve accessibility and reduce long-term delivery costs, it alone will not guarantee the future value of graduate management education. Blindly using technology is likely to be ineffective. For instance, some types of curricular content are more readily suited for technology-based instruction than others (see Rynes and Bartunek in Chapter Five). Moreover, knowledge of research-based principles for effective use of learning technology is remarkably scant among business school faculty (see Brown and colleagues in this volume).

Thus, the pertinent questions that this half-truth prompts must focus on where and how university-based graduate management education adds value *beyond* technology-based delivery mechanisms. The rise of large-scale efforts toward broader access to education (such as Massive Open Online Courses, or MOOCs) further reinforces the urgency of this issue. Only by addressing this fundamental issue can we begin to design anew our traditional approaches to graduate management education.

Half-Truth 4: New Markets Will Sustain Growth

To casual observers, the successes of the past, coupled with the emergence of regions such as Asia and Latin America that are obviously poised for expansion in the future, suggest favorable long-term prospects. Schools are accustomed to positive trend lines for enrollment, and students have high expectations for return on investment (Simon, 2013). Yet, given the trends (see Holtom and Porter in this volume), these opportunities for growth are highly unlikely to be uniform and to sustain current expectations of growth in graduate management education. Coming out the other side of the financial-crisis-inspired global recession that began in 2008 will not usher in the return of business as usual for business schools.

As outlined by a number of this volume's authors, the fallacies behind this half-truth include tuition cost plateaus, local formation of new business schools, competition from non–university-based training organizations, and so forth (see Holtom and Porter, Hay, and Kang and Stark in this volume). Indeed, in mature markets such as the United States and Western Europe, competition will likely strengthen and prosperity will become even more elusive. Thus, schools will be tempted to expand into new regions, online formats, and niches. However, relatively few MBA brands translate well in emerging markets. Thus, as Hay notes in Chapter Two, leaders would be wise to carefully consider their strengths and resources before expanding into these new arenas. When assessing themselves honestly, some schools will see the need to alter their portfolios, including shrinking or ceasing altogether some activities.

Half-Truth 5: More Programs Equal More Value

Adding new graduate programs, such as an executive MBA or a more focused master's degree such as an MS in finance, can obviously be a low-cost way to generate new revenue by leveraging existing courses and faculty expertise. Programs beyond the conventional MBA also hold the promise of increased flexibility and of career education that is more oriented toward specific industries (for example, health care, financial services, or accounting). Indeed, many readers may have already developed new programs at their own school or—at the very least—experienced pressure to do so. Despite the potential positive consequences of adding programs, however, there are numerous problems with unconditionally accepting this half-truth.

To begin with, one must seriously ask, How new are such programs? Do they really offer fresh curricular content, or are they simply repackaged, preexisting coursework? One must also consider that a majority of business schools already offer a variety of MS degrees and dual degrees, which raises questions of differentiation (see Dierdorff and colleagues in this volume). As multiple authors in this book have discussed, to make any program valuable, business schools must understand whom they serve before deciding how best to serve them (see Hay, Rynes and Bartunek, and Kang and Stark in this volume).

What is needed, then, is a strategically oriented "portfolio approach" that closely focuses attention on the quality rather than quantity of program offerings. Furthermore, we must recognize that for both specific schools and graduate management education as a whole, there are several long-term costs to pursuing programmatic variety in the absence of strategic planning. For example, adding new programs fails to address current curricular misalignment in graduate management education (see Rubin & Dierdorff, 2011); may send ambiguous signals to the market about what training students receive as part of different degrees (GMAC, 2008); exacerbates problems associated with the trend toward making knowledge a commodity (see Trank & Rynes, 2003); and fails to meet the needs of employers that frequently prefer generalist training in areas beyond accounting and finance (see Gupta, Saunders, & Smith, 2007).

Half-Truth 6: Graduate Management Education Is Value Free

The partial truth here is that it is unlikely that an all-inclusive, universal set of values could be created upon which all business school stakeholders would agree. Certainly different occupations, organizations, and nations place varying levels of importance on different values. At the same time, many have argued that graduate management education espouses a particularistic set of values, one that is predominately economic in nature and comes with several unintended negative consequences (see Ghoshal, 2005; Ghoshal & Moran, 1996; and Pfeffer, 2005). As Dierdorff and colleagues detail in this volume, there is a dire need to explicitly recognize and expand the values that graduate management education currently embraces. Moreover, it is important to realize that the values we promote, even implicitly, have broad implications for how we train, select, and evaluate business school faculty (see Spender and Khurana in Chapter Four), the types of curricula we develop and deliver (see Rynes and Bartunek, Chapter Five), and how external stakeholders view business schools in general (see Mitroff, 2004; Podolny, 2009).

Clearly, graduate management education has become unduly restricted to a rather limited set of economic-driven and self-interested values, which has seriously undermined our historical roots in social responsibility (see Augier & March, 2011; Khurana, 2007). But as Rubin and Morgeson aptly note in Chapter Eight, one would be hard pressed to find a business school that says its central purpose is simply to help students make more money. To confront this half-truth, business schools must closely examine the values they propagate against the values endorsed in the classroom and those desired by communities and society.

Half-Truth 7: Missions Make Us Unique

There is indeed some truth to the notion that business school missions are distinct. For example, empirical research shows that mission statements do vary in both content and focus (Palmer & Short, 2008). Accrediting bodies, such as AACSB, have also codified a mission-driven emphasis that presumes that a given school is unique. In Chapter Four, Spender and Khurana further posit that schools have intellectual signatures, which often distinguish the problems they seek to research as well as how these problems are studied.

Yet, we must recognize that there is also remarkable homogeneity across business schools, from the curricula and program-delivery methods to the strategies that most programs implement (see Brown and colleagues, and Rynes and Bartunek, in this volume). No doubt much of this homogeneity is driven by widespread engagement in casual benchmarking, through which schools look to top-ranked institutions for ideas and innovation. But as Pfeffer and Sutton (2006b) noted so succinctly, casual benchmarking is wholly ineffective because "the logic behind what works for top performers, why it works, and what will work elsewhere is barely unraveled" (p. 66).

The allure of this half-truth is the belief that business schools are actually following the recommendations Porter and McKibbin (1988) offered more than twenty-five years ago—namely, to avoid uniform missions across business schools and instead to capitalize on each school's individual strengths. Previous chapters have made clear that fulfilling this notion requires a systematic and self-reflective effort through which schools establish who they are and how they might best accomplish this goal (see Hay and Kang and Stark in this volume). It is also clear that there is significant room for improvement in this regard. Consider, for example, that research also shows that only one-third of business school mission statements describe the school's basic beliefs, values, and priorities (Palmer & Short, 2008). It is perhaps an understatement to point out that we can—and must—go beyond the uniqueness of mere words to deliver graduate management education in unique ways.

Parting Thoughts

The authors of this volume certainly make compelling cases for the many critical concerns that face graduate management education. What stands out most is that the current approaches, which have served business schools so well for many decades, require meaningful renovation. Escalating criticisms from multiple business school stakeholders, unprecedented competition, rising financial pressures, and shifting societal demands have created a confluence of factors that call into question the legitimacy of our current modus operandi. Yet in times when fundamental tenets are called into question, the impetus for change can become especially pressing and apparent. It seems safe to say that such times are at hand for graduate management education (Augier & March, 2011; Khurana, 2007). Further, the consequences of collective inaction appear too costly and severe. After reviewing the chapters in this volume, author Lyman Porter expressed four broad conclusions quite well:

1. The challenges graduate management education faces are many, varied, and unrelenting.
2. There seem to be no easy answers, no simple solutions, and no quick fixes.
3. A number of useful options and approaches exist to cope with these challenges.
4. Doing nothing is probably not one of those useful options.

To take action will most certainly require us to reflect on the strengths and weaknesses of our broader field, our specific institutions, and ourselves. Change will require practicing the very principles we teach in graduate management education, principles that underlie the *effective management of any organization.* That is, we must recognize that sustainability and success fundamentally depend upon how we manage various financial, technological, and human capabilities. As we so vigorously advocate in our classrooms, a necessary condition for any organization's viability is a deep understanding of purpose and of the systems and practices that align with this purpose. Institutions of graduate management education are no different in this regard.

The challenges and recommendations described throughout this book naturally span the full range of these capabilities. It is our hope that the book has done enough to expose the inflection point that we now face. To tinker at the edges is insufficient to ensure the future value of graduate management education. We must choose to disrupt, renovate, and renew our current approaches to graduate management education, lest we allow ourselves to drift into continued complacence and, ultimately, irrelevance.

References

Augier, M., & March, J. G. (2011): *The Roots, Rituals, and Rhetorics of Change: North American Business Schools After the Second World War.* Stanford, Calif.: Stanford University Press.

Barker, R. "No, Management Is Not a Profession." *Harvard Business Review,* July–August, 2010, 52–60.

Bennis, W. G., & O'Toole, J. "How Business Schools Lost Their Way." *Harvard Business Review,* May 2005, 96–104.

Brown, K. G., & Sitzmann, T. "Training and Employee Development for Improved Performance." In S. Zedeck (ed.), *Handbook of Industrial and Organizational Psychology* (Vol. 2, pp. 469–503). Washington, D.C.: American Psychological Association, 2011.

Ghoshal, S. "Bad Management Theories Are Destroying Good Management Practices." *Academy of Management Learning & Education,* 2005, 4, 76–91.

Ghoshal, S., & Moran, P. "Bad for Practice: A Critique of the Transaction Cost Theory." *Academy of Management Review,* 1996, 21, 13–47.

Gioia, D. A., & Corley, K. G. "Being Good Versus Looking Good: Business School Rankings and the Circean Transformation From Substance to Image." *Academy of Management Learning & Education,* 2002, 1, 107–120.

Gordon, R., & Howell, J. *Higher Education for Business.* New York: Columbia University Press, 1959.

Graduate Management Admission Council. *Corporate Recruiters Survey: Survey Report.* Reston, Va.: GMAC, 2008.

Gupta, P. B., Saunders, P. M., & Smith, J. "The Traditional Broad MBA vs. the MBA With Specialization: A Disconnection Between What B-Schools Offer and What Employers Seek." *Journal of Education in Business,* 2007, 82, 307–311.

Khurana, R. *From Higher Aims to Hired Hands: The Social Transformation of American Business Schools and the Unfulfilled Promise of Management as a Profession.* Princeton, N.J.: Princeton University Press, 2007.

Khurana R., & Nohria, N. "Make Management a True Profession." *Harvard Business Review,* October 2008, 70–77.

Klimoski, R., & Amos, B. "Practicing Evidence-Based Education in Leadership Development." *Academy of Management Learning and Education,* 2012, 11, 685–702.

Mitroff, I. "An Open Letter to the Deans and the Faculties of American Business Schools." *Journal of Business Ethics*, 2004, 54, 185–189.

Morgeson, F. P., & Nahrgang, J. D. "Same As It Ever Was: Recognizing Stability in the *BusinessWeek* Rankings." *Academy of Management Learning & Education*, 2008, 7, 26–41.

O'Toole, J. "The Pluralistic Future of Management Education." In S. J. Armstrong & C. V. Fukami (eds.), *Handbook of Management Learning Education and Development* (pp. 547–558). Thousand Oaks, Calif.: Sage, 2009.

Palmer, T. B., & Short, J. C. "Mission Statements in U.S. Colleges of Business: An Empirical Examination of Their Content With Linkages to Configurations and Performance." *Academy of Management Learning & Education*, 2008, 7, 454–470.

Pfeffer, J. "Why Do Bad Management Theories Persist? A Comment on Ghoshal." *Academy of Management Learning & Education*, 2005, 4, 96–100.

Pfeffer, J. & Fong, C. T. "The End of Business Schools? Less Success Than Meets the Eye." *Academy of Management Learning & Education*, 2002, 1, 78–95.

Pfeffer, J., & Sutton, R. I. "Evidence-Based Management." *Harvard Business Review*, January 2006a, 62–74.

Pfeffer, J., & Sutton, R. I. *Hard Facts, Dangerous Half-Truths and Total Nonsense: Profiting From Evidence-Based Management.* Cambridge, Mass.: Harvard Business School Press, 2006b.

Pierson, F. C., & others. *The Education of American Businessmen: A Study of University-College Programs in Business Education.* New York: McGraw-Hill, 1959.

Podolny, J. M. "The Buck Stops (and Starts) at Business Schools." *Harvard Business Review*, June 2009, 62–67.

Porter, L. W., & McKibbin, L. E. *Management Education and Development: Drift or Thrust into the 21st Century.* New York: McGraw-Hill, 1988.

Rubin, R. S., & Dierdorff, E. C. "On the Road to Abilene: Time to Manage Agreement About MBA Curricular Relevance." *Academy of Management Learning & Education*, 2011, 10, 143–161.

Simon, R. "For Newly Minted MBAs, a Smaller Paycheck Awaits." *Wall Street Journal*, January 7, 2013.

Sitzmann, T. "A Meta-analytic Examination of the Instructional Effectiveness of Computer-Based Simulation Games." *Personnel Psychology*, 2011, 64, 489–528.

Trank, C. Q., & Rynes, S. L. "Who Moved Our Cheese? Reclaiming Professionalism in Business Education." *Academy of Management Learning & Education*, 2003, 2, 189–206.

ACKNOWLEDGMENTS

This book would not have been possible without the support of the Graduate Management Admission Council® (GMAC®). We especially appreciate the support and vision of CEO Dave Wilson. We are grateful for the efforts of Rachel Edgington at GMAC. Her commitment to and coordination of the editors, authors, reviewers, and the publisher ensured the successful production of this book.

We thank the authors of this book for their enthusiasm, commitment, and expertise. Their contribution made this book impactful, meaningful, and useful to those invested in graduate management education.

We thank the faculty committee who helped shape the focus and direction of the book as well as reviewed chapters: Myrtle Bell, Grady Bruce, Thomas Hawk, Michael Hay, Jikyeong Kang, Maria Kraimer, Scott Seibert, and Jean Talbot.

Finally, we thank Jossey Bass/Wiley, especially Kathe Sweeney, for demonstrating an unwavering passion for management education and for providing encouragement and advice. We also thank Karla Tyler and Paula Bruggeman for editing the chapters.

ABOUT THE CONTRIBUTORS

Graduate Management Admission Council® (GMAC®)

Founded in 1953 by the deans and admissions officers of leading schools of business and management, the Graduate Management Admission Council (GMAC) is owner and administrator of the Graduate Management Admission Test (GMAT)—the most widely adopted and trusted admissions exam of its kind. More than 2,000 schools in nearly 100 countries today use the GMAT exam to assess applicants to more than 6,000 graduate business and management programs. With its vision on being the leader in connecting talent and aspiration to opportunity, GMAC has expanded its business and staff—as well as its membership—internationally and has adapted its role in graduate management education to include professional development, industry-wide conferences, world-class research and product development, and the global promotion of management education. Today, the proudly not-for-profit Council continues in its mission to improve the discovery and evaluation of talent and deliver on its core belief that business and management—and the teaching of both—are critical to the economic, social, and financial well-being of people worldwide.

THE EDITORS

Brooks C. Holtom

Brooks C. Holtom is associate professor of management at the McDonough School of Business at Georgetown University. He has taught at the Owen Graduate School of Management at Vanderbilt University as well as the College of Business Administration at Marquette University. He has been a visiting professor at the Munich School of Management, Ludwig-Maximilians Universität (Germany), Institut d'Economie Scientifique Et de Gestion, l'Université Catholique de Lille (France), and Colegio de Administración para el Desarrollo, Universidad San Francisco de Quito (Ecuador).

Dr. Holtom's research focuses on how organizations acquire, develop, and retain human and social capital. His more than fifty published articles have appeared in premier journals in management (Academy *of Management Journal, Journal of Applied Psychology, International Journal of Human Resource Management*, and many others). He has been a board member for a number of top journals (for example, *Academy of Management Journal, Journal of Management, Organizational Behavior*, and *Human Decision Processes*) and has received awards for this service. His thinking has appeared in many print (for example, *Business Week*, the *Chicago Tribune, Harvard Management Update*, the *New York Times*, the *Toronto Globe and Mail*, the *Wall Street Journal*, the *Washington Post*) and multimedia (for example, CBS, CNBC, CNN, FoxNews, and NPR) outlets.

Dr. Holtom received BS and MAcc degrees in accounting from Brigham Young University. After that he worked for a number of years for a large accounting firm in Seattle, Washington, where he was licensed as a CPA. Subsequently, he completed his PhD in organizational behavior and human resource management at the University of Washington.

Erich C. Dierdorff

Erich C. Dierdorff is associate professor of management in the Driehaus College of Business at DePaul University in Chicago. Erich's published research has appeared in leading management journals such as *Academy of Management Journal, Journal of Management, Journal of Applied Psychology, Personnel Psychology*, and

The Leadership Quarterly, among others. He serves on the editorial boards of *Journal of Applied Psychology*, *Personnel Psychology*, *Academy of Management Learning & Education*, *Human Performance*, and *Journal of Leadership and Organizational Studies*. He has also contributed to numerous industry and press outlets (for example, *Business Week*, the *Financial Times*, the *Chronicle of Higher Education*, and the *Washington Post*).

Erich's research regarding graduate management education has primarily focused on the various curricular challenges facing contemporary schools of business. Much of this research has centered on issues of "real-world" relevancy and has been funded by research grants from the GMAC Management Education Research Institute. In addition to graduate management education, his other research interests include improving the effectiveness of individual- and team-level learning, examining the predictors and consequences of organizational citizenship, and studying contextual factors that affect work analysis, work design, and performance effectiveness.

Erich has received several awards for teaching excellence at both the undergraduate and graduate levels of business education. Outside the university, Erich has worked with dozens of organizations in areas of human capital consulting. This work has spanned both the private and public sectors for organizations such as Nortel Networks, Siemens Systems, Law School Admission Council, U.S. Department of Labor, North Carolina State Bureau of Investigation, and the American Council for the Teaching of Foreign Languages. This work has focused on a variety of problems, including strategic workforce development, selection system design, training effectiveness, and leadership development.

THE AUTHORS

J. B. (Ben) Arbaugh is a professor of management in the College of Business (COB) at the University of Wisconsin (UW) Oshkosh. Ben's published research has appeared in leading management and educational research journals such as *Academy of Management Learning & Education, Computers & Education, Management Learning, The Internet and Higher Education*, and the *Journal of Asynchronous Learning Networks*. From 2009 to 2011, he was the Editor of *Academy of Management Learning & Education* and was Chair of the Management Education and Development Division of the Academy of Management in 2006–2007. He is a six-time Academy of Management Division Best Paper Award winner and winner of Best Article Awards with both the *Journal of Management Education* and the *Decision Sciences Journal of Innovative Education*. Ben also serves on the editorial boards for the *Journal of Management Education, Academy of Management Learning & Education, Decision Sciences Journal of Innovative Education, The Internet and Higher Education*, and *Organization Management Journal*.

Ben's research in graduate management education has primarily focused upon the delivery of management education via the Internet, with particular emphases on online course design and the influence of academic disciplines on online course outcomes, for which he received a GMAC Management Education Research Institute (MERI) faculty fellowship in 2009. He also has received MERI grants for research on career transitions of MBA graduates, women and minorities in MBA programs, and regional influences on attitudes toward MBA education. His other research interests include research methods in management education, project management, organizational growth transitions, and international entrepreneurship.

In 2011, Ben became the first UW Oshkosh College of Business faculty member since 1992 to be named a John McNaughton Rosebush Professor, UW Oshkosh's highest award for faculty. His other teaching honors include the 2008 Outstanding COB Graduate Faculty Award, the 2009 Management and Human Resources Department Teaching Award, and the 2012 UW Online MBA Consortium Outstanding Faculty Award. Outside the university, Ben has worked with organizations such as the

Hazelden Foundation and the Western Interstate Commission on Higher Education in the areas of project management and online teaching and learning.

Jean M. Bartunek is the Robert A. and Evelyn J. Ferris Chair and Professor of Management and Organization at Boston College, where she has taught since 1977. Her bachelor's degree in psychology and sociology is from Maryville University (St. Louis), where she has served on the board of trustees since 2003. Her PhD in social and organizational psychology is from the University of Illinois at Chicago. She is a past president and fellow of the Academy of Management. In 2009 she won the Academy of Management's Career Distinguished Service Award. From 2008 to 2010 she was a visiting international fellow of the Advanced Institute for Management Research in the United Kingdom.

Jean has published more than 125 journal articles and book chapters, as well as five books: *Creating Alternative Realities at Work: The Quality of Worklife Experiment at Foodcom* (coauthored with Michael Moch), *Hidden Conflict in Organizations: Uncovering Behind-the-Scenes Disputes* (coedited with Deborah Kolb), *Insider-Outsider Team Research* (coauthored with Meryl Louis), *Organizational and Educational Change: The Life and Role of a Change Agent Group* (), and *Church Ethics and Its Organizational Context: Learnings From the Sex Abuse Scandal in the Catholic Church* (coedited with Mary Ann Hinsdale and James Keenan). Her work has won best paper awards from the *Journal of Applied Behavioral Science* and *Human Relations*. Her primary research interests center around organizational change and academic–practitioner relationships. This latter interest includes how academic knowledge can be "translated" for practitioners, including students in management classes.

Jean is an associate editor of the *Academy of Management Learning & Education* and the *Journal of Applied Behavioral Science*. She serves, or has served, on the editorial boards of multiple leading journals, including the *Academy of Management Journal*, *Administrative Science Quarterly*, *Organization Studies*, the *Journal of Organizational Behavior*, and *Human Relations*. She previously was a Coeditor for the nontraditional research section of the *Journal of Management Inquiry* (1994–1997) and an Associate Editor of *Advances in Qualitative Organizational Research* (1998–2004). She has also coedited special research forums in the *Academy of Management Journal* (1993, 2001) and *Academy of Management Review* (2007, 2012).

Kenneth G. (Ken) Brown, PhD, SPHR, is currently professor and Henry B. Tippie Research Fellow in the Henry B. Tippie College of Business at the University of Iowa.

Ken conducts research on learning and motivation in workplace training and development, with an emphasis on technology-mediated learning environments. He also studies the science–practice gap as it relates to management policy and practice. Ken's published work has appeared in journals such as *Academy of Management Executive*, *Academy of Management Learning & Education*, *Human Resource Management*, *Journal of Applied Psychology*, *Organizational Behavior and Human Decision Processes*, *Personnel Psychology*, and in a number of edited books. He is coauthor (with Greg Stewart) of a human resources textbook entitled *Human Resource Management: Linking Strategy to Practice*. Ken has received research awards from the American Society of Training and Development and the Society of Human Resource Management for his research on technology-mediated training programs. He has also received best paper awards from *Human Resource Management* and the *Academy of Management Learning & Education*. Ken has served on the editorial boards of *Academy of Management Review*, *Cornell Hospitality Quarterly*, *Human Resource Development Quarterly*, *Human Resource Management*, *Journal of Management*, *Organization Management Journal*, and *Personnel Psychology*. After serving a term as associate editor of

Academy of Management Learning & Education from 2009 to 2011, he was appointed editor for 2012–2015.

Ken's teaching experiences include courses in human resources, organizational behavior, and general management across undergraduate, master's, and doctoral levels. His current teaching efforts are directed toward the mandatory, large-enrollment management course for undergraduates in the Tippie College. Ken is the recipient of numerous teaching awards, including the Dean's Teaching Award, the Collegiate Teaching Award, the President and Provost Award for Teaching Excellence, and (twice) the college's annual "Student's Choice for Faculty Excellence Award." He was selected by the University of Iowa student body to give the "Last Lecture" in 2011 and has been nominated three times by the institution for the Carnegie Foundation U.S. Professors of the Year Program.

Daniel C. Feldman is associate dean of academic affairs and Synovus Chair of Servant Leadership at the University of Georgia's Terry College of Business. He has served on the faculties of Yale College, University of Minnesota Industrial Relations Center, Northwestern's Kellogg Graduate School of Management, University of Florida, as the James Bradley Distinguished Foundation Fellow at the University of South Carolina, and as a visiting Sloan Scholar at MIT. He received his MA in administrative sciences and his PhD in organizational behavior at Yale University Graduate School.

Daniel has written six books and more than 125 articles on career development and career management. His coauthored book, *Coping With Job Loss: How Individuals, Organizations, and Communities Respond to Layoffs*, was named one of the four outstanding books of the year by the Academy of Management, and his work on job loss has been cited in the *New York Times* and the *Wall Street Journal*. In 1997, he was the recipient of USC's Educational Foundation Research Award for being the outstanding researcher in the professional schools. He has also won a J. L. Kellogg Research Professorship for his work on socialization and job change, a CIBER Fellowship for his work on expatriation, a Riegel and Emory Fellowship for his work on downsizing, the Addison-Wesley Best Paper Award from the Academy of Management for his work on early retirement incentives, the Cason Hall Best Paper Award for his work on part-time employment, and the Careers Division Best Paper Award for his work on early career indecision.

Professor Feldman has won numerous teaching awards, including MBA Teacher of the Year five times at the University of Florida. At USC, he received the Alfred G. Smith Award for Teaching Excellence (outstanding teacher in the Moore School of Business), the Michael A. Hill Distinguished Faculty Award (outstanding teacher in the Honors College), and he was named an Eli Lilly Senior Teaching Fellow (university-level award). At the University of Georgia, he won an outstanding teacher award in 2005. He has led executive education programs to a wide variety of firms, including Honeywell, Milliken, J.C. Penney, Knight-Ridder, the U.S. Health Care Finance Administration, American Red Cross, AMA, and Duke Energy.

Michael Hay is professor of management practice in strategic and international management and entrepreneurship at London Business School. He was deputy dean and secretary of the school for five years until December 2006 and acting dean of CIDA City Campus in Johannesburg in 2007. CIDA is an innovative institution that provides virtually free undergraduate business education to historically disadvantaged individuals.

Michael joined the London Business School faculty in 1987 and has held a variety of positions, including director of the Foundation of Entrepreneurial Management; associate dean of the Sloan Masters Programme; and dean of executive education. He previously spent ten years in academic publishing, principally with Blackwell, where he was deputy managing director of Blackwell Publishers, a founder and chairman of Blackwell-Polity and chairman/chief executive of Marston Book Services; and director of The Business Place in South Africa.

Michael is cofounder of the Global Entrepreneurship Monitor, which, starting with ten countries in 1999, now examines the nature and impact of entrepreneurial activity in more than fifty countries around the world. His books include *The Strategy Handbook*, with Peter Williamson; *Investing for the Future: New Firm Funding in Germany, Japan, the UK and USA* with Steven Abbott; and *The Venture Capital Handbook* with Bill Bygrave and Jos Peeters. He has worked as a consultant for the United Nations on welfare in Eastern Europe and coauthored, with Professor Sir Alan Peacock, *Social Policies in the Transition to a Market Economy*.

George Hrivnak is an assistant professor of management at Bond University in Queensland, Australia. George's research focuses on management education and development, including leadership development, experiential learning, instructional design and assessment, and transfer of learning. He and his colleagues have published their work in the *Journal of International Management*, *Journal of Management Education*, *International Journal of Organizational Analysis*, and *Small Group Research*, along with several book chapters and conference papers. He is an editorial board member of *Academy of Management Learning & Education* and a board member of Bond University's Centre for Applied Research in Learning, Engagement, Andragogy & Pedagogy. George is an award-winning teacher who teaches at the undergraduate, graduate, and executive levels regarding topics that include negotiation, leadership, organizational behavior, change management, and human resources management.

Dipak C. Jain is dean of the international business school INSEAD, a position he has held since March 2011. Jain served as dean of the Kellogg School of Management from 2001 to 2009. He joined the Kellogg School of Management faculty in

1986 as an associate professor and became an associate dean in 1996. In 1994 he was named the school's Sandy and Morton Goldman Professor of Entrepreneurial Studies and professor of Marketing.

In addition to teaching at Kellogg, Dr. Jain has served as a Visiting Professor of Marketing at Sasin Graduate Institute of Business Administration, Chulalongkorn University, Thailand, since 1989 and at Nijenrode University, Netherlands Business School, since 1995. He also serves as Visiting Professor of Marketing at the Indian School of Business, Hyderabad, India.

Jain is also a member of the board of directors for Deere & Company, Northern Trust Corporation, Reliance Industries Ltd., India, and Global Logistic Properties Ltd., Singapore.

Subhash C. Jain is professor of international marketing, director of the Center for International Business Education and Research (CIBER), and director of the GE Global Learning Center (GEGLC) at the University of Connecticut School of Business. His teaching, consulting, and research activities include marketing strategy and multinational marketing. Dr. Jain is the author of more than 100 publications, including twelve books: *Marketing Planning and Strategy, International Marketing, Export Strategy, Market Evolution in Developing Countries, Handbook of Research in International Marketing, Toward a Global Business Confederation, Multinational Corporations and Poverty Reduction, Emerging Economies and the Transformation of International Business, Global Business Negotiations,* and others.

Dr. Jain has presented seminars, both in the United States and abroad, on various marketing topics, including marketing segmentation and positioning, marketing strategy, export strategy, and global branding. He has offered seminars for the International Trade Center (WTO/UNCTAD) in Geneva. He has served as a visiting faculty at the Graduate School of Business Administration Zurich in their executive MBA program and the International University of Geneva. He has served as a consultant to such organizations as Xerox Corporation, Aetna Life and Casualty, United Technologies, Mead Corporation, General Motors, NCR, Timex Corporation, Heineken, Unilever, Pitney Bowes, and Corning Glass. He has advised government agencies in Malaysia, Chile, India, Pakistan, St. Lucia, Mexico, Iran, Kenya, and Indonesia on their trade problems.

Amy Kenworthy is the founding director of the Centre for Applied Research in Learning, Engagement, Andragogy and Pedagogy (LEAP) and professor of management at the School of Business at Bond University in Queensland, Australia.

Amy's primary research and scholarship interests are focused on the interrelated areas of service learning, community engagement, and experiential education practices. She has served as guest editor for special issues on service learning in the *Academy of Management Learning & Education*, the *Journal of Management Education*, the *International Journal of Case Method Research & Application*, and the *International Journal of Organizational Analysis* and has published numerous articles in leading academic journals. Amy's recent publications include two edited books— *Innovations in Teaching and Learning* and *Community Engagement in Contemporary Legal Education* (coedited with Patrick Keyzer and Gail Wilson).

Amy has received numerous teaching awards, including an Australian Learning and Teaching Council (ALTC) Award for Teaching Excellence and three ALTC Citations for Contributions to Student Learning. She is the first international recipient of the Organizational Behavior Teaching Society's New Educator Award and the only faculty member at Bond University who has received the university's Vice-Chancellor's Award for Teaching Excellence twice. She has presented at more than seventy-five refereed conference presentations, served as a keynote speaker at multiple international forums, and worked as a consultant to numerous business school–based service learning programs around the world.

Amy is associate editor for the *Academy of Management Learning & Education (AMLE)* and serves on the editorial boards for the *Journal of Management Education* and the *Review of Business*. She is an award-winning reviewer for *AMLE* and the AOM conferences including the Organizational Behavior Teaching Conference (OBTC) and the Management Education Division (MED) of the Academy of Management annual meeting, and has twice chaired the MED track for the Australian and New Zealand Academy of Management (ANZAM) conference.

Jikyeong Kang is currently professor of marketing and director of the DBA Programme at Manchester Business School (MBS), United Kingdom. A native of Korea, she spent eighteen years in the United States, of which nine were on the faculty of the University of Wisconsin–Madison. During the early years of her career at the University of Wisconsin–Madison, she was elected as a member of the prestigious Teaching Academy. She has also held visiting appointments at many leading business schools, including CEIBS, ESSEC, RSM, HEC, and Sogang University.

Jikyeong was director of MBA Programmes at MBS, providing strategic leadership for a suite of MBA programs. During the six years of her tenure, the MBS full-time MBA program ranking went up from forty-eighth (2002) to twenty-second (2007) in the world, according to the *Financial Times* ranking reports.

Jikyeong is a recipient of various research grants and has done consultancy work for many international organizations, including Adelphi International, the Royal Bank of Scotland, Hilti, Littlewoods, and Sears. She has also received several national and international awards for her research and actively publishes her work in various academic research journals. In addition, she has presented numerous papers at industry and academic conferences throughout the United States and Europe. In 2005, she was highly commended in the Public Sector for Asian Women of Achievement Award in the United Kingdom.

Rakesh Khurana is the Marvin Bower Professor of Leadership Development at the Harvard Business School. He is also the master of Cabot House at Harvard College. He teaches a doctoral seminar on management and markets and the board of directors and corporate governance in the MBA program.

Professor Khurana received his BS from Cornell University and his MA (sociology) and PhD in organization behavior from Harvard University. Prior to attending graduate school, he worked as a founding member of Cambridge Technology Partners in sales and marketing.

He has published articles on corporate governance in the *Harvard Business Review* and *Sloan Management Review*. His book on the CEO labor market, *Searching for a Corporate Savior: The Irrational Quest for Charismatic CEOs* was published in 2002.

His book *From Higher Aims to Hired Hands: The Social Transformation of American Business Schools and the Unfulfilled Promise of Management as a Profession* chronicles the evolution of management as a profession, with particular focus on the institutional development of the MBA. *From Higher Aims to Hired Hands* received the American Sociological Association's Max Weber Book Award in 2008 for most outstanding contribution to scholarship in the past two years. In 2007, the book was also the winner of the 2007 Best Professional/Scholarly Publishing Book in Business, Finance and Management, Association of American Publishers.

Frederick P. Morgeson is professor of management and Valade Research Scholar at the Eli Broad College of Business at Michigan State University. He received his PhD in industrial and organizational psychology from Purdue University.

Dr. Morgeson teaches and does research in human resource management and organizational behavior. His research has focused on four distinct areas. First, he has a continuing interest in leadership, particularly with respect to the role of leadership in self-managing teams and the nature of the relationship between leaders and followers. Second, Dr. Morgeson has examined fundamental questions about the nature of work, which includes how work is structured and how people perceive their work. These issues have been explored in a series of studies in the job analysis, work design, and work teams areas. Third, he has studied the effectiveness and consequences of different selection techniques. Fourth, Dr. Morgeson has explored issues of theory development and sought to produce integrative research in the substantive research areas of his interest.

Dr. Morgeson has published his research in numerous top-tier management and psychology journals, coauthored the leading job analysis book (*Job Analysis: Methods, Research, and Applications for Human Resource Management*), authored or coauthored numerous book chapters, and presented his research at universities and conferences around the world. He is editor of *Personnel Psychology* and the *Annual Review of Industrial and Organizational Psychology*, is on the editorial board of the *Academy of Management Review*, and is serving a five-year term as executive officer for the Academy of Management Human Resources Division. He was formerly a member of the Academy of Management's HR Division executive committee, associate editor of *Personnel Psychology*, a member of the SHRM Foundation Board of Directors, and has served on the editorial boards of the *Annual Review of Psychology*, *Journal of Applied Psychology*, *Personnel Psychology*, and the *Journal of Management*. Finally, Dr. Morgeson is a recipient of the American Psychological Association Distinguished Scientific Award for Early Career Contribution to Psychology in Applied Psychology.

Denis J. Nayden is a managing partner of Oak Hill Capital, a private equity firm in which Robert M. Bass is the lead investor. At Oak Hill Capital, Mr. Nayden heads the industry groups focused on investments in basic industries and co-heads the business and financial services team. Currently, he represents Oak Hill Capital on a number of boards that Oak Hill Capital has a direct investment in. He is the chairman of the boards of directors of Avolon Aerospace Ltd. and Firth Rixson Ltd. and he is on the board of Accretive Healthcare and Jacobson Companies. Formerly, he was chairman of the boards of directors of Primus International, RSC Equipment Rental, and Duane Reade, Inc., as well as on the board of Genpact Ltd., all prior Oak Hill Capital investments.

Prior to joining Oak Hill in 2003, he was chairman and chief executive officer of GE Capital, where he was responsible for twenty separate businesses representing $555 billion of aggregate assets and 90,000 employees in thirty-five countries. During his twenty-six-year tenure at General Electric Co. (GE), Mr. Nayden also served as chief operating officer (1994–2000); executive vice president (1989–1994); senior vice president and general manager in the structured finance group (1987–1989); vice president and general manager in the corporate finance group (1987–1989); and marketing administrator for air/rail financing as well as various other positions of increasing responsibility (1977–1987).

In addition to the boards of directors mentioned, Mr. Nayden serves on the board of directors of buildOn (a nonprofit organization). Mr. Nayden earned a B.A. degree in English, magna cum laude, in 1976 and an MBA in finance in 1977 from the University of Connecticut. He has served on UConn's board of trustees since 2001, currently sits on UConn's compensation committee and is chairman of UConn's audit committee. Mr. Nayden has a long involvement with UConn, including being a member of the UConn foundation board and UConn's School of Business board of advisors. Additionally, he co-chaired UConn's first-ever capital campaign, which raised more than $400 million.

Lyman W. Porter is professor emeritus of management in the Paul Merage School of Business at the University of California, Irvine (UCI), and was formerly dean of that school. Prior to joining UCI in 1967, he served on the faculty of the University of California, Berkeley, and was a visiting professor at Yale University. Currently, he serves as a member of the board of trustees of the American University of Armenia. Previously, he was a visiting professor at Hong Kong University and has served as an external examiner for the National University of Singapore.

Professor Porter is a past president of the Academy of Management. In 1983 he received that organization's Scholarly Contributions to Management Award, and in 1994 its Distinguished Management Educator Award. He previously served three terms on the board of directors of the Association to Advance Collegiate Schools of Business (AACSB).

Professor Porter is the author, or coauthor, of eleven books and more than ninety articles on topics relating to the field of management. His 1988 book (with Lawrence McKibbin), *Management Education and Development*, reported the findings of a U.S. nationwide study of business school education and postdegree management development.

Robert S. Rubin is associate professor of management in the Driehaus College of Business at DePaul University. Bob has published his work in leading academic journals such as *Academy of Management Journal, Personnel Psychology, The Leadership Quarterly, Journal of Applied Psychology, Journal of Organizational Behavior, Business Ethics Quarterly, Journal of Business Ethics, Human Resources Management, Journal of Management Education,* and *Academy of Management Learning & Education.* Professor Rubin's research has also been profiled in national publications, including *Business Week*, the *Financial Times*, and the *Chronicle of Higher Education*. Currently, Dr. Rubin is an editorial board member of the *Academy of Management Learning & Education,* and *Leadership and Organizational Studies.* Dr. Rubin coauthored a management skills textbook, *Managing Organizational Behavior: What Great Managers Know and Do.*

Professor Rubin's research regarding graduate management education has focused primarily on the content of MBA curriculum and its relevance to managerial work. His recent work has also explored issues of accreditation and assessment as well as MBA program quality. Bob's research on MBA programs has been supported in part by three generous grants from the GMAC Management Education Research Institute. In addition to his work on graduate management education, Bob has pursued research into aspects of leadership, managerial assessment and development, citizenship behavior, and emotions at work.

Beyond his academic work, Bob has been an active human capital consultant to a variety of industries engaged in improving employee selection, leadership assessment and development, change management, and executive coaching.

Sara L. Rynes is the John F. Murray Professor of Management and Organizations in the Tippie College of Business at the University of Iowa. Her research has appeared in leading management journals such as the *Academy of Management Review*, *Academy of Management Journal*, *Journal of Applied Psychology*, *Personnel Psychology*, *Harvard Business Review*, and *Academy of Management Learning & Education*. She was editor-in-chief of the *Academy of Management Journal* from 2005 to 2007 and has served on the editorial boards of the *Academy of Management Review*, *Journal of Applied Psychology*, *Personnel Psychology*, *Human Resource Management*, and the *Academy of Management Learning & Education*.

Sara's research interests are in the areas of human resource strategy, recruitment, compensation, academic–practitioner relationships, and management education. She has written about the challenges of teaching behavioral coursework in business schools, the deprofessionalization of business schools, the current state of the research literature on management teaching, the extent to which management professors teach evidence-based management, how organizational behavior is taught in MBA programs, and whether or not adding a management major to a functional area major (such as finance or accounting) improves a student's chances of receiving a job interview.

Sara is a fellow of the Academy of Management, the American Psychological Association, and the Society for Industrial and Organizational Psychology. She received the Academy of Management's 2006 Herbert G. Heneman Career Achievement Award for Research in Human Resource Management; the 2011 Dutch HRM Network Research Award, and the 2011 Michael R. Losey Human Resource Management Research Award from SHRM, the SHRM Foundation, and the HR Certification Institute. She has received research grants from the U.S. Army Research Institute, the SHRM Foundation, Cornell's Center for Advanced Human Resource Studies, the Management Education Research Institute, and the U.S. Department of Labor. She teaches courses in human resource management, organizational change, research methods, compensation, quality management, and sustainability. She is a former chair of the Department of Management & Organization at the University of Iowa and has consulted with companies such as IBM, Corning, Kodak, AT&T, Citigroup, Pearson, Merrill Lynch, 3-M, Kraft, and CIGNA. She was the 2013 Presidential Lecturer for the University of Iowa. She received her PhD from the University of Wisconsin and previously held faculty positions at Cornell University and the University of Minnesota.

John-Christopher (JC) Spender is currently a visiting professor at Lund University, Sweden; ESADE, Spain; Cranfield University School of Management, UK; Open University Business School, UK; Leeds University Business School, UK; and faculty member and chairman of the board, International School of Management, France.

Trained initially as a nuclear engineer, JC worked for Rolls-Royce & Associates at the plant for U.K. nuclear submarines 1960–1965. He later joined IBM (UK) from 1965 to 1970 as a large account team manager and worked in London as an investment banker until 1988.

Dr. Spender completed his PhD in strategic management at the Manchester Business School. His thesis won the 1980 Academy of Management AT Kearney Prize and was later published as *Industry Recipes*. After being on the faculty at various universities he retired in 2003 as dean of the School of Technology & Business at State University of New York/Fashion Institute of Technology. In addition to ongoing visiting appointments, he served as the 2007–2008 Fulbright research chair at Queen's University, Canada.

JC's current research interests include theorizing firms, managing, and markets under conditions of Knightian uncertainty. He has authored or coauthored sixty books on the history of management education, business strategy, and knowledge management, including *Strategic Conversations* (forthcoming), and *Confronting Managerialism: How the Business Elite and Their Schools Threw Our Lives Out of Balance*.

Andrew W. Stark is the Coutts Professor of Accounting and Finance at the Manchester Business School. He has held this position since 1996, having previously held faculty positions at the Yale School of Management, the University of Essex, the University of Ulster at Jordanstown, the University of Maryland at College Park, and the University of Manchester. While at the Manchester Business School, he has served for six years as the director of the full-time MBA Program and is currently head of the Division of Accounting and Finance.

He has held various leadership roles within his subject community. He has served as chairperson of the British Accounting and Finance Association. He chaired the Quality Assurance Agency Subject Benchmarking Group responsible for formulating a subject benchmarking statement for undergraduate degrees in accounting and finance in the United Kingdom.

He was a member of various U.K. research assessment exercise committees, including being a member of the 1996 and 2001 Committees for Accounting and Finance and the 2001 Committee for Business and Management. He chaired the Committee for Accounting and Finance in the 2008 Research Assessment Exercise.

He has published more than forty papers in refereed research journals. He is a past editor of the *British Accounting Review* and is a current editor of the *Journal of Business Finance and Accounting*. He has a BA in mathematics from Cambridge University and an MBA and PhD from the Manchester Business School.

NAME INDEX

SUBJECT INDEX

future, 331–339; reputation and, 311, 363–364; summary of, 340–341; system for rating, 306–307, 326–331. See also Program Quality Model (PQM)

R

Rankings: criticism of, 324–325, 338–339, 341n2; policy-makers' opinions on, 318; popularity and success of, 324–327; Program Quality Model vs., 319–321; quality dimensions emphasized in, 322–323; rating system vs., 328–331; as representation of quality, 303–304

Rating system: advantages of, 327–331; policy-makers' opinions on, 318; Program Quality Model (PQM) as basis of, 307–317, 318; proposed development of, 306–307, 326–327, 334–338

Recruiters: brought to campuses, 274; competencies sought by, 189–190, 203; as consideration when positioning business schools, 64, 65; from overseas, 61; relationships with, 81, 86, 87; variety of degree programs not understood by, 39

Relationships, as consideration when positioning business schools, 86–87

Reputation: academic signatures and, 154; developing, of young business schools, 80, 119–122, 128n2; quality and, 311, 363–364; recommendations on, 360–361; research, 124

Research: attracting faculty active in, 81; Carnegie GSIA's emphasis on, 149–150; as factor in positioning business schools, 72–74; funding for, 109–110; impact on teaching and curricula, 118–119; importance to business models, 109–119, 122–123, 124–125; management education, 230–231; orientation of U.S. business schools to, 107–109n1, 127–128n1; rigor-relevance gap of management, 155–159, 162–165

Rewards, for faculty, 231, 233–234

S

Saïd Business School, 119, 121

Salaries: of MBA holders, 25–26; for new hires at business schools, 112–115

School of Management (SOM). See Yale School of Management (SOM)

Self-efficacy, 227–228

Service learning, 191–192, 201, 243–244, 245

Size of school, as consideration when positioning business schools, 81–82

Skills: globalization-related, 203; interpersonal, 191–193; job-hunting, 274–277; soft, 269–270. See also Competencies

SKOLKOVO. See Moscow School of Management SKOLKOVO

Society, value of graduate management education to, 28–30

Stakeholder theory, 29

Stakeholders: demanding accountability for academic quality, 298–299; importance of competencies recognized by, 34; for making decisions on strategic positioning, 90–91; MBA core curriculum vs. needs of, 185–204

Stanford: critical thinking course at, 196; degree programs for executives with work experience, 69; Ford Foundation funding of, 137; leadership courses at, 191, 192–193, 241–242; MOOCs offered by, 12; online business courses, 13; reputation of, 167n4; Stanford Ignite program in India, 12

Strategic focus, 313, 349–350

Strategic positioning, 89, 90–93

Student learning and outcomes. See Learning outcomes

Students: competition to attract best, 62; demands for time and attention of, 264, 271–273; faculty ratings by, 226; personality traits influencing success of, 278–280, 356–357; selection of, for degree programs, 64–65, 313, 355–357; with work experience, 69. See also MBA student engagement